Psycho/History

PSYCHO/HISTORY

READINGS IN THE METHOD OF PSYCHOLOGY, PSYCHOANALYSIS, AND HISTORY

Edited by
Geoffrey Cocks and
Travis L. Crosby

YALE UNIVERSITY PRESS
NEW HAVEN AND LONDON

The editors gratefully acknowledge the support of the Albion College
Faculty Development Committee.

Designed by Nancy Ovedovitz and set in ITC Garamond type by David
E. Seham Associates, Inc. Printed in the United States of America by
Vail-Ballou Press, Binghamton, N.Y.

Library of Congress Cataloging-in-Publication Data

Psycho/history : readings in the method of psychology,
    psychoanalysis, and history.
    Bibliography: p.
    Includes index.
    1. Psychohistory.   I. Cocks, Geoffrey, 1948–
II. Crosby, Travis L., 1936.
D16.16.P25 1987   901'.9   86-23411
ISBN 0-300-03681-7
ISBN 0-300-03682-5 (pbk.)

The paper in this book meets the guidelines for permanence and
durability of the Committee on Production Guidelines for Book
Longevity of the Council on Library Resources.

10   9   8   7   6   5   4   3   2   1

To our students, past, present, and future

Contents

Introduction

In our teaching of undergraduates, we have discovered that psychohistory is an ideal vehicle for introducing the timeless questions of human motivation in the past. Practical difficulties in making readily available those articles which best illustrate the most important issues in applying psychological concepts to history led us to the idea of this anthology.[1] Readings found here, combined with basic readings in Freud, Erikson, and Kohut, and supplemented by other works cited in our bibliography will, we believe, offer a thorough and balanced introduction to psychohistory. The readings will also provide a springboard for a discussion of general historiographical issues.

A useful approach to the promises and problems of psychohistory lies in the opposing paradigms of Carl Hempel and William Dray. Hempel believes that history is a scientific process of empirical inquiry, verification, and prediction. Historical inquiry is thus a search for general laws which will illuminate clear lines of cause and effect for all historical events.[2] Dray, on the other hand, believes that history is not a scientific endeavor; it is instead concerned with an empathic understanding of the motives and actions of historical figures. The historian, according to Dray, should strive to see things from the subject's point of view (and not merely ask "What would I have done?") so as to make that particular historical experience come alive as a sensible and meaningful narrative.[3]

Practicing historians nowadays do not generally see themselves as purveyors of a scientific point of view, even as they have increasingly drawn models and methods from the social sciences. Historians use the term "causation" in a more tentative, less conclusive way than Hempelians would like. For most historians, the concept of causation is not an expression of, nor a search for, general laws in history. Historians make use of what Dray would call "unifying" concepts, or they may speak of "conditions" or "circumstances." Even when historians use the term "cause," they almost always mean it in a way that suggests varying degrees of determinancy.

Early psychohistorical efforts especially were often marred by an ahistorical tendency to postulate psychological causes and their law-like effects upon historical characters by seeing childhood experiences as invariantly causative upon adult behavior. In their enthusiasm, they were clearly taking a cue from Freud, who always insisted that his work was a natural science. But in so doing, they ignored Freud's own view of causal complexity, or "overdetermination," as Freud put it.

One may wonder why historians should have been drawn to an essentially therapeutic and ostensibly scientific body of psychological theory such as Freud's. There are sound reasons. The historian H. Stuart Hughes, for one, has summarized the similar convictions, concerns, and aims shared by psychoanalysis and history: the conviction that the past has an influence on the present; a concern for plural explanations drawn from the welter of small and large clues to the mysteries of human behavior; and the aim of "liberat[ing] man from the burden of the past by helping him to understand that past."[4] It has also been argued that psychoanalysis, far from being merely another aspiring natural science, employs a holistic and not a mechanical approach to the individual case history, seeking to build a coherent and meaningful narrative of a life rather than just the confirmation of general laws.[5]

Embedded within the Hempelian certainties of psychoanalysis as a therapeutic discipline, psychohistorians have also seen a role for the subjective interpretations represented by the involvement, through transference and countertransference, of analysts with their patients. Thus, as "human sciences," both psychoanalysis and history can employ a combination of objective and subjective thinking.

In its present stage of development, psychohistory clearly bears the scars of its divided allegiance between a historical tradition which sees itself as beyond the reach of general laws and a therapeutically oriented (and "scientific") field such as psychoanalysis. This fragmented theoretical framework has too often produced one-dimensional, silly, or even cruel caricatures of politicians, peoples, and geniuses. Contributing to these faulty analyses are the inherent evidentiary problems of psychohistory: the difficulty of gathering data on childhood; the resultant danger of circular reasoning in hypothesizing antecedents from adult words and actions; the absence of personal contact enjoyed by the psychoanalyst; the misuse of subjectivity; the danger of reductionism; the question of whether psychoanalytic theory is valid for other times and places (and, indeed, whether the application of any contemporary model can illuminate the special "mentalities" of earlier periods).[6] Psychohistorians must take care to recognize the limits of their approach, as a number of the selections in this anthology suggest. Paradoxically, perhaps, they must be sophisticated and daring in their use of evidence. Psychohistorians can look for clues of the irrational, for example, not merely in the absence of rationality but in the context of a life or group: clues found in self-defeating behavior, such as that of Woodrow Wilson in his campaign for U.S. entry into the League of Nations; or in patterns of expression and action;[7] or in instances of "mass hysteria."[8]

Advances since the days of classical Freudian theory have helped smooth the way for psychohistorians. The evolution within the various schools of depth psychology in the 1920s and 1930s toward a greater emphasis on ego functions, character, and object-relations operating throughout an individual's life, rather than on id impulses buried deep within the psyche and childhood, has offered the psychologically attuned historian greater interpretive flexibility.[9] If viewed as heuristic devices rather than scientific laws, the diversity of theories can help refine our knowledge of behavioral complexity in the past. An example is the ongoing work in what has become the burgeoning historical subgenre of "Hitlerature."[10]

Historians have turned away from the early easy conviction that Hitler could be understood in crude psychopathological terms alone; they have become increasingly sophisticated about the fascinating mixture of the rational and irrational, the conscious and unconscious within Hitler. A responsible portrayal of any historical figure or phenomenon must include consideration of the internal world of its subject or subjects as revealed by patterns of behavior (actions, thoughts, motives) and their origins in the whole context of a life or lives. So Hitler's life must be viewed in its phenomenological and genetic totality (that is, what he did and why) and a coherent whole must be constructed out of the interaction of his private and public worlds. Every human being constitutes the intersection of various aspects of a given historical context: family, culture, society, politics, economics—all of these environments creating a dynamic pattern of feeling, perception, and knowledge within the individual which determines motives and actions over a lifetime. These influences reach the historian in various ways, from documents to dreams. Thus when the historian reads (and accepts the accuracy of the account) that Hitler dreamed late in the war that no A-4 rocket would ever reach England,[11] the interpretation of such a dream will not reflect some crude sexual analogy but will reveal a tangle of past and present motivational conditions about Hitler's conscious considerations of technical and strategic problems and alternatives, his calculated tendency toward the histrionic, and his personal feelings about power and aggression in general and about England in paticular.

Part I of this anthology is devoted to readings which raise basic questions about the possibility of using psychoanalytic theory in historical inquiry. We begin with one of the foremost critics of psychoanalysis. In his classic 1953 statement, the English psychologist Hans Eysenck charged that psychoanalysis is riddled with theoretical and methodological errors that undermine its claim to scientific status. For Eysenck, scientific explanation in psychology must rest upon experimental evidence that builds toward a comprehension of the laws governing human behavior. Psychoanalysis, Eysenck avers, can at best only offer some commonsense understanding of human actions and characteristics.

Where Eysenck sees weakness in the psychoanalytic enterprise, the philosopher of history Hans Meyerhoff sees strength. In an address to a psychoanalytic audience in 1961, Meyerhoff outlined what he saw as the similar aim and approach of psychoanalysis and history—a convergence of concern that is distinct from purely scientific method. The historian and the scientist are distinct from each other most crucially, according to Meyerhoff, in terms of their relationship to their respective subject matters.

The historian and psychoanalyst Peter Loewenberg emphasizes the same theme in his 1977 essay. Loewenberg stresses the importance of a relativistic approach to the study of history, arguing that even within science itself positivism has given way to the recognition that scientific paradigms should be judged not so much in terms of correspondence to truth but, more like history, in terms of persuasive coherence. Like Meyerhoff, Loewenberg also places a great emphasis on the empathic means of understanding shared by history and psychoanalysis. The subjective involvement of the historian with human beings in history is similar to the phenomenon of countertransference in psychoanalysis, that is, to the process whereby the analyst reacts to the patient's memories and emotions in terms of his or her own feelings. While some analysts claim that no such genuine process of countertransference can take place outside an encounter with a living subject, historians can and do react empathically to the experiences of those whom they study. The historian does not merely report facts: he or she interprets history by means not only of intellect, but by subjective understanding as well.[12]

Every historian uses this empathic ability to determine whether certain information or interpretations "fit" in terms of an understanding of the whole of the subject's life. The relevance, indeed the existence, of Hitler's dream about his rockets never reaching England, for instance, can be confirmed at least in part in terms of the historian's sense that such a happening "fits" into the patterns of Hitler's motives and subjectivity. The goal of history is to understand specific cases, as opposed to science's mission to explain phenomena in accord with general laws. Subjectivity, in short, seems endemic in historical studies. Historians must therefore be aware of the emotional environment of their own lives and times, as well as that of the past, some arguing that psychohistorians must undergo psychoanalysis.

There are of course inherent dangers in such interpretive flexibility. Charles Strozier offers a critique of subjectivity in the psychohistorical work of Erik Erikson. As Strozier notes, Erikson's methodology is based upon what Erikson himself calls "disciplined subjectivity." Strozier observes, among other things, that Erikson never precisely defines what he means by discipline. Part I concludes with two essays by psychohistorians whose work has recently raised anew debate over historical method. The first is by Lloyd deMause, founder of the Institute for Psychohistory in New York. DeMause has earnestly insisted that psychohistory constitutes a new science. Based on a theory of the history of childhood that envisions a future utopia of adult-child harmony, deMause's work and that of his followers has been dogged by failed predictions and the unreliability of so-called fantasy-analyses of groups past and present. Binion, for his part, insists on a peculiar degree of empathy in a variation of the kind of psychohistory propounded by deMause. Binion represents one extreme end of the kind of empathic understanding of the past advocated by Dray, while deMause attempts to use Dravian means to Hempelian ends.

Psychohistory, as we have noted, is largely based upon psychoanalysis—which is itself concerned with the exploration of individual human lives. Naturally enough, then, most psychohistory takes the form of psychobiography. Part II, therefore, presents a selection of essays on the subject of psychology and historical biography. Child psychiatrist Robert Coles begins the discussion with a cautionary tale about the pitfalls of psychobiography. Too easily can psychopathological labeling become a mere device for moral condemnation or clumsy debunking. Coles also raises the troubling question of the nature of genius and whether psychoanalysis can ever contribute to an understanding of it. Although the historian Joseph M. Woods thinks that Coles may be overly harsh in some of his criticisms, Woods agrees that outdated and overly simplistic psychoanalytic approaches to the past have harmed psychohistory's credibility. Woods suggests more fruitful models may be those based either upon the narcissistic personality or upon the actions of self-defeating behavior. In a practical demonstration of how psychobiography can suggest various alternative hypotheses in explaining the life of a man of genius, the psychologist William McKinley Runyan focuses on a single dramatic incident in the painter Vincent van Gogh's life—when he cut off the lower half of his left ear as a present for a prostitute. Runyan's ingenious exercise highlights some of the problems dogging the elucidation of the motives of historical figures.

Part II concludes with a series of articles presenting different psychological intepretations of Woodrow Wilson's career. Alexander George, a political scientist, offers a valuable methodological guide to writing and evaluating psychobiographies by focusing on Wilson as an example. Robert C. Tucker, also a political scientist, presents an alternative interpretation of Wilson's motives and behavior based upon the ego psychology of the neo-Freudian Karen Horney. A major challenge to the thesis that Wilson was psychologically lamed all his life as a result of his stern upbringing by a strict Calvinist father has been mounted by the psychiatrist and neurologist Edwin Weinstein. Weinstein sees Wilson's failures—the most notable of which was his inability to lead the United States into the League of Nations after World War I—in great measure as a function of a series of disabling strokes Wilson suffered beginning in 1896.[13] In the presentation of his argument, Weinstein is joined by the clinical psychologist James Anderson and the historian and Wilson biographer Arthur Link. In a rebuttal, Juliette and Alexander George dispute the evidence for Weinstein's hypothesis, reiterating their belief in the primacy of psychological factors behind Wilson's actions. The debate raises the important issue of the role played by physiological states and disorders in the lives of historical figures.[14] While certain aspects of an individual's life can certainly be explained by the presence of a discrete medical condition, in most cases the historian will want to integrate such a factor into the broader context of the subject's motivational and developmental life.

Part III addresses the especially difficult question of the psychological study of groups in history. Biography, after all, comprises only a small portion of the historian's task. More often, historians look to the larger weave of peoples and times in the fabric of the past. How are psychohistorians to take the long step from general psychological group theories to the dynamics of particular groups? What is the psychological link between individuals constituting group behavior? What, especially, is the link between leaders and followers? This is, of course, the stuff of social psychology. Most psychohistorians have remained firmly within the psychoanalytic tradition in attempting to explain group behavior in the past.

Bruce Mazlish, a historian, concludes that Freudian approaches are more successful. Gerald Platt, however, in discussing from a sociological point of view several psychoanalytic theories as they have been applied to past societies, finds them wanting. The historian John Demos, like many others in the psychoanalytic tradition, posits the importance of the family as the mediator of social values and pressures and, drawing from the developmental ego psychology of Erik Erikson and Heinz Kohut's study of narcissism, explores here the psychological dynamics of witchcraft in the culture of early New England.

As in psychobiography, so in group psychohistory, German history has proven to be a fertile ground. Many of these works have grown up around the phenomenon of National Socialism. Harvey Asher's review of non-psychoanalytic methods of inquiry into the Nazi movement provides a concise summary of various complementary alternatives to the Freudian model. Asher's article is a call to psychohistorians to remain open to the various possibilities of psychohistorical modeling.

We conclude our anthology with an essay by Peter and Carol Stearns on the historical study of emotions as part of a broadly conceived social history. Whether their eclectic approach will enhance or transcend psychohistory remains to be seen, but their ideas are a testament to the continuing vitality of the psychohistorical debate.

NOTES

1 Early anthologies of psychohistory for our purposes are too narrowly bound to psychoanalytic theory. These include Bruce Mazlish (ed.), *Psychoanalysis and History* (New York, 1963); and Benjamin B. Wolman (ed.), *The Psychoanalytic Interpretation of History* (New York, 1971). Robert Jay Lifton and Eric Olson (eds.), *Explorations in Psychohistory: The Wellfleet Papers* (New York, 1974) is not focused on the historiographical issues that we wish to emphasize. Other anthologies are idiosyncratic in their approach to psychohistory, such as Lloyd deMause (ed.), *The History of Childhood* (New York, 1974); Lloyd deMause (ed.), *The New Psychohistory* (New York, 1975); and Rudolph Binion, *Soundings: Psychohistorical and Psycholiterary* (New York, 1981). George Kren and Leon Rappoport (eds.), *Varieties of Psychohistory* (New York, 1976) defines psychohistory too loosely through the inclusion of essays only marginally relevant to an examination of a psychologically informed historical method.

Robert Brugger (ed.), *Our Selves—Our Past: Psychological Approaches to American History* (Baltimore, 1981); and Peter Loewenberg, *Decoding the Past: The Psychohistorical Approach* (New York, 1983), while excellent in their way, are primarily collections of case studies rather than of historiographically oriented essays.

2 Carl G. Hempel, "The Function of General Laws in History," in Patrick Gardiner (ed.), *Theories of History* (Glencoe, Ill., 1958), pp. 344–55.

3 William Dray, *Laws and Explanation in History* (London, 1957).

4 H. Stuart Hughes, "History and Psychoanalysis: The Explanation of Motive," in *History as Art and as Science: Twin Vistas on the Past* (New York, 1964), p. 47.

5 Michael Sherwood, *The Logic of Explanation in Psychoanalysis* (New York, 1969), pp. 190, 231.

6 Lawrence Walker, *"Mentalités:* The Hidden Agenda of Stannard's *Shrinking History,"* *Psychohistory Review,* vol. 12, no. 4 (1984), pp. 43–48.

7 See, for example, Richard L. Bushman, "On the Uses of Psychology: Conflict and Conciliation in Benjamin Franklin," *History and Theory,* vol. 5 (1966), pp. 225–40.

8 As in John Putnam Demos, *Entertaining Satan: Witchcraft and the Culture of Early New England* (New York, 1982).

9 Peter Loewenberg, "Psychohistory: An Overview of the Field," in *Decoding the Past,* pp. 20–31.

10 Geoffrey Cocks, "The Hitler Controversy," *Political Psychology,* vol. 1 (1979), p. 67.

11 Walter Dornberger, *V-2,* trans. James Cleugh and Geoffrey Halliday (New York, 1954), pp. 91, 206.

12 Loewenberg, "Psychohistory," pp. 14–16.

13 Edwin A. Weinstein, *Woodrow Wilson: A Medical and Psychological Biography* (Princeton, 1981).

14 For another example, see Ida Macalpine and Richard Hunter, *George III and the Mad Business* (New York, 1969).

PART I

PSYCHOLOGY, PSYCHOANALYSIS, AND HISTORY

1

What Is Wrong with Psychoanalysis?

H. J. Eysenck

It is impossible to deny that Freudian theories have had a tremendous influence on psychiatry, on literature, and perhaps also on that whole complex of laws, folkways, and *mores* which we often refer to as "sexual morality." Moralists are inclined to doubt whether this influence has been essentially for the good, but after the initial outcry which was perhaps inevitable most people have settled down to an easy and even enthusiastic acceptance of psychoanalysis. This acceptance is not altogether in line with psychoanalytic teaching, which would lead one to anticipate resistance and hostility. Such resistance and hostility as there are can be found almost exclusively among psychologists and anthropologists, i.e. among those who have made a professional and detailed study of the theories and claims of psychoanalysts; among lay people the terms "psychology" and "psychoanalysis" have come to be almost synonymous, and in the literary world Freudian terms and concepts have been accepted so completely that modern novels are frequently indistinguishable from psychiatric case records.

This would appear to be an almost unique phenomenon in science. In no other science are we likely to find certain theories and hypotheses popularly accepted but rejected by many experts in that science. There are a few cases where this has been known to happen; the Lysenko affair has shown that in genetics also *vox populi* may be *vox dei*, to the extent of having genuine scientists excommunicated and threatened for not accepting views the evidence for which was practically non-existent, but which found favour with lay judges. Possibly another parallel may be found in the history of the heliocentric theory of the universe in which laymen supported those who believed the earth to be the centre of the world, against the consensus of opinion of those best qualified to judge.

Reprinted from *Uses and Abuses of Psychology* by H. J. Eysenck (Penguin Books, 1953) pp. 221–41, copyright © H. J. Eysenck, 1953.

3

In thus equating psychoanalysis with popular opinion we may seem to be moving in a topsy-turvy world. Is not Freud the great innovator, comparable with Galileo or Darwin? Is it not true that like these great scientific geniuses he also was at first stoned by the common multitude, only to be recognized and honoured after many years of persecution? Perhaps this apparent paradox is not quite as paradoxical as it may seem.

There are two kinds of psychology, just as there are two ways in which we may approach any other set of phenomena. Eddington has contracted these two approaches in his famous example of the two tables—the sensible table, which we can see and touch, which has weight and thickness, and is part of our everyday environment, and the scientific table, made up of electrons and protons, consisting essentially of nothingness interrupted by extremely fast-moving electric charges. We may accept the scientific table on the authority of the physicist's say-so, and because we have found in the past that predictions based on the physicist's view of the world tend to be correct; nevertheless, most of us find it impossible to look at the world consistently in this fashion, and prefer to deal rather with sensible entities which in some mysterious way we think we understand. It is obvious to us that the earth is flat, that the sun moves around the earth, and that you cannot make a silk purse out of a sow's ear. We may give up these views reluctantly and under protest when the factual support for the contrary views becomes too strong, but we usually do so with very bad grace, and a secret hankering after the good old ways.

The same opposition occurs with even greater force in psychology. German philosophers have brought out this point quite clearly in contrasting *verstehende* psychology with *erklärende* psychology, i.e. a common-sense psychology which tries to *understand* human beings, and a psychology which tries to *explain* their conduct on a scientific basis. It is often said that psychology has a long past, but a short history; it is the common-sense type of psychology which has been the stand-by of writers, philosophers, and all others who had to deal with human beings, and which accounts for the long past, but it is the explanatory, scientific type of psychology which arose towards the end of the last century which is referred to as having had the short history. These two kinds of psychology are so frequently mixed up that a few words may be useful in clarifying the issue.

In our dealings with people we can hardly be said to proceed on a haphazard basis of pure chance. Experience teaches us to expect certain reactions from certain types of people; close acquaintance may enable us to predict with considerable accuracy the reactions of our friends, or of members of our family. We may know quite well that Mary is a bit old-maidish, so that it is better not to tell *risqué* stories in front of her, while Joan is a bit of a fly-by-night who can always be relied upon to liven up a party. Dick is reliable and so honest that one would not be well advised to discuss in front of him ways and means of obtaining income tax relief which departed ever so little from the paths of rectitude, while Fred is forever cutting corners, and is quite likely one day to overdo it and find himself in jail. Dolores is "one for the boys" and "an easy lay"; Mac is a tightwad and High Church; Jim has no money sense at all and tends to take a scientific view of most things; Dolly is a "one-man woman" and house-proud. We all make these generalizations with respect to the people we know well, and we are quite prepared to act on them. We may even pride ourselves on our "understanding of human nature," and on the accuracy of our diagnosis. We often believe that such judgements can with accuracy be formed almost at first sight, and many people go as far as to think that external physical signs, such as a weak chin, or red hair, or a Jewish nose, are infallible signs of a person's character. We may not know consciously how we arrive at our judgements, but we will defend to the death our claim to their correctness.

Similar judgements are made every day on the physical plane also. We judge things to be heavy or light, we consider the air to be humid or dry, we expect material objects to fall when they are unsupported. We should be surprised to find that water did not wet us, or the sun did not heat us. We have a whole set of expectations built up through experience, and fortunately for us these expectations are frequently right.

Some physical concepts may appear similar to those of everyday life, e.g. those of time and space. It is, however, important to realize that they are far from identical. Newton has pointed out in the *Scholium* which precedes his *Principia,* that sensed time and sensed space, i.e. our everyday notions of these concepts, are not to be confused with "true or mathematical" time and space; anyone who confuses the two "is guilty of vulgar ignorance." Physical science does not attempt to *understand* everyday phenomena in common-sense terms, although ultimately it started out from this type of observation; physical science tries to *explain* natural phenomena in terms of laws of wide generality which subsume the individual phenomenon in question.

Exactly the same is true of psychology. The "understanding" psychologist is trying to gain an intuitive insight into the working of another person's mind on the basis of his common-sense knowledge of human nature. He may have derived his knowledge from self-observation and introspection, or from the observation of other people in a great variety of situations, or even from reading Shakespearian plays and modern novels; there is no denying that he is often amazingly astute and accurate in his intuitions. This type of insight, based on wide experience and probably natural aptitude and interest in human beings, is a very valuable quality in many walks of life, and almost indispensable in the psychiatrist, the personnel manager, the social leader, and the politician. However, valuable and useful as it may be, psychological insight and understanding by themselves have nothing whatsoever to do with psychology as a science, just as little as facility in dealing with physical "things" is an essential asset for the physical scientist. From observation I venture to assert that many of the greatest psychologists are if anything below average in this quality of "insight" into human motives and purposes, and similarly physicists of the highest standing are frequently incapable of adjusting the carburettor in their cars, or even of fixing a burned-out fuse. The expectation frequently voiced, namely, that psychologists should have learned a lot about "human nature," using the term in this sense, is quite unjustified. The psychologist knows no more about "human nature" than the next man, and if he is wise he will not let his claims outrun his discretion.

If the psychologist as a scientist is not trying to understand other people, then what precisely is he trying to do? He is trying to explain their conduct in terms of a system of general scientific laws. In doing so he may use terms which he has taken over from everyday speech, terms like intelligence, emotion, trait, type, ability, and so forth, just as the physicist took over terms like space, time, weight, mass, and many others from the language of his day. But it would be an error to equate the muddled, inexact, ill-defined terms of common usage with the exact, precisely defined, clear-cut concepts of the scientist. There are similarities, and a certain amount of overlap, but there certainly is nothing approaching complete correspondence.

This fact often leads to misunderstanding. The psychologist makes a statement regarding, say, the inheritance of intelligence, using that word in a relatively precise way to stand for a set of measurable phenomena. The layman understands the statement to refer to his own idea of intelligence, which may be and usually is rather different from that of the psychologist, and offers objections which are not at all relevant to the intent of the original statement. The psychologist finds it difficult to counter these criticisms because all the terms he uses have special connotations which would require explanation, frequently involving highly complex mathematics, and all of which can only be understood in terms of the whole system of thought of which they form a part. These bars to understanding are particularly mischievous because their presence is often quite unsuspected, and the argument may go on for hours and hours without reconciling the positions of the protagonists in the slightest. Scientific statements are highly complex statements deriving their meaning essentially from a whole set of facts, hypotheses, and theories; they cannot meaningfully be debated in the absence of full knowledge of all these facts, theories, and hypotheses.

How are these considerations relevant to psychoanalysis? Perhaps I can best make clear the connexion by stating quite briefly and dogmatically that psychoanalysis in my view is trying to *understand,* rather than to *explain;* that consequently it is essentially non-scientific and to be judged in terms of belief and faith, rather than in terms of proof and verification; and that lastly its great popularity among non-scientists derives precisely from its non-scientific nature, which makes it intelligible and immediately applicable to problems of "understanding" other people. This judgement I believe to be a statement of fact, rather than a value judgement. Religion and art are two other non-scientific disciplines which in spite of their lack of concern with scientific truth have contributed greatly to human happiness; to say that they are less valuable than science implies a scale of standards and values which itself is subjective and non-scientific. To judge

whether a given discipline is or is not scientific is possible without value implications; it necessitates nothing but a commonly agreed definition and standard
of scientific procedure. Such a definition and such standards exist, and may be
found in the writings of logicians and philosophers of scientific methodology;
those who are acquainted with these writings will agree that in spite of occasional
disagreements on minor issues there is an overwhelming amount of agreement
on the main points.

Many psychoanalysts would probably agree with this analysis, and maintain
that their work differed in many important respects from orthodox scientific
procedures. Jung is but one of a large number of analysts who consciously reject
scientific methodology in favour of subjectivity, intuition, and unconscious "understanding." There can be no argument here; those who look for religion, faith,
beauty, or other non-scientific values need fear no scientific criticism. Neither,
on the other hand, should they make any claims to having established scientific
truths; they cannot reject the methods of science and yet claim the results. This
desire to have the best of both worlds is very frequent among analysts, but it
would be difficult to proffer any logical argument in its defence. Non-scientific
analysts may, of course, quite frequently be right in their surmises, hunches, and
intuitive insights, just as many people who have never heard of psychology or
of psychoanalysis are often astonishingly astute in their understanding of human
motives. To be correct in particular instances is not necessarily a sign of the
scientific worth or correctness of one's views, theories, or hypotheses. (The obverse of this statement is more nearly true; to be wrong in particular instances
discredits a scientific theory to such an extent that it needs to be replaced completely by another, or at least heavily revised.)

While thus many analysts disclaim any intention of being scientific in their
work, no such thing could be said of the great majority who in their writings
claim that what they say is not merely useful, interesting, exciting, and ingenious,
but also true in the scientific sense of that term. Freud himself certainly held
such a view, and most of his followers would probably agree with his contention.
This makes it possible to apply our agreed criterion, and to see to what extent
psychoanalysis lives up to its pretensions.

It is here already that many analysts enter their first objection. They say that
traditional ideas as to what constitutes scientific method and scientific truth are
unduly narrow, and that the proof they are willing to offer is none the less scientific for lying outside the confines of orthodoxy. In other words, starting out
with the claim that "psychoanalytic conclusions are scientific truths," a claim
which is interesting only because we have come to appreciate that "scientific"
truths tend to be correct because they have been arrived at by a particular method, the analysts immediately proceed to alter the meaning of "scientific" in such
a way as to make it include the psychoanalytic findings in question. Such habits
of subtle redefinition are, of course, quite familiar in politics; prestige words
like "democracy" are frequently applied to dictatorships by a process of definition

which turns their customary meaning inside out. The high-priest of all who in-dulge in this pastime, of course, is Humpty Dumpty, whose discussion of the meaning of "glory" has become a classic in the art of sowing semantic confusion.

> "I don't know what you mean by 'glory,' " Alice said. Humpty Dumpty smiled con-temptuously. "Of course you don't—till I tell you. I meant 'there's a nice knock-down argument for you!' " "But 'glory' doesn't mean 'a nice knock-down argument,' " Alice objected. "When *I* use a word," Humpty Dumpty said in rather a scornful tone, "it means just what I choose it to mean—neither more nor less." "The question is," said Alice, "whether you *can* make words mean so many different things." "The question is," said Humpty Dumpty, "which is to be Master—that's all."

A well-known exponent of this practice, Mrs. Baker Eddy, redefined "science" in terms of religion, thus arriving at Christian Science. Communists redefine "science" in terms of Marxian "dialectical materialism," thus arriving at the "people's democracies" with their "dictatorship of the proletariat." The palmist of Brighton pier redefines "science" in terms of her particular mercenary art, thus arriving at "scientific fortune-telling." The claim that psychoanalysis is sci-entific has no ascertainable meaning whatever unless we define the term "sci-ence" in the way agreed on by the great majority of those who have considered the history and practice of science. This is the important question; whether psy-choanalysis is scientific in some other meaning of the term, created merely in order to enable the answer "yes" to be given, is neither here nor there.

What, then, is the evidence on which psychoanalysis is based? Essentially it is clinical rather than experimental. I have already discussed the differing attitudes of the clinician and the experimentalist in the introduction, and shall not here repeat what I have said there. Suffice it to remember that clinical work is often very productive of theories and hypotheses, but weak on proof and verification; that in fact the clinical method by itself cannot produce such proof because in-vestigations are carried out for the avowed purpose of aiding the patient, not of putting searching questions to nature. Even when a special experiment is carefully planned to test the adequacy of a given hypothesis there often arise almost in-superable difficulties in ruling out irrelevant factors, and in isolating the desired effect; in clinical work such isolation is all but impossible. The often-heard claim that "psychoanalytic hypotheses are tested on the couch" (i.e. the couch on which the patient lies during the analytic session) shows a clear misunderstanding of what is meant in science by "testing" hypotheses. We can no more test Freudian hypotheses "on the couch" than we can adjudicate between the rival hypotheses of Newton and Einstein by going to sleep under an apple tree.

What type of evidence other than the clinical do Freud and his followers ad-duce in support to their claims? There are two main varieties. The first relates to the integrated nature of the whole body of hypotheses, theories, practices, and treatments which makes up modern psychoanalysis. An integrated system of constructs in science has unique advantages; it also has considerable dangers inherent in it. The advantages lie in the mutual support which the various parts of the system given to each other; the dangers lie in the tendency for interpretations to be biased in terms of the analyst's preconceived notions. This danger is particularly marked in psychoanalysis because interpretation of observations forms such a large portion of the whole structure.

It is increased by another feature of psychoanalysis which is unique in science, and is reminiscent rather of the practices of the ancient order of Loyola. Each psychoanalyst must pass through a training analysis in which all his actions, dreams, and fantasies are interpreted in Freudian terms, and in which he forms strong emotional bonds with his teacher, bonds which predispose him to accept such interpretations as correct, and which will make it impossible for him to make objective, unbiased judgements about the true relevance of analytic concepts. That this danger is not imaginary is attested by the admission of well-known psychoanalysts. Glover, for example, in arguing against the views of another Freudian which he regarded as pernicious and dangerous, accounted for the adherence of certain analysts to these views in terms of their "emotional certainty of the truth of the analyst's views" acquired in their training analyses under the heretic. But what is sauce for the goose is sauce for the gander, and if the views of the adherents of Melanie Klein are due to their "emotional bias" acquired during the training analysis, surely the same explanation can be given of the views held by Glover and his adherents? In fact, *ad hominem* arguments of this kind form the stock-in-trade of Freudian argumentation; it is because they are recognized not to have scientific validity that they have not usually been turned back on to psychoanalysts themselves.

It is not often realized to what extent this "emotional biasing" through training analysis forms a complete barrier between analyst and critic. Thus Freud states that "the teachings of psychoanalysis are based upon an incalculable number of observations and experiences, and no one who has not repeated those observations upon himself or upon others is in a position to arrive at an independent judgement of it." Thus Freud demands effectively that one must believe in his system before one can criticize it, a demand which is hardly in line with orthodox scientific procedures! Similar claims are made by the Jungians, where Jacobi states that "theoretic conceptions and explanations are adequate only up to a certain point for the comprehension of Jung's system of thought, for in order to understand it completely one must have experienced its vital working on one's self." When it is realized that there are some fifteen or more hostile "analytic" systems making similar claims, it will be clear that no one can be competent to judge between them because no one would have enough time and money to undergo fifteen separate and incompatible personal training analyses!

Claims made for Freudian hypotheses in terms of their forming part of a "system" must therefore be rejected as irrelevant. There are quite a number of such "systems," all disagreeing on fundamental issues, and all relying on proof of the clinical ("couch") variety. But if they are all based on evidence obtained "on the couch," how can we hope to judge between their divergent claims? If the clinical experience of the claimants is the only type of proof attempted, and if these clinical experiences are in flagrant contradiction, then we must either rely on faith, declare the whole matter incapable of a solution, or ask for more acceptable proof. When Freudians claim that their patients produce in their dreams symbols clearly similar to those described by Freud, while Jungians claim with equal fervour that their patients produce in their dreams symbols similar to those posited by Jung, we must look for more experimental evidence before deciding between these claims—unless, indeed, we try to account for both findings in terms of quite a different type of hypothesis, making suggestibility to the known expectations of the analyst responsible for the results of Freudians and Jungians alike!

Such more experimental, factual type of evidence is the second variety offered by analysts, and we must look at it with particular care. Let me quote a particular argument in illustration; an argument taken from Freud's writings and selected because I have found that to many audiences it makes a very strong appeal. Freud argues for the hypothesis that all dreams are in reality wish-fulfilments, and quotes in support reports about the common experiences of explorers and others that when they are starving in their camps they tend to dream about food. Thus the need for food generates the wish for food, and the dream, ever ready to fulfil these wishes, obliges with vistas of two-pound steaks and strawberry shortcake. Here, then, we have outside support for our hypothesis, and the scientific proprieties appear to be fulfilled.

Let me restate this argument in more formal terms. On the basis of detailed observation of the dreams of many patients, we arrive at the hypothesis that "dreams are wish-fulfilments." From this hypothesis we deduce that starving men should dream of food. . If this can be shown to be so, our hypothesis is supported; if this can be shown not to be so, our hypothesis is decisively disproved. Now Freud does not provide us with experimental evidence of any kind; he relies on anecdotal evidence of the most unreliable variety, second-hand, selective, and incomplete. Little value can be attributed to it. Fortunately we have more recent reports of adequately controlled, well-carried-out experiments into human starvation, experiments in which the participants lost almost a quarter of their body weight. Detailed records were made of their dreams, and comparisons with properly-fed individuals failed to show any tendency, however small, for the starving subjects to report more food-dreams than the control group. Thus experimental procedures show Freud's anecdotal evidence up as inconclusive and irrelevant; they also disprove his fundamental hypothesis regarding the nature and purpose of the dream.

Similar findings have again and again attended the detailed investigation along experimental lines of Freudian generalizations. Orlansky, Sears, and many others have summarized the experimental literature dealing with Freudian concepts, and the outcome, by and large, has been that for every hypothesis supported there are at least two where the evidence is doubtful, or clearly contrary to expectation. This is by no means a bad average as scientific hypotheses go, but it does seem to dispose of the Freudian system as such. Much may be salvaged, and taken over into newer systems of personality description; indeed, psychology will for many years to come be deeply indebted to the intrepid genius who infused new life into a rather philosophical and academic discipline. But however highly we may value these hypotheses and insights, psychoanalysis as a self-contained system claiming to afford a scientific view of human nature is dead, even though the embalmed corpse may still be exhibited to the faithful.

How does psychoanalysis counter the factual arguments brought against it? In the first place, by claiming that its therapeutic procedures work, thus lending important support to the theories and hypotheses on which it is based. I have examined the evidence regarding the effectiveness of psychotherapy in another chapter of this book, and we may notice only the conclusion, to the effect that the available evidence, which is technically faulty and of very doubtful value, being based almost entirely on the opinion of each psychotherapist regarding the success of his own therapy, gives no support whatever to the contention that psychotherapy alleviates the mental suffering of neurotics. Some two patients out of three do tend to improve during therapy, but similarly two patients out of three improve without being given any psychotherapy at all. Thus this argument can hardly be used in order to bolster up the contentions of the Freudians.

The second defence of the psychoanalysts relates to a feature of their system which will be familiar to those who have made a study of semi-religious systems, ranging from biblical prophecy to dialectical materialism. The original statements are couched in such vague, general and complex ways that deductions cannot be made with any degree of definiteness; interpretation thus becomes necessary, and a class of self-styled "experts" arises, claiming to expound the pure truth of the original, and relating it to current problems and current thought. As Ellis, himself an analyst, points out, "analytic theory has so far been formulated in such a loose and unverifiable manner as to encourage some analysts to verge dangerously close to mysticism, than which nothing is less scientific." He goes on to direct attention to the fact that analysis has tended to attract more than its due share of individuals who seem to be mystical-minded, a fact he attributes to four main causes: "*(a)* analysis has *not* held strictly to scientific principles, but has allowed considerable non-scientific leeway to its devotees; *(b)* it has attracted to its ranks many neurotics who have great need of mystical, non-logical defences, and who must continually fall back on religio-mystical philosophies to bolster their inabilities to face the grim realities of contemporary life; *(c)* it has tolerated vague, generalized formulations which are ever but a step removed from mysticism, and which may easily be mystically interpreted; *(d)* it has frequently been cultish and obscurantist: which is precisely what mystics inevitably tend to be, too." Be that as it may, the fact is indisputable that Freudian theories are not simple, straightforward statements of hypotheses from which testable deductions can be made; they are highly involved, loose *obiter dicta* which require interpretation before being intelligible, which are frequently contradictory, and which do not easily lend themselves to processes of scientific proof and disproof. This makes them almost completely resistant to disproof; if deductions from psychoanalytic hypotheses are not verified it can always be maintained that the deduction rests on an erroneous understanding of the hypothesis, and that an alternative "interpretation" of the hypothesis would indeed predict the ex-perimentally-found facts. Thus Freudian hypotheses are indeed quite invulnerable, being too indefinite for factual deductions to be made with any certainty; by the same token they are also unscientific and useless.

It is the third defence of the psychoanalysts, however, which constitutes a master-stroke of tactical brilliance. They make use of concepts such as "reaction formation," which allow a person who theoretically should show behaviour pat-tern A to react away from this pattern to such an extent that he shows instead the opposite pattern, Z. Thus the person who because of various hypothetical childhood events is supposed to be timorous may through reaction formation be outwardly aggressive and tough; thus the hypothesis is verified regardless of whether the patient is found to be either timorous or aggressive. Jung makes use of a similar mechanism by stating that persons who are outwardly introverted are unconsciously extraverted, while those who are outwardly extraverted are unconsciously introverted—thus making it possible to "explain" any type of conduct simply by referring it either to the conscious or to the unconscious por-tion of the patient's personality. It is this feature of analytic thought, more than any other, which serves the analyst as a defence mechanism, because all reactions whatever can thus be explained after a fashion, even if none can be predicted. However, it is not *ex post facto* explanation which constitutes science, but pre-diction which can be verified. Here the concept of reaction formation is of course quite useless, because it does not help us in deciding between a number of pos-sible alternatives. Concepts like reaction formation are essentially *ad hoc* hy-potheses which inevitably explain the individual case because they have been put forward especially in order to explain it, but which do not fit into any sys-tematic framework, and which are anathema to scientists because of the ease with which they can be advanced, and the difficulty of proving or disproving them. If we make up an *ad hoc* hypothesis for every new case—which essentially is the method of psychoanalysis—then we shall never go beyond the present position where we can explain everything and predict nothing.

So far we have criticized analytic procedures on general grounds; it may be useful to particularize and state a few of the objections which psychologists have brought forward against various features of contemporary psychoanalysis. In the first place, then, *psychoanalytic conclusions are based on unreliable data*. Its data are introspections (of the analyst) and verbalized statements (of the anal-ysand). Data of this kind are essentially subjective, and therefore present special difficulties to the scientist. These difficulties are not insuperable; verbatim re-cordings can be made of the analytic session, and Roger and other non-analytic workers have shown how useful and indeed invaluable such recordings can be in tracing the course of therapy, in validating hypotheses advanced by the therapist, and in checking the accuracy of the extremely fallible memory of the therapist. In relying on his memory alone, the therapist easily becomes selective, and what is recorded by him in the case history tends to be what fits in with his preconceived ideas. Thus what is reported by the analyst in articles and books is seldom the whole evidence; it is a highly selected part of the evidence, usually taken from a few highly selected cases. No general conclusions can be drawn from such data, particularly as the analyst seldom attempts the essential cross-check of going through his data to find evidence against his preconceived notions, and in favour of a hypothesis different to the one suggested by Freudian theory.

This would not be so dangerous if the data presented by the analyst were at least direct records, however selected, of what occurred in the analytic session. But usually *psychoanalytic data prejudge the issue* by mixing inextricably raw data and analytic interpretation. The reader who is familiar with Freud's own writings, or with those of any of his followers, will be able to check for himself the ratio of fact and interpretation in the cases there reported. As Wittels admits in his biography of Freud, "Freud's specific method of investigation . . . was not suitable for setting up boundaries and strict definitions. Through insight into himself, he came to understand a psychological phenomenon, and from the beginning his discoveries carried a strong inner conviction of certitude." As Ellis comments on this passage, "while an inner conviction of certitude is indubitably a fine trait for a prophet to possess, its liabilities for a scientist should be sufficiently obvious to warrant no further comment." It is this inner conviction of certitude which presumably makes the analytic writers eager to convince by argument, rather than to prove by fact, and which leads to this inextricable combination of verbal report and interpretation.

Psychoanalysts overgeneralize their conclusions. Freud based his imposing edifice on the verbal statements of a few hundred middle-class Viennese neurotics. Instead of confining his conclusions to the population of which this was a sample—as would have been the proper scientific procedure—he extended them to all human beings, at all times, everywhere. In other words, he thought to have divined universal truth from an extremely unrepresentative sample of human beings. What is true of his neurotic patients (assuming for the moment that his observations were accurate, and his hypotheses correct) is obviously not necessarily true of non-neurotic Trobriand Islanders; indeed, Malinowsky has shown with a wealth of detailed illustrations that Freudian theories are very strongly culture-bound, and have to undergo considerable modification if they are to be applied in any way to other groups. What is true of middle-class people is not necessarily true of working-class people; in another chapter I have discussed the facts supporting this statement at some length, and will therefore not deal with them again here. Nor does the fault lie with Freud alone. Most of his followers have emulated his example, and there are several cases where what has been alleged to have been found true in one case has been generalized to the whole of humanity! Overgeneralization of this kind puts psychoanalysis outside the pale of science; before findings are extended beyond the group on which they were originally established, there must be acceptable proof that such extension is warranted.

Psychoanalysts apply their putative principles to general social phenomena without proof of their applicability. Even if Freud's theories and hypotheses were strictly applicable to human beings as individuals, it would not follow that we could account for social phenomena such as war, industrial unrest, or artistic production by their means. Many analysts, however, have extended these theories to deal with almost all the social problems which beset us, always from a theoretical point of view, i.e. without any reference to fact, and usually without the humility of the scientist presenting a hypothesis. These dubious speculations are presented as facts, and society is urged to take action accordingly.... I have seen it suggested in a serious document intended for official consumption that part of the unrest in the coalfields was due to the unconscious conflicts aroused in the miner by having to use his pick-axe (a phallic male symbol) on "mother earth" (a mother symbol). To the layman, who finds difficulties in distinguishing between psychology, psychoanalysis, and psychiatry, such far-fetched ideas are likely to bring all three into disrepute, although there is probably no serious psychologist who would subscribe to views of this type. Freud himself has issued a warning against "indiscriminate psychoanalysing" of all and sundry; it is unfortunate that his followers have not always followed this sober advice.

Where Freudian hypotheses are used to guide research, this research is often illustrative of preconceptions, rather than a crucial test of the hypothesis. Thus the hypothesis that broken homes produce neurosis may lead to a demonstration that neurotics frequently come from broken homes. This fact, of course, is not crucial unless it can also be shown that people who do not suffer from neurosis tend to come from broken homes in a significantly smaller number of cases. But this second part of the experiment is hardly ever performed by Freudians. Figures published by the American Army showed that a large proportion of neurotics did indeed come from broken homes; they also show, however, that normal and especially well-adapted soldiers also came from broken homes in almost equally large proportion. These figures indicate that the broken home had only a vanishingly small part, if any, to play in the genesis of neurosis.

This neglect of control groups to provide the negative part of the inductive argument is a very characteristic part of Freudian experimentation. Again and again a causal sequence is asserted because certain events are found to occur frequently in the early years of the lives of neurotics; hardly ever is there any attempt to show that these events occur less frequently, or not at all, in the lives of non-neurotics. The analyst may retort that we are all neurotic, after all, unless psychoanalysed according to the dictates of Freud (of Jung, or Stekel, or Adler, or whoever may be the father-figure of the analyst who is talking), and that therefore these events would be expected to occur universally. But this argument clearly proves too much; we may all be neurotic, but some of us are more neurotic than others, and it is the causes of these individual differences which we wish to know about. If the causes adduced by Freudians are universal, then by that token they cannot help us in accounting for the fact that one person has a nervous breakdown, while another overcomes his difficulties in less neurotic ways.

Psychoanalytic arguments from facts beg the question. Let us turn to the preceding argument that broken homes cause neurosis, and let us assume that it had been established beyond doubt that broken homes were more frequent in the histories of neurotics than in the histories of non-neurotics. To argue from this that the broken homes were in any way responsible for the subsequent neurosis would be a clear example of an ancient logical fallacy, namely, that of the *post hoc, ergo propter hoc* argument. To the statisticians, this fallacy is known as "arguing from correlations to causes." All that could be regarded as established would be that broken homes and neurosis are correlated; this correlation tells us nothing whatsoever about the causal sequences involved. The Freudian interpretation is an environmentalistic one; it would be just as reasonable to invoke a hereditary one, somewhat along these lines. Predisposition to neurosis is inherited—neurotic parents, neurotic children. But neurotic parents are likely to have their marriages fail, so that their children will grow up with the background of a broken home. Consequently, we shall find that neurotics will tend to come with disturbing frequency from broken homes—not because the broken home causes the neurosis, but because the parents' neurosis causes both the broken home and (through heredity) the child's neurosis. I do not claim that this second hypothesis, along hereditarian lines, is more likely to be true than the Freudian (although there is considerable evidence for the view that neurotic predisposition and emotional instability are to a considerable extent inherited traits); I am concerned with the calm disregard by psychoanalysts of non-Freudian hypotheses which might explain the alleged facts equally well. Science advances by eliminating counter-hypotheses through carefully controlled experiments; it does not advance by begging the question. When it is realized that the alleged facts themselves are of very doubtful standing, and often merely the projections of the analyst's own wishes and desires, it will be realized why scientists are chary of accepting the analytic account of human nature as anything but brilliant speculation.

Protests against these methods of conducting research and of advancing arguments and proofs are not confined to psychologists; many orthodox psychiatrists are equally severe in their censure. Elliot Slater sums the matter up extremely well when he says: "There has ... been an increasing tendency among clinicians to minimize the effects attributable to genetical causes, and to teach a psychiatry in which they receive little or no mention. This tendency has been marked in Britain, but it has assumed formidable strength in the U.S.A. Instead of a harmonious development, in which the psychoses and neuroses, constitution and environment, psychogenesis and physiogenesis receive their due share of attention, interest among practical workers has been devoted more and more exclusively towards psychotherapy, psychoanalysis, social psychiatry, personnel selection, group therapy, and preoccupations with anthropology, sociology, and political theory. In its one-sidedness, this development is not healthy.

"It would not perhaps be putting it too high to say that we are witnessing the manifestation of an anti-scientific tendency which is winning an increasing number of supporters. The customary canons of scientific reasoning are ignored by these schools. Uncomfortable facts are left unconsidered. Hypotheses are multiplied regardless of the principle of economy. Explanations which may be valid for certain members of a class of phenomena are regarded as true for the class as a whole. Interpretations which conform with theory, and which might be true, are regarded as established. Possible alternatives are not considered, and no attempt is made to seek for evidence of critical value which shall decide between them. Criticisms from outside are ignored, and only the initiate may be heard. Utterance is dogmatic and lacks scientific humility and caution. These are the mental mechanisms which we associated with the growth of a religious orthodoxy, and not with the progress of science."

If this chapter has been critical, it has been so because I am concerned about the future of psychology. However much psychologists may show their desire not to be held responsible for the views advanced by psychoanalysts, society often fails to mark the distinction between scientific statement, based on fact and rigorous logical and statistical reasoning, and the kind of *obiter dicta* discussed in this chapter, based on assumptions and loose and wishful thinking. If the latter are in due course discredited, this discredit will almost certainly attach to the whole of psychology and psychiatry, instead of only to the group responsible.

I would not like to be understood as condemning psychoanalysis hook, line, and sinker. Like most psychologists, I appreciate the breath of fresh air which Freud introduced into the musty dry-as-dust atmosphere of nineteenth-century academic psychology. The brilliance of his mind has opened doors which no one now would wish to close again, and his keen insight has given us a storehouse of theories and hypotheses which will keep researchers busy for many years to come. All this one can appreciate without accepting the totality of his views as revelations from a higher authority, and without losing one's critical sense. There is much that is supremely important in Freud's contribution to psychology, but there is also much that is bad. To eliminate the latter, without losing the former, must be the task of a scientifically-orientated psychology. The answer to the question which forms the title of this chapter—What is wrong with psychoanalysis?—is simple: Psychoanalysis is unscientific. It is only by bringing to bear the traditional methods of scientific inference and experimentation that we can hope to reap all the benefit of its founder's genius.

2

On Psychoanalysis as History

Hans Meyerhoff

There are various ways of dealing with the relationship between psychoanalysis and history, for there is much common ground between the two disciplines. Psychoanalysis, as we know, has its own philosophy of history. It is to be found primarily in the works which Freud wrote during the last phase of his life, say from *Totem and Taboo* in 1913 to *Moses and Monotheism* in 1939. We now have a considerable body of literature on this subject, chiefly by "outsiders," i.e., sociologists and philosophers, and I will not add anything to this discussion.[1]

Another link between the two disciplines is the use of psychoanalysis in history. Thus a few years ago, a distinguished historian startled his professional colleagues in a presidential address delivered before the American Historical Association by pleading seriously that a "deepening of the historical understanding" was possible only through a more extensive use of psychoanalysis.[2] Freud himself was surprisingly reluctant about applying psychoanalysis to specific problems and personalities in history. In a very thoughtful letter to Arnold Zweig, he explicitly warned against doing this sort of thing in the case of Nietzsche.[3] And while he did play the game of analyzing historical figures in his letters, he did not do so in his official works—with one notable exception: the as yet unpublished study of Woodrow Wilson which Freud wrote in collaboration with William Bullitt.[4]

Again, I will not say anything else on this interesting and difficult subject. Thus I do not discuss great speculative ideas in philosophy nor specific practical problems in history. I deal with a different topic, more modest and less exciting. Psychoanalysis and history also have a great deal in common (1) because a historical method is an integral part of psychoanalytic theory and therapy, (2) because, though formulated as a strictly psychological theory, psychoanalysis cannot be divorced from a study of history and society. The primary purpose of this paper, then, is to consider these similarities in method between the two disci-

Reprinted from *Psychoanalysis and the Psychoanalytic Review,* vol. 49, no. 1 (Summer 1962) pp. 3–20.

plines or, more simply, to look at psychoanalysis from a different perspective: not as a branch of the general sciences, biological, medical, or psychological, but as a branch of history.

It is customary to say, especially among clinicians, that psychoanalysis is (or should be) a science, no more and no less. This is a perfectly legitimate view supported as it is by Freud's own authority and by the persistent endeavors since Freud to improve the scientific status of psychoanalysis. Psychoanalysis *is* like any other science in several respects. It has developed a theoretical system of its own consisting of abstract concepts, principles, and (possibly) general laws. And this system presumably is "open": it may be revised in the light of new evidence and as a result of rethinking old concepts. The theoretical system provides the basis and support for the specific work in therapy. Thus psychoanalytic explanations are guided and controlled by psychoanalytic theory. There is a theory of dreams; there is a theory of neuroses; and, above all, there is a general theory of the mind to explain the infinite variety of individual behavior.

There is no need to belabor this point. There are, of course, many difficult problems which arise in the context of psychoanalytic theory; but that's a different topic. I do not wish to question the scientific status of psychoanalysis. Let us agree that, in principle, it is like any other science regardless of how unfriendly critics may judge its actual performance. Yet, though it has its own theory in the scientific sense, psychoanalysis, if not a branch of history, has very close affiliations with history. Moreover, these affiliations are neither accidental nor negligible. They are an essential aspect of psychoanalysis as a "science." Psychoanalysis is an interesting logical specimen because it is and must be both science and history. Thus a historical perspective may help to clarify certain problems—both logical and ideological—which haunt psychoanalysis and which seem to be peculiarly impervious to treatment by strictly scientific methods. The remainder of this paper is an attempt to make the historical dimension inherent in psychoanalysis more explicit and more respectable.

II

"Psychoanalysis is the most radically historical psychology: this is its basic challenge to all other psychologies."[5] What, then, is historical about psychoanalysis?

To begin with, psychoanalytic theory itself is historical. In contrast to other types of psychology, psychoanalysis employs a historical method and characteristically historical concepts in the study of human behavior. The method is based on the simple proposition that we know the patient when we know his history. Thus "case histories" are an integral part of psychoanalytic theory. They are not, as we shall see, symptoms of an underdeveloped science. Again, psychoanalytic concepts are historical or evolutionary: they have a temporal sense and direction built into them. They may refer to fixed points in time; they may try to catch developmental (dynamic) processes such as reaction-formations, sublimations, integrative or regressive processes; or they may simply describe crucial stages on life's way—from the oral to the genital stage of development. In brief, they deal with the vicissitudes—i.e., the historical fate—of the libido. In a striking literary image Freud, as you know, compared the mind and life of man to the historical model of the ancient city of Rome.

The basic project of psychoanalysis is historical. It consists in discovering the past as it survives in the present life of the patient. This is possible because of memory. Our patients, as Freud said, suffer from memories. Man is a distinctly historical animal because he remembers. Memory introduces a historical dimension into human life beyond the biological processes of growth, maturation, and death. Because of memory human beings are conscious of having a history. And because of memory, the "past" makes all the difference in the present and future life of the individual.

In practice, this historical (or genetic) method "works" by making and remaking the history of the patient. Thus the concrete application of history to psychoanalysis occurs in the context of clinical work. The clinical situation is essentially a historical situation; or, in Erikson's words, the "thearapeutic encounter" is a historical process. It consists in remembering, recording, and reconstructing a significant slice of human history: the patient's history as unveiled in interaction with the therapist.

Erik Erikson has paid special attention to these affinities between psychoanalysis and history as they apply to clinical work and to the psychoanalytic treatment of a historical problem.[6] Moreover, he has presented some of his own ideas by referring to the work, *The Idea of History,* by the English philosopher and historian, R. G. Collingwood. There are two major features of Collingwood's conception of history which are particularly appropriate to the work in psychoanalysis: First, for Collingwood (as for Croce) history is always "contemporary" in the sense that it is a reconstruction of the past "as it survives in the present." Thus history involves a specific reference to the present—and possibly to the future; for the present presumably always includes a direction toward the future. Second, for Collingwood (as for Dilthey) history is always the re-enactment of some *thought* of the past in the mind of the contemporary historian. Thus the task of the historian is not simply to preserve the dry-as-dust facts of the past: the assassination of Lincoln, the fate of the Armada, the burning of Moscow, the massacre of St. Bartholomew's, and so forth; the essential task of the historian is to rethink the states of mind of the human agents involved in these happenings or to explain their feelings, ideas, motivations, and intentions. In short, the historian is engaged in a "psychological" project of a highly introspective nature; for it is his task to discover the inner and hidden "meaning" behind the overt sequence of events.

Collingwood, of course, is not the only philosopher in the field of history; but his ideas on the subject have been very influential in recent years and they are obviously pertinent to the historical project in psychoanalysis. This project also aims at disclosing the inner and hidden meaning of past events: the feelings, fantasies, and ideas associated with, or repressed in, memories; and the therapist's role consists primarily in rethinking the processes, both conscious and unconscious, unfolding in the patient's mind. Moreover, a psychoanalytic inquiry into the past is always oriented toward the present—and the future. Remembering in therapy is also an act of appropriating the past in order to forget. To cure the patient of his memories is to deliver him from the tyranny of the past. In this sense, psychoanalysis serves the cause of human freedom: its primary purpose is to expand and reinforce the areas of life, both present and future, in which the individual can choose freely and responsibly because he has become the master of his own history.

The practical demands imposed upon a therapist differ, of course, from the case of a historian imbued with what Professor Lovejoy has called a "purely archaeological motive"; i.e., a pure passion for discovering the truth about the past for its own sake. Yet, even if there be such simon-pure passion—which is doubtful—it is not incompatible with the belief that more and better knowledge about the past may also be a means for a deeper insight into and a more intelligent response to the present. Thus, according to Mr. Carr, history has a dual function which corresponds closely to the basic project in psychoanalysis: "to enable man to understand the society of the past and to increase his mastery over the society of the present."[7] And even Professor Lovejoy, concerned as he is with saving the theory of history from any involvement with present interests, concedes that "history is a branch of anthropology, in the largest sense of the term, and the historian is contributing in his own fashion to mankind's effort to fulfill the Delphian imperative."[8] What else but "Know thyself" is the categorical imperative inherent in psychoanalysis? Why? Because self-knowledge is believed to be the key to human freedom and to the discovery of one's own identity. Thus what ordinary history does for the collective life of mankind, psychoanalysis does for the life of the individual.

III

These historical features of psychoanalysis give rise to two significant problems: (1) the problem of objectivity, (2) the problem of explanation. With regard to both problems, psychoanalysis finds itself in the same camp with history.

The clinical situation is unique in that it involves another person—the therapist—in the very process he is studying. I don't mean to say that he gets involved in the outside life of his patient (though, I understand, this has happened). Nor do I mean that a trained therapist cannot look upon the "case" as if it were merely an "object" for scientific study. We know that he must be capable of detachment or of what some writers in history have called an "effort of self-transcendence" or an "act of self-emptying."[9] Yet it is an open question, in history as in therapy, whether the analyst can ever detach himself so completely from the evidence he is studying that he is nothing but a free-floating, neutral observer. According to Erikson, this is not possible in the therapeutic encounter; for the "objective" study of the patient's past is a process in which the therapist is "subjectively" involved in a logical sense: his own affective and emotional responses are part of the historical process unfolding on the couch; and this situation "highlights one methodological point truly unique in clinical work."[10] The emotional responses of the clinician are part of the *evidence* for the case he is analyzing. They serve as "an evidential source and as a guide in intervention."[11] I cannot here present Erikson's reasons for making this startling assertion. In the specific case discussed by him in detail, Erikson derives this conclusion from the interpretation of a dream. This interpretation, he shows, is based not only upon an expert knowledge of psychoanalytic theory, but also upon an emotional response, more precisely, upon responding to a sense of anger felt by the therapist at a crucial juncture in the analysis of the patient.

Thus the therapist in reconstructing the specific case before him may (and must) fall back upon private resources of his own not at the disposal of anyone else. He must also "feel" his way through the evidence; or, if you prefer, he must learn to trust his unconscious. Obviously, there is no one who can double in brass for one's unconscious. Nor can the therapeutic situation, strictly speaking, be reenacted at a later time; for "later" means that time has passed and that the people concerned with a review of the case are not the same. Thus the "objective" evidence presented later, on a tape or a film, cannot be analyzed as it would or might have been during the actual process of therapy. There is no escape from this element of historicity: time and place make all the difference in psychoanalysis as in history.

Emotional responses, however, whether anger, affection, or what not, are but one aspect of this strange encounter. Even as the case before him can be reconstructed and treated only by a "psychoanalysis of the total personality"—to cite the pioneer work of Franz Alexander—so the therapist himself is involved as a whole human being in this historical process. He is engaged as a total personality as well—at least theoretically; for he must mobilize all the resources of his personality, emotional and intellectual, imaginative and moral, logical and ideological, in order to solve the particular puzzle before him. He must respond to the clinical situation in terms of his whole life. In this sense, therapy is an "existential" encounter.

A similar situation prevails in history; for what is the evidence in history? Of course, dates and documents, facts and figures—the primary sources; and nobody doubts the truth of the simple factual statement that Lincoln was assassinated in Ford's Theater in Washington on the 14th of April 1865. Yet the truth of such factual statements is not what makes history: accuracy in these matters, getting the facts straight, "is a duty, not a virtue."[12] What makes history is to explain and interpret these happenings; that is, to write a significant narrative, not a compilation of facts. In other words, facts must be selected and interpreted so that we are shown what they "mean." Evidence in history as in psychoanalysis is always interpreted evidence. Facts are significant only in a context of interpretation.

In the case of an interpretive study of Lincoln's death the evidence appealed to consists of more than primary sources. "Potentially and in principle," as Collingwood pointed out, "the whole perceptible world is evidence for the historian."[13] What he had in mind was that the evidence is found not in the documents only—or in the associations on the couch; *part* of the evidence is supplied by the historian's own personal experience. Again, what are the principles which guide the historian in his interpretations? Of course, he is guided by the "facts"; of course, he observes the principles of ordinary logic and draws upon every possible kind of knowledge in the general (scientific) sense. A historian writing about the origins of World War II must also use general laws and theories about nature, man, and society. Only in the case of ordinary history (unlike psychoanalysis which has its own theory) this general body of knowledge is usually derived from nonhistorical sources—from common sense or from some other science such as physics, geography, economics, or psychology. Yet, after these various resources have been exhausted, "the interpreting of evidence," to cite Collingwood again, "is [also] a task to which a man must bring everything he knows; . . . and not knowledge only, but mental habits and possessions of every kind; and none of these is unchanging." Why not? Because they change in his own life as in history. Thus the historian is "always a part of the process he is studying"[14]—which corresponds to what Erikson singled out as the unique feature inherent in clinical work.

It follows that, however conscientious and self-critical he may be in his work, the historian cannot be completely neutral. He cannot step outside history—his own place in history. While studying history he is also—in part—a product of history, and the ideas he employs for interpreting history are themselves part of the historical process. This creates a much more intimate relationship between observer and observed than in a study of nature where it seems to be easier to enforce a strict dichotomy between subject and object. In this sense, the historian is more involved—logically involved—in the study of history than a scientist is in a study of nature. By "logically involved" I mean that he is "at the same time both the subject and the object of historical knowledge"[15]; he is caught up in the historical process in his thinking about history; and he is indebted to history for the ideas and concepts he employs for an understanding of history.

Perhaps he is more emotionally involved as well; for a historian cannot but care about the community of men as he need not care about a colony of mice. He cannot be as indifferent about the behavior of human beings as he may be about the behavior of molecules. And "caring," of course, is an emotional term, or "subjective." It's more than that; for it is a complex attitude including emotional, intellectual, moral, and ideological components. It is a response in terms of one's whole personality—the way one thinks and feels about human life and the world in general.

It may be possible to leave this personal view of the world at home when we are doing scientific work in the laboratory. History cannot be written without it; and it would be wishful thinking to close one's eyes to the presence of a personal equation in psychoanalysis. There are many ways in which personal factors of age, sex, class, culture, and ideology intrude upon the "scientific" work in these two disciplines. Thus there is at least a *prima facie* case for skepticism.

Both history and psychoanalysis have used similar methods to cope with this threat of skepticism. Both have developed objective controls to reduce the effect of the personal equation and, if possible, to expunge it altogether. In history, these controls are known as the "critical method." Developed in the nineteenth century along with what are known as the "auxiliary sciences" of history—archaeology, epigraphy, paleography, and so forth—this method has been constantly improved and expanded. It promised to raise history to the status of "a science, no less and no more."[16] Whether this is so or not, the scientific method of history is now a *sine qua non* for doing any serious and respectable work in the field. Similarly, psychoanalysis has developed objective controls to curb capricious guesswork and private intuitions. They include a didactic analysis, a supervised analysis, controlled observations, experimental work, and objective tests of various kinds. These controls operate in conjunction with psychoanalytic theory; and both theory and controls are designed to achieve a degree of objectivity which we associate with knowledge in other sciences. The ideal goal, in history as in psychoanalysis, is to eliminate the personal equation, to make the findings in both disciplines as "objective" as possible. Thus in both fields we can and do expose crackpots, charlatans, and propagandists; we can and do distinguish between science and fiction.

Yet, after we have done all we can and should along these lines, there remains a residue which seems to be impervious to any treatment by objective methods. Take the case of disagreements in history and in psychoanalysis: they are very much like disagreements in ordinary life—or in philosophy. In fact, as the history of the psychoanalytic movement shows, serious disagreements and deviations invariably reflect basic philosophical differences. They are not caused—nor resolved—simply by appealing to the facts and the logic of the case. They are not decided on the basis of strictly objective criteria. I know we make allowance for this defect by saying that psychoanalysis, along with other human sciences, is still in a relatively primitive state as compared with the physical sciences; but, while this is true, the long record of radical and intractable disagreements in history may make us wonder whether it is the whole truth. We do not find in history any agreement upon a universal conceptual framework of interpretation as we do in the development of the physical sciences. Thus I suspect the defect is more deep-seated than we like to admit—due to the fact, as I have suggested, that in history as in psychoanalysis (or in ordinary life) we are more deeply involved in the subject matter we are studying than we are in a study of nature. This involvement may be quite nonspecific. Thus it need not be expressed in obvious prejudices and interests, whether personal or social. It may be a more general bias, an unconscious slant, as it were, derived from one's whole experience of life or one's total response to the world. Nevertheless, this is a very "subjective" sort of thing. And it is a flaw which is an integral part of the logical structure in history and in psychoanalysis.

IV

I now turn to another area, the context of explanation, in which the intimate connection between psychoanalysis and history is particularly conspicuous. Why case histories? Because the general theory—though necessary—is not enough to explain the individual case. Now it is frequently said, and correctly, that this is so in every science. We would not hail the discovery of general laws if these laws could not be used to explain, and predict, the behavior of particular events; yet in applying these laws, say, the laws of ballistics, we must always modify our calculations deduced from the laws in terms of specific conditions—type of gun, weather, wind, terrain, and so forth—which prevail at a certain time and place.

In psychoanalysis, however, this familiar problem appears in a different light. The artillery unit need not know anything about the history of the gun or how it came to be mounted at Fort Sumter in order to understand how it works. Yet psychoanalysis "works" only insofar as we reconstruct the history of the individual case. To put the matter differently, in both history and psychoanalysis, it is not only more difficult to specify the initial and boundary conditions relevant to the particular case; but this specification involves a historical analysis. Thus we do not get out of the "historical" circle. A historical method is needed in order to determine the specific conditions modifying the application of the general law. This does not mean that we can do without a general theory. To repeat: psychoanalysis does have its own (scientific) theory; and the individual case, whether a dream or a neurotic symptom, may be explained by appealing to this general theory even as the case serves as evidence for the theory. Yet a case history also employs a characteristically historical type of explanation; for it shows not only how to explain a particular case in terms of a general theory; it also shows how the pieces of evidence—like the pieces of a jig-saw puzzle or like evidence in court—fit and hang together so that the story we tell provides its own explanation. In this sense, a case history is "self-justifying" and "autonomous" as Collingwood said of a narrative in ordinary history.[17] He did not wish to say that we ever have the final truth; what he meant was that, if history is rewritten, this will be done by telling a "better" story—more complete, more coherent, more intelligible, or what not.

These two methods of explanation deserve to be distinguished; for, in the one case, we explain by showing how the evidence fits into a general theory; in the other case, we explain as we do in history, in court, in a novel, or in ordinary life: by telling a story, a coherent, intelligible story which is "true" for the individual case only. Freud's complaint that, though trying to be a pure scientist, he always came up with results that read as if they were literature, reveals something of this "logical" ambivalence inherent in psychoanalysis. For these reasons, I believe, case histories are an integral part of psychoanalysis, not a symptom of a science still in its infancy. They call attention to the fact that, in a study of human behavior, there are two kinds of knowledge and two types of explanation corresponding to them: a concept of "knowledge" in the scientific sense and an "understanding" of the individual case in the historical sense.

I know this is a controversial thesis which I cannot argue here; but it does not matter whether we say "understanding" or prefer some other expression, "perception," "insight," or what not, to describe the same phenomenon: an understanding of the particular case, the historical *Gestalt,* as it were, or the unique "life-style" of the patient in Erikson's words. What matters is that we find the same kind of language used repeatedly in both history and psychoanalysis—they cannot do without some such concept however ambiguous it may be—and that, logical critics to the contrary notwithstanding, there is no provision in the standard model of scientific knowledge for this characteristically historical type of understanding. Both ways of knowing, the theoretical and the historical, intersect in the field of human life; both interact with each other. Thus without knowledge in the scientific sense we have no theory to check on intuitive nonsense. Yet without an understanding in the historical sense we deal with abstractions only; that is, with man as an abstraction. We do not understand the concrete case, at least not in actual life. In short, to paraphrase Kant: history without theory is blind; theory without history is empty.

In psychoanalysis we cannot fail to see this dialectical schema; but a similar situation, I believe, prevails not only in history, but in other sciences of man and society as well. Scientific studies, say, in sociology, economics, or academic psychology may achieve a spurious kind of objectivity as long as they construct nothing but abstract models and theories. The price they pay for playing these games is that they must abstract from the reality of the human situation; for in actual life we are always involved—as the therapist is in a special sense—with individuals who live in history and have a history. Thus the theoretician in pursuit of the ideal of pure objectivity must deal with human beings in a very artificial setting. He must remove them from the reality in which they actually live and he must lift himself, by his own bootstraps, out of the same historical process. Without this trick he would be just as vulnerable to the historical flaw as psychoanalysis is. Thus he is safe in his science only by escaping from reality—which is an odd conception of "empiricism"; for the reality of life is not caught in the abstract, theoretical models of science, but in the concrete structure of human history.

I suggest, therefore, that psychoanalysis is actually more empirical because it is more than an abstract theory and less than objective. It is both more and less than a science in the ordinary sense because it is also a branch of history. It pays for this entanglement with human life in history as we all do in our efforts to know ourselves and others; for it would be "bad faith" to claim that, in this search for self-knowledge at home or in history, we ever achieve anything like the kind of knowledge produced in a lab. It would not even be desirable; for the ideal of objective knowledge also means that we deal with human beings as if they were nothing but "objects" for a scientific theory. Thus the historical flaw inherent in psychoanalysis may be less objectionable than methodological purists would have us believe. It makes psychoanalysis more "human," as it were; or it shows that, in addition to being an abstract science, psychoanalysis also cares about understanding individuals as we encounter them in actual life, not as we set them up for a psychological experiment. It reminds us that, in the human world, truth is never abstract as in the world of science; it is always concrete; hence, relative to a specific human situation, to time, place, and the individuals involved in it. More correctly, the abstract and the concrete intersect in human life as do theory and history. This reminder renders a significant service in our time; for it is a defense of the rights of the individual to seek his own truth and to choose his own way of life against the dark powers of abstraction prevailing everywhere in the organized systems of science and society. If psychoanalysis is to serve this human cause—an "existential" project, if you like—it must not succumb to pharmacology, but it must be conscious of its own place and function in history.

V

There is something artificial about the therapeutic situation. It is also isolated from reality. Clinical work, of course, is dictated by special needs and objectives which justify this isolation. It is based on a kind of "formal contract" according to which conditions in the outside world are largely disregarded or held in abeyance.[18]

Yet the historical process in therapy is not a private affair; it is a public event as well. Both patient and therapist are also products of the culture in which they live; and both respond not only to each other, but also to the world outside. Hence, what happens in therapy is determined, in part, by the social and cultural situation in which it takes place. "We cannot" (not even as "clinicians") "lift a case history out of history."[19] In other words, we cannot understand the history of the patient without knowing something about the world which made him sick.

A psychoanalytic study of the individual, therefore, cannot be divorced from a study of society. The fate of the libido is always decided in a concrete historical situation. This does not mean that psychological processes do not have their own "inner logic"; what it does mean is that outside conditions, both social and ideological, are built into the psychological structure of man. "We cannot even begin to encompass the human life cycle without learning to account for the fact that a human being under observation has grown stage by stage into a social world...

We cannot even begin to encompass a human being without indicating for each of the stages of his life cycle the framework of social influences and of traditional institutions which determine his perspective on his more infantile past and his more mature future. In this sense, we can learn from patients only to the extent to which we realize (and the patient realizes) that what is said and done in treatment is based on a formal contract between healer and patient and must be carefully transposed before being applied to the general human condition. This is the reason why the fragments of case histories or psychoanalytic interpretations which flutter around in increasing number in our newspapers and magazines seem lost like bats in the daytime."[20]

I have cited this long passage to make a simple point. These are not the sentiments of a Marxist critic; Erikson is not grinding an axe for professional sociologists; he is presumably working within the framework of traditional psychoanalytic theory. Yet he buries at least one controversy as artificial as it is misleading: the red herring of whether psychoanalysis is a part of biology or sociology. It is rooted in both and always has been since Freud. Biological drives always interact with historical necessities (for work and for moral restraints) imposed by society. In this sense, psychoanalysis is a branch of the social sciences.

It is also a part of the social process itself. We know something about the profound impact psychoanalysis has had upon the modern world in many fields other than clinical psychology. We have also come to acknowledge that, beyond the controlled and responsible methods of clinical work, psychoanalysis—especially in its many popular adaptations—has become an influential ideology in our culture. This ideology is a mixed blessing. "We must grudgingly admit that even as we are trying to devise ... a therapy for the few, we were led to promote an ethical disease among the many."[21] Yet, surprisingly, there are few, if any, studies which deal with the role played by psychoanalysts in society and with the ideological commitments inherent in psychoanalysis. A psychoanalyst cannot afford to close his eyes to these commitments; for they are an integral part of clinical work. Thus in order to refine the objective controls in psychoanalysis and improve its scientific status, psychoanalysis must also become "historically self-conscious."[22] It must cultivate a social consciousness, if you like, an awareness of its own place and function in the world outside the office. Otherwise, alive as the therapist may be to the unconscious processes inside the patient and within himself, he may be quite blind to the social forces without. Thus he cannot confine his study of man to the artificial isolation of the clinical situation; or if he does, he cannot but fall victim to the powers in the world that impose this isolation.

Here again we find an interesting interaction between the two disciplines. Regardless of how effective a tool psychoanalysis may be in solving specific historical problems, it is safe to say that the historian cannot simply disregard it in an effort to understand himself. "We cannot leave history," to cite Erikson once more, "to nonclinical observers and professional historians who often all too nobly immerse themselves into the very disguises, rationalizations, and idealizations of the historical process from which it should be their business to separate themselves."[23] Or, as Mr. Carr observes on behalf of the historical profession, "since Marx and Freud wrote, the historian has no excuse to think of himself as a detached individual standing outside society and outside history. This is the age of self-consciousness: the historian can and should know what he is doing."[24] The injunction holds in reverse as well: in an age of historical self-consciousness, the psychoanalyst has no excuse to think of himself as nothing but a clinical practitioner. Thus even as a historian needs psychoanalysis to become conscious of his emotional blindspots, so the therapist needs a knowledge of history to become conscious of his ideological commitments and their social implications.

When Freud returned, as he said, "after a life-long detour through the natural sciences to the cultural problems" which had "fascinated" him in his youth, this move, I suspect, was more than an excuse for indulging in fancy philosophical speculations. Throughout his life Freud was deeply imbued with a sense of culture and history. More specifically, what did he come back to in the works of his last phase? On the one hand, he revised the metapsychological foundations of psychoanalysis; on the other hand, he analyzed the function of the "cultural superego," the ideological superstructure in society. Thus these works are not merely exercises in speculative philosophy; they are also essays in applied psychology. They deal with concrete social and historical problems; e.g., with the relationship between a leader and the masses in history (as in *Group Psychology*) or with the cultural function of religion (as in *The Future of an Illusion*) or with the pathology of morality (as in *Civilization and its Discontents*). Even *Moses and Monotheism,* it is sometimes forgotten, is more than a stubborn defense of a speculative hypothesis first put forth in *Totem and Taboo;* it was also written as a contribution toward an understanding of the historical function of anti-semitism in the Western world—then erupting in its most virulent and destructive form.

These studies are, on the whole, very critical. They expose and debunk prevailing ideologies. They are a "psychoanalytic critique of society."[25] Thus the issue is not whether psychoanalysis is biologically or culturally oriented. The issue is what kind of social critique is conducted in the name of psychoanalysis; more bluntly, whether psychoanalysis is still capable of serving as a critical voice in society—say, as the biological conscience of a moribund culture.

Psychoanalysis, therefore, needs a sense of history for two reasons: first, to make the therapist conscious of his own place in society; second, to preserve the critical potential inherent in psychoanalysis. A sense of history is essential to keep psychoanalysis from becoming nothing but a "safe" science. Perhaps it is not the most promising state of affairs if psychoanalysis is simply taken for granted as it is in our culture; for as Ernest Jones observed wisely, "one cannot help suspecting that much of the so-called acceptance [of Freud's ideas] is really a subtle form of rejection, a protection against assimilation of their profound impact."[26] There is something offensive about psychoanalysis: it offends common sense and the idols of the Establishment. This is part of its heritage as a science; yet to appropriate and exercise this heritage, the psychoanalyst must be conscious of history. Without a historical consciousness he cannot be true to himself as a scientist.

NOTES

1 For some of this literature, see Herbert Marcuse, *Eros and Civilization* (Boston 1955); Norman O. Brown, *Life Against Death* (Middletown 1959); Philip Rieff, *Freud: The Mind of the Moralist* (New York 1959) and the chapters on Freud in David Riesman, *Individualism Reconsidered* (Glencoe; Ill. 1954).

2 William L. Langer, "The Next Assignment," *American Historical Review,* LXIII, no. 2.

3 Ernest Jones, *The Life and Work of Sigmund Freud* (New York 1957) vol. III, p. 459.

4 *Moses and Monotheism* may be another exception; but Freud's essays on Leonardo and Dostoevsky are not historical studies.

5 Donald Meyer in a review of *Young Man Luther* by Erik Erikson in *Theory and History,* I, 3, p. 294.

6 The two major contributions by Erik Erikson on which I have drawn heavily are: "The Nature of Clinical Evidence," in *Evidence and Inference,* ed. by Daniel Lerner (Glencoe, Ill. 1959), hereafter cited as "Evidence," and *Young Man Luther* (New York 1958), hereafter cited as *Luther.* For his statement that the "therapeutic encounter" is historical, see "Evidence," p. 77.

7 Edward Hallett Carr, *What is History?* (New York 1962), p. 69.

8 Arthur O. Lovejoy, "Present Standpoints and Past History," in *The Philosophy of History in Our Time,* ed. by Hans Meyerhoff (Doubleday Anchor: New York 1959), p. 181.

9 *The Philosophy of History in Our Time,* op. cit., p. 174.

10 E. Erikson, "Evidence," p. 93.

11 Ibid.

12 A delightful aperçu by A. E. Housman quoted by Mr. Carr in *What is History?,* op. cit., p. 8.

13 R. G. Collingwood, *The Idea of History* (Oxford 1946), p. 247.

14 Ibid., p. 248.

15 Raymond Aron, "Relativism in History," in *The Philosophy of History in Our Time,* op. cit., p. 154.

16 J. B. Bury, "The Science of History," in *Varieties of History,* ed. by Fritz Stern (Meridian: New York 1956), p. 210.

17 R. G. Collingwood, op. cit., pp. 249, 236.

18 Cf. E. Erikson, *Luther,* p. 20. The terms of this contract, as is well known, may include the condition that the patient must not make any major changes or take major decisions in his life until he has completed therapy.

19 E. Erikson, *Luther,* pp. 15–16.

20 Ibid., p. 20.

21 Ibid., p. 19.

22 Ibid., p. 18.

23 Ibid., p. 20.

24 E. H. Carr, op. cit., p. 186.

25 E. Erikson, *Luther,* p. 21.

26 Ernest Jones, op. cit., vol. III, p. 433.

3

Why Psychoanalysis Needs the Social Scientist and the Historian

Peter Loewenberg

If—which may sound fantastic today—one had to found a college of psychoanalysis, . . . analytic instruction would include branches of knowledge which are remote from medicine and which the doctor does not come across in his practice: the history of civilization, mythology, the psychology of religion and the science of literature. Unless he is well at home in these subjects, an analyst can make nothing of a large amount of his material.

FREUD (1926)

Whether or not the psychoanalysts have found the means to rescue [those whose consciousness is corrupt] or to save those in whom this evil has advanced less far, their attempt to do so is an enterprise that has already won a great place in the history of man's warfare with the powers of darkness.

R. G. COLLINGWOOD (1938)

I

There are many areas of convergence and complementarity between the modes and assumptions of the historian and the psychoanalyst which have been neglected in the usual concentration on differences and oppositions. The aim of this essay is to discuss the congruences between the disciplines of history and psychoanalysis, not to elaborate on their obvious differences. Interdisciplinary work in psychoanalysis has stressed psychodynamic insight into the humanistic and social sciences. Nearly four decades ago the anthropologist Edward Sapir

Reprinted from the *International Review of Psycho-Analysis,* 4 (1977), pp. 305–15.

(1951) wrote his seminal essay, "Why Cultural Anthropology Needs the Psychiatrist." In this important statement, written in 1938, he said:

> Culture cannot be accepted as anything more than a convenient assemblage, or at best total theory, or possible modes of behaviour abstracted from the experienced realities of communication, whether in the form of overt behavior r or in the form of fantasy. . . . We cannot thoroughly understand the dynamics of culture, of society, of history, without sooner or later taking account of the actual interrelationships of human beings. . . . It will be the future task of the psychiatrist to read cause and effect in human history (pp. 575–6).

The manifold contributions which Sapir foresaw have indeed been delivered to history and assimilated, particularly in the areas of biography, mass movements and the interpretation of cultural artifacts. No fair-minded observer can deny that these gifts have been substantial and have benefited the sophistication and complexity both of the perceptual and interpretive phases of the historical enterprise.

I wish here to develop the as yet unrealized obverse of this contribution— what psychoanalytic theory and clinical practice may gain from a familiarity with historical theory and research methodology. There is a common empathic method between history and psychoanalysis that is usually only recognized as going from psychoanalysis to history. This paper will show the reverse to be equally important. In many vital points, especially where psychoanalysis is most vulnerable *vis-à-vis* the natural sciences, the disciplines share a common methodology of empathic insight and understanding. Historians do not deal with live patients who can respond to propositions and they do not try to cure or change their subjects. Yet, there is a great deal to be gained for psychoanalysis, which is besieged by demands for empirical evidence from the side of the "hard" sciences and clinical medicine, by exploring the rich developments of humanistic and social science methodology with which psychodynamics has much in common. The methodological rationales of the humanities can buttress and fortify the intuitive and empathic realms of affect and expression which are the stuff of psychoanalytic evidence and clinical practice.

The historical sciences in particular have over the last century elaborated the justifications and cognitive foundations for the processes of deriving inference from evidence in building a longitudinal picture of events, making causal linkages and hypothesizing reconstructions of the past. A conversance with this interface is of greatest importance for psychoanalysis at this critical juncture in its history. I submit that psychoanalysis, rather than being exclusively a subspecialty of psychiatry, stands at the intersection of the humanities, the social sciences and the natural sciences in particularly crucial ways. I shall draw upon the best of historians and social scientists for my case examples, not among the mediocre, nor even upon the norm, for only the best have utilized the methodology to its full potential.

II

The most obvious, yet most controversial, lesson imparted by history is the necessity to view behaviour in a temporal and cultural context.

A graduate student writing a dissertation on Alexander the Great consulted me for a psychodynamic view of Alexander's apparent homosexuality and his instrumental use of women. According to this student's data, Alexander rarely cohabited with a woman and then only did so when it would further his political or diplomatic purposes. My response was to send the student back to fill in what were the behavioural modes of a royal house in Greek Macedonian culture in the fourth century B.C. with regard to homosexuality and the treatment of women.

The norms of 20th-century mental health cannot be trusted to tell us about average expectable or deviant behaviour in other times. Such apparent givens as the primal scene, the phases of childhood, the onset of puberty, menstruation and the vicissitudes of adolescence turn out not to be immutable at all when viewed in historical perspective. As recently as the 17th century it was normal for parents and children to live and sleep in the same room and bed. Privacy did not exist in the Early Modern European family (Shorter, 1975, pp. 39–44). Mothering was often a matter of indifference and infanticide and abandonment of children was a common practice until the late 18th century (Shorter, 1975, pp. 168–90). There is evidence that the average age of the onset of menses was 17.5 as late as the 1830s in Great Britain and has been moving progressively to earlier ages. It was 16.5 in the 1860s, 15.5 in the 1890s, 14.5 in the 1920s and 13.25 in the 1960s. Starting in 1900, the curve in the United States is roughly parallel, showing a downward tendency for the 20th century, falling among white girls to 12.5 in 1940–45 (Laslett, 1971, p. 222). J. M. Tanner finds that "menarche in Europe has been getting earlier during the last hundred years by between three and four months per decade" (Laslett, 1971, p. 222). The governing variable seems to be the quality of nutrition, particularly protein, and the quantity of calories in early infancy. The critical factor is definitely not hot climates, as was formerly believed. The median menarchical ages according to the latest figures are: 18 years in the Highlands of New Guinea, 17 years in Central Africa, 15.5 years among South African Bantu and Transkei, and 12.5 years among well-off Chinese in Hong Kong—i.e. more or less comparable with Americans and Europeans (Tanner, 1971, pp. 928–9). The consistent increase in average life expectancy, as well as the earlier onset and prolongation of adolescence, means a continuing change in the phase-specific tasks and adaptations in our patients. These temporal differences may also be seen spatially at the present time. The analogues to the historian's movement in time are the anthropologist's movement in space from one culture to another and the sociologist's movement within a culture across class and status groups.

For the psychoanalyst who works with the finest minutiae of his patient's life and communication, the nuances of the cultural variables with which he must deal are also finer. The uniqueness of each patient far transcends the gross categories of classification that social scientists use. Precisely because of this, the normative modes of behaviour against which the patient's unique acts are placed tend to be unconsciously assumed as the backdrop of behaviour.

> The patient, a lady born and raised in a Calvinist culture in north-western Europe, repeatedly presented what she termed her "drinking problem" in the course of analysis, complaining that it was not getting adequate therapeutic attention. By "drinking problem" she meant the guilt feelings she had when drinking, her fantasies of derogatory things that people watching her, including her maid, were thinking. When asked why she could not enjoy a drink she made for herself, the patient talked of not being "nice" and "respectable." At this point I initiated a cultural exploration, inquiring into attitudes towards alcohol in the patient's childhood home and culture, when she had her first drink, what the laws of the land were, including when the taverns closed, the legal age of alcohol consumption, etc. The patient found great relief in this exploration. She related various sexual attitudes, feelings about menstruation, bleeding, nudity, defecation, and what she termed "anal" sexuality, to her childhood home and social culture. The patient frequently thereafter referred to what she termed her "Puritanical" self in her analysis, relating it to various forms of denial of pleasure or the "spoiling" of gratifications.

> A patient was described in consultation as engaging in the apparently bizarre behaviour of secretly saving her earnings in order to buy a high-powered $20,000 foreign sports car for her husband. When a query elicited the information that she was from a south European country where *machismo* is a masculine ideal, her behaviour could be viewed as a grandiose and loving act in terms of her culture, rather than as aberrant as it first appeared to her analyst. Now various issues of her identification of her husband with her father could come into analytic focus.

> A patient referred to his mother as "Mrs. Jones." When I asked why he chose such an oblique way of talking about his mother, he elaborated on his image of her as a character in Samuel Richardson's novel *Clarissa, or the History of a Young Lady*: this had determined his area of academic research, his marriages, etc. It is of the greatest importance for the analyst to learn the patient's particular idiomatic terms for significant others. Did he call his father "Pop" or "Dad" or "Papa"? Was his sister "Baby" or "Betty," "Liz" or "Elizabeth"? Was his mother "Mom," "Mommy" or "Mrs. Jones"? The specific form of the name may be the key that unlocks the emotional closet of the repressed feelings of the past.

In these vignettes we see the relevance of filling in the social and cultural context of each unique clinical situation as precisely as possible. The psychoanalytic models are strong heuristic devices for pointing to the psychodynamics of a neurosis, but they cannot be applied rigidly as formulae. Each case must be fleshed out in its personal and cultural particularity. This emphasis on the unique particularity of each case is a standard canon of historical method and as such provides one of the "deep" points of contact between the disciplines of psychoanalysis and history.

III

A fundamental source of difficulty in placing psychoanalysis as a scientific discipline is a persistent misperception of the nature of science: psychoanalysts too often remain under the sway of 19th-century physicalistic notions of science. Modern science uses metaphors of varying usefulness; truth or falsity is not an issue. As Einstein (1922, p. 1) said: "The object of all science, whether natural science or psychology, is to co-ordinate our experiences and to bring them into a logical system." Freud provided universally recognized scientific achievements that posed model problems and solutions to a community of practitioners. This, the historian of science Thomas Kuhn (1970, p. viii) terms a scientific "paradigm." "Normal science," he writes, "means research firmly based upon one or more past scientific achievements, achievements that some particular scientific community acknowledges for a time as supplying the foundation for its further practice" (p. 10). How different this is from the positivistic concept of the "Yes" or "No" litmus test and the capacity to quantify which too often in clinical psychiatry passes for definitions of science! The issue here is not, "show me the location of the superego (as I can see a tubercle bacillus)," but rather, "does the concept of superego serve a useful explanatory, clinical, and research function?"

Further consequences of recent work in the nature and history of science by Kuhn, Imre Lakatos and Michael Polanyi are that the choice between competing paradigms is not rational, but is based on "all or nothing" conversion experiences, analogous to intuitive religious experiences (Kuhn, 1970, p. 150). Einstein speaks of "the search for those highly universal . . . laws from which a picture of the world can be obtained by pure deduction. There is no logical path leading to these . . . laws. They can only be reached by intuition, based upon something like intellectual love ("Einfühlung") of the objects of experience" (Popper, 1959, p. 32). Kuhn calls this a "paradigm shift." These are made not on the basis of whether a theory can be verified but on its probability of being fruitful as a research strategy. The scientist is making a choice pointing to "one of the directions in which future discussions of verification should go" (Kuhn, 1970, p. 145).

A most important point developed in the history of science during the past two decades is that falsification cannot invalidate a paradigm. Any paradigm, such as the Ptolemaic view of geocentric planetary motion or the Newtonian worldview can be stretched to subsume new data. No theory can be falsified, nor disproved within itself. As Karl Popper (1959) puts it:

> In point of fact, no conclusive disproof of a theory can ever be produced; for it is always possible to say that the experimental results are not reliable, or that the discrepancies which are asserted to exist between experimental results and the theory are only apparent and that they will disappear with the advance of our understanding (p. 50).

Kuhn (1970) stresses that all theories have anomalies:

> No theory ever solves all the puzzles with which it is confronted at a given time; nor are the solutions already achieved often perfect. On the contrary, it is just the incom-

pleteness and imperfection of the existing data-theory fit that, at any time, define many of the puzzles that characterize normal science. If any and every failure to fit were ground for theory rejection, all theories ought to be rejected at all times (p. 146).

The issue becomes which paradigm shall in the future guide research on problems which neither competitor can yet claim to resolve. These are decisions that "can only be made on faith" and "personal and inarticulate aesthetic considerations" (Kuhn, 1970, p. 158). Note how Kuhn uses the idioms of religious conversion and subjective appeal. What does a physicist mean when he says an explanation is "elegant"? One of the meanings intended by the scientist is that the proposition has the aesthetic appeal of economy, harmony and inclusiveness.

The aesthetic appeal of a psychoanalytical reconstruction consists in its logical ability to be in agreement with a narrow range of potential facts. This is what gives an interpretation accepted by the patient "truth value" for a life lived, and justifies the painstaking efforts at thorough clinical exploration and testing of prediction-statements derived from psychoanalytic theory. Likewise, the aesthetic appeal of the historical narrative moves the historian to undertake the process of historical inference and reconstruction when he seeks to establish the character of the background and initial conditions for a longitudinal development. This common aesthetic interest which motivates efforts to secure logical completeness in explanatory historical and psychoanalytical models, the relevance of testing reconstructions, and the desire for factual accuracy in narrative and explanation, should draw those who share it into effective cooperation.

Kuhn (1970) points out that in the great paradigm shifts in the history of science "most of the articulable technical arguments pointed the other way. When first introduced, neither Copernicus' astronomical theory nor De Broglie's theory of matter had many other significant grounds of appeal" (p. 158). Michael Polanyi (1958) demonstrates on a wide front that no "objective framework" can account for a scientist's acceptance or rejection of theories (pp. 12–14). The development of the science of psychoanalysis is a matter of providing the appropriate atmosphere or ecology consisting of what Polanyi (1974) terms "a fund of intuitive approaches and emotional values which can be transmitted from one generation to the other only through the medium of personal collaboration. Scientific research, in short, is an art" (pp. 22–3).

What this means is that two or more competing paradigms imply different world-views with built-in gaps in communication. We begin to see why experimental psychologists and psychoanalysts talk across chasms of mutual incomprehension. The same applies to conceptual differences among psychoanalysts, such as between representatives of the Freudian, Kleinian and object-relational schools. These are gestalt switches for conceptualizing the same clinical data analogous to the perceptual transformations of a Rorschach subject who can see bats and facial profiles from the same ink blot. I concur with Lakatos in his modification of Kuhn when he pleads for numerous paradigms: "The history of science has been and should be a history of competing research programmes (or, if you wish, paradigms), but it has not been and must not become a succession of periods of normal science: the sooner competition starts, the better for progress" (Lakatos, 1970, p. 155). Psychoanalysis can only be better for it if we abandon positivistic ideas of science and adopt a relativistic and pluralistic view of our enterprise. The difference between religion and science is the willingness to let the specific situation dictate the interpretation and the interpretive mode.

IV

Although often unaware of what they are doing, psychoanalysts actually utilize what social scientists conceptualize under the term "model-building." This social scientific tool was developed by the German historical sociologist Max Weber (1864–1920) during the same years that Freud was doing his great creative work. Weber termed these models "ideal types" or "constructed types." They are abstractions from reality, not descriptions of its particularity. Their purpose is to serve as heuristic devices to elucidate certain aspects of phenomena that will then lead to further investigation and analysis.

> The constructed scheme, of course, only serves the purpose of offering an ideal typical means of orientation. It does not teach a philosophy of its own. The theoretically constructed types of conflicting "life orders" are merely intended to show that at certain points such and such internal conflicts are possible and "adequate"... As will readily be seen, the individual spheres of value are prepared with a rational consistency which is rarely found in reality. But they *can* appear thus in reality and in historically important ways, and they have. Such constructions make it possible to determine the typological focus of a historical phenomenon. They enable us to see if, in particular traits or in their total character, the phenomena approximate one of our constructions: to determine the degree of approximation of the historical phenomenon to the theoretically constructed type. To this extent, the construction is merely a technical aid which facilitates a more lucid arrangement and terminology (Gerth & Mills, 1958, pp. 323–4).

Weber made conceptual constructs from social reality that were never encountered in such purity in the complexity of life. His ideal type of capitalist economic behaviour, for example, is a typological simplification. It is a model uniting many characteristics which give capitalism its uniqueness as an economic practice, although any particular attribute may be absent in any given historical case. The ideal type also comprises its multiple tendencies and its long-range goals in history, even if such a pure case nowhere exists.

> An ideal type is formed by the one-sided *accentuation* of one or more points of view and by the synthesis of a great many diffuse, discrete, more or less present and occasionally absent *concrete individual* phenomena, which are arranged according to those one-sidedly emphasized viewpoints into a unified analytical *construct* (Shils & Finch, 1949, p. 90).

Thus when social scientists and historians talk of "economic man," "charisma," "capitalism" or "feudalism," they are "using logically controlled and unambiguous conceptions, which are thus more removed from historical reality," rather than "less precise concepts, which are more closely geared to the empirical world" (Gerth & Mills, 1958, p. 59). Of course, the historical models of "feudalism" and "capitalism" are constantly being revised as new meanings are discovered and conceptualized in the ongoing development of the social sciences, just as psychoanalytic categories and concepts are ever being refined, torn down and rebuilt. Intellectually this is a sign of a living discipline.

Model-building is also exactly what psychoanalysts and psychiatrists do when they use diagnostic-descriptive categories such as "borderline personality," "hysterical neurosis," "schizoid" or "passive-aggressive personality." When the clinician draws upon Fenichel's (1945, ch. 14) brilliant 42-page delineation of the obsessive-compulsive neurosis, he is placing the unique individuality of his patient against an ideal type which he uses as a heuristic device to illuminate his data and to guide him to see further relationships latent in the material. Fenichel's nosology is a synthesis of many diffuse concrete individual phenomena which cannot be found in any single patient. The psychoanalytic theorist supplies a limiting construct to which the individual clinical case is compared for the presence of significant components. Social scientists have had extensive experience and have developed a sophistication in model-building which could be of use to psychoanalysts who are often needlessly defensive in their use of ideal types when dealing with their medical colleagues who rely on the "hard" evidence of laboratory tests.

V

Cultural and historical relativism, the modern history and philosophy of science, and conceptual abstraction from reality can be used to build bridges between the social sciences, the humanities and psychoanalysis. But, most importantly, those who are divided by disciplines and vocabulary can come to the other side of the chasm with firm mutal foundations in the empathic mode of understanding. This is the ultimate ground on which the disciplines meet. Here we have the unquantifiable area of personal knowledge which, as Freud (1905) said in a pungent passage on symptomatic acts in the Dora case, constitutes the essence of communication to those who wish to and know how to observe:

> He that has eyes to see and ears to hear may convince himself that no mortal can keep a secret. If his lips are silent, he chatters with his finger-tips; betrayal oozes out of him at every pore. And thus the task of making conscious the most hidden recesses of the mind is one which it is quite possible to accomplish (pp. 77–8).

This area of cognition is invoked when we say of a person "he is an experienced clinician" or when we respect the seasoned judgement of an historian who tells us a document is implausible or that an account does not "sound right."

An example is when the author was asked to review a recent biography of Adolf Hitler which, based on a manuscript account by Hitler's sister-in-law, asserts that he visited England and lived in Liverpool for a period of five months in 1912 and 1913 (Payne, 1973, pp. 93–102). From knowing Hitler's boastfulness about his authority on a wide range of matters, and knowing that in none of his speeches or writings, including the *Table Talks,* does he anywhere refer to personally being conversant with the English people, I inferred (Loewenberg, 1974) that the asserted trip never took place and the account of a stay in England is bogus. Correspondence with the Home Office (personal communication, 30 May 1975) has confirmed that there is no record of a Hitler visit to the United Kingdom.

Wilhelm Dilthey (1833–1911), the German historian and philosopher of history, early formulated the idea that the historian is himself the primary instrument of research, that he uses himself as the perceptor and interpreter of data. Dilthey said, the historian relives the past in his own mind. What makes Dilthey so strikingly modern to us, is the stress he laid on historical knowledge as an inner experience of the historian. "This conception," said Collingwood (1956) "of the historian as living in his object, or rather making his object live in him, is a great advance on anything achieved by any of Dilthey's German contemporaries" (p. 172).

Dilthey stressed that the historian's understanding *(Verständnis)* is based on his inner relationship *(innere Verhältnis)* to his subject of research, and this relationship is possible through recreation *(Nacherzeugen)* and identification *(Nacherleben).* Historians face the practical task "of the inner reliving of the development of individuation [of our subject]" ("Innerlich ... diesen Aufgang zur Individuation zu durchleben"). He called on historians to place themselves mentally in the historical situation *(Sichhineinversetzen).* "On the basis of this placing of oneself in the situation, this transposition, the highest form in which the totality of mental life can be effective in understanding, arises—imitation or identification." ("Auf der Grundlage dieses Hineinversetzens, dieser Transposition entsteht nun aber die höchste Art, in welcher die Totalität des Seelenlebens im Verstehen wirksam ist—das Nachbilden oder Nacherleben." Dilthey, 1958, pp. 213–14). Dilthey was the earliest conceptualizer of the use of sympathy *(Mitfühlens)* and empathy *(Einfühlung)* as tools of cognition in historical research.

VI

R. G. Collingwood's (1889–1943) work and method is particularly congenial to the psychoanalytic mode of experience because it highlights the tools of emotional empathy and mental identification which lead to intellectual insight as to "how it really was." He saluted Freud as "the greatest psychologist of our age" (Collingwood, 1938, p. 64). With Collingwood we may see not only a philosopher of history conceptualize what happens when an historian works, but we may also observe a first-rate historian doing his research and making his discoveries. Collingwood is closest to the psychoanalytic theory of memory when he stresses that a feeling, such as anger, when it is relived in the present, as in the transference, may be a pathway to the thoughts of the past.

> If I now think about a feeling which I had in the past, it may be true that thinking about it occasions, or else perhaps depends for its possibility on the independent occurrence of, an echo of that feeling in the present: that for example, I could not think of the anger I once felt except so far as I now experience at least a faint vibration of anger in my mind.... The actual past anger of which I am thinking is past and gone; that does not reappear, the stream of immediate experience has carried it away forever; at most there reappears something like it. The gap of time between my present thought and its past objective is bridged not by the survival or revival of the object, but only by the power of thought to overlap such a gap; and the thought which does this is memory (Collingwood, 1956, p. 293).

Collingwood was aware of, and illustrated, the psychodynamics of projection: "We learn to bolster ... self-deceit by attributing the disowned experience to other people. Coming down to breakfast out of temper, but refusing to allow that ill humour so evident in the atmosphere is our own, we are distressed to find the whole family suffering agonies of crossness" (Collingwood, 1938, p. 218).

To theorize elegantly about history is one thing. To apply a theory intelligently so that it yields solid results is quite another. It is instructive to see how Collingwood "operationalized" his empathic theory of historical research. He tried to reason as the Roman strategists did, then reconstruct the past in his own mind and test his fantasy by empirical research. His research was concerned with the purpose and function of Hadrian's Wall, a 73-mile-long structure built across the narrowest part of England on a line from the Tyne on the North Sea to the Solway on the Irish Sea and maintained by the Romans between 122 and 383 A.D. Collingwood reversed the previous scholarship by first creating a problem where there was previously only accepted dictum—that this wall, as other walls at the extremities of the Roman Empire, was a military fortification designed to keep out barbarian invaders. Collingwood asserted that he could not imagine this. His subjective fantasies and feelings led him to his problem:

> When disturbance ripened into war, when large forces from the north advanced upon the Wall and attempted (as no doubt they did, not always unsuccessfully) to penetrate it, *we cannot imagine* that the Roman cohorts actually lined up on the rampart-walk to repel them, still less that Hadrian's engineers *ever contemplated* such a proceeding [italics mine] (Collingwood, 1921, p. 9).

Collingwood tells us, he is employing his empathetic function of identification in making a reconstruction. He explicitly says that his tool of cognition is his power of imagination, his ability to get into the mind of Hadrian's engineers and, if a given pattern of thought is "unthinkable" for them in his mind, this fantasied implausibility is for him an important historical datum. Collingwood is using his educated and disciplined fantasy as a primary dimension of historical research.

Collingwood placed himself in the mental and intellectual position of the Roman generals and engineers who designed and built the wall. He immersed himself in their situation, seeking the "inward experience" of making the past object live in him. He maintained that the historian makes discoveries by rethinking the thoughts of his subjects in his own mind:

> The historian of politics or warfare, presented with an account of certain actions done by Julius Caesar, tries to understand these actions, that is, to discover what thoughts in Caesar's mind determined him to do them. This implies envisaging for himself the situation in which Caesar stood, and thinking for himself what Caesar thought about the situation and the possible ways of dealing with it. The history of thought, and therefore all history, is the re-enactment of past thought in the historian's own mind (Collingwood, 1956, p. 215).

Collingwood pointed out that those strategists who had appropriate business in the Roman province would cross the wall at one of the forts. In addition to its function as a boundary, the wall was intended as:

> an obstacle to smugglers, or robbers, or other undesirables. A man from beyond the frontier, found on the Roman side of the line, could not plead ignorance or innocent intentions if the line was clearly marked; and if, in addition, it was a slight obstacle, crossing it otherwise than at the authorized and controlled gateways was proof of a sinister purpose (Collingwood, 1921, pp. 7–8).

Now we see Collingwood, the empathic historian, at work, using his powers of identification based on an immersion in the life problems and problem-solving thought of Roman strategists in the time of Hadrian:

> [The Wall] lacks the essential characteristic of a fortification. It cannot be defended. In order to defend a wall you must be able to bring reinforcements to a threatened point; but the top of the Wall was reached only by stairways at forts and mile-castles, and by ladders (it would appear) at the turrets; and ladders 500 yards apart are a very poor means of bringing reinforcements to the top of a narrow wall. Nor was the Wall broad enough to march reinforcements along it, behind the "firing line," even if (as was not the case) the Roman soldier had been provided with *armes de jet* adequate for dealing with an attack on such a work. The walls of a fort of this period are rendered defensible by the earth bank behind them, giving access to every point, and by the frequent gates, which enable the garrison to sally out and take assailants in the rear; both these features are absent from the Wall (Collingwood, 1930, p. 78).

What then was the purpose of this large Roman work in the north of England? Making his brilliant original formulation, Collingwood tells us:

> The Wall, in spite of appearances, was not strictly a fortification. It was an elevated sentry-walk, where men patrolling the frontier were secure against sudden attack and could command a good view of the country which it was their business to watch. It was also a very effective obstacle against raiding, not because raiding parties could not get across it—for a few men with a ladder could easily overpower a sentry or two and get across before help could arrive—but because, once they were across and the alarm given, it

would be almost impossible for them to get back, especially if they were laden with plunder (Collingwood, 1959, p. 32).

The wall was a frontier work, not a military work. It was not a fortification, a work designed to resist attack by armed forces. It was a police work, designed to keep out Caledonian raiders who would be seriously impeded by such a wall.

In Collingwood's research and interpretation on the problem of the Wall, extending over two decades, we see the historian's procedure of reconstruction of the past by inferring the thoughts and feelings of particular men in the past from the historical evidence of the present. It is a process of immersion in their problems and identification with their solutions, a practice analogous to puzzle solving. And how do we know that Collingwood is right? Of course, we do not know for a certainty. Indeed we may be certain that in due course his view will be revised. But our conviction is based on the fact that for now the pieces fit. Puzzle solving, incidentally, is a methodological simile used by Freud (1923):

> If one succeeds in arranging the confused heap of fragments, each of which bears upon it an unintelligible piece of drawing, so that the picture acquires a meaning, so that there is no gap anywhere in the design and so that the whole fits into the frame—if all these conditions are fulfilled, then one knows that one has solved the puzzle and that there is no alternative solution (p. 116).

VII

The historian, like the psychoanalyst, engages in reconstruction through the method of retrogression, through retro-diction, beginning with the present, including his own emotional evidence from the present, and moving toward the past. Marc Bloch (1886–1944), one of the greatest of modern historians, made his contribution to historical method by insistence on the importance of the historian's understanding of the living as a key to the past. Bloch said:

> The lines of connection work both ways. Misunderstanding of the present is the inevitable consequence of ignorance of the past. But a man may wear himself out just as fruitlessly in seeking to understand the past, if he is totally ignorant of the present. . . . This faculty of understanding the living is, in very truth, the master quality of the historian (1953, p. 43).

He stressed that history as understood by the historian is directly related to his receptivity based on his own life awareness and openness to experience, and his ability to "resonate" emotionally with the impact of events as he lives them. He constantly emphasized the need for the historian to "know from within," just as the psychoanalyst must get in touch with his own feelings in order to resonate with what the patient is telling him. It is because the therapist has himself been a patient that he knows the nuances of what the patient is trying to communicate.

To have known and analysed the trauma of separation, the pain of humiliation, the fires of envy and the terrors of castration anxiety, is an indispensable condition for compassionately and fearlessly guiding a patient through honest inner exploration of his defences. There is more than a grain of truth in the stubborn assertion of patients from minority groups that a therapist of their own group can best understand them. An analyst who has had and "worked through" certain experiences, such as divorce, parent loss, emigration and resettlement, will have greater rapport with a patient who is dealing with those problems than a therapist who has only dealt with these life crises in theory or by way of the literature.

The analogue in historical training is the importance attached to fieldwork in the land or society one wishes to study, on the principle that, apart from the value of documents and archives, there is no substitute for direct, personal immersion in the culture and participation in the social life of the people whose history one wishes to interpret.

> As an American historian who found himself in West Berlin in August 1961 at the time of the erection of the Berlin Wall, I noted the undue anxiety of the German population about the food supply in very personalized terms. While we were concerned with whether a war between the U.S. and Soviet forces would break out, many Germans were asking, "How will I feed my family?" "Where will we get meat?" "My butcher will not take care of me, he does not regard me as a favoured customer, what will I do?" The acute food anxiety I observed being aroused by this political crisis suggested questions to which the historical experiences of Germans in the civilian deprivations during and after the two World Wars supplied at least some of the answers. A recollection of the stories of hunger recounted by my parents, who were children during the First World War, suggested further generational questions for research and phase-specific answers (Loewenberg, 1971).

Bloch was an officer in the French Army in both World Wars. He described and analysed, in what is a masterpiece of its genre, the fall of France in 1940. Bloch also described the feelings of being helpless and trapped as the German armies cut off the Anglo-French forces in Belgium in May 1940:

> Shall I ever, I wonder, forget that evening of 20 May? Just as it was getting dusk, with the flames of Arras lighting the distant horizon, my immediate superior came into the room. In a very low voice, and pointing on a school wall-map to the mouth of the Somme, he said: "The Boches are *there!*"—then, turning away, he murmured, "Don't talk about it more than you can help." I had been trying to get G.H.Q. on the telephone, and it was only after I had made the attempt several times and failed, that I realized to the full the sense of complete abandonment that comes to a soldier when he hears the word—"surrounded" (1968, pp. 12–13).

This existential experience was for Bloch a *sine qua non* of dealing with the past, for "we can truly understand the past only if we read it by the light of the present" (Bloch, 1968, p. 2). This principle is convincingly applied in Bloch's critique of the eminent medievalist, Fustel de Coulanges. Fustel had found in France "no trace" of the open field system common in the European Middle Ages. To this conclusion, Bloch (1966) commented:

Fustel de Coulanges was not a man on whom the external world made much impact. It is quite probable that he never took any special notice of the characteristic pattern of ploughlands visible all over northern and eastern France which so irresistibly call to mind the open-fields of England. And since Fustel had no particular interest in agriculture, the debates on grazing on the arable which were engaging both Chambers at the very moment ... also failed to attract his attention. Fustel based his answers on documents, very ancient documents. Now these were texts he knew very well; how was it then that they failed to reveal for him any trace of the phenomena they in fact quite plainly attest? ... Fustel concentrated solely on his documents, without considering them in the light of the more recent past (pp. xxvii–xxviii).

Bloch was calling, not only for the historian to get out and look at fields and talk to peasants, but also to listen carefully to the political issues and debates of his own time, for their benefit to him in illuminating the past. He taught (1966): "Since the facts of the distant past are also the most obscure, there is really no escape from the discipline of working back from the better to the less well-known. ... The historian ... is perpetually at the mercy of his documents; most of the time he must read history backwards if he hopes to break the secret cypher of the past" (p. xxviii). For the psychoanalyst working with a patient, this is what he does when he begins with the presenting complaint, with what hurts now, and works back to make past defences and adaptations distonic so that they may be analysed. As Bloch (1953) put it in 1941:

For here, in the present, is immediately perceptible that vibrance of human life which only a great effort of the imagination can restore to the old texts. I have many times read, and I have often narrated, accounts of wars and battles. Did I truly know, in the full sense of that word, did I know from within, before I myself had suffered the terrible, sickening reality, of what it meant for an army to be encircled, what it meant for a people to meet defeat? Before I myself had breathed the joy of victory in the summer and autumn of 1918 (and, although, alas! its perfume will not again be quite the same, I yearn to fill my lungs with it a second time) did I truly know all that was inherent in that beautiful word? In the last analysis, whether consciously or not, it is always by borrowing from our daily experiences and by shading them, where necessary, with new tints that we derive the elements which help us to restore the past (p. 44).

Psychoanalysis is, significantly, the only modern treatment modality which requires the healer to have experienced the treatment prior to himself becoming a therapist. Bloch made it a tenet of method that the historian will understand history only to the extent that he experiences in the present and understands himself as an historical subject. This, finally, is a solid ground for mutual enlightenment, support and intellectual alliance between those who pursue the spirits of Clio and Psyche as their life's work. Each discipline can make better sense of its own problems if it understands the methods of the other.

ACKNOWLEDGEMENTS

The author wishes to express his gratitude to Professors Fawn M. Brodie, Alan Dundes, John Fitzpatrick III, John Heilbron, Albert D. Hutter, Franklin Mendels,

Eugen Weber, M. Norton Wise; Drs Naomi Malin, Norman Reider and Mr David Horowitz for reading and discussing a draft of this paper.

REFERENCES

Bloch, M. (1953). *The Historian's Craft*. New York: Knopf.

———. (1966). *French Rural History: An Essay on its Basic Characteristics*. Berkeley and Los Angeles: University of California Press.

———. (1968). *Strange Defeat: A Statement of Evidence Written in 1940*. New York: Norton.

Collingwood, R. G. (1921). The purposes of the Roman Wall, *Vasculum* 8, 4–9.

———. (1930). *The Archaeology of Roman Britain*. New York: Dial Press.

———. (1938). *The Principles of Art*. London: Oxford University Press.

———. (1956), *The Idea of History*. New York: Oxford University Press.

———. (1959). *Roman Britain*. London: Oxford University Press.

Dilthey, W. (1958). Das Verstehen anderer Personen und ihrer Lebensäusserungen. In *Gesammelte Schriften,* vol. 7, Stuttgart: Teubnen.

Einstein, A. (1922). *The Meaning of Relativity*. Princeton: Princeton University Press.

Fenichel, O. (1945). *The Psychoanalytic Theory of Neurosis*. New York: Norton.

Freud, S. (1905). Fragment of an analysis of a case of hysteria. *S.E.* 7.

———. (1923). Remarks on the theory and practice of dream-interpretation. *S.E.* 19.

———. (1926). The question of lay analysis. *S.E.* 20.

Gerth, H. H. & Mills, C. W. (eds.) (1958). *From Max Weber: Essays in Sociology*. New York: Oxford University Press.

Kuhn, T. S. (1970). *Structure of Scientific Revolutions*. Chicago: University of Chicago Press.

Lakatos, I. (1970). Falsification and the methodology of scientific research programmes. In I. Lakatos & A. Musgrave (eds.), *Criticism and the Growth of Knowledge*. London: Cambridge University Press.

Laslett, P. (1971). Age at menarche in Europe since the eighteenth century. *J. interdisciplin. Hist.* 2, 221–36.

Loewenberg, P. (1971). Psychohistorical origins of the Nazi youth cohort. *Am. hist. Rev.* 76, 1457–1502.

———. (1974). Review of Robert Payne, *The Life and Death of Adolf Hitler, Comite d'Hist. de la 2e Guerre Mondiale,* Bull. no. 212, 32–34.

Payne, R. (1973). *Life and Death of Adolf Hitler*. New York: Praeger.

Polanyi, M. (1958). *Personal Knowledge: Towards a Post-Critical Philosophy*. Chicago: University of Chicago Press.

———. (1974). *Scientific Thought and Social Reality*. New York: International Universities Press.

Popper, K. (1959). *The Logic of Scientific Discovery*. New York: Basic Books.

Sapir, E. (1951). Why cultural anthropology needs the psychiatrist. In D. G. Mandelbaum (ed.), *Selected Writings of Edward Sapir in Language, Culture and Personality*. Berkeley and Los Angeles: University of California Press.

Shils, E. A. & Finch, H. A. (eds.) (1949). *Max Weber on the Methodology of the Social Sciences*. Glencoe, Ill.: Free Press.

4

Disciplined Subjectivity and the Psychohistorian: A Critical Look at the Work of Erik H. Erikson

Charles B. Strozier

As Erikson notes in *Young Man Luther,* we have to risk a "bit of impurity" in any hyphenated approach, for such efforts are the "compost heap of today's interdisciplinary efforts which may help to fertilize new fields and to produce future flowers of new methodological clarity."[1] To dwell for a moment on this metaphor, we need to understand the shape, size, and perhaps the smell of that compost heap as well as how it accumulates; we need to consider both its content and the way it is constructed. Erikson's contribution to the interdisciplinary heap is rich indeed and centers, conceptually, on his ideas of the epigenesis of the life cycle and especially the place and meaning of identity in life history and history. The assessment of such concepts and their continuing relevance—or lack of it— is an important agenda for psychohistory. But to understand and assess Erikson's ideas we must also examine systematically how he uses them. A complete treatment of Erikson's methodology would require analysis of his use of evidence, the process by which he makes inferences, his utilizations of theoretical constructs in interpretating data, and related issues. This discussion is limited by necessity and focuses on one particular aspect of Erikson's methodology: disciplined subjectivity.

From a methodological point of view, disciplined subjectivity lies at the very center of Erikson's work. He defines and develops the concept—and himself— in both *Young Man Luther* and *Gandhi's Truth,* in more theoretical books like *Childhood and Society* and *Identity: Youth and Change,* and throughout papers and speeches delivered over the years. What he means by the term is a *"specific*

Reprinted from *Psychohistory Review* 5:3 (1976) 28–31.

self-awareness" that the psychohistorical observer himself must include in his own field of perception.[2] Good historians, Erikson notes, have always expressed "some awareness of their place in history," but for psychohistorians such awareness is necessarily sharpened by psychological insight.[3] For the clinician—as for the psychohistorian—"The evidence is not 'all in' if he does not succeed in using his own emotional responses during a clinical encounter as an evidential source and as a guide in intervention, instead of putting them aside with a spurious claim to unassailable objectivity."[4]

Erikson has outlined the limits of this subjectivity most clearly in his 1968 *Daedalus* essay, "On the Nature of Psycho-Historical Evidence: In Search of Gandhi." There Erikson charts the requirement that the reviewer of a piece of history must be "reasonably clear about" the stage and conditions of his own life when he selectively involves himself in history as well as the place (or sequence) of that moment in his total life history, and the state of his community in momentary and sequential terms. By communities, Erikson means "a whole series of collective processes from which the reviewer derives identity and sanction and within which his act of reviewing has a function: there, above all, he must know himself as living in the historical process."[5]

Perhaps the most obvious reason Erikson dwells on the self-awareness of the reviewer is to caution psychohistorians not to "immerse themselves into the very disguises, rationalizations, and idealizations of the historical process from which it should be their business to separate themselves."[6] From an ethical point of view, we owe the past the same rigorous and respectful honesty that it should be our business to impose on ourselves as students, teachers, or therapists. But beyond the ethical argument the irrational counter-transference implicit in any encounter with a piece of history must be recognized and turned to methodological advantage.[7] The likes and dislikes of psychohistorians are irrelevant; but uncritical and unanalyzed identifications or petty, irrational hatred hopelessly distort understanding.

From another point of view—one that stresses the creative potential of disciplined subjectivity rather than its role in modifying counter-transference—the self-awareness of the observer permits the utilization of one's emotional responses as a source. If the analyst listens with his "third ear," the psychohistorian likewise searches his own unconscious feelings toward individual lives and collective events in the past to understand the relationship between otherwise confusing or superficially irrelevant data. Subjectivity, in Erikson's use of the term, thus permits (but is not defined by) an empathic encounter with the historical record. The methodological problem, however, is the difference between empathy in a therapeutic encounter in which two people are very much alive and present, talking, gesturing, and feeling (at least one of them is); and the experience of historians in cold, dusty archives struggling inevitably with illegible handwriting. Perhaps there is a vitality missing in the work of historians, an absence of interpersonal exchange, that makes me at least question to what extent we can really talk about empathically relating to the sources.

Part of the argument for Erikson's continued effort to place disciplined subjectivity at the center—methodologically speaking—of psychohistory is the parallel he sees between historical and psychoanalytic methodologies. Erikson has noted twice in *Daedalus* discussions the affinity he feels with the historian who, "like the clinician, must serve the curious process by which selected portions of the past impose themselves on our renewed awareness and claim continued actuality in our contemporary commitments."[8] Neither psychoanalytic nor historical methodologies are scientific in a natural scientific sense and both strive for an understanding that is loose, complex, subjective, and right only insofar as the criteria for judging the evidence are generally accepted. As John Klauber has noted—and I think Erikson would agree—that while the idea of science is unitary explanation of multiple phenomena, history and psychoanalysis attempt to find multiple explanations for single events.[9] I would only add that explanation consists in ordering all the different causes of an event. And in history, psychoanalysis, and psychohistory the most important factor is not necessarily the oldest or most repressed.

But Erikson also recognizes the distinctions between history and psychoanalysis as he simultaneously seeks to resolve the differences. The most important distinction Erikson develops is that between a case history and a life history. In a case history we learn what went wrong and why, the diagnosis which reflects the orientation of the observer; and the therapeutic suggestions for improved health. "A life history, in contrast, describes how a person managed to keep together and to maintain a significant function in the lives of others."[10] Going beyond biography—which in fact Erikson does in most of his writings—he argues forcefully, from *Childhood and Society* on, for looking at any problem from three vantage points: the somatic, the individual or ego, and the societal. In *Luther,* for example, Erikson sees an interconnectedness between the religious and political crises of the great reformer, his followers, and Western Christendom itself. Such a complex perspective requires a kind of triple bookkeeping[11] and in the end focuses more on the uncertain process of human existence than on history seen historically or psychoanalytically. Our individual place in this process makes us both observers and participants. An avowed subjectivity is therefore a more honest position but also reflects a more sophisticated understanding of life itself, of which history is a part.

It is, however, neither self-evident nor really ever explained by Erikson what precisely disciplines subjectivity. To take the question of self-analysis, it is mandated that those who make a profession of psychoanalyzing others must first have learned to analyze themselves, and this for both theoretical and ethical reasons. Psychoanalytic candidates therefore experience patienthood as an integral part of training and subsequently, in practice, learn to empathize with their individual patients in clearly articulated ways. But in history the "patients" are dead, which at least mutes the force of the ethical argument (although I agree with Erikson that it does not entirely eliminate it). Even more importantly, however, true historical understanding involves a sense of individual life history in any period *and* larger developments which shape events as we know them. Erikson, of course, is not only aware of these differences, he has discussed them at length. My point is that it is precisely because of the differences between history and psychoanalysis, that is, for both theoretical and ethical reasons, that Erikson modifies the demand for self-analytic capacity in psychohistorians. In the *Daedalus* piece Erikson argues that, "the psycho-historian will have developed or acquired a certain self-analytical capacity which would give to his dealings with others, great or small, both the charity of identification and a reasonably good conscience."[12] The word I would underline in this quote is "certain." How much is "certain?" Does that amount differ for psychobiography and group analysis? To be fair, we have to keep in mind that there is always a degree of ambiguity when discussing such an elusive concept as self-understanding. The question remains, however, whether Erikson's all-embracing humanism muddles somewhat a clear understanding of subjectivity as the methodological basis of psychohistory. As usual with Erikson—at least in my experience—he seems right. But I am also acutely aware of the unanswered questions.

A more practical but still important issue psychohistorians face in implementing what Erikson means by disciplined subjectivity is determining the criteria for judging whether a given observer has or has not adequately understood himself and, further, whether this awareness has been creatively utilized in relating to the past? A task force of the American Psychiatric Association has addressed this question recently and concluded with the mechanical recommendation that the psychohistorian should, at least, indicate in a preface the source of his particular involvement in his subject and note whatever biases were relevant to the research. But such a position assumes self-awareness is present before the preface is written. And, as I have already asked about self-knowledge, how much revelation is enough? Is the demand for such self-revelation equally relevant for all forms of psychohistorical inquiry? And, finally, as Erikson himself has noted, how can we be sure effusive self-revelation is not serving as an ingenious cover-up and/or disarming propaganda?[13] For Erikson the issue seems relatively simple. He is a practicing analyst, self-aware and sophisticated, able to introduce himself into his writings carefully, selectively, judiciously. His personal asides are, to me, rich and enlightening. But for psychohistorians generally, it is more complex. Most are not analyzed (though I have no knowledge of the relevant statistics), but in any event to require a personal analysis of a psychohistorian would make the field merely an adjunct of psychoanalysis, a position Erikson does not support. We are left, it seems to me, urging self-awareness without defining it; hoping for creative utilization of the self in psychohistorical inquiry without establishing the criteria by which it will be judged; and failing to establish the relevance of disciplined subjectivity for areas such as group analysis.

I find, in conclusion, that I have raised more questions than I have answered. Such is the challenge of working in a new field. Disciplined subjectivity and its role in psychohistorical inquiry is an issue that interests me professionally and personally. I approached the subject after my own analysis and as I begin training as a research candidate at the Chicago Institute for Psychoanalysis. I rather hoped in re-reading Erikson's writings that I would find a greater consistency, a more coherent argument for the training course I am in fact following. That I found some ambiguity is the subject of this short paper. That the issues are so intelligently joined, that the contradictions are developed with such complexity, is a tribute to Erikson.

NOTES

1 Erik H. Erikson, *Young Man Luther: A Study in Psychoanalysis and History* (Austen Riggs Center, Monograph No. 4, New York: Norton, 1958), p. 16.
2 Erik H. Erikson, *Insight and Responsibility* (New York: Norton, 1964), p. 52.
3 Erik H. Erikson, *Dimensions of a New Identity: The 1973 Jefferson Lectures in the Humanities* (New York: Norton, 1974), p. 15.
4 Erikson, *Insight and Responsibility*, p. 73.
5 Erik H. Erikson, "On the Nature of Psycho-Historical Evidence: In Search of Gandhi," *Daedalus* 97, No. 3 (Summer 1968), p. 709.
6 Erikson, *Young Man Luther*, p. 20.
7 Erikson, *Daedalus*, p. 707.
8 Ibid., p. 695.
9 John Klauber, "On the Dual Use of Historical and Scientific Method in Psychoanalysis," *International Journal of Psycho-Analysis* 49:80–88, 1968.
10 Erikson, *Dimensions of a New Identity*, p. 13.
11 Erik H. Erikson, *Childhood and Society* (New York: Norton, 1950), p. 46.
12 Erikson, *Daedalus*, p. 709.
13 Erik H. Erikson, " 'Identity Crisis' in Autobiographic Perspective," *Life History and the Historical Moment* (New York: Norton, 1975), pp. 17–47.

5

The Independence of Psychohistory

Lloyd deMause

Ever since 1942 when the philosopher Carl Hempel published his essay "The Function of General Laws in History,"[1] it has been recognized by most philosophers of history that history cannot be a science in any strict sense of the term and that history can never regard it as part of its task to establish laws in the Hempelian sense. Written history may, in the course of its narrative, use some of the laws established by the various sciences, but its own task remains that of relating the essential sequence of historical action and, *qua* history, to tell what happened, not why.[2]

Psychohistory, it seems to me, is on the contrary specifically concerned with establishing laws and discovering causes in precisely the Hempelian manner. The relationship between history and psychohistory is parallel to the relationship between astrology and astronomy, or if that seems too pejorative, between geology and physics. Astrology and geology are disciplines seeking sequential orders in the sky and the earth, while astronomy and physics are not narrative at all, but are sciences attempting to establish laws in their own respective areas. Psychohistory, as the science of historical motivation, may concentrate on the same historical events that written history covers, but its purpose is never to tell what happened one day after another. When the first astronomers came along and found astrologers describing the positions of the stars day by day and trying to explain all the relationships between them, they created a revolution by saying, "Forget about the sequence of the skies. What interests us *qua* scientists is this one dot of light and whether it goes in a circle or an ellipse—and *why*. In order to find this out, we will have to drop the narrative task of astrology."

What is more, science never did pick up this task of narration—because it couldn't. Astronomy, even if it finally discovers all the laws of the universe, will still not narrate the sequences of skies, any more than psychohistory will ever

Reprinted from *The New Psychohistory* by Lloyd deMause, pp. 7–27, Psychohistory Press, New York: 1975.

narrate the events of this or that period. Psychohistory, as a science, will always be problem-centered, while history will always remain period-centered. They are simply two different tasks.

It does not, of course, follow that psychohistory simply uses the facts historians have narrated up to now in order to construct laws of historical motivation. Like astronomy and physics, psychohistory finds it necessary to conduct its own search for material peculiar to its own interests in both past and present society. Whole great chunks of written history are of little value to the psychohistorian, while other vast areas which have been much neglected by historians—childhood history, content analysis of historical imagery, and so on—suddenly expand from the periphery to the center of the psychohistorian's conceptual world, simply because his or her own new questions require material nowhere to be found in history books. ·

Now I am well aware that in claiming the field of historical motivation exclusively for the psychohistorian I immediately run up against the oft-repeated claim by historians that they work with motivations all the time, so there is nothing new in that. I had heard this claim so often in the two decades since I first studied the philosophy of history that I was finally moved to measure exactly how often historians actually do examine motivations in their works. I therefore kept a tallysheet as I read 100 history books of varying kinds and recorded exactly how many sentences were devoted to any kind of motivational analysis whatsoever— not just psychoanalytic, but any level of attention at all. In no case did this motivational content reach as much as 1% of the book—so the field seemed to be ours by default. What wasn't pure narrative of one event after another turned out to be mainly the recitation of as many economic facts as possible in the hopes that their mere conjunction with the historical narrative would be mistaken for explanation.

Now anyone who has read any portion of the over 1,300 books and articles contained in the "Bibliography of Psychohistory"[3] will soon realize that psychohistory has reversed this 1-to-99 ratio, so that the bulk of psychohistorical writing is devoted to an intense concentration on motivational analysis while the physical events of history are necessarily given quite sketchy background treatment. There is, for instance, only one page at the beginning of Runciman's three-volume *History of the Crusades*[4] describing how the participants decided to begin four hundred years of wars, and then several thousand pages devoted to the routes, battles and other events which make up the "history" of the Crusades. A psychohistorian would *assume* the history, and spend his decades of research and thousands of pages in the most fascinating question for psychohistory—why so many set off on such a strange task as relic-saving. That the historian, when reviewing such a psychohistory, would accuse it of "ignoring" the full history of the Crusades should bother the psychohistorian as little as the accusation by the astrologer that Galileo "ignored" all the other stars in describing the path of one mere planet. It wasn't his task, and narrative history isn't ours.

What seems not to have occurred to the critics of psychohistory is that we might choose to focus on the historical evolution of the psyche because only thereby can we reach the unsolved problems of precisely these same fields of politics, economics and sociology, fields which are shot through with unproven psychological assumptions and which have failed to become reliable sciences precisely because of the unsolved psychohistorical problems within them. Professionals in each of these fields recognize this quite well, and even admit it to each other in their journals—it is only historians, ignorant of the shaky psychological underpinnings of the fields from which they uncritically borrow, who imagine there can be "economic, political and social factors" which are somehow apart from "psychological" factors in history. As one instance, it is probably true that my own work on the evolution of childhood was at least partly a response to problems encountered in the theory of economic development, as set forth in such books as Everett E. Hagen's *On the Theory of Social Change: How Economic Growth Begins,* where the crucial link needed to produce a take-off in economic development is shown to be just the kind of personality which I was later able to trace in the history of childhood as the result of the "intrusive mode" of parenting. Just as surely is the study of class intimately tied up with evolving psychohistorical patterns of dominance and submission, and the study of power dependent upon an understanding of group-fantasy needs and defenses. The notion that psychohistory somehow "ignores" economics, sociology or political science is possibly the most ignorant charge that could be leveled against it.

When the *Times Literary Supplement* attacks the *Journal* for "seeing behind every action a hidden motive,"[5] all one can answer is "Of course! Action is simply behavior, and since only psyches can have motives, motivation, hidden or not, must be examined in and of its own right to give meaning to all action." Historians habitually skip this examination, as when A. J. P. Taylor describes why Hitler did not intend to go to war in 1939:

> Many however believe that Hitler was a modern Attila, loving destruction for its own sake and therefore bent on war without thought of policy. There is no arguing with such dogmas. Hitler was an extraordinary man; and they may well be true. But his policy is capable of rational explanation; and it is on these that history is built. . . . In considering German armament we escape from the mystic regions of Hitler's psychology and find an answer in the realm of fact. The answer is clear. The state of German armament in 1939 gives decisive proof that Hitler was not contemplating general war, and probably not intending war at all.[6]

The sleight-of-hand involved in this way of writing history is never to examine the actor's actual motives at all, but simply to conclude from looking at material reality, here armaments, what his motives were. That this eliminates the possibility that Hitler might have intended war regardless of the state of his armaments is simply overlooked. Historians are presumed to be unable to "do psychology," which is "mystical" anyway, so they are forced to accept the most "rational" explanations. . ."and it is on these that history is built."

These and many other reasons integral to the logic of psychohistory lead me to believe that it will sooner or later be necessary for psychohistory to split off from history and form its own department within the academy in much the same way that sociology broke off from economics and psychology from philosophy in the late 19th century. As a matter of fact, there is a real sense in which psychohistory never was the exclusive or even the major possession of history departments: the majority of the books and articles in the "Bibliography of Psychohistory" were written by scholars who were not professional historians at all, and this is also the case for the articles written for this *Journal,* the contributing editors of which include psychiatrists, political scientists, educators, psychologists, psychotherapists, humanists and anthropologists as well as historians. Only a minority of the subscribers to the *Journal* are in fact historians. Courses in psychohistory are being offered today in many different departments, and even when offered in the history department they are likely as not conducted jointly by a historian and a psychoanalyst. Therefore my suggestion that separate psychohistory departments should be established is less a schismatic device than it is a move to unite the fractured parts of psychohistorical inquiry, so that all those who are really in the same field can communicate with each other, rather than their being minorities in separate departments and thinking of themselves as "political psychologists," "psychoanalytic sociologists," "applied psychoanalysts," and so on. The choice of *problems*—not the material studied—defines the discipline, and all these scholars are working on the same kinds of problems.

In uniting these many fields, psychohistory would, it seems to me, for the first time make some sense out of the crazy-quilt pattern of separate disciplines presently studying "the psychology of society." It would assume, of course, that "psychohistory" is not a narrower term than "psycho-social," and that in fact the term "psycho-social" is simply redundant, since the "social" is not "out there" but only "in here," in the head. The usual accusation that psychohistory "reduces everything to psychology" is philosophically meaningless—*of course* psychohistory is reductionist in this sense, since all it studies is historical motivations. Only when the "social" is admitted to being part of the "psychological" can the paradigm for psychohistorical study be recognized as follows:

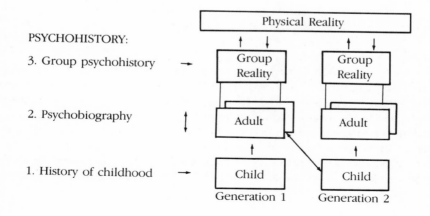

Besides defining the three divisions of psychohistory, this paradigm does two things that distinguish it from the other social sciences, particularly sociology. First, it reverses the relationship between physical and psychological reality, so that instead of material progress setting the pace of history and somehow dragging behind the psyches of its actors, human psychology is made primary—setting Marx on his head and Hegel back on his feet—and material reality is viewed as primarily the outcome of man's decisions, past or present, conscious or unconscious. Secondly, the major basis for historical change is the *interrelations of persons,* not forgetting the relations between generations, and man is viewed for the first time not as *homo faber* but as *homo relatens.*

There are other differences in psychohistory that are only now becoming apparent. First of all, as a science, psychohistory proceeds not by patient accumulation of piles of facts, but by first defining problems interesting to its own internal development, then formulating bold hypotheses from available evidence to solve these problems, and finally attempting to test and *disprove* (not prove—proofs are for high school chemistry students) the hypotheses from new evidence now painstakingly acquired. In fact, psychohistory has a double burden of proof, for it has to conform not only to all the usual standards of historical research, but it must also be psychologically sound—unlike the usual shoddy psychology now found in every historical journal which makes one want to shout at every page, "But people just don't *work* that way!" This double burden of proof will require its own special kind of training, of course, with thorough grounding in the full range of tools of historical research and developmental psychology, since both are essential to the job of cracking open the clam-shell of historical motivation.

It is of course quite true, as historians have pointed out, that psychohistory has no special method of proof that is unavailable to the historian or to any other discipline for that matter. Like all sciences, psychohistory stands or falls on the clarity and testability of its concepts, the breadth and parsimony of its theories, the extent of its empirical evidence, and so on. What psychohistory *does* have which is different is a certain *methodology of discovery,* a methodology which attempts to solve problems of historical motivation with a unique blend of historical documentation, clinical experience and the use of the researcher's own emotions as the crucial research tool for discovery. Let me give a personal example to illustrate this.

For the past decade, I have been intensely interested in the small but growing literature on the causes of war which has begun to be produced by social scientists of many disciplines. I had long ago discovered that historians, wrapped up in the specifics of one particular war or period, were little interested in generalizing on their narrative. In fact, it seemed as though historians used the words "desire for power" as terminations of thought as though the sight of millions of people organizing themselves for years in order to gobble up millions of their hostile neighbors at enormous sacrifice to themselves was the most transparent of human actions, requiring no explanation of motivation whatsoever. Those few historians who went beyond their narrative jumped immediately into economic "explanations," something not too difficult to do, since no war failed to have an economic dispute hanging around somewhere nearby. But they simply never got around to asking why war was the means by which this or that economic dispute was resolved. Neither did they seem to notice that the war was in fact never economically beneficial, and that when the leaders were deciding to go to war they simply never bothered to sit down and draw up a list of economic objectives, assign them a dollar value, subtract the costs of the war, and come up with a "war profit statement" (the very rationality of such an act makes it laughable). Yet the historians continued to pour out whole libraries describing economic conditions prior to wars, never bothering to examine the actual words and actions of the leaders who made the decision to go to war to see if all those economic factors actually had any causal effect on their motivations.

I was as little able to make any sense out of other kinds of historians' explanations for war, which were not only psychologically naive but often as not logically contradictory. Given "diplomatic" causes, opposite conditions were supposed to cause identical results, World War I having been caused by the "inflexibility" of the alliance system, so that when one little fight broke out all of Europe was dragged in, while World War II was caused by the "over-flexibility" of the alliance system term, allowing Hitler to pick off one country after another without fear of bringing in others. Similarly, "social" causes were cited with contradictory results: the cause of France's going to war with Austria in 1772 was the revolutionary turmoil within her borders, while her war with England in 1803 was caused by the *end* of revolutionary turmoil, thus allowing her energies to be turned outward

My own studies of the causes of war centered on the actual motivations of those who made the decisions, and of those around them who created the climate of expectation which allowed them to carry the decision into actuality. During the past year, I collected a large stack of photocopies and notes on the actual words of leaders and others during the times decisions to go to war were being made—a task which is not as simple as it may sound, since historians generally remove from their narrative much of the most important material a psychohistorian needs to determine motivation, such as personal imagery, metaphors, slips, side comments, jokes, scribbles on the edges of documents, and so on, and these were not too easily recovered from their original sources in a limited time span. Still, at the end of the year I had accumulated a wide range of material, and had even learned from it a few new things about war.

The first thing I learned was that these leaders seemed to me to be less fatherfigures in the Oedipal sense than garbage-disposal directors, being expected by those around them to handle huge amounts of projected emotions which the individuals were unable to keep bound by means of the usual intra-psychic defenses. Large groups seem to present a different level of problem to the psyche than interpersonal relations, so that intrapsychic defenses become less effective and the psyche is thrown back on modes of relating that prevailed in pre-verbal infancy, when problems were handled by projecting them into the mother's body and re-introjecting them back into one's own ego. The individual relates to a large group with similar massive projection devices, and delegates leaders and other role-players to assist him in this task. This process is continuous throughout the history of all large groups, and requires specific *group-fantasies* to carry it out and to defend against the primitive anxieties that result. One group-fantasy leaders are expected to carry out is to find places to dump these huge quantities of projected emotions, which I took to calling external and internal "toilet-objects." That the emotions thus dumped were of infantile origin goes without saying, but to my surprise I found that they seemed to come from all levels of the psychic organization, so that in 1914 German leaders could call the Serbs not only "regicidal" (Oedipal), which one could understand, but also "poisonous" (oral), "filthy" (anal) and "licentious" (phallic).[7] Once the leaders had designated which countries were to be the toilet-objects for these projected emotions, the emotional dumping could continue as a regular part of the political system, and it was then the task of diplomacy to see to it that these now-dangerous objects were fully controlled, in the same manner that little children, favorite toilet-objects for adults, are controlled by being now "chastised," now "brought to their knees," now "taught a lesson," and so on. As long as these external toilet-objects did not threaten to get out of control, war could be kept at a distance, and "diplomacy" seemed to work.

But something always seemed to happen to disturb the delicate process of emotion-dumping, and a group-process began which inexorably led the way to war, even when all those concerned seemed to want to avoid it. This "helpless drift" toward war was the predominant emotional tone for every war I was studying, so that it seemed as though some extremely powerful group-fantasy was being acted out which even the most powerful of leaders was quite helpless to change once it got rolling. To use a German example once again, Kaiser Wilhelm II, who had been encouraging Austria-Hungary to go to war with Serbia, was so startled when Serbia agreed to virtually all of Austria's excessive demands that, having announced that "every reason for war drops away," he gave orders for Vienna to be told to be conciliatory. But the pull of the group-fantasy was too great. His subordinates acted as though *they simply did not hear what he he said,* and the war began anyway. As Bethmann-Hollweg remarked at the time: "All governments . . . and the great majority of their peoples are peacefully inclined, but the direction has been lost, and the stone has started rolling."[8] War seemed to be a group-psychotic episode, with patterns of thinking, levels of imagery, and degrees of splitting and projection that are usually only found in the limited psychotic episodes of individuals, but which are temporary and which sooner or later appear quite incomprehensible to those same people. The manic optimism and inevitable under-estimation of the length and severity of the war, the increase in paranoia as to the motivations of the enemy (an "index of paranoia" has even been constructed and graphed[9]), the total absence of awareness that in going to war real people would actually *die,* these and other seeming irrationalities are all indications that a powerful group-fantasy is being acted out. But just what this relentless group-fantasy was completely stumped me. Some controlling process held together all these images and insights that I had picked up from the material in front of me. But I had no idea what it was, and why it seemed so compelling to all the participants.

As in previous cases when I had been bewildered by the material before me, I was convinced that personal defensive reasons were behind my inability to find an answer, and I tried many ways to break my defenses down. I attempted to identify with those leaders on whom I had the most complete material, reading every biography from Napoleon to Hitler that I could get hold of, trying to listen to their "free associations" to the events around them. I immersed myself in the mass of material for weeks at a time and analyzed my dreams each morning for my *own* "associations" and defenses. Nothing seemed to work. I was completely stuck for several months.

In January of this year, I was reading *Business Week* and noticed the interview with Henry Kissinger in which he explained that he had learned that "it is easier to get into a war than to get out of it" and that the only case in which the U.S. would go to war again was "where there is some actual strangulation" occurring. This imagery struck me as familiar. It particularly reminded me of something Kaiser Wilhelm and those around him kept saying in 1914, that "the Monarchy has been seized by the throat and forced to choose between letting itself be strangled and making a last ditch effort to defend itself against attack," and that a "net has been suddenly thrown over our head, and . . . we squirm isolated in the net."[10] I remembered that when I initially read them I was struck by how inappropriate these feelings were, since Germany was in no way strangling and since England, who was accused of throwing the net over her head, was at that time quite friendly toward Germany. Since I was familiar with the many "encirclement" theories with which nations justified their going to war, I was once again tempted to pass off the imagery as rationalization when I stopped myself and said "No! Both Henry and Wilhelm seem quite sincere here. They are reporting to me that it *felt* as if they were being strangled and that consequently they had to go to war, and for once I ought to *trust* their feelings and see where they take me." I once again pulled out my pile of notes, and soon found that this had indeed been the controlling fantasy I had overlooked for so long—images of being "strangled" and "choked" leaped up from every page I had before me. What was more, the strangulation of war seemed to be caused by a fantasy of being in the birth canal, "unable to draw a breath of relief," "unable to see the light at the end of the tunnel," but nevertheless "against one's will" beginning "the inexorable slide towards war," starting with the inevitable "rupture of diplomatic relations," moving with "naked force" into "the descent into the abyss" and finally "breaking out" into the "war that is the price of one's freedom."

Needless to say, I was still extremely reluctant to accept the reality of such an unlikely, even bizarre group-fantasy as "war as birth." Yet even a provisional emotional acceptance of the basic birth thesis made all the difference in the world to how I proceeded with my research. For one thing, only now could I begin to use my knowledge of the psychoanalytic literature on common birth images in dreams, in which suffocation and claustrophobia always represent being trapped in the birth canal, facts which completely eluded me during the prior year while trying to make sense of the historical material. I had noticed, of course, that leaders said they felt "small and helpless" during the slide towards war, but had thoroughly blocked out the importance of the imagery. That there was a life-and-death struggle going on for "some breathing space" was apparent—as Bethmann-Hollweg told the Reichstag in announcing war on August 4, 1914: "He who is menaced as we are and is fighting for his highest possession can only consider how he is to hack his way through."[11] But there was also present all the imagery of birth-dreams familiar to psychoanalysts—choking, drowning, hanging, suffocating, being crushed in rooms or tunnels. In psychoanalysis, these images represent the patient's attempt to repeat and by repeating to master the fearful pressure of labor contractions and the gasping for air after birth. This reliving indicates that birth traumata are still very much alive in most adults, especially those whose regressive need to re-merge with the mother has been kept alive by inadequate parenting.[12] Not only have psychoanalysts traditionally found these images in dreams,[13] but more recently Arthur Janov has discovered that patients in Primal therapy regularly have "birth Primals" in which they re-experience their own births in great detail, and with enormous psychological and physical changes taking place after these re-livings.[14]

In somehow trying to make sense out of all these strands of thought, I noticed that it didn't seem as though *reality*—physical reality—was forcing leaders to feel like strangled babies. Henry Kissinger and the Kaiser were actually no more in danger of war when they began voicing feelings of choking in a birth canal than they had been a year earlier when they did not voice such feelings. What was actually "strangling" the American economy was more the effects of the 1.5 trillion dollars spent on war goods in the previous two decades than the current oil situation, and the notion that little Serbia was actually able to "strangle" central Europe was wholly fantastic. In fact, when I checked my material I found that nations who were *actually* surrounded, like Serbia herself, or Poland in 1939, did *not* voice such images, while countries which *do* say they feel encircled when going to war, like Germany in 1939, do *not* then say so when the war goes against them and they in fact become encircled (for instance there is not a single birth image in *Hitler's Secret Conversations,* running from July 1941 to November 1944). It is *group-reality,* a psychic reality, not material reality, which for reasons yet unknown causes nations to pour into their leaders feelings of being strangled in a birth canal, and which causes these leaders to then feel that only the extreme solution of going to war and hacking their way through offers the possibility of relief.

It was now not long before I became aware that wars proceed in the same sequence as birth. They develop out of a condition resembling pregnancy, the air heavy with feelings of great expectancy, what William Yancey, head of the Alabama delegation to the secessionist Democratic Convention in 1860, before a hushed convention, referred to as "a dormant volcano" which threatened to become "a great heaving volcano."[15] Soon it seems that "every day is pregnant with some new event."[16] The nation's leaders find themselves in what Kaiser Wilhelm termed "the nervous tension in the grip of which Europe has found itself during the last few years,"[17] or what Admiral Shimada in a pre-Pearl Harbor meeting described as a "tight, tense, and trapped feeling" in the air. The nation soon found that it had to "relieve herself of the inexorable pressure to which he has been subjected . . . to extricate herself from the desperate position in which she was entangled . . . to at least gain a breathing spell."[18] The nation seems to be gripped, as Congressman Brinton said in 1917, in what felt like an "invisible energy-field." "There is something in the air, gentlemen," he told his fellow Congressmen, "something stronger than you and I can realize or resist, that seems to be picking us up bodily and literally forcing us to vote for this declaration of war."[19] Shortly thereafter, diplomatic relations are "ruptured," "the past placed its hand on the shoulder of the present and thrust it into the dark future"[20] and the "descent into the abyss" begins as the nation starts its "final plunge over the brink."

When war is finally decided upon, the feeling is inevitably one of enormous relief. When Germany declared war on France in 1914, it came, said the Crown Prince, as a welcome end to the ever-increasing tension, an end to the nightmare of encirclement. "It is a joy to be alive," rejoiced a German paper the same day; Germany was "exulting with happiness."[21] And in America, half a century earlier, when Fort Sumter fell, both North and South experienced the same relief that "something unendurable had ended." Crowds went wild with laughter, waving banners, being swept up in the excitement. "The heather is on fire. I never before knew what a popular excitement can be," wrote a Boston merchant, watching the jubilant crowds, and the *London Times's* correspondent described the same thing in the South—"flushed faces, wild eyes, screaming mouths" outshouting the bands playing "Dixie."[22]

If the announcement of war was equivalent to the actual moment of birth, I wondered to myself how far this concreteness of detail could be carried. For instance, would it be too far-fetched to imagine that one might find in the historical material evidence of the actual explosive first gasp for breath of the newborn, usually accompanied by a slap on the back. I did not have to look far for confirmation of my hunch. Searching my notes once again for the actual feelings expressed by those present at the precise moment that war had been declared, I discovered several clear instances where an *actual birth explosion* had been hallucinated. For instance, when Lincoln issued his proclamation calling for troops to defend the Union, an action recognized by all as the beginning of the Civil War, he retired to his room alone, "and a feeling came over him as if he were utterly deserted and helpless . . . he suddenly heard a sound like the boom of a cannon . . . The White House attendants, whom he interrogated, had heard nothing . . . . He met a few persons on the way [outside], some of whom he asked whether they had not heard something like the boom of a cannon. Nobody had heard anything, and so he supposed it must have been a freak of his imagination."[23] Similarly, when Chamberlain stood before the British Cabinet in 1939 and announced: "Right, gentlemen, this means war," one of those present remembered: "Hardly had he said it, when there was the most enormous clap of thunder and the whole Cabinet Room was lit up by a blinding flash of lightning. It was the most deafening thunder-clap I've ever heard in my life. It really shook the building."[24] The birth-explosion seemed to take place only after the emotional recognition that the birth crisis was terminated—it did *not* take place, for instance, upon the first actual shooting, at the siege of Fort Sumter. In fact, the birth-explosion could be hallucinated even if the message that war had started was in error. When Hitler in 1938 was handed the message that Czech forces were mobilizing, and it looked as though the long-avoided European war would begin, Paul Schmidt, his interpreter, said it seemed as though a "big drum-bang" had sounded in the dead silence of those few minutes.[25] This birth-explosion was so necessary, in fact, that leaders, including both Woodrow Wilson and F.D.R., always carefully delayed bringing their countries into wars until they could feel the exaltation (and exhalation) of the war-cry of birth. As Wilson put it, when one of his Cabinet told him in early 1917 that America would follow him if he led them to war:

> Why that is not what I am waiting for; that is not enough. If they cannot go in with a whoop, there is no use of their going in at all.[26]

The more I examined the words of leaders the more I recognized that all of them seemed to *realize* that war was a group-fantasy of birth against which one struggled almost in vain. During the Cuban missile crisis, for example, it was only after Khrushchev wrote to Kennedy pleading that the two nations not "come to a clash, like blind moles" battling to death in a tunnel[27] that war between them could be averted. Even more explicit is the code-word used by Japanese ambassador Kurusu when he phoned Tokyo to signal that negotiations had broken down with Roosevelt and that it was all right to go ahead with the bombing of Pearl Harbor. Forced to invent a voice code on the spot which Tokyo would recognize as meaning that war should begin, Kurusu announced that the "birth of a child" was imminent and asked how things were in Japan. "Does it seem as if a child might be born?" "Yes," came the reply, "the birth of the child seems imminent." The only problem was that American intelligence, listening in, spontaneously recognized the meaning of the war-as-birth code.[28]

The imagery of war as birth seemed to reach back to earliest times. Numa erected a bronze temple to Janus, the Roman god of doorways and archways, and whenever Rome went to war the huge double doors were opened, a common dream-image of birth. Thereafter, whenever a war began, nations borrowed the Roman imagery and declared, as did the *Chicago Tribune* the day Lincoln called for troops: "The gates of Janus are open; the storm is on us." Certainly no American war has seemed to lack birth-imagery, beginning with the American Revolution, filled with images of birth and separation from the mother-country and what Samuel Adams termed the fight for "the child Independence ... now struggling for birth[29] right down to the Vietnam war, which began as "a swampy hole you got sucked into," soon turned into a "bottomless pit" and a "tar baby" you couldn't let go of,[30] and ended with a baby airlift.

While some of the symbolism of war is quite open and transparent—it hardly needs a psychoanalyst to interpret the message General Groves cabled to President Truman to report that the first A-bomb was successful ("The baby was born") or to see the imagery of the Hiroshima bomb being called "Little Boy" and the plane from whose belly it dropped being named after the pilot's mother—still some of the symbolism of war only becomes intelligible when one becomes familiar with psychoanalytic clinical research into dreams of birth. Although I was familiar with much of this literature, from Rank's essay on the birth-trauma to Janov's extensive work on the re-experiencing of birth during primal therapy, I discovered a whole new range of images once dreams. For instance, I discovered a little-known book written 25 years ago by the psychoanalyst Nandor Fodor entitled *The Search for the Beloved: A Clinical Investigation of the Trauma of Birth and Pre-Natal Conditioning,* a book which was ignored at the time it was published only because it was so far in advance of its time. It includes, for example, a complete description of the violence of "normal" birth methods that anticipates at every point that of Frederick Leboyer,[31] plus a proposal for psychotherapy to heal the birth trauma that spells out in advance much of the work of Arthur Janov.

One of the birth symbols that Fodor calls attention to is the image—or rather more often the nightmare—of fire. According to both Leboyer and Fodor, the neonate's skin is extremely sensitive, and feels as though it is burning up both during the long hours of labor and immediately after birth, especially when the room is colder than 98°F. or when the baby is wrapped in rough clothes.[32] Once this is realized, the historical image of war as a "ravaging fire" is more easily comprehended. Moreover, just as in dreams birth can be symbolized by being caught in a burning house, much of warfare involves simply setting fire to people and things, even when it costs more to do so than the benefit involved, as in the case of the "strategic bombing" of Europe in World War II. War and burning seem so intimately connected that troops are driven to set fire to villages even when the latter belong to those who are supposedly allies, as in Vietnam. The impulse to set people and places afire seemingly transcends any other objective in war.

Similarly, Fodor's book contains many references to another dream image for birth—falling or jumping out of towers. This is, of course, a repetition of the moment of birth itself, which involves falling upside down and activates the baby's instinctual fear of falling and reflexive hand-grasping. Only if one keeps one's "inner ear" tuned for this imagery does it become obvious that leaders at crucial moments use the "jumping out of towers" theme to convey war-as-birth messages. For instance, just as Japan was deciding to go to war with America, its leaders were presented with a voluminous report containing well-documented evidence that Japan was outnumbered by America in every area of war potential and actuality by at least 10 to 1 and therefore couldn't possibly win. Since they were in the group-process stage that made the "slide to war" inexorable, Tojo looked at this overwhelming proof that Japan couldn't win the war and announced: "There are times when we must have the courage to do extraordinary things— like jumping, with eyes closed, off the veranda of the Kiyomizu Temple!"[33] Similarly, the French Foreign Minister, at the time of the Munich Agreement, referred to war as "jumping from the Eiffel Tower."[34]

By the time I had finished re-examining my historical material, it had become obvious that all the "innocent babies" killed—and sometimes rescued—during wars were not merely side issues, accidents of war, but rather that *babies were the heart of war's central fantasy.* Consider how often wars open with rumors of the enemy "disemboweling pregnant women," whether by Turkish bayonet or Khmer Rouge wooden stake.[35] Consider how often wars end with "baby-saving" missions, whether by American baby-lift from Vietnam or Nazi Lebensborn projects in Europe, where babies from occupied countries were stolen, measured with obstetrical-type instruments for racial fitness, and either killed as unfit or sent back to Germany for raising as Aryan. Consider how often the killing of babies—as in the Calley trial—becomes the emotional turning-point of a war, and how once it was recognized that *Americans were actually killing babies* (which of course they had been doing all the time) the public removed its support from the war. It soon becomes apparent that, as Fodor found in his birth-dream research[36] and as Melanie Klein discovered clinically,[37] breaking out of the birth canal involves simultaneously breaking *into* the mother's body, and that the merging of these two fantasies is the essence of the war-as-birth fantasy in which neighboring countries must be invaded to escape from "encirclement" while at the same time the invader has the need to control and destroy the bad babies in the mother's body, the hated siblings, the damaged contents of the womb. That foreign countries contained infantilized bad-babies who had to be eliminated—or sometimes saved—was indicated by far more than my Kleinian proclivities. The historical material was full of such imagery. For instance, Hitler began World War II not only because he felt Germany needed *Lebensraum,* "room to live," but also because he had to save the good (German) babies in neighboring states and kill the bad (Jewish, Polish, etc.) ones. The blood-ties binding the mother to those babies who were to be saved was clear in the imagery of the opening words of *Mein Kampf:*

German-Austria must return to the great German motherland, and not because of economic considerations of any sort. . . .*Common blood belongs to a common Reich.* As
long as the German nation is unable even to band together its own children in one
common State, it has no . . . right to think of colonization.[38]

But aside from those few good babies who deserve to be saved, most babies are
hated occupiers of the mother's body, and must be eliminated. In fact, even the
use of poison gas for genocidal purposes began (in early 1939) with the gassing
of mentally ill and deformed *children,* and only two years later was extended
to include Jews and others,[39] all equally bad-babies, all made bad by the very
same emotional dumping described earlier in the section on external and internal
toilet-objects. For in the end the baby must die after all, and modern war has
been quite as effective in carrying out the filicidal impulses of humanity as child
sacrifice and infanticide used to be.[40]

Now the point of this side trip into the methodology of psychohistorical discovery is that far more is involved in contributing to a specific moment of discovery in psychohistory than the technical training of the psychohistorian.
Certainly both my historical and psychoanalytic knowledge helped—I had to
know how to get around in the literature of both fields—but in a more profound
sense every moment of my own emotional development led to the breakthrough
in recognizing the birth imagery in war. This goes beyond my own obvious interest in the causality of war over the past two decades, and has nothing at all
to do with any theoretical bent toward birth trauma imagery, since I was neither
a Rankian nor a Janovian. Far more crucial were, for example, the long hours
somewhere around the seventh or eighth year of my personal psychoanalysis
when I struggled to re-experience and find meaning in dreams of drowning and
sinking in a whirlpool or quicksand, or, when my son was two years old, those
hundreds of hours I spent with him pretending we were babies in mommy's
belly, crawling around in the dark under the bedclothes and pretending to fall
off the bed crying "Help! Save me!," because that was the endless game that
seemed to give him a strong sense of the pleasure of mastery. Psychohistory,
like psychoanalysis, is a science in which the researcher's *feelings* are as much
or even more a part of his research equipment than his eyes or his hands. Like
eyes, feelings are not infallible; they often introduce distortions, and so on, but
since psychohistory concerns human motivation and since the discovery and
weighing of complex motives can *only* be accomplished by identification with
human actors, the usual suppression of all feeling preached and followed by
most "science" simply cripples a psychohistorian as badly as it would cripple a
biologist to be forbidden the use of a microscope. The *emotional* development
of a psychohistorian is therefore as much a topic for discussion as his or her
intellectual development. That it includes personal psychoanalysis as a foremost
prerequisite goes without saying, as in the case of the psychoanalyst. But I think
it goes beyond this formal requirement.

I must candidly report that as a result of my own personal contacts over the past decade with perhaps a thousand historians from all over the world, both in connection with the history of childhood project and in starting this *Journal,* I no longer believe that most traditional historians are emotionally equipped, even with training, to use their feelings as psychohistorical research tools, although there is a whole new generation of psychohistorians just now beginning to write who *are* able to do so. To expect the average historian to do psychohistory is like trying to teach a blind man to be an astronomer, so averse are they to psychological insight into themselves or their historical material from *any* school of modern psychology. There are complex historical reasons for this fact, having to do with the differential process of self-selection within the universities in recent decades and with the process whereby departments of history have lost so many emotionally open students to psychology. In light of this fact, whenever I speak to a scholar of the emotional development necessary to make a good psychohistorian and get a blank look of total incomprehension, I try to find a way to leave the subject of psychohistory altogether. My listener usually is in another world of discourse where emotional reactions are not considered crucial to the results.

A final illustration will further demonstrate this point. For many years I wondered why I, a radical and anti-nationalist, was nevertheless moved almost to tears when I stood with my son watching a parade with marching bands. The temptation was to shrug off the feeling or to give it a label that would deflect the discomfort, but I was so concerned with this feeling of being swept up by military music that I took to leaving my table at the New York Public Library each time I heard music from a military band going down Fifth Avenue just to see if I could catch my feeling and locate its power over me. If I seemed a bit odd to associates who were with me at the time, so be it—I had to try to answer this question, which was psychohistorical to its core. It was only after the discovery of the war-as-birth thesis that my mind returned to the question of why the bands moved me so—I now had a hunch that I knew the answer. I took a stop-watch out to the next parade and timed the beats of the band. They occurred at about 110–130 beats per minute. Then I timed some popular music, of the usual soothing quality, on the radio—from 70 to 80 beats per minute. When I checked with my wife's obstetrician, I found that the normal heartbeat is about 75 beats per minute and that the elevated heart-beat of a woman during a contraction in labor is between 110–150 beats per minute. I obviously was a baby being born while watching the parade, being picked up and carried along by my mother's heart-beat whether I felt like it or not, and the tears in my eyes were for the impending separation from my mother! Perhaps not the most important discovery in the world, but one thoroughly psychohistorical—and though its *confirmation* might be open to anyone using usual scientific canons of truth, its *discovery* was only open to the psychohistorian with the quite peculiar personality patterns and even lifestyle necessary for using one's emotions as tools for the investigation of group reality.

All of which is not to indicate that I felt satisfied that I had found the ultimate "cause" of war with the war-as-birth paradigm. Oddly enough, science doesn't specifically aim at discovering causes—it tries to solve problems interesting to its own internal development, and causes are often the byproduct of this problem-solving. What I had done by my research was, I think, something even more crucial to psychohistory than finding a cause: *I had changed the question I was asking*. I had defined a new problem, embedded in a new theoretical structure which I felt could be both fruitful and empirically testable, and I was now able to ask a whole series of new questions such as: Why do nations project birth feelings into their leaders at some moments in their histories and not at others? What means are used to communicate these projections? Are these birth images defenses against other psychic conditions in the leadership group or in the nation? Were some wars exceptions to the war-as-birth paradigm, and if so what motivational imagery did they substitute for it? Are there differential evolutionary patterns of war imagery? Why do group-fantasies occur in such grotesquely exaggerated slow-motion, taking months and years to act out events that originally took hours, while exactly the same images in dreams are condensed into minutes?

The ability to generate new questions is precisely the hallmark of a science. Physical science expanded so rapidly in the seventeenth and eighteenth centuries not because scientists were somehow brighter than those around them. In some senses, these early scientists were quite limited in their education and in a wide knowledge of the world around them. The same principle holds for psychohistorians, who hope to succeed where historians have failed by giving scientific explanation to historical motivation. Psychohistorians can achieve this, not because they are smarter than historians but because they conceive of their task in a wholly different way and have access to research tools and scientific models unavailable to the historian. Just as there was no way for even the most learned astrologers to understand the motions of the planets as long as they (1) conceived of their task as essentially narrative- rather than problem-centered, and (2) refused to use a telescope, so even the most learned historian cannot understand the causality of history as long as he (1) conceives of his task as narrative- rather than problem-centered and (2) refuses to use his own emotional-identification capacity in a scientific way at every step in the research process.

Other psychohistorians have, I believe, found ways similar to mine to intensify this emotional-identification and defense-stripping process. Rudolph Binion, in researching his psychobiographies of Lou Andreas-Salomé and Hitler, spent several years accumulating mountains of primary source material on their motivational patterns and then locked himself up for months with his evidence and read and re-read every detail until "the pieces . . . *all* fit together, with the facts *all* stacked up behind them: this alone carried final conviction."[41] Henry Ebel surrounds himself with his historical material and "Primals" for hours while free-associating to the material in front of him, in a concentrated effort to reach deeper levels of motivation than the usual reading reveals.[42] All these methods, like my own dream-interpretation to remove defenses against discovery, are attempts by psychohistorians to fashion research tools that, like microscopes and telescopes, give access to material hitherto denied them. For psychohistory is more a *re-discovery* than a discovery—*it is a process of finding out what we all already know and act upon.* Our discovery of exterior conditions is wholly dependent on how much we can strip away of our interior defenses against recognition of what we are doing all the time. Every person going to war speaks in birth imagery, responds to birth drumbeats, and communicates in birth symbols to others going to war, and every historian fills his books with writing that tells of "the pulse-beat of the coming violence growing louder and faster as the nation moves inexorably to the birth-pangs of war." We all know it—yet no one knows it. Only the psychohistorian who trains himself to use what is "in here" to discover what is going on "out there" can hope to succeed where so many have failed in understanding and bringing under control those group-fantasies we choose to call our history.

NOTES

1 Carl Hempel, "The Function of General Laws in History," in Herbert Feigel and Wilfred Sellars, ed., *Readings in Philosophical Analysis.* New York: Appleton-Century-Crofts, 1949.

2 Alan Donagan, "Explanations in History," in Patrick Gardiner, ed., *Theories of History.* New York: The Free Press, 1959.

3 Lloyd deMause, ed., *Psychohistory: A Bibliographic Guide.* New York: Garland Publishing, 1975.

4 Steven Runciman, *History of the Crusades.* 3 vols. Cambridge: Cambridge University Press, 1950.

5 Elie Kedourie, "New Histories for Old," *Times Literary Supplement,* March 7, 1975, p. 3.

6 A. J. P. Taylor, *The Origins of the Second World War.* New York: Atheneum, 1968, pp. 216, 217.

7 Max Montgelas and Walter Schücking, eds., *Outbreak of the World War: German Documents Collected by Karl Kautsky.* Oxford: Oxford University Press, 1924, pp. 63, 307, 266, 161.

8 Montgelas and Schücking, eds., *Outbreak of The World War,* pp. 250ff. The inexorability of the movement to war, as well as most of the other irrationalies of the war process, is best summarized and adequately referenced in Geoffrey Blainey, *The Causes of War.* New York: The Free Press, 1973.

9 Ole R. Holsti and Robert C. North, "The History of Human Conflict," in Elton B. McNeil, ed., *The Nature of Human Conflict.* Englewood Cliffs, N.J.: Prentice-Hall, 1965, p. 166.

10 Luigi Albertini, *The Origins of the World War of 1914.* Vol. II. Oxford: Oxford University Press, 1952, p. 132; Imanuel Geiss, ed., *July 1914: The Outbreak of the First World War: Selected Documents.* New York: Charles Scribner's Sons, 1967, p. 295.

11 Ralph H. Lutz, *Fall of the German Empire, 1914–1918: Documents of the German Revolution.* Vol. I. Stanford: Stanford University Press, 1932, p. 13.

12 For the various levels of parenting throughout history, see Lloyd deMause, ed., *The History of Childhood.* New York: The Psychohistory Press and Harper & Row, 1974 and 1975.

13 Nandor Fodor, *The Search for the Beloved: A Clinical Investigation of the Trauma of Birth and Pre-Natal Conditioning.* New Hyde Park: University Books, 1949, pp. 35–45.

14 Arthur Janov, *The Feeling Child: Preventing Neurosis in Children.* New York: Simon and Schuster, 1973, pp. 41–81.

15 Bruce Catton, *The Coming Fury.* Garden City, N.Y.: Doubleday & Co., 1961, p. 32.
16 William Eddis, *Letters from America.* Cambridge, Mass.: Harvard University Press, 1969, p. 151.
17 Montgelas and Schücking, ed., *Outbreak of the World War,* p. 56.
18 Herbert Feis, *The Road to Pearl Harbor.* Princeton: Princeton University Press, 1950, pp. 293, 265.
19 Richard W. Leopold and Arthur S. Link, eds. *Problems in American History.* New York: McKay, 1965, p. 762.
20 Feis, *Pearl Harbor,* p. 293.
21 Barbara Tuchman, *The Guns of August.* New York: The Macmillan Co., 1962, p. 121.
22 Catton, *Fury,* p. 325.
23 Carl Sandburg, *Abraham Lincoln: The War Years.* Vol. 1. New York: Harcourt, Brace & Co. 1939, pp. 236–37.
24 Sidney Aster, *1939: The Making of the Second World War.* New York: Simon and Schuster, 1973, p. 387.
25 Paul Schmidt, *Statist auf diplomatischer Bühne 1923–45.* Bonn, 1949, p. 413.
26 Joseph P. Tumulty, *Woodrow Wilson As I Knew Him.* New York: Doubleday, 1921, p. 235.
27 Robert F. Kennedy, *Thirteen Days: A Memoir of the Cuban Missile Crisis.* New York: W. W. Norton, 1969, p. 89.
28 John Toland, *Rising Sun: The Decline and Fall of the Japanese Empire.* New York: Random House, 1970, pp. 174–75.
29 Henry Steele Commager and Richard B. Morris, eds., *The Spirit of Seventy-Six* Vol. I. New York: Bobbs-Merrill Co., 1970, p. 294.
30 David Halberstam, *The Best and the Brightest.* New York: Random House 1969, pp. 249, 601, 617.
31 Frederick Leboyer, *Birth without Violence.* New York: Alfred Knopf, 1975.
32 Personal communication with Dr. Leboyer at the Tarrytown Conference on Birth without Violence, April 19, 1975; Fodor, *Search,* pp. 16, 93–103.
33 Toland, *The Rising Sun,* p. 112.
34 Laurence Thompson, *The Greatest Treason: The Untold Story of Munich.* New York: William Morrow & Co., 1968, p. 112.
35 Robert Sam Anson, "Withdrawal Pains," *New Times,* March 21, 1975, p. 25.
36 Fodor, *Search,* p. 253ff.
37 Melanie Klein, *Narrative of a Child Analysis.* New York: Basic Books, 1960.
38 Adolf Hitler, *Mein Kampf.* New York: Reynal & Hitchcock, 1939, p. 3.
39 Lucy S. Dawidowicz, *The War Against the Jews, 1933–1945.* New York: Holt, Rinehart and Winston, 1975, p. 132.
40 As I was writing up this article I found that I had encountered the essence of the baby imagery more than a year earlier in *The First Part of the Revelation of Moses the Son of Jehoshar* (Fort Lee, N.J.: Argonaut Books, 1973, pp. 58–59, 102, 106) in the brilliant aphorisms of Henry Ebel describing how "Dresden, Berlin, Hiroshima and Nagasaki were also made chokewomb hot-wombs" and how "men wonder at the calm bestiality with which the Nazi murdered babies and infants and children. But that was the whole point. The helpless adults they butchered were equally 'children' to them. If they baby-phagged as hard as they could, then perhaps they wouldn't be babyphagged themselves. If they pushed more babies into the chokewomb hotwomb, then perhaps Mama would spare THEM."
41 Rudolph Binion, "Hitler's Concept of *Lebensraum,*" *History of Childhood Quarterly: The Journal of Psychohistory* 1 (1973):196; "My Life with Frau Lou," in Perry Curtis, ed., *The Historian's Workshop.* New York: Knopf, 1970, pp. 293–306.
42 Henry Ebel, "Primal Therapy and Psychohistory," *History of Childhood Quarterly: The Journal of Psychohistory* 2 (1975):563–70; and *The First Part of the Revelation of Moses the Son of Jehoshar.*

6

Doing Psychohistory

Rudolph Binion

A universe permanently unconscious of itself in all its parts, existence everywhere and forever unexperienced, boundless being in a sensory void: this is inconceivable. Such incognizance is spoiled just by being imagined. To envision even bygone worlds of unsuspecting, unsuspected matter, or an oblivious cosmos to come, is for the mind's eye to supply the defect. Because existence cannot be unthought, philosophers tend to suppose that it is inherently known. For Anaxagoras already, psyche was the containing and ordering principle of the universe, so that awareness of things was one with their cause. Many a master of modern historical thinking has followed Anaxagoras in this. Thus for Hegel, human history had meaning; its meaning was expanding consciousness; its contents was what consciousness required to expand. Here is where Karl Marx claimed to set Hegel aright. Marx argued instead that what was developing in the long haul was the economy, with human relations, institutions, and finally consciousness tagging along. But modes of production developed logically and intelligibly for Marx just as consciousness did for Hegel. For Marx too history made sense, and for him too the point of it was to be understood. Relative understanding ("class consciousness") lent history its dynamics; absolute understanding would be its fulfillment. It was Darwin who dealt such age-old human presumption its hardest blow. In Darwin's scheme, consciousness had evolved from more rudimentary sensibility and, behind that, insensibility. Darwin's derivation of mind from brute matter by way of accidents adding up (through "natural selection from random variations") turned Anaxagoras inside out. Anaxagoras's containing and ordering principle reappeared accordingly—in the exact adaptation of consciousness to nature and the possibility of systematizing the messy facts of life.

Ours is Darwin's world. Our consciousness no longer fools us about its mindlessness. Our species' history merges with natural history. Our species' future is open: its natural lot is to change continually, with or without mutations, de-

Reprinted from *The Journal of Psychohistory,* vol. 5 (1978) 313–23.

pending on who survives to reproduce. Our animal instincts of survival and re-production have us coming and going, even where they miscarry or where we refine them beyond recognition. Our creatural consciousness is distinguished in the main by being reflexive. We do not want something without knowing that we want it—or refusing to know. Our faculty of refusing to know what we want was Freud's province. Prying into its pathology, Freud uncovered a human reserve of instinctual thinking unfit for consciousness beyond infancy, and that in a nether realm of disclaimed memories and inexpressible stirrings out of the individual and racial past. Here was a whole new germinal source of history. Freud well realized this. But Freud approached history through his clinical findings imaginatively extended instead of using history to extend them. Psychoanalysis has yet to repair his omission. Historians can look to psychoanalysts, Freud foremost, for object lessons in interpreting human folly, but not for interpretations ready-made.

Human history is what people did. To understand it is to understand why people did what they did. This is possible because mind is enough of a kind for its workings to be inwardly intelligible at any historic remove. Understanding history through motives and motives through history: this is psychohistory. Psyche causing history, making it intelligible: this updates Anaxagoras.

For such intelligibility the records must suffice. There is a no telling in advance when they will. They could be bulky with the key pieces missing. My own odd experience has been that the key pieces always survive, however little else does. But I have stuck to richly documented history for safety's sake. This precaution is hardly restrictive, as just about any topic is worth doing, or redoing, in the present crude state of the art. A more restrictive consideration in the choice of topics is that they must be lived with at emotionally close quarters for years. My own intended next topic was the traumatic aftereffects of the Black Death as re-flected in the outbursts of social violence, convulsive and contagious, that spread in its wake a generation after. But then I balked at absorbing myself in that morbid matter after five years with Hitler's Germany. In any case the project was infel-icitously conceived. Proper psychohistorical procedure is to pursue causes rather than effects. A researcher can probe a given event, say young Napoleon's flight from Corsica, for unconscious input, but not for unconscious output. Should a link be suspected with Napoleon's flight from Egypt six years later, this would need to be probed in its own right.

As a rule, the aspirant psychohistorian is best advised to pick a biographic subject. This rule is highly breakable. But the individual psyche remains the basis of our conceptualizations until further notice. So it were as well for the trainee to train by penetrating one or another historic life in full. Actually there is no penetrating a historic life except in full, as nothing significant in a life is detached from the rest subjectively. The life need not be written up in full when the time comes. But its thrust or drift at any juncture must fall in with its thrust or drift overall—with its controlling purposes, its dominant patterns, its recurrent mo-tifs—when they are read as (as Nietzsche's phrase) "a sign language of the affects."

To grasp a life inwardly requires mastery of its full documentary remains. It also calls for conversance with the whole run of personalities, institutions, and events, and the whole congeries of ideas, usages, and values, involved. To top that off, it takes an intellectual and emotional stunt both strenuous and delicate. The researcher must emphatize and analyze at once. He must imagine himself Napoleon setting sail from Alexandria and ask himself: "What am I doing *unconsciously* in setting sail from Alexandria?" His empathy must be perfect to yield Napoleon's answer, yet only partial for him to catch the answer when it comes. That is, he must make believe in earnest and still know that he is making believe. This comes to an artificial, controlled ego-split.

As good a passage of an assumed life as any to probe first in this posture is one with a suspected precedent, such as Napoleon's flight from Egypt: the precedent will never simply fall into place associatively without leading beyond itself. Another good starter is quirks or foibles except that they can easily get magnified out of proportion. Better are lapses or aberrations from a smooth course of action or system of thought: they will be found to expose its underpinnings. Fictionalists offer an ideal point of departure in their fiction, the rule being that every element of it has at least one referent in their lives. Take Ibsen. Inquiry on him would almost have to begin with his impregnating a servant girl when he was eighteen. This misadventure looms even larger behind his later dramas than the two unsettling circumstances of his childhood: his rumored illegitimacy and his father's financial ruin. All three come into *The Wild Duck* practically undistorted in the backdrop to the sorry menage of a photographer and dreamer (read: naturalist and poet). Tragedy ensues when an idealistic illusion-destroyer (Ibsen again) drags the old misadventure upstage center. Ibsen took his own hint here and returned to disguising his experience of the unwanted child again and again until his last heroine went mad from reliving it again and again in disguise. Here, in *When We Dead Awaken,* the child is a statue for which she has posed in the nude. Traumatized by the sculptor's mere thanks for the chaste episode, she relives it in reverse as a nude artist who teases men to despair.

Not only characters and situations, but also themes and techniques, have their antecedents in a creative writer's life. Bertolt Brecht's shock at the surgical butchery he witnessed as a medical orderly in 1918 went into pacifist plays aggressively staged, then didactic plays justifying violence, before he mastered it in a theater balancing both modes and messages. Jean Genet's obsession with his own homosexuality shows behind the dominant devices of his theater: the play of false identities and the inversion of customary relations and values. Philosophers for their part work up private experience into ideas. Witness Malthus conceiving of "moral restraint" as a corrective to his fearful "power of population" while on a chaste research trip abroad with his future wife. Or witness Søren Kierkegaard, the last child of a seduced housemaid: his pious father's shattering disclosure of this transgression eventuated in S.K.'s concept of a "teleological suspension of the ethical" whereby Abraham suspended ethics to the roundabout end of getting his son Isaac (S.K.). This equivalence was full of dialectical twists: Abraham was tempted to be ethical; he surmounted his temptation; he got by renouncing. A writer's life too has its themes with their concealed allusions to his past. They go by the same rules of origination as those in his works: it is as simple as that. Take Kierkegaard renouncing his fiancée untouched by pretending to have been only trifling with her: this repeated in the negative his father's seduction of the wench he then dutifully married. Repudiated masters are imitated like repudiated parents. Auguste Comte wound up enunciating a new Christianity like Saint-Simon. John Stuart Mill followed Comte in finding a mismated muse to humanize his theories.

But such fragments of a life may not go to the heart of it. What counts is how it cohered, beginning with what it cohered around. An activist who was also a theorist invites a focus on the action his theorizing served. The simple sense of a lifelong course of action takes exceeding care to discern. What was a Lenin's basic endeavor? It was something like a use of coercion for the sake of final deliverance from coercion. Here are the two terms of a classic bout with the father ghost, the proper sequence—deliverance from, then succession to, the coercionist—being simply reversed. This reversal was offset in practice by the need to end the Czar's despotism before Lenin's could begin. And yet I would expect Leninism to have been actuated less by the father complex than by "a shattering experience"[1] of seventeen-year-old Vladimir Ilyich: his elder brother's execution for plotting to kill the Czar. Both brothers had become intellectual rebels upon their father's death a year earlier. The elder one alone had turned to politics. He espoused Marxism, but resorted to terrorism against "a system which permits no freedom." So he explained at his trial, adding: "Terror is our answer to the violence of the state. It is the only way to force a despotic regime to grant political freedom to the people."[2] His avenger, even while liquidating Czarism, perfected its repressive methods from inside the Kremlin on the theory that freedom would someday ensue. Here is a tempting paradox. Only the paradox may be mine rather than Lenin's—a function of my formulation rather than his intention. There is no telling from the biographic outside. To know what values or aims, attitudes or methods, were vital to Lenin, and discover what they meant to him deep down, I would need to become Lenin artificially, with the whole Lenin corpus down pat.

But even then, how would I know the right answer if I found it? Right answers come piecemeal, each piece a breakthrough with a compelling rush of unsuspected associations. Psychohistorical analysis proceeds about like dream analysis on a grand scale except that the associations thrown up involve new material facts that then check out. This is retrodiction. It dispels any and all self-doubt on the researcher's part. I worked through the known Hitler records by empathic introspection to missing experiences that I documented only afterwards, including Hitler's Pasewalk hallucination, his mother's poisoning, and her maternal trauma. Through Hitler's calls for Germany's eastward expansion I even heard the muted reference to Germany's lost eastern conquest of World War I before I could pin it down archivally. I say "even" because I heard it on the receiving end of his calls, by thinking and feeling myself into the public to which he appealed. But when is such an inquiry complete? Loosely put, when nothing puzzles us any longer about a Lenin or a Hitler—when we know what was bothering him inwardly, and how he handled it outwardly, with all his crucial utterances and decisions and moves as forced consequences. Perhaps more formal criteria can be defined. Informally it is again as in dream analysis: the mystery is exhausted— and the self-analyst with it.

Breakthrough, retrodiction, exhaustion: these are conclusive for the researcher. They prove nothing for anyone else. He can show that his solution fits to the nth degree of irrefragability. That will establish it as possible, no more. He can show further how to confirm or disconfirm it. But no subsequent empirical support will carry final conviction either. Here the psychohistorian is uniquely up against it. His special problem is not, as the clinical-minded insist, the risk of "countertransference" so long as the data keep running his way. Any other historian also risks reading his own *meshugas* into his materials. So for that matter does the natural scientist. Einstein may well have had a world womb at heart when he conceptualized his plenum universe finite and unbounded, self-contained and expanding, quasi-spherical and quasi-elliptical like a mollusk. The payoff is whether kinetic energy does equal $mc^2/\sqrt{1-v^2/c^2}$. With the psychohistorian too the proof is in the pudding. But the psychohistorian's pudding cannot be just measured and weighed. It must also be tasted to be tested. That is, others must step inside his subject after him and try out his reading of the evidence on themselves in turn. This costs emotional strains on top of critical pains, though none that begin to approach the researcher's own. With affective material, feeling is believing. In any case belief is "something *felt* by the mind," as David Hume remarked.[3] That is doubly so in psychohistory.

But the problem is not simply one of belief as against disbelief. An open-minded reader will ordinarily believe a right psychohistorical solution only to underweight it. Granted your derivation of a Lenin's politics, he will say, was there nothing *else* agitating the agitator? And what about hard objective forces shaping his will?

This second question embarrasses many a psychohistorian into an unmeaning methodological pluralism. The hedging preface would have it that the psychohistorical is one factor among many—that it adds one new dimension. An unfortunate influence this way would seem to be the *Annales* school with its aim of *histoire totale*. In practice *histoire totale* means that to describe past social reality anything goes, from climate to the id. The key word here is "describe": *histoire totale* is total description of past social reality slowly changing. To explain such change is another matter. The law of parsimony applies to all explaining. More, social change must be seen for what it is, people doing things differently, or it will forever resist explanation. Statistics are no way around this imperative.

The fall of a net fertility rate way back when means that some women were copulating less or breastfeeding longer or something. All that statistical analysis can show is who and what. The psychohistorical "Why?" remains. To reply to it in the negative, whatever people did not act *from* or *on* does not help explain their acts. By *"from"* I mean the inner impetus inwardly regulated; by *"on"* I mean a resistant or compliant medium. The rest is beside the explanatory point. Gravitation and respiration are vital to human enterprise, but not for understanding it. The same goes for social context as distinct from social motives or purposes. Inquiry is inclusive, explanation exclusive.

That principle of exclusion applies to motivational material itself. Unless we can pick out the crucial pieces behind a historic performance we slip into itemization tending toward a *psychohistoire totale*. The psychohistorical catchall has its advocates. Their catchword is "overdetermination." This was Freud's peculiar term for mutlidetermination in mental life—peculiar because it implies that some determinants are expendable and so are not determinants after all. But, terminology apart, Freud recognized that, say, a tightly condensed dream is not caused by all the latent material stacked up behind it, let alone by all the modes of concealed expression employed in it. In his scheme, a dream is caused by a preconscious thought that combines with an unconscious wish or vice versa. The rest just gets in on the act. Roughly these same rules apply to a psychic economy waking as sleeping except that awake means oriented to outer reality at the level of consciousness. Short of pathology, routine living is governed by the reality principle in accordance with unconscious intent, while the twists and turns of a life's course are governed by unconscious dictates in keeping with the reality principle. This causality as per Freud holds in psychohistory if room is made in his scheme for unconscious demands arising out of postinfantile experience. And what counts in psychohistory are causes, not the whole range of "overdeterminants," though these too must be rehearsed in print now and again—behind a mind set or a brain storm, a decision or an inspiration, analyzed or reconstructed in full for illustrative purposes.

To the same point, psychotherapy will rightly deal in infantile material that is wrong for psychohistory. Consider Kierkegaard again. Why did his father's disclosure about his mother's seduction hit him so hard? The answer would have mattered to him on the couch. It is immaterial to his "teleological suspension of the ethical" if this is directly accountable by that disclosure affecting him unconsciously (and his broken engagement consciously). Or consider Ibsen again. His theater appears to have been haunted most by the erotic and financial casualty of his unwanted child, with his rumored illegitimacy and his father's business failure brought in by association. Such a traumatic setback to a highminded, ambitious youth is irreducible to infantile material. In Lenin's case, the father complex is conspicuous in his marked ambivalence toward his elder brother as the new head of their family after their father's death. That brother's execution was no less a powerful experience in its own right that certainly shaped his striving in more ways than he knew. And where was the generative center of Hitler's politics? "The Jew" was his mother's last doctor, "living space" was Ludendorff's lost conquest; the rest was peripheral.

Emotional shock-absorption comes into the clinical texts only in its failing form: the traumatic neurosis. But its normal form, unconscious reliving, is the ferment of endless historic storm and stress. Therein lies another warning against simply applying clinical theory to history. But no more warning should be needed against this misguided procedure than that the most to be gained by it is less than nil. Imagine a psychobiographic sleuth on the trail of a narcissistic personality disorder behind Stalin's seemingly paranoid rule. Instead of entering into his subject in all its vastness, he would be documenting Stalin's irritability, his whims and rages, his grandiosity, his intolerance of frustration and dissent. However strong a presumption he might finally establish that baby Djugashvili resented his severance into self and other, that primal upset leads nowhere in particular careerwise or otherwise. So he could not turn around and derive Stalinism from it. Besides, Stalin's terror arose with his victims' eerie compliance. To be seen into, it would need to be seen arising. It were probably best approached through his crude debut as terrorizer in Tsaritsyn in 1918. Causes show most distinctly through beginnings. When I could not trace Hitler's calls for eastward expansion to a personal source, their beginnings led me to their source in his audiences prompting them. To have tapped that source is my proudest research coup. That would be the lure of a Stalin, a Lenin, a Napoleon, as psychohistorical subject: their unconscious rapport with those they ruled.

Twice now I have cited Hitler's unconscious rapport with his public: *jamais deux sans trois!* The clue to it came from *Mein Kampf.* There Hitler related that in his agitational incunabula he had delivered two stock speeches in ever new versions by reading corrections off his listeners' faces. Reports by Party and press, by Army and police, of his early speech-making attested to his intense interaction with his audiences. His one stock speech denied German war guilt; the other vindicated the Treaty of Brest-Litovsk as a gracious partnership with the defeated Soviet Union. Both connected *a contrario* with his project, first published in *Mein Kampf* of 1924–1926, for a German conquest of the Soviet Union with Britain's concurrence. I had already found this project expounded in private utterances recorded over the year preceding the Putsch of November 1923. Could it have developed out of his two early oratorical repertory pieces following the indications from his listeners' faces? I thought and felt myself back into his audiences in the Munich area before the Putsch and across Germany in the late 1920s. After long months of straining my mind's ear I could all at once hear, and shrilly, where his call for eastward expansion resonated with a traumatic national experience. This was the 1918 defeat, for which Germans were the less prepared since Ludendorff's subjugation of Soviet Russia had seemed to render them invulnerable. That trauma did not, then, just pop up behind Hitler's expansionist project and introduce itself. It erupted convulsively, a pent-up panic so overpowering when released that I blocked it out again and again before I could admit it to consciousness sufficiently even to identify it. With it, disparate elements of Weimar Germany's troubled and confusing politics rushed to mind, connected up, fell into place. These included a missing link in my evidence that I then had to hunt down: the transition from Hitler's two early repertory pieces to his project for a new eastern conquest. This project was now intelligible as an invitation to a traumatic reliving—one designed ostensibly to undo the 1918 defeat, actually to outdo it. A year or more passed before I realized that I was taking that transition for granted. Then I scouted for documentation. I found it for May 31, 1921, when Hitler delivered those two repertory speeches combined, both for the last time. In vindicating Brest-Litovsk on that occasion he blurted out that the big German loss from the defeat in the west had been the land conquered from the Soviets. And he grounded the point in the very arguments that he later advanced to urge a reconquest.

That documentary find confirmed for me my intuition of the German trauma. True, my final proof of it lay with Hitler registering it and reacting.[4] But the insight had been won through self-projection into his national public. This opened mass phenomena to direct psychohistorical inquiry. Such effects may be only sporadic and transitory in modern times—repercussions of group shock or fear for a few generations. Or all large-scale human developments may be collaborative at the unconscious level. Take a broad cultural movement such as Romanticism. Why did Romantic values spread across Europe in the decades around 1800? All at once youngsters sought out the common path and the rare destiny; exalted community and aloneness; affected enchantment and estrangement, exuberance and languishing, yearning and pining; swooned over their sister if they had one, and felt burnt out by twenty-some if they lived that long. Gerald N. Izenberg is studying several important Romantics against a background of changing familial circumstances. If that is where the stimulus to Romanticism came from, he can be trusted to find it. But I wonder. A proto-Romanticism burgeoned early along in the Age of Reason with its bursts of tears and brooding over ruins, as if the regnant formalism and rationalism were not wholly tolerable. The binding constraints and restraints had rigidified beyond easy endurance. The Romantics repudiated them in a surge of passion (and posturing), often enough without having experienced them at first hand. This emergence of Romanticism out of "the stirrings of unchanneled emotion . . . disrupting the old order"[5] makes culture look continuous on the level of nerves, with one century's moodiness developing into the mannered mood of the next. Jacques Barzun stretches that line of descent farther back. Referring to "romantic" exploration and creation in the sixteenth century, he adds that "when classicism had twinges, they were like pre-natal recollections of romanticism."[6] This image is psychohistorically overdrawn, to be sure. Yet it is meaningful within a time-honored, universal frame of reference: that of collective historical experience, with collective memories to match. The psychological truth to this ever-current scheme of history requires to be explored. Its exploration would seem to offer at least as promising an approach to broad movements in history as the search for patterns of change in private cirumstances.

I do not say more promising. The only thing wrong with psychoprosopography is the word. Collective experience involves individuals. How it involves them is part of what requires exploring. So the comparative study of individual Anabaptists or Abolitionists can only complement the exploration of those mass manifestations per se. The same holds for more generalized historical studies of formative influences on children, from nurturing and socializing practices[7] to great existential upheavals.[8] Such studies yield norms and aggregates—types and tendencies of personal development. These cannot be searched out for the motives that make history. Only specific individuals can for individual motives, specific collectivities for collective motives.

Such collectivities run large so far as can tentatively be told. Monster-ridden medieval Europe was one for Walter Abell in *The Collective Dream in Art*.[9] The convenient access to collective traumas or anxieties through common motifs in art has been neglected since this pioneering work. But Paul Monaco found in the popular cinema of the 1920s, with its relatively closed national markets, a comparable medium for penetrating national group process. By analyzing the French and German filmic fantasy wares of those years, he established that the Germans were then haunted by the war they had lost in 1918 and the French by their subsequent national insecurity.[10] And now Lloyd deMause has spotted a new locus of national fantasy in the imagery interspersed in public rhetoric. It, he holds, signals unconscious national imperatives to responsive political leaders.[11] No doubt it does. But do the signals come in perinatal crisis cycles as deMause contends? That is too schematic for the few glimpses we have had of group process. My own guess is that collective identities are vestigial—that they were the giants and many-headed monsters of yore. If so, they will draw researchers to prehistory. Only this much is already certain: that they await further insight before theoretical bearings can be taken.

For such insight, the more genius the better. But the first thing needful is expertise—in history generally, and in individual-based psychohistory—as distinct from small-minded professionalism. Historical professionalism, like any other, is defined by what has been and is being done. Psychohistory itself is infested with a would-be professionalism oriented toward clinical models. Such models of individual personality disserve it because of their tangential relevance. Not even tangential relevance can be found for the psychoanalytical theories of group process drawn from self-observing artificial groups.[12] With collective causality, psychohistory comes into its own. That puts it farther beyond the professional pale than ever before. Its big, and only, hope is that, with a whole uncharted realm of human reality open before it, it is also more exciting than ever before.

NOTES

1 Louis Fischer, *The Life of Lenin* (New York, 1964), p. 9. See also ibid., p. 17: "a lasting shock."
2 Quoted in David Shub, *Lenin* (Baltimore, 1966), pp. 15–16. See further Fischer, pp. 14–17,

and, on young Lenin and revolutionary terrorism, Richard Pipes, "The Origins of Bolshevism: The Intellectual Evolution of Young Lenin," in *Revolutionary Russia: A Symposium*, ed. Richard Pipes (New York, 1968), pp. 33–66.

3 David Hume, *A Treatise of Human Nature*, Book I, Part III, Section VII.

4 Rudolph Binion, *Hitler among the Germans* (New York, 1976), pp. 58–66.

5 Jacques Barzun, *Classic, Romantic and Modern* (New York, 1961), p. 53.

6 Ibid., p. 56.

7 As fine a monograph as any is John Demos, *A Little Commonwealth: Family Life in Plymouth Colony* (New York, 1970). The grand overview is Lloyd deMause, ed., *The History of Childhood* (New York, 1974).

8 The best differentiated cohort analysis of the aftereffects of a social calamity is Glen H. Elder, Jr., *Children of the Great Depression: Social Change in Life Experience* (Chicago, 1974).

9 Walter Abell, *The Collective Dream in Art: A Psycho-Historical Theory of Culture Based on Relations Between the Arts, Psychology, and the Social Sciences* (Cambridge, Mass., 1957; New York, 1966).

10 Paul Monaco, *Cinema and Society. France and Germany during the Twenties* (New York, 1976).

11 Lloyd deMause, "Jimmy Carter and American Fantasy," in Lloyd deMause and Henry Ebel, eds., *Jimmy Carter and American Fantasy* (New York, 1977).

12 Here the great source is W. R. Bion, *Experience in Groups* (New York, 1959). The single, signal application of small group theory to history is in the pre-Bion school deriving from Georg Simmel and based on "the development of the attitudes of the individuals concerned": see R. C. Raack, "When Plans Fail: Small Group Behavior and Decision-Making in the Conspiracy of 1808 in Germany," *Conflict Resolution*, Vol. 14, pp. 3–19.

Part I
Bibliography

The argument about the scientific validity of psychoanalysis has sparked a lively debate. The most convenient and comprehensive source book is *Psychoanalysis, Scientific Method, and Philosophy,* ed. Sidney Hook (New York, 1959). A more recent and detailed examination of the scientific status of psychoanalysis, which focuses on such specific aspects as dream theory, personality types, and Oedipal dynamics is Seymour Fisher and Robert P. Greenberg, *The Scientific Validity of Freud's Theories and Therapy* (New York, 1977). This may be complemented by Paul Kline's *Fact and Fancy in Freudian Theory* (London, 1972). Eysenck himself returns to the attack in "Psychoanalysis—Myth or Science?" *Inquiry,* vol. 4, no. 1 (Spring 1961), pp. 1–15. Paul Meehl supports Eysenck, emphasizing the importance of refutability or disconfirmation as the best criterion in demarcating science from other kinds of cognitive enterprises such as metaphysics. If an experiment cannot be replicated exactly, it cannot be disconfirmed: it is here that experimental psychology parts company with psychoanalysis. See Meehl's article, "Some Methodological Reflections on the Difficulties of Psychoanalytic Research," in *Minnesota Studies in the Philosophy of Science* (University of Minnesota Press, 1970), vol. 4, pp. 403–16. The historian Saul Friedlander, clearly sympathetic to psychoanalysis, has strong reservations about its role as a scientific means of explanation. His first chapter, "The Theoretical Framework," in *History and Psychoanalysis* (New York, 1978) sets forth his argument. Even some analysts doubt that the work of Freud and his followers can be considered scientific as that term is defined according to the canons of natural science. This is Fritz Schmidl's view in his "Psychoanalysis and History," *Psychoanalytic Quarterly,* vol. 31 (1962), pp. 532–48.

The consensus seems to be that psychoanalysis no longer has, if it ever had, the status of a scientific field of endeavor. This is an important issue as it relates to psychohistory. If psychohistorians believe that the dictates of psychoanalysis have the force of general laws in history, they will naturally assign it a significant causative role. This no doubt accounts for the previously mentioned tendency among some psychohistorians to accept uncritically the equation: if x (childhood experiences), then y (adult behaviors). To think of psychoanalytic theory in terms of an ineluctable model of human actions, rather than as a heuristic device for understanding human behavior, may distort the contributions that psychoanalytic theory could make to the study of history. Thus some critics, influenced by what they see as the scientific pretension of psychoanalysis, dismiss psychohistory out of hand. See, for example, Jacques Barzun, *Clio and the Doctors* (Chicago, 1974) and David Stannard, *Shrinking History* (New York, 1980). A thoughtful and moderate counter to Barzun and Stannard is Peter Gay's *Freud for Historians* (New York, 1985). In it, Gay pleads for a history that is "an elegant, fairly rigorous aesthetic science" (ix).

It is important to remember that not all explanation is scientific, a point made by (among others) John Passmore, "Explanation in Everyday Life, in Science, and in History," *History and Theory,* vol. 2, no. 2 (1962), pp. 105–23; and George Miller, "Is Scientific Thinking Different?" *Bulletin. The American Academy of Arts and Sciences,* vol. 36, no. 5 (Feb. 1983), pp. 26–37. The ideal of descriptive or narrative explanation in history as opposed to a scientific explanation has recently been given attention by Lawrence Stone, "The Revival of Narrative: Reflections on a New Old History," *Past and Present,* vol. 85 (Nov. 1979), pp. 3–24; and Hayden White, "The Question of Narrative in Contemporary Historical Theory," *History and Theory,* vol. 23, no. 1 (1984), pp. 1–33. The implications of a narrative explanation for psychohistory are clear: it may be a more workable approach to the past than a scientific explanation. As Michael Sherwood reminds us, Freud himself used different kinds of explanations, among them unified narratives based upon minute detail to lend coherence, through patterning, to a patient's life. Sherwood's argument in full may be found in *The Logic of Explanation in Psychoanalysis,* cited in our introduction. See also Thomas A. Kohut, "Psychohistory as History," *American Historical Review,* vol. 91 (1986), pp. 336–54.

PART II

THE PSYCHOLOGY OF THE INDIVIDUAL IN HISTORY

7

On Psychohistory

Robert Coles

In a letter dated October 9, 1898, Freud made mention of Leonardo da Vinci: he was "perhaps the most famous left-handed individual," and he "is not known to have had any love affairs." The letter was one of many addressed to Wilhelm Fliess. As Freud step by step began to formulate what we know today as psychoanalysis, he turned to his friend to present his thoughts openly and with some passion, as if he needed to ask whether all those ideas made any sense or were hopelessly out of kilter—useless notions prompted by the disturbed minds a psychiatrist sees, not to mention his own dreams and fantasies, which he had relied upon rather significantly in *The Interpretation of Dreams.*

That book, published in 1900, was unquestionably Freud's masterpiece; rich with years of clinical observations, written in a forceful style, it is by no means out of date now, nor will it ever be. A writer had sensed something important about human experience and found for himself an original language—a means by which his ideas might take hold of the reader's imagination. Soon after its publication Freud broke with Fliess. Why write letters about ideas when they are already set down in a book? Why discuss possible discoveries when they have been made, and are even attracting a limited but impressively brilliant cadre of admirers? Anyway, if Freud had once overestimated Fliess extravagantly, soon enough the latter's distinct limitations became apparent, and that was that—no awful scene, just a moment or two of recognition that became much more only as time passed.

Leonardo da Vinci was harder for Freud to put aside. Though by 1907 he was caught up in psychoanalytic work (by then the Vienna Psychoanalytical Society had been established), there is evidence that the achievements and the spirit of one genius were very much on the mind of another. Freud was reading a study of Leonardo that year, and called it one of his favorite books. On December 11,

1907, he spoke at some length about the general subject of psychoanalytic biography. Two years later he again referred to Leonardo, this time in a letter to Jung dated October 17, 1909: a patient under treatment had the same "constitution," the same psychological makeup, as the famous artist, but not his genius. He also told Jung that he was hoping to obtain a book, published in Italy, on Leonardo's youth.

In early December of 1909 Freud spoke to his Vienna colleagues at the Psychoanalytical Society about Leonardo, not the first time, incidentally, that such a presentation had been made. Isidor Sadger, one of the earlier members of the society (he joined in 1906, the same year Rank did), had studied the lives and writings of Heinrich von Kleist and C.F. Meyer. A short story of Meyer's, "Die Richterim," had also interested Freud; he once wrote to Fliess about that, too, remarking how Meyer's own life seemed to come across in the fiction he wrote.

By 1910 Freud was engaged in more than a casual inquiry; he went through every book on Leonardo he could lay his hands on, and he started writing one of those inviting, even charming essays of his that have a way of stirring up far more controversy than they seem meant to. In America the essay was translated by A.A. Brill and published as *Leonardo da Vinci: A Study in Psychosexuality*. More recently Alan Tyson has made another translation that is more faithful to the German at points, yet reads much better in English: *Leonardo da Vinci and a Memory of His Childhood*. In 1957, nine years before the surprise publication of *Thomas Woodrow Wilson*, supposedly a collaborative "study" by Freud and William Bullitt, the editors of the Standard Edition of the *Complete Psychological Works of Sigmund Freud* described the short book on Leonardo as "not only the first but the last of Freud's large-scale excursions into the field of biography."

It is an excursion well worth looking at today. What Freud tried to do over a half century ago still is being done, sometimes under the name of "psychohistory." Moreover, both his successes and his difficulties as an analyst of a long-dead historical figure's mental life are being experienced by others in our time. The Leonardo book stirred up an immediate reaction of disapproval—"more than the usual amount," we are told.[1] In 1910 everything Freud wrote was met with incredulity or anger by his colleagues. With the appearance of this new book many could find him guilty of an additional crime: not content with declaring the behavior of his patients to be the result of sexual tensions deviously expressed, he was now implicating one of the greatest artists of all time.

In fact Freud took pains to express his admiration for Leonardo. He was not writing an exposé. He had no intention of hurting the reputation of a great man. He was writing of "one who is among the greatest of the human race," and doing so because he firmly believed that "there is no one so great as to be disgraced by being subject to the laws which govern both normal and pathological activity with equal cogency."

Freud was intent on finding at all costs a way of looking at the human mind. He had started doing so with a few patients, then had the courage and honesty to include himself in their company, and around the time of the Leonardo study was ready to look elsewhere: at ordinary men and women who have no symptoms and never see psychiatrists; at patients with disorders other than those he would be likely to see in his office; and in this instance, at a historical figure whose life in certain respects seemed to lend itself to the kind of investigation Vienna's psychoanalysts were making with (as they saw it) astonishing success.

The point was to move from the given clinical case to the broader statement, from the specific to the universal—the "laws" Freud mentions. He wanted to move from the apparent, the readily observable, to "deeper layers"—to those unconscious forces he was convinced control just about every aspect of our lives. He wanted to leave the psychiatrist's office and find in the life of a man who was never a patient further evidence that it is correct for analysts to deny that "health and disease, normal and nervous, are sharply distinguished from each other, and that neurotic traits must be considered proofs of a general inferiority." And finally, he wanted to go back far in time, find in the remains, so to speak, of a man of great historical importance—his words, remarks attributed to him, his sketches and paintings—evidence that explains some of the contradictions and ambiguities of his life.

Freud acknowledges that not much is known about Leonardo's childhood. He refers to "the obscurity" of the artist's boyhood. Still, in his scientific notebook Leonardo did mention a childhood memory:

> It seems that I was always destined to be so deeply concerned with vultures; for I recall as one of my very earliest memories that while I was in my cradle a vulture came down to me and opened my mouth with its tail, and struck me many times with its tail against my lips.

When mentioning the bird Leonardo used the word *nibio,* which in the modern Italian form *nibbio* refers to a kite, not a vulture. Freud keeps on using the German word *geier,* meaning vulture. He was misled by several German translations.

There is no doubt that this memory of Leonardo's stirred Freud's imagination. He argues his case not only forcefully but elegantly. He does indeed make the sexual interpretations that by now are unsurprising to those who have experienced psychoanalysis firsthand. The vulture is the mother, yet Leonardo, strangely, has "succeeded in endowing precisely this bird which is a mother with the distinguishing mark of masculinity." Such a paradox is explained, and soon (if we are disposed to go along) a man's memory is made the clue to his later psychological characteristics.

Nor does Freud stop there. Immensely learned, and especially so about the various ancient cultures, he makes what Alan Tyson calls "the Egyptian connection." Leonardo was not alone, and may well have known so, Freud suggests, because the hieroglyph for the Egyptian word for "mother" also happens to represent a vulture. Moreover, Freud's friend Oskar Pfister came up with another notion, and in 1919 Freud added it as a footnote to his book's argument: in Leonardo's *St. Anne with Two Others,* at the Louvre, Mary's "curiously arranged and rather confining drapery" turns out to have the "outline of a vulture." Pfister called it an "unconscious picture-puzzle," and by the time he was through with his analysis one part of the drapery is "a bird's outspread tail, whose right-hand end, exactly as in Leonardo's fateful childhood dream, leads to the mouth of the child, i.e., of Leonardo himself."

It is easy to scoff at all this. Freud was not altogether won over to Pfister's imaginative vision, as it could be called; but apart from Pfister's contribution Freud had constructed his own elaborate interpretation on what turned out to be, in retrospect, rather shaky ground. Still, the immediate response to his book had nothing to do with the details of the argument, but rather was moral: how dare these psychoanalysts, their minds always so grimly centered on pathology, most of it sexual, take on a much revered man, dead several hundred years, and saddle him with a host of psychiatric complexes and disorders? No matter how generous Freud was to Leonardo's genius, no matter how carefully and incisively he tried to connect the artist to every single one of us, the anger and mockery continued; nor were they without effect.

Irrational rejection breeds even in the best of men disappointment and sadness. Freud often reassured his colleagues that some day the world would take seriously their various formulations and conjectures—and one measure of his genius was just that self-assurance. On the other hand, under constant assault he and his coworkers became victims of their effort to defend themselves. Wrongly dismissed, they in turn dismissed others, however well intentioned such skepticism and misgivings were. Well-educated and cultivated men, they couldn't help becoming cliquish, even parochial, and highly self-protective. The next step, alas, was a kind of arrogance that demolishes all criticism as "irrational," or treats such criticism with a barrage of unnecessarily self-justifying counterargument—for example Kurt Eissler's effort to challenge the more cautious and justifiable criticism of Freud's Leonardo study.

Eissler's *Leonardo da Vinci* is a long book, in comparison to which Freud's own seems a mere monograph. Much of Eissler's argument is set forth, far less polemically and legalistically, by the four editors (James and Alix Strachey, Anna Freud, and Alan Tyson) in their introduction to Mr. Tyson's translations of Freud's book. They grant that certain "arguments and conclusions are invalidated by careful analysis of Freud's assumptions." (A kite is not a vulture.) Still, assuming a certain psychoanalytic sensibility in their readers, the editors quite justifiably refuse to give way completely. Leonardo's memory or fantasy or daydream (who can ever know exactly which?) seems justifiably of psychological interest, as does the "interesting problem" of how it came about that the Egyptians linked the ideas of "vulture" and "mother." Egyptologists attribute the connection to chance: a phonetic coincidence. Psychoanalysts have a right to speculate otherwise, though not at Leonardo's or anyone else's expense, unless with some evidence.

Most important, for all his ambitiousness and speculative ingenuity, Freud never lost the guardedness that clinical work demands. "The aim of our work," he said at the end of his study, "has been to explain the inhibitions in Leonardo's sexual life and in his artistic activity." To a degree he succeeded. Leonardo's hopes and his fears make a good deal of sense to the receptive reader by the time he has read the various interpretations offered by a writer who had more than a touch of the novelist in him: the text is clean and direct, its narrative power hard to resist. Very important, there are discussions that amount to a separate contribution; Leonardo's life stimulated Freud to think about a number of psychoanalytic issues he had not before dealt with very seriously, and for the first time he broached the subject of "narcissism." Later on that aspect of human development would prompt in him and other analysts no end of concern.

On the other hand, he ran into difficulties, some of them not unforeseen. Leonardo had himself in his own language admitted to the "sexual inhibitions" Freud calls to our attention repeatedly, so he was not in the position of making a case that may well be false. Perhaps on that account the writing at times is so relaxed and satisfactory: we are not being nervously grabbed by the collar and told to ignore all existing documents and legends in favor of a premise that can never be proved, only believed.

However, quite another tone appears when the second part of the author's "aim" is being fulfilled. We are warned that some critics, and even more significantly some of Leonardo's contemporaries, simply didn't look upon his "artistic activity" as "inhibited"—not that they were likely to use such a word. Instead, they offered excuses for his failure to finish much of his work, or were frankly puzzled by it, or felt prompted to remember that others (like Michelangelo) also worked slowly, even enigmatically. They also have insisted that Leonardo was a man of the very widest interests; when he was not painting he was occupying himself with an astonishing range of scientific investigations and forecasts, often wedded to his artistic capabilities through intricate sketches or drawings.

Such efforts to look at Leonardo as a thoroughly successful and productive artist and scientist, entitled to make his own decisions about what to work on and for how long at a time, are to Freud "excuses," admittedly "valid" but not sufficient. Whereas he freely admits that little is known about Leonardo's childhood and youth, he is less willing to stress what is nevertheless true: that absolutely nothing is known about any thoughts or "associations" Leonardo may have had about his decision to pursue careers as an artist and a scientist, and to do so at his own speed. His problems as a child and later as a man who feared sexual relations with women and sought out intense relationships with men are treated sensitively by Freud, and in such a way as slowly to produce a plausible picture: against considerable odds a particular man struggled hard to find the best kind of life he could, given impediments he simply could not shake off.

In contrast, when Freud considers Leonardo the man of Western scientific and cultural history, a rather different approach becomes evident. Things are not so much clarified and furnished a perspective as made the subject of all too fixed and unqualified interpretations. Leonardo's interest in how birds fly, his prophecies that man may one day do the same, move Freud to ask: "But why do so many people dream of being able to fly?" The answer: the wish to be able to fly is nothing else than a "longing to be capable of sexual performance." Leonardo's career as a sharp naturalistic observer is explained this way: "His rebellion against his father was the infantile determinant of what was perhaps an equally sublime achievement in the field of scientific research." True, the *Mona Lisa* is a portrait, the product of observation and imagination, but the artist found his model's smile so powerful and unforgettable "for the reason that it awoke something in him which had for long lain dormant in his mind—probably an old memory.

The memory, of course, had to do with his mother, and her influence on Leonardo's later life is put this way: "For his mother's tenderness was fateful for him; it determined his destiny and the privations that were in store for him." Elsewhere Freud is more restrained; Leonardo's mother is connected only to *part* of his destiny—as a celibate and lonely man. But at the end, after pointing out modestly that "psychoanalysis does not throw light on Leonardo's artistic powers," Freud feels he has to insist that both the "manifestations" and "limitations" of those "powers" are indeed made "intelligible" to us by psychoanalytic inquiry—and then he goes on to make this claim:

> It seems at any rate as if only a man who had had Leonardo's childhood experiences could have painted the Mona Lisa and the St. Anne . . . have embarked on such an astonishing career as a natural scientist, as if the key to all his achievements and misfortunes lay hidden in the childhood phantasy of the vulture.

That last phrase is, of course, not at all substantiated, nor has the fate of any psychoanalyst ever since been to find such a "key" to anyone's career, however "astonishing." It can be argued that the same holds for anyone's life, even that of a terribly hurt and suffering mental patient who can barely stay quiet long enough to read a book or look at a painting with any concentration. Ironically and without prejudice one might observe that it is a key dream of the author's that is revealed in such a comment: somewhere a person's creativity—his or her "astonishing career," all the achievements that get recorded in history—can be located and then exposed.

Yet the study throughout works against such a conclusion. Again and again Freud connected Leonardo's presumed childhood experiences and his later psychological characteristics to those that millions of other people have. Health and illness, he emphasized, are not so "sharply distinguished from each other," nor are the so-called normal from those referred to as "neurotic." Insofar as each of us is a "civilized human being," he points out, we are susceptible to one or another neurotic tendency; the repressive function of the mind, so constantly in operation, guarantees such an outcome. Leonardo was indeed "obsessional," but so are millions of other people. The real question, of course, is what Leonardo did with his life; not just with his neurosis, but with his remarkable energy—

his emerging intelligence, his perceptiveness, his sensitivity, his imagination, his resourcefulness of spirit, his artistic sensibility, his capacity to take note of how all sorts of things (including the body's muscles and joints) work.

These are not words or phrases Freud uses. He more or less takes for granted Leonardo's genius. He mentions it but does not "analyze" it. That is not the kind of analysis he is up to. Mostly he is willing to admit that as a psychoanalyst he will never be able to make such an analytic attempt. He calls his study a "pathographical review" and defends it as such against those who would call it "a piece of useless impertinence." Such people, he insists with some truculence, really want utterly untarnished heroes. Such people go about idealizing certain gifted historical figures and for that reason "find all pathography unpalatable." Still, he puts in the mouths of such people an argument that he never answers, intent as he is on analyzing their "real" (worshipful) intent. The argument is that a psychoanalytic study of a great man "never results in an understanding of his importance and his achievements," so there is no point in making "a study of things in him that could just as easily be found in the first person one came across."

As one reads Freud carefully in this important psychoanalytic biography his dilemma becomes apparent. He wants to comprehend an elusive and gifted man. He has a limited amount of information to go on. He is not interested in undercutting his subject, turning him into some perverse eccentric whom everyone without his talents can pity. He is a man of discrimination and refinement. He wants to learn—from his own frailties, as they come across in dreams, slips of the tongue, fantasies, as well as from Leonardo's life, in so far as it can be discerned.

On the other hand he is in his own way as insatiably curious as Leonardo was; he wants answers—and not just to small questions. He once likened himself to a conquistador, but like all conquistadors, there was just so much territory he could conquer. He had at his disposal a nineteenth-century mechanistic view of nature, a cause-and-effect mentality that scientists of his day found helpful in the course of their work. This produces that. One thing brings about another. X lies at the root of Y. And if it doesn't *seem* that way, if there are many other forces at work and all of them make for a murky atmosphere, then the greater the challenge. With more knowledge comes increased specificity—and that is the direction a scientist travels. So, back and forth he goes, even from paragraph to paragraph. One moment he says he is trying to fathom Leonardo's "trivial peculiarities" and the "riddles of his nature" so as to discover "what determined his mental and intellectual development." The word "determined" stands out, especially when it is used in connection with Leonardo's *intellectual* development. No wonder, a page or two on, we encounter quite another line of thinking:

In Leonardo's case we have had to maintain the view that the accident of his illegitimate birth and the excessive tenderness of his mother had the most decisive influence on the formation of his character and on his later fortune, since the sexual repression which set in after this phase of childhood caused him to sublimate his libido into the urge we know, and established his sexual inactivity for the whole of his later life. But this repression after the first erotic satisfactions of childhood need not necessarily have taken place; in someone else it might perhaps not have taken place or might have assumed much less extensive proportions.

We must recognize here a degree of freedom which cannot be resolved any further by psychoanalytic means. Equally, one has no right to claim that the consequence of this wave of repression was the only possible one. It is probable that another person would not have succeeded in withdrawing the major portion of his libido from repression by sublimating it into a craving for knowledge; under the same influences he would have sustained a permanent injury to his intellectual activity or have acquired an insurmountable disposition to obsessional neurosis.

We are left, then, with these two characteristics of Leonardo which are inexplicable by the efforts of psychoanalysis; his quite special tendency towards instinctual repressions, and his extraordinary capacity for sublimating the primitive instincts.

One can try to pin a life down, but only so far. There is that "degree of freedom"—frustrating to a scientist who wants to have every possible "variable" tracked down and fitted right in its place. Even more vexing, that "quite special tendency" and that "extraordinary capacity" were by no means only Leonardo's, nor are they only the property of a few geniuses. Those tendencies or capacities are widespread. Many talented people respond to thousands of different childhood experiences through their own unique blend of repressions and sublimations. Anyway, as Freud goes on to say, there is a biological element in all this that defies our comprehension—even now, decades later. He writes of "the organic foundations of character on which the mental structure is only afterwards erected."

His language here is as vague as the state of knowledge warranted. What I suppose he might have said, were he less of a hopeful, ambitious scientist and of a more philosophical nature, would go something like this: we can understand some of this man's psychological troubles, but his gifts as an artist and a scientist are beyond anyone's ken; they are God-given or part of Nature's mysterious design, though maybe someday, centuries later, we'll know more—and meanwhile let's not try to do the impossible with the valuable but thoroughly limited tools available. If he sometimes approaches saying that, he also backs into quite another corner: *only* a man with Leonardo's kind of childhood could have painted the *Mona Lisa.*

The difficulties Freud faced and candidly admitted in his study of Leonardo have persisted, despite the efforts of psychoanalytically sophisticated biographers. Nor have all of Freud's successors been as fair and self-critical as he was when he wrote about Leonardo. In the name of "applied psychoanalysis" the lives of an assortment of political leaders, generals, artists, and writers, not to mention characters in novels, short stories, and plays, have been examined; and as one goes through those attempts, dozens and dozens of them, one keeps coming back to the Leonardo study—and to Freud's superior qualities as a thinker and a writer.

He may not have been able to transcend the limits of his own historical era. He may have made mistakes of fact, even at times of judgment. He may have tried unsuccessfully to harness language to a number of ambitions. As a scientist searching for tangible discoveries, but also as a man of artistic temperament, especially sensitive to the opportunities and hazards that words present, he was not unlike Leonardo, caught between opposing directions of his own making. But Freud did not in frustration, resentment, and envy turn on the man he was trying to learn more about. Words like "oral" or "anal" or "phallic" are not fastened upon Leonardo. His ideas about religion are discussed in the context of the fifteenth and sixteenth centuries in which he lived.

If Freud shows pride and more than a dash of the messianic explorer, determined at fifty-three to find an intellectual New Jerusalem, he is also able to be tentative, and frankly so. Almost inadvertently, and ironically just at the point when he becomes categorical, we are given a chance to see the confines of his own thinking. When we are told that psychoanalysis finds "inexplicable" Leonardo's particular bent for repression and his remarkable powers of sublimation we are confronted with the author's own impasse. Freud can describe Leonardo in new ways but in the end that impasse remains: a man's various gifts defy the imagery of pathography. If I am able to play tennis all day and score quite well at it, too, I do so not because tennis has a symbolic meaning to me, based on a "problem," or because I lack various diseases or handle certain physiological stresses in a way that differs from that of many others, who find that their symbolic sense of what tennis "means," based on their past or still present "problems" and their physiological makeup, however like mine, do not get translated into my kind of game.

To put it differently, infirmities, or the thoughts they prompt, or even the absence of infirmities don't explain the presence of assets. Here words and phrases come to mind that Freud for his own reasons learned to distrust: will, determination, ingenuity, spirit, ambitions—dreams of a broader kind than he tended to analyze. He had found it necessary to move away from those ways of speaking (and looking at the world) because many of his first patients had for years been slapped on the back or kicked somewhere and told to find willpower, shape up, and get better. The more he listened to his patients the less respect he had for the moralistic pieties of Victorian consciousness. He wanted to expose all that for the sham it was. Anyway, he was not a fuzzy or abstract philosopher, certainly not a theologian, but a neurophysiologist become psychiatrist become a new kind of scientist, a psychoanalyst, so he did not wish to talk about Leonardo's willful spirit, which at times had given way to indifference or apparent apathy.

In a sense, then, Freud's study was a dramatic standoff. There was Leonardo, across the centuries, a man whose obvious capacities and achievements could not be taken for granted or buried under an avalanche of terminology developed in response to the plight of seriously disturbed patients. And there was Freud, anxious to extend his observations to include people like Leonardo, but smart enough to hold back, or venture out only for so long on thin ice.

The best psychoanalytic theorists, first Freud himself, then his daughter Anna, and Heinz Hartmann, have tried to find concepts that would make it easier for them to consider not only Leonardo but those many people who may have their moments of tension, but who in general live useful and untroubled lives. The ego has been emphasized; its capacities have been described in detail. The id may exert its pressures, but we have those various "mechanisms of defense" to call upon. Moreover, the ego is not only in the position of reacting to demands or outright assaults made upon it. The ego has its own energy, some of it "conflict free." When we mobilize our intelligence, use the mind's power of logic and analysis, we are summoning "conflict-free" energy.

The expression "conflict free," used so often by Heinz Hartmann, is a revealing one; with respect to man's everyday work, his various successes as a competent and resourceful creature, it is as far as psychoanalysis can go conceptually, given its history, its concerns, and not least, the nature of its imagery. Hartmann, like Freud, was a man of vast knowledge, and sensitive to the respect and good manners, if not admiration, that novelists or artists, like other human beings, have the right to assume from those who study them. The same can be said for Ernest Kris, a colleague of Hartmann's who had a special interest in artists and the sources of their creativity; and for Anthony Storr, whose recent book[2] shows that such an interest continues to preoccupy certain analysts. Kris worked hard at distinguishing between the paintings or drawings of hospitalized psychotics and those done by artists, and Storr emphasizes the difference between what he calls "pornographic images" and "great art."

But one wonders whether there is any need for psychoanalysts to bother themselves with such distinctions, however well intended. Critics, maybe even ordinary viewers, are quite able to do so on their own. No doubt both of those analysts were angered by and ashamed of what some of their colleagues have done in the name of psychoanalytic "interpretation" of writers, artists, political leaders. Yet at a certain point, all these psychological efforts at biography, literary criticism, or the "analysis" of artistic production come upon the very stumbling blocks Freud had the good sense to discuss openly in his Leonardo book. Here, for example, is Dr. Storr, writing about "creativity" over half a century after that book was published:

> Man is a creature inescapably, and often unhappily divided; and the divisions within him recurrently impel the use of his imagination to make new syntheses. The creative consequences of his imaginative striving may never make him whole; but they constitute his deepest consolations and his greatest glories.

Always it is trouble, problems, conflicts, "divisions" that generate novels and paintings, or for that matter, the efforts of history's gifted leaders. A phrase like "impel the use of his imagination" may be an attractive way of putting it, but the cause-and-effect assertion is both utterly clear and utterly unsubstantiated— and the use of such a phrase only serves to show that those of us who are trained to dwell upon psychopathology, to think of people as variants of one or another "psychiatric model" (the anal or oral or phallic "character,") are also "impelled" to use our imaginations for certain reasons.

To his credit Kurt Eissler has furthered discussion of this issue substantially, as I mentioned in a previous essay:

> The question, however, has not been answered, what connection exists between the genius's psychopathology and his achievements. Psychopathology, in general, is looked upon as defect. . . . Observation of the genius, however, suggests the possibility that psychopathology is indispensible to the highest achievements of certain kinds.

He then takes the next logical step:

> Consequently if what we observed in the genius struck us as neurotic or psychotic or perverse or even criminal, we would then have to reconsider our classification under these accustomed headings. If, for example, an apparently obsessional symptom was indispensable to geniushood . . . there would be no sense in calling it a neurotic symptom. Whatever the essence of neurosis may be, the concept of neurosis makes sense only when it is correlated with a deficit.

Needless to say, what goes for the genius goes for the near-genius and on down. One has a right to ask the broader question: What connection is there between an ordinary human being's daily achievements and his psychopathology, or between a psychiatrist's, a lawyer's, a politician's accomplishments and the various emotional upsets he as a human being is bound to have? Open-minded on this issue as Eissler is, he can't give up the conviction that psychopathology is a *sine qua non* of life—as Freud among others (Job, Isaiah, Saint Paul, not to mention some of those geniuses Eissler mentions) has made quite clear. Why is its presence in anyone, gifted or not, an occasion for surprise, and more than that, aggrandizement—the insistence that other elements in a person's life are tied to, or are expressions of, or are causatively linked with "deficits" or neurotic developments in childhood or "mechanisms of defense," such as sublimation?

For some reason it has been psychoanalysts, among psychological theorists, who have been most anxious to study the lives of creative men and women, or of historical figures. Piaget, whose studies of intelligence as it develops over the years might be considered particularly well suited to such studies, has avoided them, perhaps because his speculations always follow from what he has watched and heard, even as Anna Freud has in recent years insisted that "direct observation" ought to precede theoretical formulation and elaboration. Perhaps a scientist like Piaget knows full well that the "variables" that make up a man's creative life—be it a writer's or a political leader's or a psychoanalyst's—defy the language and concepts of any particular psychological theory.

Anna Freud once referred to "the universally envied gift of creative energy."[3]

There is no point in turning that gift into an unapproachable mystery. Scientists have a right to move closer toward any "phenomenon" they happen to find interesting. Nor need such an approach be insulting, abusive, or destructive. The issue is one of evidence—is there enough of it?—but also of motives, as Miss Freud has mentioned; and envy is only one of them. Theorists, like the presidents and dictators they study, can be overcome by ambition and a kind of intellectual aggressiveness that has to be checked by the prudent skepticism of critics.

In this regard, some of Freud's most valuable discoveries—the nature of "resistance" and the workings of "transference" and "countertransference" in psychoanalytic therapy—have become ironic instruments in the most narrow kind of ideological self-justification. Doubts or misgivings are chalked up to a lack of psychoanalytic experience or sophistication, if not to outright "hostility" or "ambivalence" of one or another kind. This *ad hominem* tendency obviously undercuts the possibility of any rational argument, except for the kind sanctioned by those who do the thinly disguised name calling.

Even friends can get caught in such intellectual warfare, where sides are taken and one is considered either a friend or a foe. Referring to an interesting and suggestive biography, *Woodrow Wilson and Colonel House,* the editor of a collection of essays called *Psychoanalysis and History* makes an interpretation of sorts: "Brodie's review-essay of the Georges' book about Wilson points up the overtly psychoanalytic aspects of their work, which they felt constrained to conceal in a footnote."[4] The editor himself notes a few sentences later that the book's subtitle is "A Personality Study." Furthermore, in an author's note at the very beginning, even before the table of contents, Alexander and Juliette George acknowledge forthrightly the influence Harold Lasswell and Nathan Leites had on their study of Wilson's relationship to his longtime principal adviser. A special "Research Note" discusses that influence for six pages—before the section called "Notes and Bibliography" even begins.

What have they concealed—or rather, why are they described as concealing anything? True, they write as historians. That is to say, they want to examine the psychological quality of a particular president's involvement with one of his aides, but they also want to move from one point in time to another, and carry their readers with them. In other words, their interests are chronological and narrative as well as psychological. They have a broad view of American political life to present and, just as important, to document convincingly—in a way that will make the reader understand what he is reading and feel satisfied that a sincere effort has been made to start with facts, assemble them into a point of view, and present the latter as that and only that, not as the answer to a "problem."

No doubt about it, psychoanalytic terminology is avoided by the Georges. We are not told, as we are in *Thomas Woodrow Wilson: A Psychological Study* by William Bullitt and Sigmund Freud, that "the libido insulated in his [Wilson's] reaction-formation against his passivity to his father had been without outlet and had reached such a pitch of intensity that it had to break out against someone."

We are told much about Wilson and his father, considerably less but nevertheless much about Colonel House. The President and his aide found in each other a fateful dovetailing of psychological qualities. Certainly they worked out "neurotic needs" through one another, as we all do, and eventually (when things were going downhill on other accounts) at each other's expense. But the Georges can't seem to forget that the involvement of the two men has to be viewed from other directions: the nature of the presidency, the social and cultural characteristics of a given moment in American history, the particular stresses that wars, accidents, unexpected tragedies (the death of Wilson's first wife) can bring upon a man's character and personality, whatever the determinants of childhood that bear down on him, on all of us.

I doubt very much that even the most eager proponent of "applied psycho-analysis," or one of its contemporary equivalents or closely related "areas" of inquiry, "psychohistory," would want to change the perspective the Georges have given us. How might they have made their debt to psychoanalysis more explicit? As other historians and essayists have done over the centuries, they have drawn upon knowledge that is available, traditional modes of study or reflection and new modes, and made of it all an exercise in exposition, explanation, and comment.

If they conceal anything from the reader it is any temptation they may have felt to fix static labels on the men they were studying or to come up with sweeping, unqualified statements such as this: "In fact, psychoanalytic theory fully accounts for the observation that no known charismatic leader can be described as a genuine genital character."[5] Or, "The personality of the charismatic leader can be characterized briefly, since we already indicated that his behavior must conform to childish fantasies about how omnipotent adults behave."[6] Or, with regard to Robespierre: "Unfortunately, the implacable superego coupled with the released sadism and the projective paranoid mechanisms common to the Leader and the masses created the need for further human sacrifices, and thus the Revolution in a truly cannibalistic way devoured its own children."[7]

Nor is Robespierre unique: "The psychological truth expressed in this last speech of the doomed leader exceeds his singular case and applies to every revolutionary leader and to every dictator."[8] In this century the love they give us, the good and decent intentions they possess and offer to us as something to imitate and make our own, the cultural heritage they hand down—so many facts, so many assumptions, so much that has to do with proficiency and self-assurance and comprehension of the world—all of that somehow is either taken for granted or overlooked in favor of "complexes" of various kinds.

There is, further, a pejorative streak in the language of psychopathology that not only demeans the "object" of description but the writer doing it and his or her "discipline." There is also a stinginess of spirit in some of the descriptions psychiatrists and psychologists (and those who follow their lead in other disciplines) give to individuals of the most obvious attainments. Which contemporary historians or critics advocate unthinking, reflexive sentiment or glorification? These days the danger comes from quite another direction: will the application of psychological "insight" to history or the arts be done in such a way as to produce caricatures of human beings—and those only to be turned into proof of some larger generalization about the "laws" that govern the human mind?

Or will one kind of knowledge be called "superficial" simply because it possesses its own richness and complexity of vision—in contrast to another kind of knowledge that somebody else happens to find congenial or happens to be trained to call upon? Or will a book's manner of organization and language be pushed into intellectual arguments or vendettas that really have nothing to do with what an author has intended?

In the case of the Georges' book on Wilson, two historians have nicely drawn upon psychoanalytic principles without in any way doing an injustice to their own responsibilities. To imply that they are hiding something out of fear is to be less than fair not only to their profession but to their scholarship. No one would deny that some historians, like some doctors or lawyers or writers, have no use for *any* effort to look at historical figures from a psychoanalytic perspective—overtly or otherwise. Still, it is absurd at this time for analysts and those interested in "applying" psychoanalysis or developing a "field" called "psychohistory" to imagine themselves embattled, scorned outcasts, neglected on all fronts—rather as Freud and his first followers were.

Psychoanalysis and its various "applications" have been embraced all too ardently by the American public—and not only by its so-called "lay" segment. Sometimes that enthusiasm was for the bad: it is astonishing, for example, how many writers submitted willingly to the brutal, stupid lashings an analyst like Edmund Bergler gave them in his books supposedly meant to "explain" writers and their "personality structure." But sometimes much of value came of this enthusiasm: it is remarkable how openly and generously many important American medical schools welcomed analysts during the 1930s and 1940s, often to good effect so far as the education of young doctors goes. In any event, to this day a historian or political scientist, not to mention a psychoanalyst, who writes a biography or discusses some contemporary issue, or one connected with the remote past, from a psychological point of view stands at the very least an excellent chance of getting the public's attention.

Walter Langer's "secret wartime report," now become *The Mind of Adolf Hitler,* has hardly been ignored. In view of the substantial scholarship on the Nazis that has gone relatively unnoticed—the work of historians, economists, political scientists—one has to look not only at the book itself but at the reasons for its appeal. Nor has Bruce Mazlish's "psychohistorical inquiry" into Richard Nixon's life been ignored—any more than will the portentously named *The Kennedy Neurosis: A Psychological Portrait of an American Dynasty.* Each of them is yet another variant of the kind of inquiry Freud began long ago: harnessing psychology to an understanding of certain people who have taken a significant part in history.

To start with the worst, the book on the Kennedy family is, alas, an exercise in nastiness, and an instructive lesson in how psychological words and phrases, presented as a means of scientific exposition, can become in certain hands instruments of moral condemnation, and even malicious abuse. The author of *The Kennedy Neurosis,* Nancy Clinch, refers to her "study of the Kennedy's characterology" as a "form of psychohistory"; it is even "psychohumanism." People have what she calls "self-actualizing needs." There are "parental patterns" and a "specific cultural milieu," and they, of course, affect a "hierarchy of needs." When things go wrong a neurosis develops: "a self-defeating defense pattern of feeling and behaving." Something called a "pseudo-self" comes into being. There is "basic anxiety" and it keeps generating "unconscious hostility." After we learn about all that, we are told where we are going:

> It is my purpose to analyze what the historical record seems to reveal: that the Kennedy drive to power was largely neurotic in origin and thus largely neurotic in goal; and that when power was obtained, the Kennedys were severely limited in the use of their authority for positive aims because of emotional conflicts and ambivalences.

Note the word "because": assertive, unthreatened by any modifiers, anxious to make its connection. There is no point in looking at the structure of our government, let alone at our society. Those political scientists and journalists who try to figure out what presidents can and cannot do, those historians who try to apprehend the subtleties of America's development as a democracy, the regional tensions, the push and pull of economic and social forces—they have been seduced by complexity, ambiguity, even uncertainty. The author says we need "autonomy, self-direction, and freedom." Those observers and scholars of American history need the freedom to use the word "because" more boldly—though one can drop the word and get the same startling result:

> The Kennedys, like American scientists, achieved the "impossible" through teamwork in their election triumphs. But once elected, they seemed to "fall under a fairyland spell" that kept them from accomplishing any significant part of their professed aims.

The "spell" is next defined: "neurotic conflict." It seems that Mr. and Mrs. Joseph P. Kennedy (called "Joe and Rose") made "excessive demands for perfection and social success" on their sons and daughters. The result: a need on the part of those children for their own "frustration, punishment and even destruction":

> I do not see the Kennedy failures in performance as caused mainly by bad luck or by the vagaries of politics and human nature. Rather, the factual failures were largely the result of psychohistorical circumstances that existed for the Kennedy sons even before they were born and that strongly affected the shaping of their individual characters.

So much for "bad luck" or the "vagaries of politics and human nature"—the stuff of novelists or playwrights, the passing fancy of newspapermen, the preoccupation of old-fashioned, overly scrupulous scholars or essayists, who may be aware of "unconscious emotional conflicts," but who get side-tracked by their search for facts, their insistence on maintaing detachment as well as respect for those they study.

Perhaps this book has its place; some day social historians will want to study its by no means unique mixture of Nichols and May psychology, non sequiturs, simpleminded social commentary, and dizzying historical overstatement. For example, Mr. Joseph P. Kennedy is singled out from the rest of us parents for "unconsciously" projecting "his needs and longings onto his sons." Even though the author admits that some of the book's points "may seem strained, and even cruel," she persists, in the interest of truth. Thus, "Jack, Bobby, and Teddy" (as they are called by this expert on their lives who has never even met them) "would all take up cigar smoking, the Freudian symbol of potency and power."

Then there was President Kennedy. Here is what his White House staff was all about:

> Thus Kennedy was not only in close and constant touch with his family, but he also created a new family of staff retainers who seem to have served partly as substitute parent images daily filling the old dual role of nursemaids and slave drivers.

One of them was Kennedy's secretary, Mrs. Lincoln. He may have liked her, but his general attitude toward women, along with a few other things, is summarized in the following four sentences:

> Kennedy essentially disliked and distrusted women. Therefore his strong emotional need for support and approval led him to follow the counsel of male authority figures. Unfortunately, a large number of these authority figures—such as McNamara, Rusk, Acheson, Taylor, Bundy, and Rostow—were as confused and misguided as Kennedy about national values and priorities. The 1971 publication of the Pentagon Papers clearly revealed this about their Vietnam policy.

There it is: from sexism to Vietnam in less than a paragraph. Not that the author forgets other parts of the world. She says the President had "an emotional fixation" on Castro, who was "Kennedy's alter-ego: the bold leader Kennedy longed to be but could not bring himself to become." Why could he not? "Making laws may arouse unconscious resistance in the lawmaker who has suffered much in his own life from rigid legalisms."

As for the President's brother and trusted adviser, he was similarly "neurotic." Did he have compassion for the poor and vulnerable in this nation? Yes, but "this is understandable in view of his 'underdog' position in the family and the emotional insecurity he never lost." Did he like athletics and inspire young people to follow suit? True, but there was a reason:

> Here we can see a belief in the masculine mystique of physical toughness, and also a probable need for reassurance and affection through physical contact with other males that was more difficult to express directly. Football for the Kennedy sons—and especially Robert, who even kept a football in his Attorney General's office and often tossed it around with his staff—carried deep psychological undertones of emotional need and gratification.

Finally, the author, who can toss a few passes of her own, reserves the longest throws for the book's last paragraphs: "Yet the Kennedy mystique can also be seen as essentially the outcome of some four thousand years of the Graeco-Judeo-Christian ethos which has directed and energized Western civilization, and which has now spread over the world." There is cause for hope, though: "By studying the lives of national leaders, such as the Kennedys, we can find reflections of our own search for identity and confirmation, and help change both ourselves and our nation toward maturity and health rather than neurosis."

There are other reasons to study the lives of important men of history. As Walter C. Langer makes clear in his book on Hitler, the Office of Strategic Services was interested in winning the war; "maturity" and all the rest could come to Germany (and America) later. Colonel William J. ("Wild Bill") Donovan knew Dr. Langer, then a Boston psychoanalyst, and asked him to put together a psychological appraisal of Hitler, including an estimate of what he might do if things should go badly for him, as they already were going in 1943 when Langer began his hurried job. Yet, for all the rush, this book is decidedly better than the one on the Kennedys. Langer's portrait of Hitler is far more thoughtful and sensitive than Miss Clinch's caricatures of the Kennedy family.

Langer avoids psychiatric name calling.[9] He emphasizes Hitler's strengths, his abilities, his obvious capacity to mesmerize and lead a nation. There are mistakes of judgment or emphasis, but these are usually owing to false information which was supplied to the relatively uninformed analyst and his quickly assembled staff. The prose is clear, a clue to the author's essential modesty and common sense. Once in a while there is an utterly fatuous remark, but it is usually delivered in a way that makes one less angry than regretful:

> I may be naïve in diplomatic matters, but I like to believe that if such a study of Hitler had been made years earlier, under less tension, and with more opportunity to gather first-hand information, there might not have been a Munich; a similar study of Stalin might have produced a different Yalta; one of Castro might have prevented the Cuban situation; and one of President Diem might have avoided our deep involvement in Vietnam. Studies of this type cannot solve our international problems. That would be too much to expect.

At only one point does the author reveal the smugness and arrogance that are all too common in such efforts, and even then they derive from a remark of one of Langer's colleagues: "Now I know what his [Hitler's] perversion is." Not that anyone *knows*. We are never given any hard, concrete evidence—only guesses and secondhand speculations, some from highly unreliable sources, as the historian Robert G. Waite makes clear in his useful afterword. "It just came to me out of my clinical experience," the surprised Dr. Langer heard when he asked his colleague how she had come to that conclusion. Fortunately, it was Dr. Langer and not his colleague who tried to figure out the personality of a man whom he had never met and about whom he had only the most shadowy and suspect of information. Professor Waite says that such an attempt is justified: "Basically, he is convinced the perversion existed because he knows as an experienced analyst widely read in the literature of abnormal psychology that many patients with the same patterns of behavior as Hitler have exhibited a penchant for the same perversion."

Once again we are back to the same problem. Clearly those "patterns of behavior" Hitler had (shiftlessness for a while, anxiety, phobias, sexual inhibitions) have been and are shared by millions of people. *Some* of them may end up, as conjecture about Hitler would have it, lying on the floor and pleading with women to empty themselves (the nearer the better, and all over, if possible), but some may choose other ways to find pleasure, and by no means do all those with Hitler's "patterns of behavior," or anyone else's share his supposed "penchant." A million prior interviews with disturbed men and women would not enable anyone to know the facts of a particular person's private life. Nor does Dr. Langer's prediction that Hitler would probably commit suicide when and if he were cornered constitute "dramatic and convincing evidence of the validity of his approach to an understanding of Hitler's personality." But Dr. Langer mentions several other possibilities, and is unwilling to pin himself down—a refreshing trait, in view of the certainties that other writers are drawn to.

Hitler himself repeatedly mentioned his intention; he would go down to death on his own rather than surrender, bringing all of Germany with him, if he had the choice. Clearly Dr. Langer was right in suggesting suicide as "the most plausible outcome," though he lists insanity and death in battle as other possibilities. But then, my ninth-grade Latin teacher made a similar prediction—he was more unequivocal—in class around the same year, when we were reading Caesar's *Gallic Wars;* and so did the journalist Dorothy Thompson, who mentioned the very same likelihood several times in her syndicated columns during the early 1940s. I would imagine that thousands of people thought about Hitler as a probable suicide when they read their newspapers and saw how desperate his situation had suddenly become.

With Langer's study of Hitler we face once more the nagging questions other "psychohistorical" inquiries pose; and Dr. Langer can no more settle those questions for us than could Freud in the case of Leonardo. How did a wretched, deeply troubled, at times pathetic youth—the "neurotic psychopath" of this book—end up Führer of the Third Reich, a man not only possessed of authority and power but believed and heeded by millions? If not Hitler, might it have been someone else? If only Hitler, then surely it was not his "perversion" or his disordered mind (the province of the psychoanalyst) that accounts for his successes.

Hitler's life, like many other lives, presents several purely psychological mysteries, apart from the "psychohistorical" one of his particular rise to power. After the First World War, this nondescript, pitiable ne'er-do-well suddenly turned into a remarkably persistent and adept politician, then into a charismatic leader, finally the Füher of most of Europe. Langer refers to a "transformation of character," as well he might. But how to account for it? We are told that there is an explanation: the weak and panicky Hitler, "in order to quiet his fears," suddenly "imagined himself as a person who far surpassed his enemies in all the 'virile' qualities." We are given the name for such a psychological maneuver, "identification with the aggressor," and its importance is described in language not unlike that used by Freud in connection with Leonardo: "This is the key to an understanding of Hitler's actions since the beginning of his political activities to the present time."

Presumably Hitler was thereby freed to become what he eventually did become. If only that maneuver worked as well for thousands of other nobodies, who have tried desperately to convert their vulnerability and self-hate into something they can use on others. The Weimar Republic was full of such people; America has its share: people who "identify" with various "aggressors"—and, having done so, get nowhere. As for psychological recovery or "transformation," psychiatrists can spend long, intimate months, if not years, with patients and not know why at a particular moment a person is suddenly, it seems, "better." *In retrospect,* we come up with formulations, explanations: such and such was "interpreted." We are less likely to mention the many times we have offered similar "insights" to other patients, even to the same patient, all to no avail.

Langer was no doubt right about the turn of mind Hitler experienced. But he goes way beyond the bounds of logic—and his own profession's knowledge— when he makes that commonly indulged-in "mechanism" the "key" to an understanding of Hitler's "recovery," let alone all the subsequent "actions" of that satanic genius. Nor is the "messiah complex," also cited by him, very helpful— as any psychiatrist knows who works with the severely disturbed and utterly ineffectual "paranoid schizophrenics" who inhabit our state hospitals, insisting every day that they could save the world, if they were only heeded.

No one wants to circumscribe the continuing attempt of psychologists and psychiatrists to make sense of the irrational and bizarre, the seemingly normal but in fact pathological. It is when a more polemical, even aggrandizing tone enters the discussion that the possibility of a rational distinction between different objectives becomes hard to maintain. In this regard, Kurt Eissler is at least candid in his book on Leonardo. The first section of the book is frankly called "Polemics," and in a chapter called "The Historian vs. the Psychoanalyst" Eissler makes no bones about what he believes and, moreover, expects of those who disagree with him:

> There can, of course, be no doubt that the psychoanalyst has to know the results of historical and iconographic research; but what he does with that knowledge in order to reach psychological conclusions will more frequently than not strike the historian as far-fetched and inconclusive. [Meyer] Schapiro dismisses us with the admonition that the analyst should inform himself better about Leonardo's life and art and the culture of his time before applying his science to the psychological study of that life. Wohl and

Trosman, with their little understanding of the subtleness of the genius, believe the problem could have been solved if Freud had "allowed his manuscript to be scrutinized" by an expert in history. These writers bypass the essential question that is at issue between the historical sciences and psychoanalysis and that cannot be resolved as long as the historian and philologist do not acquire full insight into psychoanalysis and are restrained by the bias of our time from obtaining maximum knowledge of the structure of the human mind by consistent and long-lasting clinical work.[10]

No doubt somewhere there is a historian prepared to insist that any psychoanalyst who wants to write about history take a full graduate course and spend a few years doing "proper" historical research. But some scholars have to some degree combined the two disciplines—the historian Bruce Mazlish, for example, or the political scientist E. Victor Wolfenstein. Both men have psychoanalytic knowledge—of an order Dr. Eissler would doubtless find acceptable—as well as training in their professions.

Professor Mazlish has been an especially active proponent of what he and others (Robert Jay Lifton, Joel Kovel, John Demos) call "psychohistory." Each of these men has his own particular way of working with historical materials from a psychological (more precisely, psychoanalytic) point of view. They share a common interest in drawing upon several disciplines in the hope of seeing human experience more broadly, and escaping the rigidities and biases inherent in any particular psychoanalytic formulation. Robert Wallerstein has perhaps made the best case for such activity:

> Consider the impact on the assessment of an individual's psychological functioning if the limiting social postulate were changed from that of the "average expectable environment" to that of a "systematically fluctuating or a turbulent environment"; compare a campus in unrest set within a world in turmoil. That is, the simplifying assumptions made for its purposes by one behavioral science, if *looked at as variables* as they are in another behavioral science which makes them its central subject matter, would influence the explanations arrived at in important ways.[11]

Yet as one goes through Mazlish's *In Search of Nixon: A Psychohistorical Inquiry* or Wolfenstein's *The Revolutionary Personality: Lenin, Trotsky, Gandhi*, it seems clear that both scholars have as many dangers to avoid as opportunities to grasp. In both books we are warned that psychoanalytic "reductionism" is offensive and perhaps a thing of the past. Nevertheless, Nixon is called "oral" and "anal" at various points, as are Lenin, Trotsky, and Gandhi. Ambivalences are discussed, problems with mothers and fathers are described at length.

In the case of Mazlish's book an interesting dialectic of sorts takes place. First the President is described or typed. ("Orality is an important element in Nixon's character.") Then the reader is informed that such a description merely makes Richard Nixon a human being. If he has used a "genital metaphor and an anal one," then "others frequently use similar metaphors." After we have read two-thirds of his book, in which words or phrases like "passivity," "death anxiety," and "survivor guilt" are pervasive, Mazlish makes this statement: "What we have been discussing up to now may be thought of as the psychological banalities of Nixon's character." One wonders, at this point, why the author has bothered to write this book at all, especially since the rest of the book offers nothing else about the President's "character," only an extensive justification of the value of "psychohistory" as "science."

Understandably, Professor Mazlish has singled out Nixon, who has, after all, singled himself out. This "search" for Nixon ends with the discovery of "three traits," which he characterizes as "role identification," "ambivalence," and "denial." We have already been informed that any of us can possess these qualities. But Nixon apparently has more of them: "ambivalence, of course, is in all of us. Yet as a scholar I have never dealt with a public figure as ambivalent as Nixon." Exactly how does one quantify "ambivalence?" Has Mazlish studied other public figures? If so, which ones, and on what basis has he made his judgment? How are we to compare Nixon's "ambivalence" with, say, Wilson's? How does a psychiatrist distinguish among the degrees of ambivalence he finds in his various ambivalent patients? If the "degrees" of those three traits are at issue, one can find many patients who qualify as intensely ambivalent and who are also inclined to "deny" and resort to "role identification."

Nor do such patients become, on that account, hard to "know," as the President is claimed to be. "The three traits have made Nixon one of the most difficult political figures to analyze." Maybe the problem lies elsewhere; maybe the tools of psychoanalysis are inappropriate to the task at hand. In contrast, intelligent political journalists like Jules Witcover or Garry Wills, whose mind has been disciplined by the Jesuits, can "analyze" Nixon suggestively. Wills has evoked brilliantly those aspects of America's social reality that President Nixon has, one suspects, never overlooked or failed to understand. Wills understands the power of a certain kind of religious piety, even when it has become thoroughly secularized.

Richard Nixon's carerr—assisted, one should not forget, by Lee Harvey Oswald and Sirhan Sirhan—can be seen as the discerning response of an able and ambitious man to currents in American life he fully appreciates, and even manages to evoke with some credibility, in spite of the widespread distrust he also generates. When Wills analyzes our country's conflicting ideals and assumptions he gets as close to the "real" Nixon as any of us may find possible or desirable.

It is sad to find toward the end of Mazlish's book this remark: "Earlier we acknowledged that many people are wary of applying psychoanalysis to historical figures (and usually distrust therapy as well, a problem with which we cannot deal here)." It may be that many clinicians, who every day trust "therapy" enough to show up in an office and try hard to work with other human beings, have good reason to be wary: to repeat, so much that goes on in "treatment" is mysterious, intangible, elusive; one hesitates to apply to politics concepts already of very circumscribed or indeterminate value. Perhaps some of those wary clinicians would want to say what the psychoanalyst Leslie Farber did in response to the way human beings, from great men of history to ordinary workers and citizens, continue to be treated by members of his profession:

> Without examining these normative statements in detail, the reader can see why psy-chiatry is so often charged with being reductive. For while the creatures described above may bear some resemblance to animals or to steam engines or robots or electronic brains, they do not sound like people. They are in fact constructs of theory, more hu-manoid than humans; and whether they are based on the libido theory or on one of the new interpersonal theories of relationships, it is just those qualities most distinctively human which seem to have been omitted. It is a matter of some irony, if one turns from psychology to one of Dostoyevsky's novels, to find that no matter how wretched, how puerile, or how dilapidated his characters may be, they all possess more humanity than the ideal man who lives in the pages of psychiatry.[12]

True, psychiatric jargon can be defended: it is a kind of shorthand for busy doctors who are not interested in describing "life," as novelists like Dostoevski are, but in understanding and "curing" patients. Even assuming that such a way of thinking and speaking about people helps clinical understanding and doesn't itself affect "treatment"—an assumption I would certainly not want to make— one has to insist on the obvious, so far as men like Leonardo or Nixon go: they are not "patients" in treatment by "psychohistorians" and so nothing absolves us of the responsibility to measure up to the standards Dr. Farber suggests.

When the theoretical intent of the writing Farber describes becomes more ambitious, as it does in Wolfenstein's book, among others—when we are after the roots of genius or the specific "drives" or "psychohistorical contexts" that make for a gifted artist or writer or politician, we are likely to find the same sorry results. Generalizations are heaped on one another and they turn out to be mirages, deceptively intriguing, but ultimately susceptible to being dismissed on the most elementary logical grounds. Lenin, Trotsky, and Gandhi, we are told, "each had an unusually ambivalent relationship with his father." Even the word "unusually" does not deprive those men of the company of thousands and thou-sands of others. Because those men were "ambivalent" they couldn't take orders. But they must be singled out even further, the author knows:

> the inability to be a follower, of course, does not account for the ability to be a leader. For this something more is needed, namely a firm identification with parental authority, an underlying feeling of connection with the moral standards and behavior of one parent or another.

Does that formulation work, though? Are those leaders thereby distinguished from many men and women who have become "doctors, lawyers, Indian chiefs," fac-tory workers and white-collar workers, maybe even psychiatrists and historians?

No discussion of "psychohistory" can even begin without mention of Erik Er-ikson, yet I come to him toward the end of this essay. Most of the "psychohis-torians" I have mentioned refer to him constantly. His influence rivals Freud's; on those historians and political scientists I have discussed, I think it is fair to say his influence surpasses Freud's. Philosophers and theologians, also, have been especially indebted to him. "Religion," he writes in *Young Man Luther,* "elaborates on what feels profoundly true even though it is not demonstrable: it translates into significant words, images, and codes the exceeding darkness which surrounds man's existence, and the light which pervades it beyond all desert or comprehension.

One can look at such a sentence and be grateful for the subtlety of its content and expression. One can note the absence of heavy-handed "interpretations"; it is clear the writer does not intend to denigrate religion as an "illusion"; to "get" Luther, "explain" him, "expose" him, use him to prove a theory of his own— but rather to write a biography, an imaginative response to a series of facts about a particular person's life. Those facts are assembled to tell a story, to interest and maybe bestir the reader, to allow a writer with, say, psychological or philosophical interests (and how many writers are without such interests?) a medium for self-expression through another's life.

But there are obligations: to the letter and to the spirit of the subject's life. Though *Young Man Luther* has been widely praised, it has also been subject to serious criticism. Roland H. Bainton, Professor of Ecclesiastical History at Yale Divinity School, and an authority on Luther, has taken strong issue with a number of Erikson's assumptions. He has emphasized how vague, ambiguous, and sometimes severely distorted are those "sources" which even the best of Luther scholars ultimately have had to rely upon.

Bainton is not opposed to psychological speculation—with regard to Luther or anyone else. He mentions in what respects *Young Man Luther* was helpful to him, even suggests further issues Erikson might have profitably explored. But he insists that much of Erikson's thesis necessarily has to depend on his translation of remarks by Luther, and on the validity of various statements attributed to Luther, often at second-, third- and fourthhand. He takes issue with several of Erikson's translations. He also points out that sometimes there is contradictory information about Luther—so much so that several different yet plausible conclusions can be drawn, depending on which sources, letters, anecdotes are cited.[13]

Even so, in spite of such hazards Erikson's book provides opportunities: to connect the past with the present, to show with discretion how the application of a particular discipline, psychoanalysis, developed in the twentieth century, makes more intelligible to us events that had a different kind of coherence for others who lived long ago. It is not enough to call Erikson a gifted writer or an unusually sensitive psychoanalyst. He is more than these. He has dared to bring up subjects like "virtue"; not just "conflict-free" or "neutralized" energy or "ego-strengths," but various ethical strivings. He has insisted that those who would write about historical figures openly examine what their own prejudices might be, what their purposes are in studying a particular "life" or historical issue.

Erikson's prose is the product of careful struggle because he knows the damage that has been done, particularly in psychology and the social sciences, by the use of "becauses," "contexts," and "interrelationships." Erikson talks about "trust" and "initiative" and "industry," plain and risky words that bring us closer to life and imply judgments on human experience. By doing so, he is also choosing not to rely on an evasive technical vocabulary. "Conflicts" there are; but also resolutions to them—and beyond that, affirmations that have their own authority, momentum, and, yes, psychohistory: a thoughtful father here, a kind-spirited mother there, a friend who helped, a husband or wife who helped even more, a time that begged for something from someone.

In Wolfenstein's book we are told that Lenin lacked "trust" in comparison to Trotsky and Gandhi, and all three went through an "exceptionally stormy" adolescence, which, we are told, is "the period of the 'crisis of identity'." Here a phrase of Erikson's has been turned into a new label. His ability to pull together in a single formulation many observations or ideas can be a mixed blessing. What is meant to inspire in others one kind of response (does this way of putting things fit? is it helpful? or ought I look elsewhere, perhaps use my own words, or simply keep looking and listening?) gets quite another response (that is the answer, or what I want to prove, or what I had better well prove, since everyone else these days is doing so).

In December of 1871, the first book of George Eliot's *Middlemarch* was published; within a year the eight sections of that long and demanding novel had appeared. She had spent years preparing for the writing, and as an unashamed moralist, she wanted not only to tell a story but to instruct. She hoped in *Middlemarch* to show how certain individuals live—and thereby raise the old philosophical questions that some of us in psychiatry claim to have new ways of approaching: Who am I? What makes me behave as I do?

Middlemarch is "about" life in the English provinces from 1829 to 1832; it offers a detailed picture of a nation on the brink of political reform, social upheaval, economic change, and it also offers an astonishing breadth of sociological "data": dialects, customs, beliefs, prejudices. A novel of manners, a philosophical novel, a psychological novel, a Victorian novel, a novel which, as Henry James said, "sets a limit" to what "the old-fashioned English novel" can be—it is all of those, but is is also in class by itself.

George Eliot combed through the available medical literature to prepare for her study of Dr. Lydgate. She knew English provincial life from personal experience, but she read newspapers, books, articles to supplement her knowledge. She paid especially close attention to historical sources; like Tolstoy in *War and Peace* she was writing about a generation that immediately preceded her own, and she was aware that sometimes it is harder to be accurate about the recent past than about a more distant time. She knew theology and religious archaeology, and as a result Casaubon is unforgettable; he draws our sympathy as well as our scorn. She had a thorough grasp of the workings of the unconscious mind, so that Bulstrode's agonizing struggle with himself is presented with a keen eye for psychological nuance.

As she wrote she kept a notebook, published some time ago as *Quarry for Middlemarch*. All the facts in it, all the information she had gleaned, all her ideas and theories about human nature, all the historical veins she had tapped somehow came together in a story, in her characters. She condensed an era into a book. She transformed psychological characteristics into people—men and women who are not mechanisms or bundles of reflexes or drives or "needs." In *Middlemarch* history lives through the individuals whose lives, large and small, go to make up history.

I suppose we could call Eliot a psychological novelist, or a novelist interested in how social forces mold individual "behavior" or how particular men and women respond to the demands of a given era. Certainly she knew how to "integrate" her "perspectives." She meticulously fitted her knowledge into the novel, as Jerome Beatty in "History by Indirection: the Era of Reform in *Middlemarch*," *(Victorian Studies,* December, 1957) and Asa Briggs in "*Middlemarch* and the Doctors" (*Cambridge Journal,* pp. 749–762) have shown. It might be useful for some of us today to study how she went about her work, rather than to try to figure out her "personality." Maybe she was just a woman of broad sensibility who had taste and diligence and an extraordinary capacity to evoke the human complexity she saw about her.

In the same way, when one reads C. Vann Woodward's *Tom Watson* or Isaac Deutscher's three-volume biography of Leon Trotsky, one gets a notion of how that impoverished Georgia youth or that Russian student, so fiercely determined and so high-minded, slowly came to terms with themselves—and with the historical currents of their times. We are not given the "mind" of Tom Watson or Leon Trotsky; rather their lives, their concrete struggles, their disappointments, their blind spots, their inevitable pride. Eventually we come to know them well, as well as we can know anyone we have not met or spent time with.

True, not all scholars can glimpse as much as. C. Vann Woodward; few can give biography the power and drama of a novel, while providing the most vivid and searching kind of history. We certainly need more psychologically sophisticated historians—and more psychiatrists with a sense of history. But will that need be met by creating yet another "field" called "psychohistory"? One suspects that good historians like Woodward have no need of old or new psychological terminology or "perspectives," even as an analyst like Erikson calls upon history naturally and wisely because he is an intelligent and learned man—possessing a quality of mind which no college degree, and maybe no course of study, necessarily provides.

Meanwhile Bruce Mazlish may well have offered us an "objective" when he described the historian William L. Langer's suggestion that historians take a greater interest in psychology as an appeal for such an attempt on "a rather low level of theory." That would do—along with plain old thoughtfulness, tact, and the hope that a measure of grace, so mysterious in origin, so impossible to define, so evident and satisfying when present, will somehow come to inform what is written.

NOTES

1 Volume XI of *Complete Psychological Works of Sigmund Freud* (Macmillan, 1964).
2 *The Dynamics of Creation* (Atheneum, 1972).
3 Foreword to *Vincent Van Gogh: A Psychological Study* by Humberto Nagera (International Universities Press, 1968).
4 *Psychoanalysis and History,* edited by Bruce Mazlish (Grosset & Dunlap, 1971).
5 "Charismatic Leadership in Crisis" by George Devereux, in *Psychoanalysis and the Social Sciences,* edited by Warner Muensterberger and Sidney Axelrad (International Universities Press, 1955).
6 Ibid.
7 "Dictatorship and Paranoia" by Gustav Bychowski, ibid.
8 Ibid.
9 We are spared the absurd generalities of Gustav Bychowski's study a few years later on the same man (*Dictators and Disciples: A Psychoanalytic Interpretation of History,* International Universities Press, 1948).

The repressions of his psycho-sexual development did not permit the proper integration and sublimation of his aggressive-sadistic drives, which, to begin with, were not utilized for the construction of normal erotic aggression. The intended identification with his father was not even psychically successful, and instead of the expected masculinity, the constantly competing passive, female attitude appeared.

10 One wants to read Eissler with respect and detachment but his persistent arrogance and rudeness make it hard to do so. We have reason to be grateful to Meyer Schapiro for the first-rate critical essays in which, without rancor, and with great sensitivity, he showed how Freud had erred. Eissler's book on Leonardo was largely prompted by Schapiro's observations, particularly his essay "Leonardo and Freud: An Art-Historical Study," first published in the *Journal of the History of Ideas,* Spring, 1956, and reprinted in *Renaissance Essays,* edited by P. Kristeller and P. Wiener (Harper & Row, 1968), and in *Ideas in Cultural Perspective,* edited by P. Wiener and A. Noland (Rutgers University Press, 1962).
11 *The Psychoanalytic Forum,* Vol. 4 (International Universities Press, 1972).
12 "Martin Buber and Psychiatry," *Psychiatry, A Journal for the Study of Interpersonal Processes,* XIX (1956), p. 110.
13 "Psychiatry and History: An Examination of Erikson's *Young Man Luther,*" *Religion in Life,* Winter, 1971.

8

Some Considerations on Psycho-History

Joseph M. Woods

In recent years an increasing number of historical works have been making use of psychoanalytic concepts in an effort to explain individual and group behavior in history. Despite the scepticism of many historians, it would seem that psycho-history, as it has come to be called, is winning a place for itself, or at the very least forcing those who write biographies or study political and social movements into the asking of some fresh questions. But there is another side to the development of psycho-history. In reviews by psychoanalysts of psycho-historical works and in debates among the practitioners of psycho-history itself there has come to the fore considerable argument about how this new discipline should be practiced. What does a historian need to know, and what training should he have to write psycho-history? Contrariwise, if only an analyst can write psychoanalytic history, what of his training in history? Or is the only fruitful path that of collaboration between analysts and historians? And how can this best be achieved? In short, before psycho-historical works can be critically examined, something must be known about the arguments over the nature of the discipline. It is to some of these arguments that the present essay will largely address itself. Its emphasis will be on psycho-biography.

Early in 1973, Robert Coles, a psychiatrist and the author of a recently published study of the work of Erik Erikson as well as several other works, published two essays on psycho-history in *The New York Review of Books*.[1] His arguments and viewpoints are a useful jumping-off place for discussion of the subject and some of its dilemmas.

Some of Coles' arguments have value, his criticism of jargon, for instance. Perhaps historians, unsure of their professional identities, of what history means, and what it means to be a historian, have embraced psychoanalytic jargon uncritically, as if the use of a private and developed professional language could endow them with a professional identity. The question of jargon is an especially

Reprinted from *The Historian,* vol. 36 (1974), pp. 722–35.

significant one because even among "classical" or "orthodox" psychoanalysts,[2] crucial terms such as depression, masochism, and narcissism, are not used in the same way.[3] But Coles' argument about psycho-history seems questionable at many points. He charges the psychologists and those historians who apply psychoanalytical concepts with envy of the creative energy displayed by great artists and historical leaders, with stinginess in praise, with negativism, with reducing the achievements of the great to weakness, problems, conflict.[4] No doubt he has a point, but should he not be equally alarmed about historians who idealize the figures they are writing about, who seem to endow historical personages with all the great qualities they themselves desire to possess, who minimize, leave unexamined, or put into footnotes the acts of selfishness, cruelty, self-deception, and self-destruction of their heroes? As Naomi Bliven has pointed out in a recent review of Antonia Fraser's *Oliver Cromwell*,[5] biographers of politicians are not as hard on their subjects as biographers of artists. Artists do not get credit for their unfulfilled intentions, but politicians do. They are praised for what they achieved and usually they are not blamed for what they promised but did not achieve. At least psychoanalysis provides a theory for noticing these facts, and perhaps understanding why a leader's reach exceeds his grasp.

One gets the impression from Coles that the insights of such thinkers as Pascal, Kierkegaard and Nietzsche, and of the great novelists, may instruct the historian about the human condition but that the developed body of psychoanalytic theory cannot do so for it is a set of concepts "of very circumscribed and indeterminate value,"[6] but one is not clear why Coles believes the insights of thinkers he admires should be more useful to the historian than a developed body of clinical evidence. Presumably it is because psychoanalytic concepts were devised to deal with sickness, and since the psycho-historian is hardly attempting to cure a patient, he cannot and should not apply them, and in applying them give us historical figures that are "more humanoid than human." But psychoanalytic concepts are not merely concepts devised for treating the sick. There are two branches in psychoanalytic literature: papers concerned with the technique and practice of psychoanalysis, and theoretical statements which purport to offer a general theory of mind and personality.[7] Coles does not give reasons for rejecting the claim of psychoanalytic theory to be a general psychology.[8] His argument also seems to ignore the fact that psychoanalytic theory has been built on the study of many patients who, whatever their sickness, have been successful in their careers even though they have not been made content or happy by their success.[9] But on the other hand many so-called great men in history have failed to take satisfaction in their successes—Luther, Rousseau, Lincoln, Woodrow Wilson to name a few— however much they longed for success. It would seem that psychoanalytic theory again enables the historian to notice and perhaps explain this fact.

Coles argues in criticizing Walter Langer's recently published *The Mind of Adolf Hitler*[10] that Hitler's weaknesses do not explain how he became Führer of all Europe. How many thousands of others who employed such mechanisms as "identification with the aggressor" got nowhere, and how many paranoid schizophrenics have "messiah complexes"? Such a criticism is not, however, a valid criticism of psycho-history alone, but of any explanation of why any figure, in Erikson's phrase, "daydreams his way into history." Every historian comes up with some notion of the motives of the character he is dealing with, and one can always argue that ten or ten thousand other people in that time and place had (or might have had) the very same motives, and yet did not take the historical stage. No historian can really explain this mystery of why X, instead of these ten thousand other people, who may have had similar motives, becomes noteworthy. It seems to me one of those unproductive questions like why does Shakespeare have the Friar leave the tomb in *Romeo and Juliet*. We are reminded by Coles that whereas psycho-historians have, by and large, given us persons who are illustrations of theory, it is the great novelists like Dostoevski and George Eliot who give us people in all the fullness of life. But what historian of any school can rival the great novelists in characterization? It is hardly a just criticism of psycho-historians to say that they are inferior to major novelists. Furthermore, Coles, decrying the negativism of the psycho-historian, tells us that historical figures have been given more by their parents and bring more from their childhoods than burdens, complexes, conflicts, and inhibitions. To be sure. But the remark may well be beside the point. The point is rather that many great artists and famous historical figures do not acknowledge those debts to parents and others, and the biographer, often with the aid of psychoanalytic theory, attempts to explain why. Surely one of the major findings of psychoanalysis is that children internalize distorted images of early authority figures, having invested those figures with their own hostile and sadistic impulses, and that in many cases these images are lasting and unmodified by experience. Thus V. S. Pritchett's recent biography of Balzac, which seems to me to understand Balzac in a psychoanalytical way (although Pritchett does not acknowledge any influence and writes a prose unhindered by jargon), notes that Balzac was given to presenting himself—usually to women—as someone deprived of a mother's love and as "ruined" by his mother, whereas it would be more accurate to say that he had ruined his mother, financially at least.[11]

Many psychoanalysts, however, would seem to believe that psychoanalytic theory can contribute to the understanding of historical personages.[12] To be sure these psychoanalysts are critical of those historians who have not seriously studied psychoanalytic theory and who seem to be, at this late date, laboring under the impression that psychoanalytic theory begins and ends with Freud and who are almost completely unaware of the revisions and elaborations in theory since the 1940s.[13] What has been criticized is that psycho-biographers have often not taken into account the shift in emphasis in psychoanalytic theory from (a) the instincts and their vicissitudes to (b) the development of the ego and the early object-relationships, especially the importance of the mother in the development of the child—that is to say, the importance of the pre-oedipal stages of life. These developments in theory would seem to be of special importance to the historian because they provide an explanation of how one relates—or fails to relate—to others. Assuming that "good enough mothering" takes place in the pre-oedipal mother-child relation, the child moves from a phase in which there is no awareness of self apart from the other to the phase where the other is regarded by the child as existing only to gratify his needs, to the phase where the other is regarded as a person in his own right with needs and feelings of his own. In the relationship with the mother, the child's ego, availing itself of its own inherent energies and with additional neutralized energy from the drives, begins to build up "internalized object relations"—that is, good and bad self-images and good and bad object-images. These images "result from continuous daily contact with the mothering person and reflect countless pleasureable and frustrating experiences in the infant's daily life."[14]

These images must become (a) differentiated and (b) stabilized. In normal development, the self-images are differentiated from the object-images, and the good and bad self-images are integrated as are the good and bad object-images. The differentiation between the self and object-images and the respective integration of the good and bad self and object-images constitute the basis for (1) individual identity and relationship with others, (2) the achievement of "psychological birth"—that is, psychological separation from the mother and the continuing process of becoming a separated individuated person, (3) the ability of the child to make necessary identifications with others, which are the basis for a developing identity and expansion of the functioning of the ego by acquiring skills and roles, (4) the appropriate development of the superego—that is, the development of a structure in which (a) personal goals, ideals and aspirations (called the ego-ideal) are toned down from the magical, grandiose aspirations of the child and (b) the internalized versions of the punitive parents have also been toned down by more realistic perceptions of parental demands and prohibitions and (c) the idealized and punitive aspects of the superego are harmonized.[15] Disturbances in the mother-child relationship of the pre-oedipal period are usually regarded as the cause of those character disorders which fall on the scale of pathology between psychosis and neurosis—the "borderline" states and certain narcissistic personality disturbances. These disorders have received much attention in psychoanalytic literature over the last decade.[16]

Because of the importance, then, of the mother-child relationship for the development of personality, psychoanalysts have been critical of much work done in psycho-biography on the ground that all too confidently the biographer focuses on the Oedipus complex of a given figure—as if all problems and conflicts were rooted in an unresolved oedipal conflict, and as if the pre-oedipal stages of development were not significant. As Gertrude and Rubin Blanck point out, if a father is resentful of a male child and of the attention the child receives from its mother, that may indicate that the father has not resolved his own Oedipus complex. But the father's behavior may also be "a manifestation of pre-oedipal object relations and of need-gratification wishes which render the individual unable to take the needs of either wife or son into account."[17] Which of these interpretations is true depends on the other evidence the clinician has available about the life of the patient. Since the biographer of an historical figure does not have direct access to his subject and has no way of uncovering repressed material, some analysts believe that he cannot be certain about the source of the character's "problems."[18] Psychoanalysts are agreed in criticizing the biographer who goes beyond the evidence and fabricates unconscious desires and fantasies.[19]

Since, then, the biographer often does not have, and cannot get enough information about his subject, some psychoanalysts believe that full analytic study of an historical figure is not possible and that the psycho-historian should restrict himself to "partial efforts, highlighting what general biographers have ignored and failed to understand, to undo denials and idealizations and to correct distortions aided by freedom from unconscious reactions to our subjects."[20] But must psycho-historians restrict themselves to critical corrections? The method used by Miles F. Shore in his essay on Henry VIII is suggestive.[21] Instead of speculating about what Henry's feeling for and early relationships with parents and siblings "must have been," Shore points out that Henry received treatment at the hands of tutors and servants that vacillated between extravagant adulation and brutal discipline, and that the hypocrisy and self-serving nature of this adulation by what were in effect "paid foster parents," had the result that his upbringing did not offer the possibilities for forming permanent important relationships. All of these conditions fostered the development of Henry's pathological narcissism. Shore then goes on to show how Henry's narcissism operated: how a series of defeats and disappointments offended Henry's grandiose self-image, and caused the series of actions which led to the break with Catherine and with Rome, and to later events in Henry's career as well.

Actually, is it necessary to postulate anything about a subject's childhood to do an analytic study? This is a central question because there is rarely enough reliable and available evidence about any given childhood and about a subject's feelings about the significant figures in childhood. But psychoanalytic theory enables the biographer to see, in examining the mature life of a character, behavior that he might not otherwise notice: alteration between active and passive states, how he relates to people, or whether his behavior indicates that he has not relinquished fantasies of omnipotence, whether he is burdened with an unconscious sense of guilt; and to show how these constructs enable us to understand the character more clearly. One does not, in short, have to know the earliest reasons why a character seems incapable of regarding other people except as "there" to meet his needs, in order to notice that he does relate to people in such an infantile way. Furthermore, psychoanalytic writing makes clear that the same effects (or "symptoms") do not always result from the same early "causes." Ralph Greenson has pointed out that compulsive gambling can be the result of (a) deprivation, (b) over-gratification, or (c) a combination of these in childhood.[22] Since this is true, the biographer is hardly—given the lack of evidence about a subject's childhood—entitled to assume causes.

The psychoanalytic work done over the last decade or so on the narcissistic personality may be useful to the historical biographer in understanding certain so-called "great men" in history.[23] What are the features of this type of character? A defective superego or conscience. Instead of having ideals, standards, values, goals, narcissistic personalities are possessed by fantasies of omnipotence, dreams of limitless greatness. They do not have ideals; rather, as Edith Jacobson says, the demandingness and exhibitionism of His Majesty the Baby are masquerading as ideals.[24] The narcissistic personality has not renounced infantile fantasies of omnipotence—more precisely, he has not renounced the wish for magical participation in the omnipotence of idealized early authority figures.[25] As Ralph Greenson points out, these personalities do not simply long for omnipotence, they feel they are omnipotent.[26] Unconsciously, their wishes are facts. They want to have their cake and eat it. They act upon their grandiose fantasies to be assured that they are superhuman. Their participation in the omnipotence of early figures may manifest itself in a belief in a special relationship with God, Fate, History, the mystical Nation, the General Will. They are subject to rapid oscillations of mood, feeling at times that they are God, at other times that they are nothing.[27] Usually narcissistic personalities deceive themselves into believing that they are serving noble causes, making nations great, rescuing and avenging the oppressed. Actually they are preoccupied with their own greatness.

Nevertheless, the grandiose self-concept which the narcissistic personality tries to live up to often does make for real achievement. As Max Weber said of charismatic leaders, because they attempt the impossible they attain the possible. Historians have often recognized the absence in so-called "great men" of any genuine values, standards, commitments, and of any coherent identity. They have recognized that one looks in vain for a consistent ideology, that great men often lack fidelity to the values of their group, their class, or their nation. Of Lloyd George, John Maynard Keynes wrote that he was "rooted in nothing"; General Beck said of Hitler, "this fellow has no Fatherland at all"; of Napoleon III, Marx wrote, "being nothing himself, he could be everything to everyone." Going along with the self-preoccupation of narcissistic personalities is the absence in them of any feeling that other persons are persons in their own right with needs and feelings of their own. Others are regarded instead as existing to meet their needs and demands, or as mirrors before whom they display themselves, or as containers into which the narcissistic personality deposits his own characteristics when they do not accord with his idealized self.[28] One is always right, good, and superior: others are wrong, bad, and inferior. These narcissistic types may be extremely dependent on other people but they really use them to live up to their own dreams of glory. Those on whom they depend are soon devalued and blamed if reality proves resistant (as reality usually does). Other helpers are often soon substituted—as if people were interchangeable parts; notice, for example, Henry VIII's succession of *alter rexes*. There is little human give-and-take in these relationships. Above all, this personality type usually does not experience conscious guilt feelings for greed, selfishness, hostility and aggression against others. Absence of conscious guilt feelings is one of the leading characteristics of their pathology.[29] They are given to projecting the guilt they should feel or the feelings and actions they should feel guilty about. Hitler, for instance, who had sponged off his mother and had earned no money until he was twenty-two, accused the Jews of being parasites on the German nation.[30] Yet the very defects of the narcissistic personality may be an advantage to a political leader.[31] The absence of any real values and principles and of any center seem to make it possible for him to play many roles and to tell other people what they want to hear in order to get their support. He pretends to be conservative to conservatives and radical to radicals. The defects in the structure of his superego make it possible for him to lie, exploit, manipulate, divide and conquer, crush opposition— not to speak of provoking wars and inaugurating "final solutions." Political leaders of this type seem to have an uncanny ability to use their "sickness" for purposes of gaining public support and attention. As Erikson writes of Hitler, "It is hard to say where personal symptom ends and shrewd propaganda begins."[32]

There is no need to dwell on the inadequacies of Walter Langer's *The Mind of Adolf Hitler*. It was written in 1943 as a secret report for the OSS but not published until 1972. It was composed before many of the developments in and revisions of psychoanalytic theory that I have been discussing had taken place. It emphasizes Hitler's pervasive Oedipus complex which was developed "to an extraordinary degree." The interpretation, and the evidence and reasoning behind it, have been criticized by clinicians and historians alike.[33] More recent analytic work on Hitler focuses on the pre-oedipal period and on a disturbed mother-child relationship.[34]

Of more interest to historians than speculating on childhood traumas is the theory recently proposed by a psycho-historian that Hitler unconsciously wanted (or needed) to fail. That theory holds that because of Hitler's unconscious guilt feelings about the possibility of his having Jewish blood, about his incestuous desires, and about his "massively masochistic sexual perversion," Hitler had to punish himself by "bringing about the kind of global war that he could not conceivably win."[35] But we do not really know what Hitler's unconscious guilt feelings were "about." They might just as well have been about his destructive wishes and deeds. But that is not the important point. The important point is rather that recent psychoanalytic theory has, on the basis of more and more clinical evidence, cast doubt on the earlier theory that self-destructive behavior is caused by unconscious guilt feelings seeking punishment. There may be some cases where self-defeat is produced by guilt needing punishment, but those cases involve neurotics with overly severe superegos.[36] An overly severe superego was hardly Hitler's problem. If it had been, as Erikson has pointed out, Hitler would have been "paralyzed"; he would not have been one of the great actors and destroyers in history.[37] Rather Hitler's case might correspond to those borderline person-alities whose self-destructive tendencies are the product of inner structural de-fects. Neither the ego nor the superego are well enough constructed to tame and regulate aggressive impulses. As a result aggression is released both against the world and against the self.[38] This is but one possible explanation for Hitler's self-destructiveness.

There has been almost an embarrassment of riches in explaining self-defeating behavior in recent psychoanalytic literature—none of them stressing guilt in search of punishment. Some of these are: self-defeat may result from grandiosity, from the need to be beyond limits. Gamblers going for broke—and Hitler so characterized himself—do not necessarily need to lose. They may lose, but that is not the intention of the gambling. Proving themselves omnipotent *is* the in-tention. That Hitler committed suicide when he didn't get away with it might also be ascribed to shame because of failure to live up to his exalted self-image.[39] Or a person may invite defeat in order to rescue self-esteem—paradoxical as this may seem. Unconsciously he can say to himself: I control the circumstances; I have arranged for failure; it did not come upon me from outside myself.[40] Or a person may be self-defeating not just to punish himself but to punish someone else—"victory through defeat"—whether the someone else be hated and envied early figures or later figures.[41] I do not know which of the many current psy-choanalytic explanations for self-destructiveness might work in Hitler's case. I am simply saying that an explanation that stresses guilt seeking punishment is, given the state of theory today, the least plausible.

Much has been written on methodology in psycho-history—how to proceed, what evidence to credit, which psychoanalytic model to apply, what to do in the absence of the evidence that an analyst has available in healing a patient, whether the historian must have clinical experience as well as formal study in psychoan-alytic theory, whether psycho-history must be a collaborative effort between his-torians and psychoanalysts. One can hardly imagine a line of inquiry more likely to vex the founder of psychoanalysis. Freud had little love for discourses on method. Those who were preoccupied with methodology were, he said, forever polishing their glasses and never putting them on.

It may be true that psycho-history cannot be written except as a collaborative effort. This surely depends on what is meant by psycho-history. Isn't any work that makes use of psychoanalytic theory to understand a given individual or group movement, a work of psycho-history? Could not Edmund Wilson, "Our American Plutarch,"[42] be called a psycho-historian? Certainly he used psychoanalytic theory not only to understand the creative process in literature but also to understand historical figures such as Marx, Lenin, Lincoln, Woodrow Wilson. His use of psy-choanalytic theory has always shown tact and judgment. It was never used ex-plicitly, let alone self-consciously. Wilson did not invoke diagnostic labels or worry about what level of pathology a given character displayed. Nor did he use psy-choanalysis in such a way that his subject became an illustration of a theory. Nor was he inclined to go beyond the evidence, imagining what childhoods "must have been." He criticizes, for example, Carl Sandburg's trumped-up version of Lincoln's childhood. Wilson himself is content to establish Lincoln's towering ambition, his heroic conception of himself by referring to one of his speeches in 1838: "Towering genius . . . thirsts and burns for distinction; and, if possible, it will have it, whether at the expense of emancipating slaves or enslaving free men."[43] Wilson interprets: "it is evident that Lincoln has projected himself into the role against which he is warning [his audience]."[44] He was "describing this figure with a fire that seemed to derive as much from admiration as from apprehension."[45] Wilson shows that to justify his ambition and the aggression that it involved Lincoln grew increasingly to believe that God was on the side of the Union and against slavery and had willed the Civil War. And Wilson believes that this religious mysticism about the Union was not merely contrived by Lincoln "to express himself in phrases congenial to his public" but was a "vision" that had imposed itself. Yet while thirsting and burning for distinction at the expense of sending "thousands to their deaths" and referring one's will and actions to God is hardly a flattering picture of Lincoln, the reader at no point feels that Lincoln has been put down, reduced, or that Edmund Wilson is attacking a national idol or moralizing about his faults. Wilson's tone, his ability not to trivialize or patronize a figure seems to spring from his sense that "thirsting and burning for distinction" or sadistic and masochistic tendencies (which Wilson so clearly brings out in his treatment of Marx) are human qualities, not occasions for shocked surprise of outraged morality or disappointment that some of history's movers and shakers have "base" motives. He realizes that achievement has its price, and writes of Karl Marx:

> Certainly his character was domineering; certainly his personality was arrogant, and abnormally mistrustful and jealous; certainly he was capable of vindictiveness and of what seems to us gratuitous malignity. But if we are repelled by these traits in Marx, we must remember that a normally polite and friendly person could hardly have accomplished the task which it was the destiny of Marx to carry through—a task that required the fortitude to resist and to break off all those ties which—as they involve us in the general life of society—limit our views and cause our purposes to shift.[46]

One doubts if many psychoanalysts would agree with this favorable verdict on Marx, would agree that his isolation, aggression, and cruelty are to be excused, still less explained, by his "destiny," though they may have made possible his achievement. Wilson seems to admire those figures who need to be great, who thirst and burn for distinction at whatever cost; but he does not withhold or suppress whatever information is available to him that makes possible a harsher or different judgment. Psychoanalysis is not an orthodoxy; two psychoanalysts regarding the same historical figure will not necessarily come to the same interpretation of his behavior or to the same judgment of his goodness or badness.[47] Thus Erik Erikson has been criticized by a psychoanalyst for "idealizing" Gandhi, for not giving enough attention to his sadism and to the irresponsibility, given the poverty of India, involved in his contempt for science, birth control, industrialization, and mass education.[48] It would seem, then, that psychoanalysis is not going to make history itself different from what it has always been and what Pieter Geyl said it was: "argument without end."

NOTES

1 February 22, and March 8, 1973.
2 We refer here to psychoanalysts who have received their training at Institutes accredited by the American Psychoanalytic Association. For further detail see *A Glossary of Psychoanalytic Terms and Concepts,* ed. by Burnes E. Moore and Bernard D. Fine (2nd ed.; New York, 1968), 9–11.
3 Myer Mendelson, *Psychoanalytic Concepts of Depression* (Springfield, Ill., 1960), 137. Mendelson points out that there is "but limited consensus among psychoanalytic writers on depression. Disagreement is acute on numerous issues."
4 Coles, *New York Review of Books,* Feb. 22, 1973, 18, 19, 21.
5 *The New Yorker,* Jan. 14, 1974.
6 Coles, *New York Review of Books,* Mar. 8, 1973, 27.
7 Lionel Trilling, Introduction to *The Life and Work of Sigmund Freud* by Ernest Jones. Edited and abridged by Lionel Trilling and Steven Marcus (New York, 1963), vii.
8 See *Makers of Modern Social Science: Sigmund Freud,* ed. Paul Roazen (Englewood Cliffs, N.J., 1973), editor's introduction.
9 See Helen H. Tartakoff, "The Normal Personality in Our Culture and the Nobel Prize Complex," in R. M. Loewenstein et al., *Psychoanalysis: A General Psychology* (New York, 1966), 222–52; and Annie Reich, "Pathologic Forms of Self-Esteem Regulation," *Psychoanalytic Study of the Child,* 25 (1960), 215–32.
10 *The Mind of Adolf Hitler: The Secret Wartime Report* (New York, 1972).
11 V. S. Pritchett, *Balzac* (New York, 1973).
12 Panel. "The Methodology of Psychoanalytic Biography," reported by John E. Gedo, *Journal of the American Psychoanalytic Association,* 20 (1972), 638–49. Cited hereafter as Gedo. Also Bernard C. Meyer, "Some Reflections on the Contributions of Psychoanalysis to Biography," in *Psychoanalysis and Contemporary Science,* I, ed. R. R. Holt and E. Peterfreund (New York, 1972), 373–91. Cited hereafter as Meyer.
13 By psychoanalytic theory here, I mean that body of theory which, to speak only of the United States, is taught at psychoanalytic training institutes accredited by the American Psychoanalytic Association and to the literature which appears in such journals as *International Journal of Psychoanalysis, Journal of the American Psychoanalytic Association, Psychoanalytic Quarterly, American Imago,* and such annuals as *The Psychoanalytic Study of the Child.*
14 Rubin Blanck and Gertrude Blanck, *Marriage and Personal Development* (New York, 1968), 12.
15 This brief summary of the importance of the mother-child relationship for the development of personality is derived from Rubin Blanck and Gertrude Blanck, *Marriage and Personal Development,* especially Chapters 2, 5, 6, and 7 and from Otto F. Kernberg, "Early Ego Integration and Object Relations," *Annals of the New York Academy of Science,* 193 (August 25, 1972), 233–47. Some of the major contributors to ego psychology and object relations theory are John Bowlby, Erik Erikson, W. R. D. Fairbairn, Anna Freud, Heinz Hartmann, Edith Jacobson, Otto Kernberg, Melanie Klein, Margaret Mahler, René Spitz, D. W. Winnicott. A list of significant writings will be found in the bibliography of the Blancks' book and in the footnotes of the Kernberg article.

16 Otto F. Kernberg, "Borderline Personality Organization," *Journal of the American Psychoanalytic Association*, 15 (1967), 641–85; "Factors in the Psychoanalytic Treatment of Narcissistic Personalities," *Journal of the American Psychoanalytic Association*, 18 (1970), 51–85; and "A Psychoanalytic Classification of Character Pathology," *Journal of the American Psychoanalytic Association*, 18 (1970), 800–822.

17 Blanck and Blanck, *Marriage*, 78.

18 See Gedo, "The Methodology of Psychoanalytic Biography," 641–43. It would seem that analytic biography may be more successful with literary figures than with generals and politicians for the works of the former allow access to their fantasies.

19 Rudolf Binion's *Frau Lou: Nietzsche's Wayward Disciple* (Princeton, 1968) has been criticized by Bernard F. Meyer, for instance, as an example of "wild analysis" because Binion with neither evidence nor argument "unhesitatingly announces the cause of his subject's unhappy childhood: 'a craving for her father excited by excretion and attended by darkling visions of re-entering his bowel-womb to repossess his penis.' [p. 6] Now aside from wondering what this sentence might mean [Dr. Meyer continues] the reader may justly ask by what route the author arrived there, for there is nothing in the text up to this point—31 lines of the book so far—that has paved the way for any conclusion whatever, let alone this somewhat extravagant one. Psychoanalysis is not an arcanum for an exercise in revealed truth; neither is it in the nature of its methodology nor in that of any scientific discipline, for that matter, to initiate a study or an experiment with an unproved conclusion." Meyer, "Some Reflections ...," 374. Later in his essay, Meyer notes that Binion, in his preoccupation with Frau Lou's "charged up obsession with famous men, overlooks or minimizes the role of maternal influences both in his subject and in those who moved about her." Ibid., 378–79.

20 Gedo, "The Methodology of Psychoanalytic Biography," 641.

21 Miles F. Shore, "Henry VIII and the Crisis of Generativity," *Journal of Interdisciplinary History*, 2 (Spring, 1972), 359–90.

22 Ralph Greenson, "On Gambling," *American Imago*, 4 (April 1947), 70. Myer Mendelson has pointed out that there is disagreement among analysts about "the period in childhood which is most critical for the predisposition to depression." Mendelson, *Psychoanalytic Concepts of Depression*, 138.

23 Not all narcissistic personalities have the same degree of pathology. This category of mental illness falls between neurosis and psychosis, but some are closer to neurosis and some to psychosis (borderline personality disorders). Hitler, for instance, has been diagnosed as a "narcissistic personality with overt borderline characteristics." See Norbert Bromberg, "Hitler's Character and Its Development," *American Imago*, 28 (1971), 289–303. It should be noted that the narcissistic personality represents pathological narcissism. Normal narcissism is evident in "healthy self-esteem."

24 Edith Jacobson, *The Self and the Object World* (New York, 1964), 203–04.

25 Helen H. Tartakoff, "The Normal Personality in Our Culture and the Nobel Prize Complex," in Loewenstein, *Psychoanalysis*, 233, 242.

26 Ralph Greenson, "On Gambling," 68.

27 Annie Reich, "Pathologic Forms of Self-Esteem Regulation," 226.

28 Paulina F. Kernberg, "The Course of the Analysis of a Narcissistic Personality with Hysterical and Compulsive Features," *Journal of the American Psychoanalytic Association*, 19 (1971), 453.

29 Ibid.

30 Norbert Bromberg, "Hitler's Character and Its Development," 298.

31 Alexander and Juliet George suggest that high accomplishment in political life may be positively correlated not only with neurosis but with even more pathological states. *Psychology Today* (June 1973), 98.

32 *Childhood and Society* (New York, 1963, paperback edition), 341.

33 See Coles, *New York Review of Books,* March 8, 1973, 25–26; Hans Gatzke, "Hitler and Psychohistory," in *American Historical Review,* 78 (April 1973), 394–401. See also Erik H. Erikson, *Childhood and Society,* 329–30. Erikson is not criticizing Langer's book directly, and his essay gives no indication that he has seen the original report; he is criticizing, however, the view that Hitler's behavior can be adequately explained by the "Oedipus complex."

34 Norbert Bromberg, "Hitler's Character and Its Development."

35 R. G. L. Waite, "Adolf Hitler's Guilt Feelings: A Problem in History and Psychology," *Journal of Interdisciplinary History,* I (Winter, 1971), 229–49. This article gives many instances of Hitler's self-defeating behavior which historians might ordinarily pass over, but not all of them are equally plausible.

36 Otto F. Kernberg, "Prognostic Considerations Regarding Borderline Personality Organization," *Journal of the American Psychoanalytic Association,* 19 (1971), 610.

37 *Childhood and Society,* 329.

38 Otto F. Kernberg, "Early Ego Integration and Object Relations," 242, and "Prognostic Considerations Regarding Borderline Personality Organization," 608–11.

39 Charles Rycroft, *Neurosis and Anxiety* (London, 1971, Pelican paperback), 54.

40 L. Eidelberg, "Humiliation and Masochism," *Journal of the American Psychoanalytic Association,* 7 (1959), 274–84.

41 Otto F. Kernberg, "Prognostic Considerations Regarding Borderline Personality Organization," 610.

42 The phrase is Alfred Kazin's.

43 Edmund Wilson, *Patriotic Gore* (New York, 1969, paperback edition), 107.

44 Ibid., 108.

45 Ibid., 129.

46 Wilson, *To the Finland Station* (New York, 1972), 178–79.

47 For a discussion of different interpretations by two analysts of an important episode in Goethe's life and the impossibility of deciding which interpretation is valid, see Gedo, "Methodology of Psychoanalytic Biography," 640.

48 H. Robert Blank, review of Erikson's *Gandhi's Truth, Psychoanalytic Quarterly,* 41 (1972), 123–27.

9

Why Did Van Gogh Cut Off His Ear? The Problem of Alternative Explanations in Psychobiography

William McKinley Runyan

Late Sunday evening December 23, 1888, Vincent Van Gogh, then thirty-five years old, cut off the lower half of his left ear and took it to a brothel, where he asked for a prostitute named Rachel and handed the ear to her, requesting that she "keep this object carefully."

How is this extraordinary event to be accounted for? Over the years a variety of explanations have been proposed, and more than a dozen of them will be sketched below. Is one of these explanations uniquely true, are all of them true in some way, or perhaps, are none of them true? What criteria and procedures are there for critically evaluating and deciding among these alternative interpretations? This incident is examined in order to explore the problem of alternative explanations in the study of individual lives, a problem of central importance in psychobiography (Anderson, 1981a; Crosby, 1979), in personality psychology (Allport, 1961; Hogan, 1976; Murray, 1938), and in the clinical professions (Horowitz, 1979; Spence, 1976).

A VARIETY OF EXPLANATIONS

1. One explanation of Van Gogh's behavior is that he was frustrated by two recent events: the engagement of his brother Theo, to whom he was very attached, and the failure of an attempt to establish a working and living relationship with Paul Gauguin. The aggressive impulses aroused by these frustrations were first directed at Gauguin, but then were turned against himself (Lubin, 1972).

Reprinted from *Life Histories and Psychobiography: Explorations in Theory and Method* by William McKinley Runyan. Copyright © 1982 by William McKinley Runyan. Reprinted by permission of Oxford University Press, Inc.

2. A second interpretation is that the self-mutilation resulted from a conflict over homosexual impulses aroused by the presence of Gauguin. According to this account, the ear was a phallic symbol (the Dutch slang word for penis, *lul,* resembled the Dutch word for ear, *lel*), and the act was a symbolic self-castration (Lubin, 1972; Westerman Holstijn, 1951).

3. A third explanation is in terms of Oedipal themes. Van Gogh was sharing a house with Gauguin, and Gauguin reported that on the day before the ear mutilation Van Gogh had threatened him with a razor but, under Gauguin's powerful gaze, had then run away. According to this interpretation, Gauguin represented Van Gogh's hated father and that, failing in his initial threat, Van Gogh "finally gratified his extraordinary resentment and hate for his father by deflecting the hatred onto his own person. In so doing Van Gogh committed, in phantasy, an act of violence on his father with whom he identified himself and at the same time he punished himself for committing the act" (Schnier, 1950, p. 153). Then "in depositing his symbolic organ at the brothel he also fulfilled his wish to have his mother" (pp. 153–54).

4. Another interpretation is that Van Gogh was influenced by bullfights he had seen in Arles. In such events the matador is given the ear of the bull as an award, displays his prize to the crowd, and then gives it to the lady of his choice. The proponent of this interpretation, J. Olivier (in Lubin, 1972) says: "I am absolutely convinced that Van Gogh was deeply impressed by this practice. . . . Van Gogh cut off the ear, his own ear, as if he were at the same time the vanquished bull and the victorious matador. A confusion in the mind of one person between the vanquished and the vanquisher" (p. 158). Then like the matador, Van Gogh presented the ear to a lady of his choice. (The following explanations, unless otherwise noted, are also from Lubin's (1972) comprehensive analysis.)

5. In the months preceding Van Gogh's self-mutilation, there were fifteen articles in the local paper about Jack the Ripper, who mutilated the bodies of prostitutes, sometimes cutting off their ears. "These crimes gave rise to emulators, and Vincent may have been one of them. As a masochist instead of a sadist, however, it is conceivable that he would reverse Jack's act by mutilating himself and bringing the ear to a prostitute" (Lubin, 1972, p. 159).

6. Van Gogh was emotionally and financially dependent on his brother Theo, and usually spent the Christmas holidays with him. This year, however, Vincent learned that Theo would spend the holiday with his new fiancée and her family. One interpretation suggests that Van Gogh's self-mutilation was an unconscious strategy for holding on to his brother's attention, and a way of getting Theo to come and care for him rather than spending the holidays with his fiancée.

7. Van Gogh had recently been painting a picture of a woman rocking a cradle, using Madame Roulins as his model. He felt great affection for the Roulins family and may have envied the love and attention their children received. In mutilating himself, Van Gogh may have been attempting to obtain care and love from these substitute parents. The immediate response of Madame Roulins is not known,

but Monsieur Roulins came to Van Gogh's aid on the night of the injury and helped to care for him afterward.

8. Van Gogh had a great sympathy for prostitutes and identified with their status as social outcasts. One suggestion is that his self-mutilation was a reflection of this identification. "In June, just a few months before butchering his ear, he had written that 'the whore is like meat in a butcher shop': when he treated his own body as 'meat in a butcher's shop,' he reversed their roles, identified himself with the whore, and showed his sympathy for her" (Lubin, 1972, p. 169).

9. Vincent felt that his mother saw him as too rough and as a bad boy. During the psychotic state surrounding this incident, primitive symbolic thought processes may have led Van Gogh to cut off his ear from a desire to be perceived more positively by his mother. "Because the unconscious mind tends to regard protuberances as masculine and aggressive, removing the protuberant part of the ear may have been to inform the prostitute, a substitute for his mother, that he was not an aggressive, hurtful male—the 'rough' boy whom his mother disliked—but helpless, penetrable, the victim of a hurt" (Lubin, 1972, p. 173).

10. It is likely that Van Gogh experienced frightening auditory hallucinations during his psychotic attack similar to those he experienced in other attacks. Afterward, while in the sanatorium, he wrote that other patients heard strange sounds and voices as he had and speculated in one case that this was probably due to a disease of nerves in the ear. Thus, in a psychotic state, Van Gogh could have felt that his own ear was diseased and cut it off to silence the disturbing sounds.

11. In the Garden of Gethsemane scene in the Bible, Simon Peter cut off the ear of Malchus, a servant of the high priest, who had come to seize Christ. This scene had been on Van Gogh's mind. He attempted to paint it in the summer of 1888, and also mentioned it in a letter to his sister in October. In his delirium, Van Gogh may have acted out the scene at Gethsemane, carrying out the roles of both victim and aggressor.

12. Another explanation is that Vincent identified with the crucified Jesus and that the Virgin Mary lamenting over the dead body of Christ represented Vincent's mother. "In giving the mother surrogate, Rachel, a dead segment of his body, Vincent symbolically repeated the scene on Calvary" (Lubin, 1972, p. 179).

13. Vincent Van Gogh lived in the shadow of a dead brother, also named Vincent, who died at birth exactly one year before Vincent the painter was born. It is suggested that Vincent had the feeling he was unloved by a mother who continued to grieve over an idealized lost son. Killing part of himself may have been an attempt to win his mother's love. Vincent's self-mutilation "represented a symbolic death, exhibiting Vincent in the image of his dead brother, the first Vincent—someone mother adored. As a gift, the severed ear was specifically the gift of a baby, a dead baby. Thus it was both a reliving of wishes to unite him with mother and a bitter mockery of his mother's attachment to her dead son" (Lubin, 1972, pp. 182–83.)

What to Make of These Alternative Explanations?

Here are thirteen different psychodynamic explanations for why Van Gogh cut off his ear and gave it to a prostitute, and additional interpretations have been proposed (Lubin, 1972; Nagera 1967; Schneider, 1950; Schnier, 1950; Untermeyer, 1955; Westerman Holstijn, 1951). There is a substantial list of explanations for Van Gogh's disturbances which also consider biological factors (Monroe, 1978; Tralbaut, 1969). How should we interpret these alternative explanations? Are all of them true, are some true and some false, or, perhaps, are none of them true? Do the various explanations conflict, so that if one is chosen then one or more of the others must be rejected, or do a number of them supplement each other? Is there, perhaps, some other explanation that would replace all of these possibilities? Do we end up with a feeling that we understand Van Gogh's behavior, that we know why he acted as he did?

Individuals may vary widely in their responses to this material. From one point of view, it is a richly woven tapestry connecting a single event to many themes, conflicts, symbols, and unconscious wishes and processes in Van Gogh's life. According to the principle of "overdetermination," which suggests that actions typically have multiple causes and meanings, this material can be seen as a rich set of complementary explanations for Van Gogh's behavior. Lubin (1972) for example, after discussing a number of possible explanations, suggests that "there may be truth in all of these suggestions. One's motivations include the superficial factors that are well known to oneself as well as deep, troubling factors that one would vehemently deny when confronted with them. Man carries his conflicts from one period of life to the next, and each stage of development puts its mark on the next" (p. 163). From the standpoint of overdetermination, it would be surprising to find a single explanation for any human action, and events can be expected to have more than one cause, more than one meaning. At other points, Lubin states that "various aspects of Vincent's life converged in this single episode" (p. 155) and that what we have is a set of "interrelated" explanations (p. 182).

A second way of making sense of these multiple explanations is to note that several of the different explanations are concerned with different aspects or features of the larger episode. For example, the choice of an ear may have been related to Van Gogh's observation of bullfights, the fact that it happened at Christmastime may have been associated with the presentation of the ear as a gift, and his choice of a prostitute as the recipient may have been related to recent publicized accounts of Jack the Ripper. A substantial number of interpretations, however, are concerned with similar aspects of the event. His choice of the ear has been related to his observation of bullfights, the newspaper accounts of Jack the Ripper, the ear as a phallic symbol, a belief that auditory hallucinations may have come from diseased nerves in the ear, and his concern with the Gethsemane scene.

A third approach is to work from the assumption that several of these explanations may be valid while the others are not, and that procedures for critically evaluating alternative explanations are needed in order to assess their relative credibility. The doctrine of overdetermination may be correct in that psychological events often have multiple causes and meanings, but to assume that all possible interpretations "are ultimately members of one happy family is to abandon critical thinking altogether" (Hirsch, 1967, p. 164). For therapeutic purposes, it may be useful to explore as many meanings as possible for a single event, but for scientific or explanatory purposes, it is necessary both to critically assess the plausibility of alternative explanations and then to examine the extent to which the remaining explanations supplement or conflict with one another.

A fourth possible response is to think that all of this symbolic interpretation is somewhat arbitrary, perhaps even hopelessly arbitrary. If interpretations can be generated merely by noting similarities between the event in question and earlier events and experiences, then connections "are embarrassingly easy to find" and "the number of possible (and plausible) explanations is infinite" (Spence, 1976, pp. 377, 379). It can be argued that the process of interpretation is so loose and flexible that it can be used to explain anything, and its opposite, not only once but in many different ways. A milder version of this criticism is that the process of psychodynamic interpretation is perfectly legitimate but that it has been used with insufficient constraint in this particular example.

THE CRITICAL EVALUATION OF EXPLANATORY CONJECTURES

This incident forcefully raises several basic questions about the logic of explanation in psychobiography. What procedures exist, or can be developed, for critically evaluating alternative explanations of life events? How can we know whether we do or do not have a "good" explanation of a particular event or set of events in a life history? The Van Gogh example is useful in that it pushes the explanatory endeavor further than usual by suggesting a wide range of possible interpretations, with supporting evidence for each. In doing so, it raises with unusual clarity questions about the generation of explanatory hypotheses, about the critical evaluation of such hypotheses, and about the choice among, or integration of, a variety of explanatory possibilities.

It seems helpful, following Popper (1962), to distinguish between the processes of conjecture and refutation and to make a distinction between the processes of generating and critically evaluating explanatory conjectures. The literature on Van Gogh provides an excellent example of the processes of explanatory conjecture, and can also be used to illustrate the process of critically evaluating such conjectures. Consider, for example, the hypothesis that Van Gogh may have been influenced by contemporary newspaper accounts of Jack the Ripper. This particular explanation depends on the assumption that Van Gogh read these stories in the local paper, that he noticed the ear-cutting detail mentioned in two of the fifteen stories, that it made a lasting impression on him, and that it influenced him the night he mutilated his own ear. This explanation depends on a chain of assumptions, none of which has direct empirical support, which leaves this particular conjecture relatively unsubstantiated.

In comparison, the probability that he was influenced in his actions by visions of a matador and bull may be somewhat higher (although still perhaps low on an absolute basis) in that his letters indicate that he had attended bullfights in Arles. There is evidence that he had at least witnessed this scene, and that it had made an impression on him, whereas we can only presume that he may have read about Jack the Ripper and his cutting of ears.

Consider also the theory that he identified with a prostitute by treating his own body like meat in a butcher shop. The phrase "the whore is like meat in a butcher's shop" occurred in a letter in June of 1888, six months before the ear-cutting incident. Without further supporting evidence that this image occurred to Van Gogh nearer in time to the ear-cutting incident, there is little reason to believe that it played a significant part in his self-mutilation.

Part of the evidence supporting an Oedipal interpretation of the incident also seems open to question. Gauguin did not report that Van Gogh threatened him with a razor until fifteen years after the incident; indeed, in Gauguin's account to a friend four days after the event, this was not mentioned. Gauguin left Arles for Paris immediately after Van Gogh's self-mutilation. It has been suggested by Rewald (1956) that Gauguin was concerned about the propriety of his conduct, and may have invented the threat story later as a justification for having abandoned Van Gogh in a moment of crisis.

In yet another explanation, Untermeyer (1955) suggested that Van Gogh "had cut off an ear and sent it to one of the prostitutes he and Gauguin had visited. It was a Christmas present, a return for being teased about his over-sized ears" (p. 235). There are several reasons for being suspicious of this particular explanation. As far as I have been able to determine, there is no evidence that Van Gogh was teased by the prostitute about the size of his ears. This highly relevant circumstance is not mentioned in such primary sources as Van Gogh's letters or Gauguin's memoirs or in far more extensive biographies of Van Gogh, such as Tralbaut's (1969) or Lubin's (1972), which contain detailed analyses of the ear-cutting episode. Furthermore, the same paragraph containing this assertion has at least two other factual errors in its description of the incident. Instead of supposing that Untermeyer's book of ninety-two biographical sketches has access to information unavailable to scholars such as Tralbaut, who has spent more than fifty years studying and writing about Van Gogh, it seems more reasonable to conclude that there is no reliable evidence supporting this explanatory conjecture and that the evidence was fabricated in order to produce a plausible account. Similar criticisms may be made of Meier-Graeffe's (1933) story that the prostitute had earlier asked Van Gogh for a five-franc piece, he had refused, and that she then said that "if he could not give her a five-franc piece he might at least honour her with one of his large lop-ears for a Christmas present" (p. 163).

An explanation not based on such unreliable evidence rests on Van Gogh's report several months later in the sanatorium that other patients heard words and voices, just as he had, probably because of diseased nerves of the ear. Such beliefs may have played a part in the ear-mutilation episode.

The evidence presented must, in addition to being reliable in itself, be shown to have explanatory relevance or explanatory force in relation to the events in question. This explanatory relevance may, according to various construals, be obtained through deductive use of a theory or law relating the available evidence to the event to be explained (Hempel, 1965), through identifying reasons that the agent had for acting as he or she did (Dray, 1957), or through constructing a coherent narrative linking the evidence to the event to be explained (Sherwood, 1969). Consider, for example, the explanation which suggests that Van Gogh identified with the crucified Jesus, and that in giving the mother surrogate, Rachel, a dead segment of his body, he symbolically repeated the scene on Calvary. In his presentation of the ear, Van Gogh hoped that his mother would adore him as Mary adored the crucified Jesus (Lubin, 1972, p. 180). This explanation is based on a set of symbolic equivalencies, with Vincent representing Jesus, the severed ear representing the dead body, and Rachel representing the Virgin Mary. The events of his ear-mutilation can be translated into these terms, but what is the explanatory force of such a translation? It is not sufficient to suggest such possible symbolic equivalences; it is also necessary to provide reasons for believing that such representations were causally relevant to the actual course of events, in other words, that Van Gogh, either consciously or unconsciously, made such symbolic connections and that they influenced his actions. At various times in his life, such as in his struggles to be a minister and in his compassion for the downtrodden, Van Gogh did indicate an identification with Jesus; but that the severed ear represented to him the dead body of Christ, that Rachel represented the Virgin Mary, or that images of the Calvary scene influenced his self-destructive actions that night remains to be demonstrated.

Perhaps the single most strongly supported explanatory factor in Vincent's breakdown was the perceived loss of his brother's care. Specifically, the ear-cutting incident and two later mental breakdowns coincided with learning of Theo's engagement, his marriage, and the birth of his first child. In each case, Vincent was threatened by the prospect of losing his main source of emotional and financial support, as it seemed that Theo might redirect his love and money toward his new family (Tralbaut, 1969).

A masochistic response under situations of rejection or loss of love was not alien to Van Gogh. In 1881, he had visited the parents of Kee Voss, a woman he loved but who was avoiding him. When he heard that Kee had left the house in order to avoid seeing him, Van Gogh "put his hand in the flame of the lamp and said, 'Let me see her for as long as I can keep my hand in the flame' " (Tralbaut, 1969, p. 79). They blew out the lamp and said that he could not see her. These other incidents make it seem more likely that Van Gogh's self-mutilation was influenced by a perceived loss of love from his brother.

It is no easy task to winnow through a range of explanatory hypotheses, and given limitations in the accessible evidence about historical events, it is sometimes impossible to directly test every explanatory conjecture. However, substantial progress can still be made in identifying faulty explanations and in gathering corroborative evidence in support of others. Explanations and interpretations can be evaluated in light of criteria such as (1) their logical soundness, (2) their comprehensiveness in accounting for a number of puzzling aspects of the events in question, (3) their survival of tests of attempted falsification, such as tests of derived predictions or retrodictions, (4) their consistency with the full range of available relevant evidence, (5) their support from above, or their consistency with more general knowledge about human functioning or about the person in question, and (6) their credibility relative to other explanatory hypotheses (Bromley, 1977, chap. 8; Cheshire, 1975; Crosby, 1979; Hempel, 1965, 1966; Sherwood, 1969).

For each explanatory problem we can imagine a tree of explanatory inquiries, with the trunk representing the initial question or puzzle, each limb representing an explanatory conjecture, and smaller branches off the limb representing tests of that particular hypothesis or conjecture. Any single explanatory hypothesis can be submitted to a variety of tests, with each test providing partial, although not definitive, corroboration or disconfirmation of the hypothesis.

The least developed inquiries would consist of a trunk with a single bare limb, representing a single explanatory conjecture that has received little or no critical examination. A comprehensive explanatory inquiry would resemble a well-developed tree, filled out with limbs and branches, representing a great variety of explanatory conjectures, with extensive testing of each explanatory hypothesis. This picture of an ideal tree, or of a fully rational explanatory inquiry, provides a framework for assessing the progress of particular explanatory inquiries and for visualizing what has been done in relation to what could be done.

THE SEARCH FOR SINGLE EXPLANATIONS

Psychobiographical studies of individual lives are often criticized for being open to a variety of explanations. For instance, it is claimed that Freud's case studies "suffer from the critical flaw of being open to many interpretations" (Liebert and Spiegler, 1978, p. 50). Popper (1962) states: "Every conceivable case could be interpreted in the light of Adler's theory, or equally of Freud's. . . . I could not think of any human behavior which could not be interpreted in terms of either theory. It was precisely this fact—that they always fitted, that they were always confirmed—which in the eyes of their admirers constituted the strongest argument in favour of these theories. It began to dawn on me that this apparent strength was in fact their weakness" (p. 35). Similarly, Gergen (1977) says: "The events of most people's lives are sufficiently variegated and multifarious that virtually any theoretical template can be validated. The case study simply allows the investigator freedom to locate the facts lending support to his or her pre-formulated convictions" (p. 142).

These criticisms are, I believe, overstated and apply most readily to poorly developed explanatory inquiries. It may be possible to interpret any life with any theory, but often only at the cost of distortion or selective presentation of the evidence. Any explanatory conjecture *can* be made, but not all of them stand up under critical examination. In legal proceedings, self-serving explanations of the course of events by a guilty defendant often crumble under rigorous cross-examination. Similarly, explanations of a life history using a particular theory sometimes fail to stand up under critical examination. For example, the disorders of George III had widely been seen as manic-depressive psychosis until Macalpine and Hunter (1969) persuasively reinterpreted them as symptoms of porphyria, a hereditary metabolic disturbance. Even if some evidence can be found in a life history that is consistent with a wide variety of theories, this does not mean that all of these theories provide an adequate interpretation of the events in question.

Critical testing of the claims and implications of various explanations can lead to the elimination of many of them as implausible or highly unlikely. Ideally, this process will lead to a single well-supported explanation. In some cases, though, even after a great number of unsatisfactory conjectures are eliminated, more than one explanation that is consistent with the available evidence may remain. We are sometimes faced with "many possible explanations, all of which may be equally valid theoretically and which the facts equally fit, and when this happens there is no way we can say which explanation is the most correct" (Pye, 1979, p. 53).

This problem may not be frequently encountered in everyday practice, where minimal resources are available for inquiry, where investigation ceases once a single plausible explanation is reached, or where inquiry stops once an interpretation consistent with a prevailing theoretical orthodoxy is produced. However, if an explanatory problem is extensively investigated, if it is approached from a variety of theoretical perspectives, or if it touches on conflicting social and political interests, it becomes more likely that a variety of alternative explanations will be generated.

CONCLUSION

It is sometimes suggested that the interpretation of single cases is little more than an arbitrary application of one's theoretical preferences. No doubt this happens at times, but *any* method can be poorly used. Effective use of the case study method requires not only the formulation of explanations consistent with some of the evidence but also that preferred explanations be critically examined in light of all available evidence, and that they be compared in plausibility with alternative explanations. After the implausible alternatives have been eliminated, more than one explanation consistent with the available evidence may remain, but this is far different from saying that the facts can be adequately explained in terms of any theoretical conjecture.

When faced with a puzzling historical or clinical phenomenon, investigators are sometimes too ready to accept the first psychodynamic interpretation that makes previously mysterious events appear comprehensible. The case of Van Gogh's ear illustrates the dangers of this approach, as further inquiry often yields a variety of other apparently plausible explanations. When this happens, it is not sufficient to suggest that all of the explanations may be simultaneously true; rather, the situation requires that the alternative explanatory conjectures be critically evaluated and compared in terms of their relative plausibility.

REFERENCES

Allport, G. W. *Pattern and growth in personality.* New York: Holt, Rinehart and Winston, 1961.

Anderson, J. W. The methodology of psychological biography. *Journal of Interdisciplinary History,* 1981, II, 455–75.

Bromley, D. B. *Personality description in ordinary language.* New York: Wiley, 1977.

Cheshire, N. M. *The nature of psychodynamic interpretation.* London: Wiley, 1975.

Crosby, F. Evaluating psychohistorical explanations. *Psychohistory Review,* 1979, 7(4), 6–16.

Dray, W. H. *Laws and explanation in history.* Oxford: Oxford University Press, 1957.

Gergen, K. J. Stability, change, and chance in understanding human development. In N. Datan & H. Reese (Eds.), *Life-span developmental psychology: Dialectical perspectives on experimental research.* New York: Academic Press, 1977.

Hempel, C. G. *Aspects of scientific explanation.* New York: Free Press, 1965.

———. *Philosophy of natural science.* Englewood Cliffs, N.J.: Prentice-Hall, 1966.

Hirsch, E. D., Jr. *Validity in interpretation.* New Haven: Yale University Press, 1967.

Hogan, R. *Personality theory: The personological tradition.* Englewood Cliffs, N.J.: Prentice-Hall, 1976.

Horowitz, M. J. *States of mind: Analysis of change in psychotherapy.* New York: Plenum Medical, 1979.

Liebert, R. M. & Spiegler, M. D. *Personality: Strategies and issues.* Homewood, Ill.: Dorsey Press, 1978.

Lubin, A. J. *Stranger on the earth: A psychological biography of Vincent Van Gogh.* New York: Holt, Rinehart & Winston, 1972.

Macalpine, I., & Hunter, R. *George III and the mad business.* New York: Pantheon, 1969.

Meier-Graeffe, J. *Vincent Van Gogh: A biographical study.* (J. Holroyd-Reece, Trans.). New York: Blue Ribbon Books, 1933.

Monroe, R. R. The episodic psychoses of Vincent Van Gogh. *Journal of Nervous and Mental Disease,* 1978, 166, 480–88.

Murray, H. A., et al. *Explorations in personality.* New York: Oxford University Press, 1938.

Nagera, H. *Vincent Van Gogh: A psychological study.* London: Allen & Unwin, 1967.

Popper, K. R. *Conjectures and refutations.* New York: Basic Books, 1972.

Pye, L. Letter to the editor. *Psychohistory Review,* 1979, 8 (3), 50–53.

Rewald, J. *Post-impressionism from Van Gogh to Gauguin.* New York: Museum of Modern Art, 1956.

Schneider, D. E. *The psychoanalyst and the artist.* New York: International Universities Press, 1950.

Schnier, J. The blazing sun: A psychoanalytic approach to Van Gogh. *American Imago,* 1950, 7, 143–62.

Sherwood, M. *The logic of explanation in psychoanalysis.* New York: Academic Press, 1969.

Spence, D. P. Clinical interpretation: Some comments on the nature of evidence. In T. Shapiro (Ed.), *Psychoanalysis and contemporary science* (Vol. V). New York: International Universities Press, 1976.

Westerman Holstijn, A. J. The psychological development of Vincent Van Gogh. *American Imago,* 1951, 8, 239–73.

10

Some Uses of Dynamic Psychology in Political Biography: Case Materials on Woodrow Wilson

Alexander L. George

More so than historical writing at large, biography is selective. By choosing a single individual as his concern, the biographer can focus on those aspects of the historical process which interacted most directly with his subject. The nature of this interaction and, particularly, the extent to which it is reciprocal, is one of the central problems of biography. To what extent was the behavior of the subject culturally and situationally determined? To what extent did it reflect the individuality of his personality? Though variously worded by different writers, this twofold task of the biographer is a familiar and perplexing one.

In a brief but acute statement of the problem, the Committee on Historiography emphasized that the writing of biography requires both a systematic field theory of personality and hypotheses as to social roles.[1] While agreeing with this twofold emphasis, we have chosen for several reasons to focus attention in the present article upon the need for a systematic approach to personality factors. First, it would appear that historians generally are already more favorably disposed to the cultural approach, and better prepared to employ it, than to a systematic handling of personality components in biography. Second, we wish to show by introducing concrete case materials that a systematic personality approach may be necessary and particularly rewarding in the biographical study of innovating leaders, those who attempt to reinterpret and expand the functions of existing roles or to create new roles. We are particularly interested, that is, in "role-determining" as against "role-determined" leadership. At the same time, we agree that the creation or reinterpretation of leadership roles can only be understood in the context of social-historical dynamics and the institutional setting. The "great leader," as Gerth and Mills observe, has often been a man who has successfully managed such institutional dynamics and created new roles of leadership.[2]

We shall draw upon our previously reported study of Woodrow Wilson[3] in order to demonstrate how the personality component in a biography may be handled in a systematic fashion. And we shall attempt to show that dynamic psychology provides a number of hypotheses which can supplement a cultural or role analysis of Wilson's interest in constitution-writing and which permit the biographer to view the relationship between his "Presbyterian conscience" and his political stubbornness in a new light.

SOME DEFICIENCIES OF PSYCHOLOGICAL BIOGRAPHIES

In the past three or four decades historians have occasionally turned to the new field of dynamic psychology for assistance in this task. At the same time, specialists in psychology, especially psychoanalysts, have themselves occasionally attempted to apply the insights and theories of their practice to historical figures.[4] The results of such efforts, from both sides, to merge history and psychology in the writing of political biography have not been encouraging. Even when their purpose was not to debunk a historical figure, most psychoanalytical biographies suffered from pronounced and basic deficiencies.

Three major deficiencies in this type of biography may be briefly mentioned. In the first place, in varying degrees such biographies exaggerate the purely psychological determinants of the political behavior of their subjects. In the cruder of these studies, the subject is represented as if in the grip of powerful unconscious and irrational drives which dictate his every thought and action. Even in more discriminating analyses, the revelation of human motive resulting from incisive insights into the subject's personality can easily oversimplify the complexity of motivation and political action.

Secondly, in viewing adult character and behavior as the legacy of certain early childhood experiences, psychological biographies often oversimplify the process of personality formation and the intricacy of personality structure and functioning. Such a psychological approach is by today's standards inadequate for it overlooks the relevance of important developments in "ego psychology" in the past few decades.[5] Contemporary students of personality emphasize that in the course of his development the individual develops a variety of defenses against underlying anxieties and hostilities. He may learn ways of curbing and controlling tendencies which handicap him in various situations; and he may even devise *constructive* strategies for harnessing personal needs and motivations and directing them into fruitful channels. In other words, the individual attempts to cope simultaneously with the demands of impulse, conscience and reality in developing a philosophy of life, a system of values, a set of attitudes and interests, and in choosing in various situations from among alternative courses of action.[6]

And, finally, to conclude this brief review of the major deficiencies encountered in psychological biographies, one is struck by the fact that the actions of the subject are often interpreted in ways which seem highly speculative and arbitrary. Few investigators in this field have come to grips with the admittedly difficult problem of making rigorous reconstructions of personality factors and plausible interpretations of their role in behavior from the types of historical materials usually available to the biographer. The result is that the use which the biographer makes of dynamic psychology often appears to consist in little more than borrowing certain terms and hypotheses, and superimposing them, more or less arbitrarily upon a smattering of the available historical materials concerning the subject.

PERSONALITY TYPES: THE PROBLEM OF DIAGNOSIS AND CLASSIFICATION

Typologies of personality or character are provided by most of the various schools of psychoanalysis and dynamic psychology. The depiction of a type is usually on the basis of one or more traits, or behavioral tendencies. Often, the characterization of types also includes some indication of the origins and underlying psychodynamics of that type of behavior, which enhances the usefulness of the typology to the biographer. We do not propose to review these typologies here or to attempt to assess their relative worth to the biographer.[7] Rather we wish to consider the status or nature of these personality types and some of the problems which arise in efforts to utilize them in biography.

Most of the types in question are to be understood as being general constructs, or *ideal types*. Though derived from empirical observation, they abstract and deliberately oversimplify reality.[8] Accordingly, their value to the biographer is necessarily limited, since his task is to describe and explain a particular individual in all his concreteness and complexity.

The biographer cannot be satisfied merely to label his subject as constituting an instance of, or bearing a certain resemblance to, a certain personality or character type. To do so oversimplifies the task of making fruitful use of the theories and findings of dynamic psychology and yields results of a limited and disappointing character. Many investigators whose initial attempt to use a personality approach in biography is of this character become disillusioned and abandon the task. They sense that to type their subject, as a "compulsive" for example, tends to caricature him rather than to explain very much of the richness, complexity and variety of his behavior throughout his career.

We are concerned here with a problem not always clearly recognized in the writing of psychological biographies. *Classification* is often confused with *diagnosis*. To tag the subject of the biography with a label or to pigeonhole him in one of a number of existing categories does not in itself provide what the biographer will need most: namely, a discriminating "theory," i.e., a set of assumptions or hypotheses, as to the structure and dynamics of his subject's personality system.

The "diagnosis *vs.* classification" problem also exists in clinical psychiatry where a distinction is sometimes made between the "sponge" and the "file-drawer" clinician.[9] The "sponge"-type clinician attempts to approach his patient with a relatively open mind, trying to derive a theory about that particular patient from an intensive analysis of his behavior and case history. In contrast, the "file-drawer"-type of clinician is more inclined to orient himself to the patient on the basis of general theories and past experience. The one attempts to construct a theory about the patient *de nouveau,* a theory that, as a result, may be highly particularistic; the other stresses gaining insight into the patient by making an astute classification of him on the basis of accumulated theory and experience.

The difference between these clinical approaches is mentioned here in order to point up alternative approaches available to the biographer. As will become clear, we are suggesting that though the biographer should indeed be familiar with available personality theories, he should nonetheless approach his subject as does the "sponge"-type clinician and undertake to develop as discriminating and refined a theory as possible of that particular personality.

In attempting to account for the subject's actions throughout his career, the biographer will have to make specific diagnoses of the operative state of his personality system in numerous situations. To this end, the biographer starts with as good a theory of the subject's personality as he can derive from secondary accounts and from a preliminary inspection of historical materials. Then he reviews chronologically, or developmentally, the history of his subject's behavior, attempting to assess the role that situational and personality factors played in specific instances.[10]

In utilizing a preliminary theory of the subject's personality to make specific diagnoses the biographer in a real sense also "tests" that theory. Detailed analysis of the subject's actions in a variety of individual situations provides new insights into the motivational dynamics of the subject's behavior; these insights, in turn, enable the biographer to progressively refine and improve the theory of the subject's personality with which he started. What the biographer hopes to achieve eventually is an account of the subject's personality that gives coherence and depth to the explanation of his behavior in a variety of situations and that illuminates the more subtle patterns that underlie whatever seeming "inconsistencies" of character and behavior he has displayed.

TWO USES OF PERSONALITY TYPES IN BIOGRAPHY

Despite the general nature of personality and character types, they may be of substantial use to the biographer in several ways. First, knowledge of these types assists the biographer in developing the kind of *preliminary* theory about the personality of his subject to which reference has already been made. Second, familiarity with the psychodynamics of behavior associated with a particular personality or character type provides the biographer with hypotheses for consideration in attempting to account for the actions of his subject, especially those that cannot be easily explained as adequate responses to the situation which confronted him. Let us consider these two general uses in somewhat greater detail.

A major shortcoming in many conventional biographies, including those of Wilson, is that they lack a systematic theory about the subject's personality and motivations. The biographer is usually satisfied to catalogue individual traits exhibited by the subject without exploring their possible interrelationship and their functional significance within the personality as a whole.[11] Various of Wilson's biographers,[12] for example, have called attention to his marked "conscientiousness," "stubbornness," "single-track mind," and various other traits. They have done so, however, without indicating awareness that, according to Freudian theory, these traits are commonly exhibited by "compulsive" persons.

The term "compulsive" today is commonly applied to persons whose lives are regulated by a strict super-ego, or conscience, which dominates their personalities. Perhaps not generally known, however, is the fact that this type of behavior has been carefully studied over a period of many years by many clinicians; as a result, there are a number of detailed analyses and theories of compulsiveness and the compulsive type that attempt to account for the genesis and underlying dynamics of this type of behavior. Later in this paper we shall attempt to show how this rich body of observation and theory can be used by the biographer. It suffices here to observe that biographers of Wilson, being generally unfamiliar with such materials, have not been in a position to assess the significance of individual traits displayed by Wilson in terms of their underlying dynamics.[13]

Occasionally biographers of Wilson have been able, on the basis of an intensive analysis of a particularly well-documented episode in Wilson's career, to infer or to suggest that his choice of action in a particular situation was apparently governed by personal motives other than the aims and values which he was publicly espousing.[14] But generally they have hesitated to make diagnoses of the operative state of Wilson's personality system in specific situations, to explore in any systematic fashion the complexity and deeper levels of his motivation, or to postulate in detail the role of his personality in his political behavior. Therefore, while these biographers have sensed Wilson's personal involvement in politics and called attention to his many contradictions, their portraits of Wilson's personality are inevitably somewhat flat, even though accurately depicting behavioral tendencies at a surface level.

A familiarity with personality and character types identified in the literature of dynamic psychology will assist the biographer to construct a *preliminary* theory, or model, as to the structure and functioning of his subject's personality. For this purpose there are available to the biographer a variety of typologies of personality and character. Some of these are predominantly sociopsychological rather than clinical in their conception and orientation. Not all typologies of personality are comparable, since they have been constructed from different theoretical standpoints, for different purposes and applications. An overlapping can be noted, however, particularly among some of the typologies provided by various schools of psychoanalysis. Thus, for example, the "aggressive" person in Karen Horney's system bears a substantial resemblance to the Freudian concept of the compulsive type. Similarly, Alfred Adler's central emphasis upon the drive to power and superiority as a means of compensation for real or imagined defects finds a place in many other personality theories as well.

Given the variety of alternative typologies available, the biographer must obviously consider a number of them before choosing the type or types that seem most appropriate to his subject and most useful for the specific questions about the subject's motivations and behavior he is trying to clarify.

Personality theorists, Freudian and non-Freudian, have emphasized that the type-constructs formulated by them are not pure types. Rather, they view the personality functioning of an individual as a mixture of several trends, or types, in a more or less dynamic relationship to each other. This observation applies with particular force to Wilson, in whom several diverse trends can be detected.[15] Nonetheless, the present account is limited to discussing the applicability of the compulsive type to Wilson, partly because of limitations of space and partly because we feel that the compulsive component of his personality is particularly important for illuminating the self-defeating aspects of his behavior.

In any case, having found much evidence of compulsiveness and of the compulsive syndrome in the historical accounts of his life and career, we felt justified in adopting as a tentative working theory that Wilson had a compulsive personality.

We then considered his development and behavior in detail from this standpoint, examining the voluminous documentation of his career that is available to the biographer. In doing so, we encountered increasing evidence of behavior on his part that could not easily be subsumed under the simple model of the compulsive type. This forced us to refine and elaborate the theory as to his compulsiveness, and to attempt to state the *conditions* and to characterize the *situations* in which he did and did not behave in a way (for example, stubbornly) that was in accord with the expectations explicit or implicit in the personality model with which we were working.[16]

Gradually, then, the general construct of the compulsive type (which, as already mentioned, is to be taken as an abstraction and deliberate oversimplification of reality) was modified and brought into consonance with the complexities encountered in the individual case at hand. The point was reached when the picture of Wilson's personality that was emerging became too complex to be retained within the bounds of the compulsive model with which we had started. What remained of that model or theory was the notion of an important compulsive component in his personality and functioning. This component, we shall attempt to show, remained of considerable value as an explanatory principle for some of Wilson's political behavior that has puzzled and distressed many of his contemporaries and biographers.

Another major use of typologies and theories of personality to the biographer is that of providing alternative hypotheses for consideration in attempting to account for the actions and behavioral patterns of his subject. Such general hypotheses are not ready-made explanations to be employed arbitrarily or to be superimposed upon the data. Rather, as a statement of the dynamics of behavior and motivation often or typically associated with a certain personality type, they may serve to orient the biographer's effort to explain the actions of his subject.[17] A familiarity with such hypotheses broadens and deepens the biographer's assessment of the aims and values that the subject pursues in a given situation or in a series of situations. Furthermore, it sensitizes him to historical evidence of the possible operation of unconscious or unstated motives he might otherwise overlook.

During the preparation of our study of Wilson we combed the technical literature for hypotheses about the dynamics of motivation and behavior associated with compulsiveness that might illuminate the nature of Wilson's personal involvement in political activities.[18] We hoped to find clues to certain inept and apparently irrational actions on his part and to discover, if possible, a consistent pattern or thread in the various. inconsistencies of behavior and character he displayed.

If Wilson is not the simple clinical stereotype of a compulsive, neither can he be regarded as a full-blown neurotic. True, one cannot read, for example, Karen Horney's insightful and penetrating descriptions of neurotic drives and of the neurotic character structure without being struck by the applicability of much of what she says to Wilson. But these descriptions are applicable only to a certain point and, upon reflection, one is on balance equally or more impressed with the extent to which Wilson's behavior and career *diverge* from those of her patients. This divergence from the clinical picture concerns precisely the critical question whether the neurotically disposed individual is able to deal adequately with his conflicts and hence retains the ability to function effectively.

For Wilson was, after all, a highly successful person. He was able to overcome a severe disturbance in childhood development; thereafter, not only did he keep fairly well in check the compulsive and neurotic components of his personality but he succeeded in large measure in harnessing them constructively to the achievement of socially productive purposes.[19] To the clinical psychologist, therefore, Wilson is interesting as much because he was able to overcome childhood difficulties and to perform as successfully as he did in public life, as he is because of the pathological pattern of self-defeating behavior he tended to repeat on several occasions during his public career.[20]

COMPULSIVENESS AND THE COMPULSIVE TYPE

To indicate briefly what is meant by compulsiveness and the compulsive type of personality is not an easy task since these concepts are employed somewhat differently within the various theoretical schools which comprise dynamic psychology. The point to be made here is that the existence of different theoretical orientations and, particularly, of important lacunae in knowledge and theory within the field of dynamic psychology need not prevent the biographer from making fruitful use of systematic personality theory as a source of hypotheses that serve to orient and give direction to his own research.[21]

In any case, the usefulness of the technical literature to the biographer will be enhanced if the distinction is kept in mind between the question of the *origins* of compulsiveness and compulsive traits, about which there are various views, and the *dynamics* of such behavior, about which there is less disagreement. Similarly, the biographer will observe that specialists seem able to agree more readily on a characterization of the quality of compulsive behavior than on a list of specific traits common to all compulsive persons.

In Freudian theory various correlations are predicted between disturbances of different stages in libido development and the emergence of certain adult character traits. Disturbances in one of these stages of development leads, according to the theory, to the presence of orderliness, stinginess, and stubbornness in adult behavior.[22] These are general traits, or broad tendencies, that manifest themselves more specifically in a variety of ways. By combing the technical literature one can easily construct a richer, more elaborate list of traits which together comprise the syndrome or constellation.[23]

Thus, for example, the general trait "orderliness" may manifest itself in (a) "cleanliness" (corporeal, symbolic); (b) "conscientiousness" (single-track mind, concentration, drive, pedantism, reliability, punctuality, punctiliousness and thoroughness); (c) "regularity" (according to spatial and temporal aspects); (d) "plannedness"; (e) "norm conformity."[24]

Most personality and character types are usually described, at least in the first instance, in terms of certain manifest behavioral traits such as those that have been listed. If the description of a type does not link the traits in question with a theory of personality structure and motivational dynamics, the type-construct will obviously be of little value for motivational and situational analysis of an individual's behavior. At the same time, however, it is overly sanguine to expect that relationships between most manifest behavior traits and their inner, subjective functions for the personality will be of a simple one-to-one character. For, as clinical psychologists have particularly emphasized, the same item of manifest behavior may fulfill different functions for different personalities or, at different times, for the same individual. Particularly the political and social behavior of an individual, in which the biographer is most interested, is not likely to reflect single motives; it is more likely to be the outcome of a complex interplay of several motives and of efforts on the part of the person to adjust inner needs and strivings to one another as well as to external reality considerations.

A personality type construct is potentially more useful, therefore, if it is associated with a more or less distinctive type of motivational dynamics, whether or not this be invariably accompanied by a set of distinctive behavioral traits.

From this standpoint, leaving aside for the present the question of its validity, the Freudian concept of the compulsive type is a particularly rich one in that it includes, in addition to the syndrome of traits already noted, a rather explicit and detailed set of structural-dynamic hypotheses of this kind.

We shall not attempt to recapitulate the rather involved and technical set of structural-dynamic hypotheses associated with the compulsive type in Freudian theory. Of immediate interest here is the fact that orderliness and stubborness in persons of this type are said to derive in part from a desire for power or domination, which in turn is said to be related to a more basic need for self-esteem, or security.[25] Thus, according to the technical literature compulsives often show a marked interest in imposing orderly systems upon others, an activity from which they derive a sense of power. They also hold fast obstinately to their own way of doing things. They dislike to accommodate themselves to arrangements imposed from without, but expect immediate compliance from other people as soon as they have worked out a definite arrangement, plan or proposal of their own.

In the spheres of activity in which they seek power gratifications, compulsives are sensitive to interference. They may take advice badly (or only under special circumstances). Often they exhibit difficulties in deputing work to others, being convinced at bottom that they can do everything (in this sphere) better than others. This conviction is sometimes exaggerated to the point that they believe they are unique. Negativeness, secretiveness and vindictiveness are traits often displayed by compulsives. (Considerable evidence of most of these traits and tendencies, too, can be found in the historical materials on Wilson, many of them being noted by contemporaries and biographers.)[26]

While particularly that aspect of Freudian theory that regards interferences with libido development as the genesis of adult character traits has been criticized, the existence of certain constellations of adult traits, as in this instance, is less controversial and, in fact, appears to enjoy some empirical support.[27]

In revisions and elaborations of Freudian theory somewhat less emphasis is often placed upon specifying a distinctive content of compulsive behavior. Karen Horney, for example, regards compulsiveness as a characteristic quality of all neurotic needs. Thus, the craving for affection, power and prestige, and the ambition, submissiveness and withdrawal which different neurotics manifest all have a desperate, rigid, indiscriminate and insatiable quality, i.e., the quality of compulsiveness.[28]

Much of common to various of these formulations has been summarized in Harold D. Lasswell's account of the functional role of the compulsive dynamism in the personality system and of the general character of the circumstances in which it is adopted.[29] Thus, the compulsive dynamism is one of several possible defensive measures a child may adopt as a way out of an acute tension-producing situation that may arise during the course of socialization and learning. Tension is produced when a relatively elaborate set of requirements are imposed upon the child and reinforced by a system of rewards and punishments of a special intensity and applied in such manner so that deprivations and indulgences are balanced. One possible defensive measure against the ensuing tension is the adoption of a blind urge to act with intensity and rigidity, i.e., the dynamism of compulsiveness.

The reasons and conditions for the emergence of compulsiveness are, as has been suggested, somewhat difficult to formulate precisely. However, in making use of available knowledge of the compulsive personality for purposes of political biography, an answer to the causal question is not essential. Whatever creates a given personality dynamism, the dynamism itself—which is what interests the biographer the most—can be fairly readily identified in accounts of the subject's behavior.

In Wilson's case, even the circumstances under which the compulsive dynamism was adopted are richly suggested in materials collected by the official biographer.[30] Thus, accounts of early efforts at the boy's education, in which the father played a leading role, strongly suggest the sort of acute tension-producing situation that, we have already noted, is considered by specialists as predisposing to the adoption of the compulsive dynamism. This, however, evidently was not Wilson's initial method of coping with the tension-inducing situation; rather, for quite a while his method of defense took the form of a tendency to withdraw from the situation. For the time being the boy was unable, perhaps out of fear of failure, or unwilling, perhaps out of resentment, to cooperate with his father's efforts to advance his intellectual development. Wilson's early "slowness" (which specialists today might well consider a case of reading retardation based on emotional factors) was a matter of considerable concern to his family; it manifested itself most strikingly in his not learning his letters until he was nine and not learning to read readily until the age of eleven.[31]

At about this time the boy showed signs of beginning to cooperate actively with his father's efforts to tutor him and to make prodigious efforts to satisfy the perfectionist demands that the Presbyterian minister levied upon his son.[32] One can only speculate at the reasons for the change at this time; possibly it was connected with the birth of a younger brother when Wilson was ten. (Wilson had two older sisters but no younger brothers or sisters until this time; he himself recalled that he had clung to his mother and was laughed at as a "mama's boy" until he was a great big fellow.)

In any case, it is easy thereafter to find evidence of a compulsive bent to the young adolescent's personality. It requires no great familiarity with the technical literature on such matters to detect indications of compulsiveness in the youth's extreme conscientiousness, the manner in which he drove himself repeatedly to physical breakdowns, and the singleness of purpose he displayed in applying himself to the task of achieving knowledge and skill in the sphere of competence—politics and oratory—with which he quickly identified his ambitions.[33]

WILSON'S INTEREST IN CONSTITUTIONS

In the remainder of this paper we should like to develop the case, mainly by way of illustrative materials from the study of Wilson, for supplementing cultural and historical components in biography by an intensive and relatively systematic appraisal of personality.

A number of Wilson's biographers, including the official biographer,[34] have been struck by the interest in constitutions he displayed from early youth. Beginning in his fourteenth year he wrote or revised a half dozen constitutions, an activity that culminated in the Covenant of the League of Nations. It is our thesis that this activity on his part reflects the type of interest in order and power that compulsive persons often display. (See above, p.140.) In other words, he was motivated in part (though not exclusively) by a desire to impose orderly systems upon others, deriving therefrom a sense of power or domination.

The historian will quickly object, and rightly so, offering a more obvious counter-hypothesis, which is certainly plausible; namely that Wilson's interest in writing constitutions was culturally determined. After all, it was part of the belief system of the age that progress in human affairs was to be achieved by such instrumentalities as better constitutions, institutional reform, etc. The fact that Wilson wrote or revised many constitutions, therefore, does not necessarily attest to a personal interest in order and power.

Is it possible to demonstrate that Wilson's motivation in the matter did not stem exclusively from identification with a role that was socially approved? Or is such a question entirely out of the reach of the historian? In the following remarks we shall attempt to show that such questions are capable of being dealt with on the basis of the materials and method of the historian.

First, why Wilson and not someone else? Why, in other words, did the belief system in question impress itself particularly on Wilson? Is it not more than a coincidence that in every club he joined as a youth he seized the earliest opportunity, often making it the first order of business, to revise its constitution in order to transform the club into a miniature House of Commons? Granted that constitution-making was part of the existing cultural and political ethos and that admiration for the British system was already widespread among American students of government, why should the task of revising the constitution and political structure of these groups always fall to Wilson? Why were none of these constitutions revised along desirable lines by others, before Wilson joined these clubs? It would seem that among his contemporaries it was Wilson who found constitution-making a particularly attractive occupation. The readiness with which he accepted for himself a role that was, to be sure, culturally sanctioned makes the inference plausible that personal motives were strongly engaged by the possibility that constitution writing afforded of ordering the relations of his fellow-beings.[35]

Secondly, what evidence can be found of an unconscious motive or need to impose orderly systems upon others? If such a motive exists, we may expect appropriate pleasurable feelings to ensue from its gratification. However, we cannot reasonably expect that the pleasure experienced by the individual in such instances will be fully articulated under ordinary circumstances. Hence, in the type of historical materials on the subject's inner life usually available to the biographer we can expect only episodic and fragmentary evidence of the fact that an activity on his part has satisfied deeply felt personality needs. This is in fact what we find in this case. For example, after rewriting the constitution of the Johns Hopkins debating society and transforming it into a "House of Commons," Wilson reported to his fiancee the great pleasure he had derived from the project: "It is characteristic of my whole self that I take so much pleasure in these proceedings of this society. . . . I have a sense of power in dealing with men collectively that I do not feel always in dealing with them singly."[36]

That constitution-writing had a deep personal meaning for Wilson is further suggested by the fact that such activities were always instrumental to his desire to exercise strong leadership. It is rather obvious even from historical accounts that rewriting constitutions was for Wilson a means of restructuring those institutional environments in which *he* wanted to exercise strong leadership. He wished to restructure the political arena in these instances in order to enhance the possibility of influencing and controlling others by means of oratory. This was a skill in which he was already adept as an adolescent and to the perfection of which he assiduously labored for years. In the model House of Commons which Wilson created, and in which as the outstanding debater he usually became "Prime Minister," independent leadership was possible and, as Wilson had foreseen, the skillful, inspirational orator could make his will prevail.[37]

From an early age, then, Wilson's scholarly interest in the workings of American political institutions was an adjunct of his ambition to become a great statesman. He wished to exercise power with great initiative and freedom from crippling controls or interference. The relationship between Wilson's theories of leadership and his own ambitions and changing life situation, which we cannot recapitulate here, is revealing in this respect.[38] Suffice it to say that when Wilson's career development is studied from this standpoint considerable light is thrown on the intriguing question of the role of personal motivations in political inventiveness and creativity. Political psychologists have hypothesized that a compulsive interest in order and power is often to be found in strong political leaders who were great institution-builders and who made it their task to transform society. The case study of Wilson lends support to this general hypothesis.

To posit such personal, unconscious components in the political motivation of some leaders by no means excludes the simultaneous operation of cultural determinants. There is no doubt in Wilson's case that his personal interest in order and power was defined and channelized by the cultural and political matrix of the times. Moreover, concrete opportunities to rewrite constitutions and to exercise and perfect his talents as orator-leader were provided by existing situations in which he found himself or that he actively sought out.

Thus, the external situation in which the individual exists necessarily defines and delimits the field in which personality develops and in which personality needs and traits find expression. On the other hand, the interaction between the personality of a political leader and the milieu in which he operates may be, in an important sense, a reciprocal one. A leader's basic needs and values, his motives and dispositions, shape his perception of the situations that confront him and influence his definition and evaluation of the choices of action open to him.[39]

What is gained by attributing motivations of this character to a political leader? In this case, what difference does it make whether Wilson's interest in writing constitutions had the type of personal motivation in question? The postulate of a deep-seated, unconscious interest in imposing orderly systems upon others as a means of achieving a sense of power, we believe, accounts in part (but only in part) for Wilson's peculiar involvement in the League Covenant and in the making of the peace, the many strands of which we have attempted to document in our book. The biographer who is sensitive to the possible role of unconscious motivation is struck, for example, by the fact that it was Wilson's constant concern to reserve to himself final authorship of the Covenant, even though none of the ideas that entered into it were original with him, and that he appeared to derive peculiar pleasure from giving his own stamp to the phraseology of the document.[40]

Similarly, the postulate that Wilson derived from constitution-writing gratification of unconscious personal needs for power and domination may account in part (again only in part) for the tenacity with which he resisted efforts by various Senators to rewrite parts of the Covenant, which in some cases amounted merely to an alteration of its wording. Wilson appears to have subconsciously experienced all such efforts as attempts to "interfere" with or "dominate" him in a sphere of competence that he regarded as his own preserve.

Such an interpretation, taken alone, will seem highly speculative. The reader, we hope, will find it more plausible in the context of the theory of Wilson's personality that we have worked out and utilized in detail for purposes of analyzing Wilson's entire development and career. Briefly paraphrased here, the theory is that political leadership was a sphere of competence Wilson carved out for himself (from early adolescence on!) in order to derive therefrom compensation for the damaged self-esteem branded into his spirit as a child. Particularly when performing in his favored role as interpreter and instrument of the moral aspirations of the people, he considered himself as uniquely endowed and virtually infallible. His personality needs were such that in the sphere of competence, which he regarded as peculiarly his own, he had to function "independently" and without "interference" in order to gain the compensatory gratification he sought from the political arena. These we believe to have been the underlying dynamics of his somewhat autocratic style of leadership to which many contemporaries and biographers have called attention.[41]

THE RELATIONSHIP BETWEEN WILSON'S MORALITY AND HIS STUBBORNNESS

The extraordinary role of "conscience" and "stubbornness" in Wilson's political behavior has been noted by numerous of his contemporaries and biographers. It has often been said that Wilson's refusal to compromise on certain notable occasions, particularly as President of Princeton and as President of the United States, was a reflection of his "Presbyterian conscience." When great principles were at stake, as on these occasions, he could not bring himself to compromise. In such situations Wilson characteristically portrayed himself as confronted by a choice between dishonorable compromise of principles and an uncompromising struggle for moral political goals. Accordingly, for him, there could be no alternative but to fight for truth and morality against all opposition, whatever the consequences.

No matter that others (including careful historians such as Arthur S. Link)[42] find his characterization of the situation in these terms unconvincing; that in fact Wilson was not really confronted by such an unpleasant either-or choice. The fact remains that *Wilson* saw it thus. However much one may deplore the political consequences of his refusal to compromise, so the argument goes, surely the only valid conclusion that can be drawn is that Wilson was possessed by an unusually strong sense of morality and rectitude that exercised a determining influence upon his political behavior.

It has seemed plausible, therefore, to attribute great importance to the Presbyterian culture in which Wilson was reared and from which, to condense this familiar thesis, he derived his unusual conscience and sense of morality.

Such a thesis must cope with various questions that can be legitimately raised. For example: If Wilson's refusal to compromise in certain instances is simply a matter of his Presbyterian conscience, then what of the numerous instances in which that same conscience was no bar to highly expedient, if not opportunistic political behavior on his part?[43] Clearly, at the very least a more refined theory as to the nature of the Presbyterian conscience and of its influence on political behavior is needed.

This general question is merely posed here. Instead of pursuing it further on this occasion let us consider, rather, the usefulness of looking at the relationship between Wilson's morality and his political stubbornness in terms of what is known about the dynamics of the compulsive type. To examine the problem of Wilson in these terms is not to deny the importance of his Presbyterian upbringing or related cultural factors. Nor does it thereby ignore the possibility, which need not be explored here, that compulsive personalities are or were frequently to be found among members of the Presbyterian subculture. Indeed, the Presbyterian ethos no doubt provided reinforcement and rationalization for Wilson's stubbornness. We have elsewhere observed that such a creed produces men of conviction who find it possible to cling to their principles no matter what the opposition. The feeling that they are responsible, through their conscience, only to God, gives them a sense of freedom from temporal authority and the opinions of their fellow men.[44]

The problem of Wilson's convictions that he was "right" in refusing to compromise, and was acting in conformity with moral standards, however, is more complex than it appears at first glance, as we will try to show.

The analysis of "stubborn" behavior in compulsive personalities indicates that it is often a form of aggression. Thus aggressive tendencies, usually repressed, find expression in situations that actually comprise, or can be represented by the individual to himself as comprising, struggles on behalf of goals that receive strong endorsement by the conscience. The operative mechanism is referred to as "idealization" and has been described in the following terms: "The realization that an ideal requirement is going to be fulfilled brings to the ego an increase in self-esteem. This may delude it into ignoring the fact that through the idealized actions. There is an expression of instincts that ordinarily would have been repressed. . . .the ego relaxes its ordinary testing of reality and of impulses so that instinctual [in this case, aggressive] impulses may emerge relatively uncensored."[45] One is reminded in this connection of Wilson's repeated expressions of his "pleasure" and "delight" at an opportunity for a good fight, on behalf of a good cause, and his highly aggressive outbursts against opponents who blocked his high moral purposes. The instinctual nature of these eruptions is suggested by their extreme and intemperate quality; they were often personally unbecoming as well as politically inexpedient, and on occasion left Wilson shortly thereafter much chagrined at his loss of self-control.

Whatever the satisfactions of an uncompromising fight for what is "right," it may lead the compulsive person into essentially immoral behavior, behavior which strongly conflicts with role requirements and expectations. Given a culture in which political power is shared and in which the rules of the game enjoin compromise among those who participate in making political decisions for the community, to insist stubbornly that others submit to your own conception of what is truth and morality may in fact contravene political morality. The "right" thing for Wilson to do in the critical phases of his struggles at Princeton and with the Senate in the League matter, in terms of the prevailing political mores, was to have worked together with others who legitimately held power in order to advance as far as possible towards desirable political goals.

Wilson was well aware of this requirement. As a historian and astute student of American political institutions, he knew very well that the "right" thing for a statesman to do is to be practical and accomplish what he can. And he had expressed himself often on this very problem. In an address before the McCormick Theological Seminary, in the fall of 1909, for example, he had said: "I have often preached in my political utterances the doctrine of expediency, and I am an unabashed disciple of that doctrine. What I mean to say is, you cannot carry the world forward as fast as a few select individuals think. The individuals who have the vigor to lead must content themselves with a slackened pace and go only so fast as they can be followed. They must not be impractical. They must not be impossible. They must not insist upon getting at once what they know they cannot get."[46]

However, at several critical junctures in his public career, when he found his righteous purposes blocked by opponents who would not bend to his will, Wilson did not do the "right" thing; he did not compromise or accommodate, even when friends and political associates enjoined him to do so. Rather, he stubbornly persisted in his course and helped bring about his own personal defeat and the defeat of worthwhile measures which he was championing.

It seems, then, that we are confronted here by a form of self-defeating behavior in which the role of "conscience" in political stubbornness is perhaps much more complex than is implied in the familiar thesis of Wilson's "Presbyterian conscience" and his stiff-necked "morality."

But why must stubborn refusal to compromise be pushed to the point of self-defeat and the frustration of desirable legislation if not for Wilson's stated reason that he would have found it immoral to compromise great principles? Once again the literature on compulsiveness provides an alternative set of hypotheses with which to assess the available historical data. It is our thesis, which we have tried to document elsewhere,[47] that Wilson's stubborn refusals to compromise in situations where true morality and the requirements of his role demanded accommodation created feelings of guilt within him. He was vaguely disturbed by what he subconsciously sensed to be his own personal involvement in the fights with his opponents. The greater the stubbornness (a form of aggression against his opponents), the greater the inner anxiety at violating the moral injunction to compromise, which was a very real requirement of his political conscience.

This predicament was worked out in the following manner: stubborn refusal to compromise was maintained to the point where Wilson could demonstrate his "moral superiority" over his opponents. This could be achieved by manipulating the situation so that his opponents were also involved in "immoral" behavior, for example, by permitting their dislike of Wilson to warp their political good sense, by conspiring to defeat Wilson despite the merits of the issue at stake, by refusing to support desirable proposals just because he was championing them, etc. Thus, stubbornness was maintained so that, should it not succeed in forcing the capitulation of his opponents, it would provoke his defeat by selfish and immoral opponents. Thereby, he could at least assuage his anxiety and guilt for, whatever his "crime," it was outweighed by the demonstration in defeat of his "moral superiority" over his opponents.

These, we believe, were the underlying dynamics of the search for martyrdom which other writers[48] as well have seen in Wilson's ill-fated Western speaking tour on behalf of the League of Nations. Whether the available historical materials which we have cited in support of this thesis render it sufficiently plausible and convincing must be left to individual judgment. Instead of rephrasing the evidence and reasoning already presented on its behalf in our book, we shall confine ourselves here to noting that the mechanisms described above, as underlying the possible quest for martyrdom, are very well described in the literature on compulsive stubbornness.

> What is usually called stubbornness in the behavior of adult persons is an attempt to use other persons as instruments in the struggle with the super-ego. By provoking people to be unjust, they strive for a feeling of moral superiority which is needed to increase their self-esteem as a counter-balance against the pressure of the super-ego.[49]

> The stubborn behavior is maintained the more obstinately, the more an inner feeling exists that it is impossible to prove what needs to be proven, and that one is actually in the wrong. . . . The feeling, "Whatever I do is still less wicked than what has been done to me," is needed as a weapon against the super-ego and, if successful, may bring relief from feelings of guilt.[50]

In brief, therefore, the very "morality" in terms of which Wilson could initially legitimize the open expression of pent-up aggression and hostility ensnared him in profoundly immoral political behavior. His repeated protestations as the struggle with his opponents wore on that he had to do what was "right" and what conscience demanded were, in fact, a cloak for activity that was contrary to the requirements of his leadership role and some of the demands of his own conscience. The repeated protestations that he was acting merely as an instrument of the people's will and had no personal stakes in the battle were the external manifestation of desperate efforts to still inner doubts of the purity of his motivation in refusing compromise and to controvert the knowledge that gnawed from within that he was obstructing his own cause.[51] We have here an instance not of stern morality but of a type of rationalization which has been labelled the "moralization" mechanism, i.e., a tendency to interpret things as if they were in accord with ethical standards when they are actually (and subconsciously known to be) in striking contrast to them.[52]

Thus did Wilson go down to tragic defeat. A subtle personal involvement in political struggle prevented him from anchoring his actions in the profound wisdom of the maxim: "There comes a time in the life of every man when he must give up his principles and do what he thinks is right."[53]

THE SELF-DEFEATING PATTERN IN WILSON'S CAREER

The thesis of a self-defeating dynamism in Wilson's personality gains in plausibility from evidence that it was part of a pattern which tended to repeat itself under similar conditions during his career.[54] A number of Wilson's biographers have noted that Wilson's defeat in the fight for the League fits into a pattern of behavior he had displayed earlier in public life. Thus, after a painstaking analysis of the bitter and unsuccessful struggle Wilson waged with his opponents at Princeton, Professor Link was led to remark that "a political observer, had he studied carefully Wilson's career as president of Princeton University, might have forecast accurately the shape of things to come during the period when Wilson was president of the United States." Calling the former period a microcosm of the latter, Link ascribed to Wilson's uncompromising battles both in the graduate college controversy and in the League of Nations battle with the Senate "the character and proportions of a Greek tragedy."[55]

Similarly, writing many years before, Edmund Wilson, the distinguished man of letters, saw in the same events of Wilson's career evidence of a curious cyclical pattern that can be detected in the lives of other historical figures as well:

> It is possible to observe in certain lives, where conspicuously superior abilities are united with serious deficiencies, not the progress in a career or vocation that carries the talented man to a solid position or a definite goal, but a curve plotted over and over again and always dropping from some flight of achievement to a steep descent into failure.[56]

The type of enigmatic personality described here by a humanist is one which has been of long-standing interest to the clinician as well. Influenced by Freud's earlier description and analysis of neurotic careers, Franz Alexander in 1930 presented what has become a classical psychoanalytical account of this general character type.[57] In many cases, driven by unconscious motives, persons of this type alternate between committing a transgression and then seeking punishment. Thereby, their careers may exhibit "alternating phases of rise and abrupt collapse," a pattern indicating that "aggressive and self-destructive tendencies" run along together. "The neurotic character," Alexander continues, "has fired the literary imagination since time immemorial. They are nearly all strong individualities who struggle in vain to hold the anti-social tendencies of their nature in check. They are born heroes who are predestined to a tragic fate."

Let us examine more closely the repetitive pattern of behavior that observers working from different standpoints have detected in his career.[58] As President of Princeton, Governor of New Jersey, and President of the United States, Wilson gained impressive early successes only to encounter equally impressive political deadlocks or set-backs later on. He entered each of these offices at a time when reform was the order of the day, and with a substantial fund of goodwill to draw upon. In each case there was an initial period during which the type of strong leadership he exercised in response to his inner needs coincided sufficiently with the type of leadership the external situation required for impressive accomplishment. He drove the faculty and trustees at Princeton to accomplish an unprecedented series of reforms. The New Jersey legislature of 1911 was a triumph of productivity in his hands. Later, he exacted a brilliant performance from the Sixty-Third Congress of the United States.

We are forced to recognize, therefore, that Wilson's personal involvements contributed importantly to the measure of political accomplishment he attained. In each position, however, his compulsive ambition and imperious methods helped in time to generate the type of bitter opposition that blocked further successes and threatened him with serious defeats. Wilson was skillful in the tactics of leadership only so long as it was possible to get exactly what he wanted from the trustees or the legislature. He could be adept and inventive in finding ways of mobilizing potential support. He could be, as in the first year of the Governorship and in the "honeymoon" period of the Presidency, extremely cordial, if firm; gracious, if determined; and generally willing to go through the motions of consulting and granting deference to legislators whose support he needed. It is this phase of his party leadership that excited the admiration of contemporaries, historians, and political scientists alike. It is essential to note, however, that Wilson's skillfulness in these situations always rested somewhat insecurely upon the expectation that he would be able to push through his proposed legislation in essentially unadulterated form. (As Wilson often put it, he was willing to accept alterations of "detail," but not of the "principles" of his legislative proposals.)

Once opposition crystalized in sufficient force to threaten the defeat or marked alteration of his proposed legislation, however, Wilson was faced with a different type of situation. Skillful political behavior—the logic of the situation—now demanded genuine consultation to explore the basis of disagreement and to arrive at mutual concessions, bargains, and formulas that would ensure passage of necessary legislation. In this type of situation Wilson found it difficult to operate on the basis of expediential considerations and at times proved singularly gauche as a politician. Once faced with genuine and effective opposition to a legislative proposal *to which he had committed his leadership aspirations,* Wilson became rigidly stubborn and tried to force through his measure without compromising it.[59] The greater the opposition, the greater his determination not to yield. He must win on his own terms or not at all!

Personally involved in these struggles, Wilson was incapable of realistically assessing the situation and of contriving skillful strategies for dividing the opposition and winning over a sufficient number to his side. Both at Princeton and later in the battle with the Senate over ratification of the treaty, Wilson was incapable of dealing effectively in his own interest with the more moderate of his opponents. In the heat of the battle, he could tolerate no ambiguity and could recognize no legitimate intermediate position. He tended to lump together all of his opponents. In such crises, therefore, his leadership was strongly divisive rather than unifying. He alienated the potential support of moderate elements who strongly sympathized with his general aims but felt some modification of his proposals to be necessary. Instead of modest concessions to win a sufficient number of moderates over, he stubbornly insisted upon his own position and rudely rebuffed their overtures, thus driving them into the arms of his most bitter and extreme opponents.[60] It was his singular ineptness in the art of political accommodation, once the battle was joined, which was at bottom responsible for some of Wilson's major political defeats at Princeton and in the Presidency.

In these situations—when opposition crystalized and threatened to block Wilson's plan—the desire to succeed in achieving a worthwhile goal, in essence if not in exact form, became of less importance than to maintain equilibrium of the personality system. He seems to have experienced opposition to his will in such situations as an unbearable threat to his self-esteem. To compromise in these circumstances was to submit to domination in the very sphere of power and political leadership in which he sought to repair his damaged self-esteem. Opposition to his will, therefore, set into motion disruptive anxieties and brought to the surface long-smouldering aggressive feelings that, as a child, he had not dared to express. The ensuing struggle for his self-esteem led, on the political level, to the type of stubborn, self-defeating behavior and the search for moral superiority over his opponents that we have already described.

NOTES

1 *The Social Sciences in Historical Study: A Report of the Committee on Historiography,* Social Science Research Council, Bulletin 64, 1954, pp. 153–54. By "field theory of personality" the Committee had in mind one which takes into account the fact that " 'external factor,' not just childhood training, set norms and incentives and influence motivation and codes of conduct," (See also ibid., p. 61.).

2 Hans Gerth and C. Wright Mills, *Character and Social Structure* (New York, 1953), chapter xiv, "The Sociology of Leadership," See also fn. 35, pp. 87, 88.

3 A. L. George and J. L. George, *Woodrow Wilson and Colonel House: A Personality Study* (New York, 1956). (Hereafter referred to as *WW & CH.*)

4 For a recent review of such studies see John A. Garraty, "The Interrelations of Psychology and Biography," *Psychological Bulletin* 51, No. 6 (1954): 569–82. See also Gordon W. Allport, *The Use of Personal Documents in Psychological Science,* Social Science Research Council Bulletin 49, 1942.

5 For a brief review of this development see Calvin S. Hall and Gardner Lindzey, *Theories of Personality* (New York, 1957), pp. 64–65, 271–72.

6 For a useful statement of major trends in social psychology and personality theory see Chapter 2, "Converging Approaches," in M. Brewster Smith, Jerome S. Bruner and Robert W. White, *Opinions and Personality* (New York, 1956).
For a useful summary and synthesis of the ways in which unconscious needs find expression in political behavior see Robert E. Lane, *Political Life* (Glencoe, Illinois, 1959), chapter 9.

7 Useful accounts of some of these typologies, and others drawn partly from social-psychological standpoints, are available in Ruth L. Monroe, *Schools of Psychoanalytic Thought* (New York, 1955); Harold D. Lasswell, *Power and Personality* (New York, 1948); Robert E. Lane, "Political Character and Political Analysis," *Psychiatry* 16(1953):387–98. On trends in the study of political leadership, see Lester G. Seligman, "The Study of Political Leadership," *American Political Science Review* 44(December 1950):904–15.

8 On this general point, see Gardner Murphy, *Personality: A Biosocial Approach to Origins and Structure* (New York and London, 1974), pp. 749–52.

9 I am indebted to Dr. David Hamburg, Chairman, Psychiatry Department, Stanford University, for bringing this to my attention.

10 The need for developmental analysis of personality that starts with some preliminary theory, or set of hypotheses, has been frequently emphasized by those writing on the problems of biography. See for example the following statement by the historian Thomas C. Cochran: "Faced with the task of constructing an interpretive biography, the investigator trained in

psychological methods would formulate hypotheses as he started work on the early life of his subject-hypotheses as to what sort of person the man would prove to be when he later became involved in different types of situations. A systematic testing of these hypotheses against the evidence provided at different stages in the life history would not only provide clues to the understanding of motives but would also focus the biography sharply on the processes of personality development." (In *The Social Sciences in Historical Study: A Report of the Committee on Historiography,* Social Science Research Council, Bulletin 64, 1954, p. 67.)

11   Much dissatisfaction has been expressed in recent times with the conventional "trait" approach to the study of personality and leadership. See, for example, Cecil A. Gibb, "The Principles and Traits of Leadership," *Journal of Abnormal and Social Psychology* 42(1947):267–84: Alvin Gouldner, *Studies in Leadership* (New York, 1950).

12   Among the many useful personality sketches and interpretations of Wilson see particularly those recently provided by Arthur S. Link, *Wilson: The New Freedom* (Princeton, 1956), pp. 61ff., 93–144; John A. Garraty, "Woodrow Wilson: A Study in Personality," *The South Atlantic Quarterly* 56, No. 2 (April, 1957):176–85; John Morton Blum, *Woodrow Wilson and the Politics of Morality* (Boston, 1956).
The importance of personality is emphasized particularly in Garraty's account, which runs parallel to our own at many points.

13   Thus Blum refers only parenthetically to Wilson's "compulsiveness" and his "obsessive sense of unrest" (op. cit., pp. 5, 11, 75). Though he has explored the technical literature on compulsive behavior, Blum did not attempt a methodical exploitation of it in preparing his study of Wilson. (Personal communication to the author.)
The compulsive nature of Wilson's ambition and political style, his inability to pace his demands for reform more expediently, was earlier grasped by the official biographer (Ray Stannard Baker, *Woodrow Wilson: Life and Letters* (New York, 1927), II, pp. 153, 244–45; V. p. 119); by Link (see for example Wilson: *The Road to the White House* (Princeton, 1947), pp. viii–ix, 45, 90); by Edmund Wilson, "Woodrow Wilson at Princeton," *Shores of Light* (New York, 1952), pp. 312–13; and by Edward S. Corwin, in *Woodrow Wilson: Some Princeton Memories,* ed. William Starr Myers, pp. 34–35.

14   See, for example, Arthur L. Link's perceptive account of Wilson's highly revealing reaction when his opponents at Princeton unexpectedly offered to accept a compromise proposal to which he had earlier committed himself. (Op. cit., pp. 69–71, 75–76; see also *WW & CH,* 42–43.)

15   Thus, a fuller statement of the personality trends or types that can be detected in Wilson's personality would, in Freudian terms, probably have to include reference to the "oral character" and the "neurotic character" (see pp. 92–93), as well as to the compulsive type. Similarly, if Karen Horney's typology is employed Wilson would probably have to be described as an amalgam of her "compliant," "aggressive" and "detached" personality types. See K. Horney, *Our Inner Conflicts* (New York, 1945).
It should be noted that some of the "contradictions" in Wilson's character, often noted by contemporaries and biographers, can be understood in terms of the combination of trends, or types, of which his personality was composed.

16   See *WW & CH,* pp. 115–22.

17   I have omitted from this paper a discussion of the historian's method for explaining the "subjective" side of action (the "logic-of-the-situation" approach), and of the prospects for merging it with that of the clinician's. These prospects are not unfavorable, though the task is admittedly difficult. Both the historian and the clinician (as well as the political scientist!) are interested in intensive causal analysis of the single case and employ for this purpose a variant of the same type of interpretive procedure.

18   A useful, detailed summary of theories about the dynamics of behavior in compulsives is provided in Otto Fenichel, *The Psychoanalytic Theory of Neurosis* (New York, 1945), pp. 268–310, 487–88, 530–31.

19 On this point see also *WW & CH,* p. 320.
20 We must reserve for another occasion an effort to account for Wilson's development of a viable personality organization and the ability to function as successfully as he did.
21 The fact that there are various specialized terminologies within the field of dynamic psychology and that members of the various schools at times state their differences polemically tends to obscure the wide area of fundamental agreement among them and the fact that an important body of knowledge and insight into human behavior has been gradually developed around a common dynamic point of view. Moreover, dynamic psychology has based itself more recently upon a core of assumptions common to a number of approaches to the study of behavior: psychoanalysis, social anthropology, social psychology and learning theory. (See, for example, O. H. Mowrer and C. Kluckhohn, "Dynamic Theory of Personality," in J. McV. Hunt, ed., *Personality and the Behavior Disorders,* I (New York, 1944), pp. 69–135.)
22 These traits, comprising the so-called "anal" or "anal compulsive" character, are sometimes formulated in different terms as instances of sublimations or reaction formations. Freud's statement of the type appears in his "Character and Anal Erotism," *Collected Works,* II (London, 1950), pp. 45–50. For more recent formulations, see Fenichel, loc. cit., especially pp. 278–84.
  An important restatement and interpretation of Freud's libido theory is provided by Erik H. Erikson in his *Childhood and Society* (New York, 1950). See also the attempt to clarify and elaborate operationally the Freudian character types in Henry A. Murray, *Explorations in Personality* (New York, 1938), pp. 361–85.
23 For this purpose, in addition to the sources cited in the preceding footnote, see for example, William Healy and Augusta F. Bronner, *The Structure and Meaning of Psychoanalysis as Related to Personality and Behavior* (New York, 1930); William C. Menninger, "Characterologic and Symptomatic Expressions Related to the Anal Phase of Psychosexual Development," *Psychoanalytic Quarterly* 12, 1943: 161–93.
24 In the initial phase of our research we collected a large amount of evidence of the presence of most of these orderly traits in Wilson. Contemporaries and biographers have been impressed by various orderly traits in Wilson. For example, Wilson was "a stickler for accuracy" (David Lawrence, *The True Story of Woodrow Wilson,* p. 342); he had an extraordinary ability to concentrate and compartmentalize (Baker, op. cit., II, p. 44) and himself often referred to his "single-track" mind (Alfred Maurice Low, *Woodrow Wilson—An Interpretation,* p. 282); he attempted to rigidly separate thinking and emotions and leaned over backwards to prevent private and personal considerations from interfering with public duties (Baker, op. cit., II, p. 2; III, pp. 160–61; Edith Bolling Wilson, *My Memoir,* p. 162; Joseph Tumulty, *Woodrow Wilson As I Know Him,* pp. 473–74); he was pedantic, dogmatic and fastidious as a teacher (C. W. Mosher, Jr., "Woodrow Wilson's Methods in the Classroom," *Current History* 32(June 1930):502–03; Baker, op. cit., II, p. 13); he was reliable and scrupulous in keeping his word, no matter what the inconvenience (E. B. Wilson, op. cit., p. 171; Tumulty, op. cit., p. 469); his punctuality was well-known and it was said that one could set one's watch from his comings and goings (Eleanor Wilson McAdoo, *The Woodrow Wilsons,* pp. 22, 60, 213; Lawrence, op. cit., p. 126); he was punctilious, thorough and methodical (Baker, op. cit., I, pp. 86–87, 182; E. W. McAdoo, op. cit., pp. 24, 188; E. B. Wilson, op. cit., pp. 90, 307, 347; A. S. Link, *Wilson: The Road to the White House,* p. 94); he was strikingly neat, orderly and regular in personal working habits (Baker, op. cit., II, p. 46; V. p. 138; E. W. McAdoo, op. cit., p. 20; E. B. Wilson, op. cit., p. 79).
25 The hypothesis that certain types of (compulsive or neurotic) personalities pursue power as a means of obtaining compensation for low self-esteem can be and has been divorced from the distinctive structural-dynamic framework and terminology of the Freudian school. Various versions of a similar hypothesis are provided by other schools of dynamic psychology. (See fn. 25).
26 In his personality profile of Wilson, Arthur S. Link, for example, identifies the following traits: a demand for unquestioning loyalty, egotism and a belief in the infallibility of his own

judgment, vanity and a belief in his own superior wisdom and virtue, inability to rely upon others, indulgence in narrow prejudices and vindictiveness, intolerance of advice and resentment of criticism, a tendency to equate political opposition with personal antagonism, susceptibility to flattery. (*Wilson: The New Freedom,* pp. 67–68.) In his *Wilson: The Road to the White House,* the same biographer referred to his subject as possessing an "imperious will and intense conviction," a "headstrong and determined man who was usually able to rationalize his actions in terms of the moral law and to identify his position with the divine will" (p. ix).

In compulsives, too, an overrevaluation and high development of the intellect is often found. At the same time, however, intellectualization is curiously combined with archaic features (superstitiousness and magical beliefs). It is noteworthy, therefore, that many writers (e.g., ibid, p. 94) have been struck by the curious streak of superstitiousness in Wilson, a man otherwise noted for his emphasis on the intellect and on being guided by reason.

27 See, for example, Robert R. Sears, *Survey of Objective Studies of Psychoanalytic Concepts,* Social Science Research Council Bulletin 51, 1943, pp. 67–70.

28 Karen Horney, *The Neurotic Personality of Our Time* (New York, 1937); *Our Inner Conflicts* (New York, 1945).

29 H. D. Lasswell, *Power and Personality* (New York, 1948), pp. 44–49.

30 Some of these materials are presented in volume I (pp. 36ff.) of Ray Stannard Baker, *Woodrow Wilson: Life and Letters* (New York, 1927). However, other relevant materials on Wilson's childhood, and, especially, on his relationship with his father were not included in the official biography and are to be found in the Baker Papers, Library of Congress. A fuller summary and interpretation of this material than is possible here is given in *WW & CH,* Chapter I.

31 The significance of this childhood developmental problem has been overlooked in the otherwise authoritative biography by Arthur S. Link. There is no reference to it in Link's account of Wilson's formative years. On the contrary, Link asserts that "Wilson's boyhood was notable, if for nothing else, because of his normal development." (*Wilson: The Road to the White House,* p. 2.) The fact of Wilson's "slowness" is also omitted in the biographies by Garraty and Blum, though it is mentioned (and glossed over) by Baker, op. cit., I. pp. 36–37. The stern, domineering and caustic manner of Wilson's father, a source of acute tension and discomfort for Wilson, is also muted in Baker's published account, though not in the materials which Baker collected for his biography. (See note 30 above.)

32 A belated identification with his father appears to have accompanied Wilson's adoption of the compulsive dynamism at this time. The identification with the father was extremely strong on the manifest level and was rigidly maintained throughout Wilson's lifetime. At the same time, however, feelings of inferiority vis-á-vis the father, who had been the chief instrument of Wilson's damaged self-esteem, persisted throughout Wilson's life. For this and other reasons, accordingly, we have felt it necessary to postulate that the father-son conflict persisted in Wilson at an unconscious level. (Readers familiar with the technical literature will be reminded of the Freudian theory of the Oedipal basis of the inferiority complex.) We have also postulated that aspects of Wilson's behavior in the struggles with Dean West and Senator Lodge constituted a displacement, or "acting out," of the unconscious hostility that he had experienced towards his father as a child but had not dared to express. (For a fuller statement of the thesis concerning the father-son relationship, see *WW & CH,* Chapter I, also pp. 46, 114–15, 270–73.) On the conditions under which Wilson's latent aggressive impulses could find overt expression against political opponents, see the discussion of "idealization," p. 90.

33 Baker, op. cit., I.

34 Baker, op. cit., I, pp. 45, 75–76, 94, 123–24, 148, 198–200, 302–03.

35 In more general terms we are asserting the possibility that personality needs and motives of an unconscious character may govern an individual's selection of social and political roles and that these needs and motives may infuse themselves into the individual's performance

of those roles. The fact that a person's behavior can be interpreted in terms of role theory, therefore, does not relieve the investigator from considering the possibility that aspects of basic personality are also expressing themselves in such behavior. It is incorrect, therefore, to define the problem as some proponents of role theory tend to do in terms of "role vs. personality." Rather, the interplay of role and personality needs to be considered.

36 Baker, op. cit., I, p. 199; *WW & CH,* p. 22.

37 Ibid.

38 See *WW & CH,* pp. 144–48, 321–22.

39 *WW & CH,* p. xvii.

40 See *WW & CH,* pp. 208–10, 223, 226–28.

41 This theory is a special application of a general hypothesis concerning the pursuit of power as a means of compensation for low self-estimates, which Harold D. Lasswell has extracted from the findings and theories of various schools of dynamic psychology. (See his *Power and Personality,* p. 39ff.) The hypothesis is evidently of wide, though not universal application in the study of political leaders.

We have discussed some of the problems of applying this general hypothesis to someone like Wilson, who pursued other values as well as power, in *WW & CH,* pp. 319–22, and in the paper, "Woodrow Wilson: Personality and Political Behavior," presented before a panel of the American Political Science Association, Washington, D.C., September, 1956.

As already noted, the pervasiveness of power strivings as compensation for organic or imagined defects was given early emphasis by Alfred Adler. The fruitfulness of Adler's theories for subsequent social psychological approaches to personality is now widely recognized. See, for example, Gardner Murphy, op. cit., Chapter 24, "Compensation for Interiority."

42 Wilson: *The Road to the White House,* p. 76.

43 See particularly Arthur S. Link, *Wilson: The Road to the White House,* and *WW & CH,* chapters III and IV.

44 *WW & CH,* pp. 4–5.

45 Otto Fenichel, *Psychoanalytic Theory of Neurosis,* pp. 485–86.

46 Baker, op. cit., II, p. 307.

47 *WW & CH,* pp. 290–98.

48 See, for example, Richard Hofstadter, *The American Political Tradition,* 2nd ed. (New York, 1954), pp. 281–82; Thomas A. Bailey, *Woodrow Wilson and the Great Betrayal* (New York, 1945).

49 Fenichel, op. cit., p. 279.

50 Ibid., p. 497. See also Christine Olden, "The Psychology of Obstinacy," *Psychoanalytic Quarterly* 12(1943):240–55.

51 *WW & CH,* pp. 297–98.

52 See, for example, Fenichel, op. cit., p. 486.

53 It might be added that we have encountered no evidence that Wilson subsequently ever expressed or experienced any self-doubts as to the wisdom or correctness of his refusal to compromise in the struggle to ratify the peace treaty. On the contrary, his defeat and physical breakdown seem to have provided relief from the feelings of uneasiness experienced at the time.

54 It should be emphasized that whether, to what extent, and how often the self-defeating dynamism referred to here finds expression depends upon the character of the situations encountered by the subject during his lifetime. Similarly, we have postulated that this destructive tendency was held in check to some extent by the development in Wilson's personality system of a constructive strategy whereby he generally committed his need for domination and achievement only to political projects which were about ready for realization. (On this point, not discussed further in this paper, see *WW & CH,* pp. 118, 320–22.)

55 Arthur S. Link, *Wilson: The Road to the White House,* pp. 90–91. A similar observation is made by Blum, op. cit., p. 36.

56 Edmund Wilson, "Woodrow Wilson at Princeton," reprinted in his *Shores of Light* (New York, 1952), p. 322.

57 "The Neurotic Character," *International Journal of Psychoanalysis* 11(1930):292–311. In contrast to true neurotics who squander their energy in futile inactivity, Alexander noted, persons of this character type live active and eventful lives; they "act out" repressed unconscious motives that are unacceptable to their ego. The neurotic element in such persons appears, that is, not so much in the form of circumscribed symptoms but permeates the personality and influences their entire behavior.

58 The following paragraphs are a brief paraphrase of materials presented in *WW & CH*, pp. 116–21, 320–22, and in a paper at the meetings of the American Political Science Association, Washington, D.C., September, 1956.

59 The italicized phrase is an important qualification to the general proposition. In the case of legislative proposals which were not "his" or to which he had not committed his aspirations for high achievement, for example the military "preparedness" legislation of 1915–16, Wilson was more flexible when confronted by effective Congressional opposition. (*WW & CH*, pp. 116, 121.)

60 *WW & CH*, pp. 38, 45; chapter XIV, especially 286–89.

11

The Georges' Wilson Reexamined: An Essay on Psychobiography

Robert C. Tucker

ON PSYCHOBIOGRAPHY

Forty-five years have passed since Harold Lasswell wrote into the first paragraph of *Psychopathology and Politics* the ringing declaration that "political science without biography is a form of taxidermy." The kind of biographical study needed in the discipline, if taxidermy was not to be its fate, was not conventional biography but biography as "life history." Biography as "life history," or "natural history" as Lasswell also called it, would be "concerned with facts which are *developmentally* significant,"[1] i.e., what nowadays is generally described as "psychological biography."

The distinction between psychological biography (or psychobiography for short) and conventional biography is real though not absolute. Conventional biography has been characterized by one of its scholarly practitioners as ". . . the simulation, in words, of a man's life, from all that is known about that man."[2] That is to say, it is a form of portrait painting, where the subject is a person's life and the medium of expression is language. As such it has had not only a very long history but one that shows many significant changes in life-writing conventions. Thus English biography in the nineteenth century, unlike much biography in England and elsewhere in the twentieth, observed the convention that "the fundamental reason for writing a man's life was that he was admirable."[3] Whatever the prevailing conventions, however, conventional biography has rarely been devoid of some psychological characterization of its subject—typically as an informed mind's intuitive judgment of character expressed in terms of everyday discourse.

What is distinctive of psychobiography as a scholarly enterprise is that the biographer is attempting to make sense out of the subject's life-course, or key

Reprinted from the *American Political Science Review,* vol. 71 (1977), pp. 606–18.

phases of it, *in terms of a consciously thought-out psychological interpretation of that subject's personality.* This is not to say that he will be oblivious of the role of circumstance in the life course, or that his study will not contain descriptive passages or whole sections which might just as easily appear in a regular biography of the same individual.

It follows that all psychobiographies have in common a mooring in personality theory, either in one of its particular forms (Freudian, post-Freudian, or non-Freudian) or in some eclectic combination of interpretive-theoretical orientations. Beyond this, we can draw a distinction between two different ways in which the psychobiographer may make use of the theoretical position he has selected in the effort to "make sense" out of the subject's life-course psychologically. He may, on the one hand, treat the subject as an illustrative example of a general psychological formula or paradigm that he believes is applicable, e.g., the "compulsive personality" as conceptualized in Freudian thought or the "paranoid personality" as described in clinical textbooks. Or, having used one or another formula or paradigm as a *springboard* for interpretive analysis of the individual case at hand, he may work out an individualized psychological theory or set of hypotheses concerning the personality of his subject—referring, for example, to that person's life-goal or goals as rooted in a particular character structure, pattern of motivation, and modes of response to people and situations. It seems to me that psychobiography as a form of scholarship is developing, and fruitfully so, from the first to the second sort of approach. As Alexander George has expressed it, "to tag the subject of the biography with a label or to pigeonhole him in one of a number of existing categories does not in itself provide what the biographer will need most: namely, a discriminating 'theory,' i.e., a set of assumptions or hypotheses, as to the structure and dynamics of his subject's personality system."[4]

Since, in either of these two approaches, personality theory will give guidance to the psychobiographer's interpretation of his subject, the question arises whether it matters very much which personality theory or whose psychological perspective is chosen for this purpose, so long as the psychobiographer adheres to it as rigorously as possible and follows it as far as it will take him in his interpretive quest. In short, isn't any one of the major psychological perspectives acceptable in principle as a guideline, and what possible basis is there for preferring one over another?

One could argue that it is best to avoid a comparative analysis of different theoretical perspectives, given the overlap among them and given the inevitable difficulties of adjudication. Alternatively, one may take the view, as I do, that despite difficulties, the critical task in psychobiography is to compare alternatives and try to discover which of various possible theoretical perspectives is most fruitful for dealing with the case at hand. But then the question arises: by what criteria do we decide which theoretical perspective can do more, interpretively or explanatorily, than the alternative preferred and used by the psychobiographer whose work is under consideration?

Two criteria appear particularly applicable. First, which of the two leaves the psychobiographer with a smaller residue of refractory material, of actions, characteristics, etc., that do not easily submit to explanation in terms of the given perspective? Second, which of the two is more effective for interpreting the key points or key patterns in the subject's life, those phenomena which are most significant for the subject's influence upon people and events and hence most in need of explanation by the psychobiographer of a political leader? From the standpoint of a psychobiography that attempts to be, likewise, a psychohistory— that is, a contribution to history writing as well as to life-writing—the matter of key points or patterns is often very important; and this is where the comparison of alternative modes of psychological interpretation may be most needed and most useful for scholarship.

GETTING OFF THE GROUND

Lasswell proved excessively optimistic in his early belief that biography as "natural history," or psychobiography, was close at hand.[5] Progress has in fact been slow. We might compare the recent past and present in psychobiography in political science with the dawn of the age of the heavier-than-air flying machine. Such a contraption had been conceived by various minds, inspired by a belief in its possibility, and here and there an effort was being made to construct one that would fly. Finally, a success occurred: the Wright brothers, at Kitty Hawk, got their machine off the ground and it flew. Alexander and Juliette George have in a way been the Wright brothers of psychobiography in political science. Their *Woodrow Wilson and Colonel House* has been widely appraised as a psychobiographical effort that succeeded.[6]

It may be helpful to pinpoint the sense in which the Georges succeeded. There has not been anything approaching a consensus among political scientists that a political leader's personality is a factor of potentially great or even decisive importance in explaining his conduct in the leader-role that he acquires. Many believe that the pressures and role requirements of political office, along with the political logic of the situations encountered, suffice to explain the leader's conduct; and that an individual not disposed to be responsive to these pressures and situational demands is also not likely to rise to power at all, owing to the screening process involved in any society's mode of leader selection.

The Georges demonstrate impressively, in the single but significant case of Wilson, that his performance in a succession of leader-roles was deeply affected by the psychodynamics of his personality; and portentously so, since what was involved in his personality-determined conduct in the nation's presidency was ultimately nothing less than United States entry into the League of Nations. As one early reviewer appropriately remarked in the light of such considerations, "this book is a good antidote to the irrepressible tendency of political scientists, as well as laymen, to think of high politics as something carried on by disembodied spirits, whose larger actions may vary in degree of shrewdness and fore-sight but are seldom affected by submerged and hidden passions."[7]

I fully share the view just cited, and propose to reexamine the Georges' *Wilson* in the belief that it is a work of outstanding scholarly merit and a path-finding achievement which has done much to inaugurate the psychobiographical en-terprise as a vital part of political science. Moreover, I believe any genuine classic requires to be re-reviewed from time to time as scholarship develops sufficiently to permit fresh assessment. My treatment will focus on three themes: the book's underlying Lasswellian hypothesis about political man; the Georges' application of the hypothesis; and a comparison of the resulting psychological interpretation of Wilson's character and political conduct with an alternative possible inter-pretation based upon Karen Horney's conception of the neurotic personality.

LASSWELL'S ASSUMPTIONS ABOUT POLITICAL MAN

Woodrow Wilson and Colonel House was the product of fifteen years of study and research. From the outset, it was conceived as a psychobiography as defined above. In the early phase, the Georges worked with the hypothesis that Wilson was a "compulsive personality" as that type has been conceived in Freudian the-ory. At length, they found this approach inadequate and adopted a new theoretical point of departure in Lasswell's psychological characterization of political man.

Over many years, Lasswell's effort to give the study of politics a psychological foundation issued in a search for a psychologically defined "political type," a *"homo politicus."* In *Psychopathology and Politics,* political man was characterized as one who displaces "private affects" onto "public objects" and rationalizes this in terms of the public interest.[8] Eighteen years later, in *Power and Personality,* Lasswell moved to a more Adlerian position in his continuing effort to concep-tualize political man. In Alfred Adler's post-Freudian "Individual Psychology," a person with one or another form of congenital weakness or organ inferiority is seen as compensating for the resultant inferiority feelings by developing a life-goal of superiority and a corresponding "style of life." Adapting this idea to his purposes as a political scientist, Lasswell now hypothesized that, apart from dis-placing private affects onto public objects, political man seeks power "as a means of compensation against deprivation," and specifically that: *"Power is expected to overcome low estimates of the self,* by changing either the traits of the self or the environment in which it functions."[9] The Georges adopted this "compen-sation" hypothesis as the basis for psychological interpretation of Wilson. In their words, "power was for him a compensatory value, a means of restoring the self-esteem damaged in childhood."[10]

In a later methodological essay, Alexander George has spoken in broader terms about the Lasswellian formula, attributing to it a general usefulness to the political scientist concerned with psychobiography. While the hypothesis provides, he writes, a "relatively 'shallow' account of the origins of the need for power," still:

The problems of interest to the political scientist do not require the same level of explanation in matters of this kind that the psychoanalyst is interested in. Moreover, the political scientist lacks the data, observational opportunities and diagnostic skills for making fuller in-depth reconstructions. Under these circumstances, attempts to do so are likely to be difficult, frustrating and unduly speculative—as well as often being unnecessary.[11]

I am not convinced that the political scientist as psychobiographer is in any better position to dispense with fuller in-depth reconstructions than any other psychobiographer,[12] although it may be true in some instances. Moreover, Lasswell's conception of the politician as one who seeks power to overcome low estimates of the self, useful though it may be up to a point, presents a serious problem.

The conception has value insofar as it takes us beyond the old stereotype of the politician as one who seeks power simply for power's sake. It makes allowance for what is probably the frequent fact that people seek the power of political office for motives other than power *per se*. What needs to be called into question is the assumption that the power-drive of would-be political leaders derives from low estimates of the self. This seems *prima facie* doubtful. "Low estimates of the self" would take the form of conscious feelings of self-depreciation or self-belittlement. Very possibly, there have been exemplars in political history. But it would seem that in most cases, political power-seeking is a form of activity that appeals to expansive personalities, to people who possess very considerable (if not unusually strong) self-esteem and self-confidence, reflecting high rather than low estimates of self. Those in whom feelings of self-belittlement or self-depreciation are salient would tend to shun active involvement in the political arena, and not to be successful if they ventured into it.

Curiously, Lasswell himself, in one place, recognizes or half-recognizes this. He writes that "the accentuation of power is to be understood as a compensatory reaction against low estimates of the self *(especially when coexisting with high self-estimates)* ..."[13] But he does not explain, psychologically, the paradox of high self-estimates coexisting with low ones. He could have done so, however, had he referred to the work of Karen Horney on the neurotic personality. This form of personality, as she analyzes it, shows high *and* low estimates of the self coexisting.

In the revision of psychoanalysis made by Horney, human beings are endowed with a growth tendency or urge toward actualization of their capacities and potentialities as persons. When, however, psychologically adverse experience in early childhood results in a condition of "basic anxiety," defined as a "feeling of being isolated and helpless in a world conceived as potentially hostile," the child typically responds by, among other things, forming an "idealized image" of himself to make up for his inadequate sense of personal identity and insecurity about his personal significance.[14] The idealized image is a picture of himself as a perfect or superhuman being along one or another line as dictated by the tendency to move *against* others in a drive for "mastery," *toward* others in search for "love," or *away from* others in quest of "freedom."

Unless the psychic conditions generating the basic anxiety change for the better, the individual in time takes a fateful further step: he identifies the idealized image as the person he really is. In Horney's terms, the idealized image turns into an "idealized self." When and if this happens, the energies available for growth or self-realization are henceforth invested in the effort to prove in action, i.e., to demonstrate to himself and others, that he *is* in fact the idealized self. Since any failure along this line incurs painful anxiety, the effort to actualize the idealized self (Horney calls this the "search for glory") takes on a compulsive character, meaning that the person in question feels driven involuntarily to prove himself (i.e., the idealized self) in action. Failures are, however, unavoidable given the individual's human fallibility, on the one hand, and the godlike or absolute character of the idealized self on the other.

Awareness of such discrepancies causes the person—again compulsively—to turn in a fury of self-accusation, self-condemnation and self-hatred against his "empirical" self, which begins to seem to him an alien being. Hence the neurotic personality is above all the victim of an inner conflict, a person "at war with himself." Being thus at odds with himself, moreover, he is virtually certain to be at odds with others. For others, if only unwittingly, are likely to inflict painful blows upon the neurotic person's "pride system" by failing, in word or deed, to treat him in accordance with the claims of the idealized self. Whence his hypersensitivity to criticism (an implicit denial of the idealized self's lofty attributes or perfection) and the vindictive hostility aroused in him toward those enemies (as he perceives them) who have given him affront by criticism or other forms of failure to affirm the idealized image. To gain a vindictive triumph over them by hitting back at them is his way of attempting to restore the injured pride. Furthermore, one of his unconscious ways of dealing with the self-hatred aroused in him by his violations of his impossibly high standards is to "externalize" it, i.e., to project it outwards and experience it as his hatred of *other* persons—against whom it is realistically possible to fight and win a pride-restoring triumph. This increases the likelihood that the neurotic's inner conflict will impair, at least at certain times in life, his relationships with others.

Here, then, in the neurotic personality, we see the coexistence of both unnaturally high and unnaturally low estimates of the self. The high ones take the form of an idealized self-image possessing attributes of imagined genius, perfection, or greatness along one or another line; the low ones, in a despised empirical self experienced as an offensive stranger because of its inevitable inability to fulfill the superhuman demands and specifications of the idealized self. Through such inner mechanisms as repression, externalization, and rationalization, the neurotic does his best to preserve the pride system intact and act out successfully the role of greatness and glory in which he has cast himself in his self-idealization. But no matter how herculean his efforts along this line, he is virtually condemned to suffer a series of experiences which bring the despised self into the forefront of his self-consciousness or threaten to do so. On the one hand, he strives by every possible means to keep the "high" self-estimate salient in his experience of himself; on the other, the "low" one keeps threatening to intrude.

Although references in *Power and Personality* show that Lasswell was at the time of writing familiar with the views Horney had expressed in various writings then available, his parenthetical mention of coexisting high and low self-estimates did not betoken an attempt to make use of her theory of the neurotic personality for his purposes. His formula for "the political type" remained the one already cited: the power-seeker pursues power in order to "overcome low estimates of the self."

THE GEORGES' APPLICATION OF LASSWELL'S HYPOTHESIS

The first question I want to raise is: how consistently do the Georges follow Lasswell's compensation hypothesis in their psychological interpretation of Wilson, and how well does it serve them? They do postulate, as already indicated above, that Wilson's desire for power and for a career of political leadership was motivated by a desire to overcome the low self-estimates generated during his early childhood. Wilson's father humiliated the boy by regularly making him the target of a caustic wit. The son "never retorted and he never rebelled. Instead, he accepted his father's demands for perfection, tried to emulate him, and interpreted his stinging criticisms as humiliating evidence that, try as he might, he was inadequate."[15] The Georges note that the boy did not learn the written alphabet until he was nine and couldn't read readily until he was eleven. Wilson's recollections of his youth, the authors go on,

> furnish ample indication of his early fears that he was stupid, ugly, worthless and unlovable.... It is perhaps to this core feeling of inadequacy, of a fundamental worthlessness which must ever be disproved, that the unappeasable quality of his need for affection, power and achievement, and the compulsive quality of his striving for affection may be traced. For one of the ways in which human beings troubled with low estimates of themselves seek to obliterate their inner pain is through high achievement and the acquisition of power. The trouble is that no matter how dazzling, their accomplishments are likely to prove only momentarily satisfying because the deep-seated low estimates persist and in short order begin to clamor anew for assuagement.[16]

Thus for the Georges, Lasswell's compensatory hypothesis explains the urge for power and achievement which made Wilson dissatisfied with being a professor (in this connection, they quote him as saying: "I want to *do* something!") and drove him to win a succession of important leader-roles: the presidency of Princeton University (1902–10), the governorship of New Jersey (1910–12), and finally the presidency of the United States (1913–21). Lasswell's compensation hypothesis serves more as a generalized explanation of Wilson's lifelong quest for leader-roles than as a means of explaining specific actions taken along the way. From time to time, however, the authors invoke the hypothesis in concrete explanatory contexts. For example, they write in one place that the need to struggle against the self-depreciating tendencies from Wilson's early years "crippled his capacity to react objectively to matters at hand."[17] Again, in dealing with his troubled relations with Congress in 1913, they suggest that what dictated his leadership tactics was "his need for domination as a means of countering his low self-estimates."[18]

Wilson's impressive successes in winning leader-roles were counterbalanced and ultimately overshadowed by a number of failures in his performance as a leader, most notably the long and losing battle with Dean West at Princeton over the location of the projected new Graduate College and the battle with Senator Lodge and others over ratification of the Versailles Treaty by the United States Senate. Even in his short career as governor, his successful passage of reforms in the New Jersey legislature of 1911 was followed by what Arthur Link calls "the debacle of the session of 1912," which was (writes Link) "the result of his own failures and personal limitations." Apart from his absences from the state at the time, the failure of leadership reflected Wilson's "temperamental inability to cooperate with men who were not willing to follow his lead completely; he had not lost his habit, long since demonstrated at Princeton, of making his political opponents also his personal enemies, whom he despised and loathed."[19]

The explanation of this pattern of recurrent leadership failure is an obvious major challenge for any psychobiography of Wilson. The Georges recognize this fact. They begin their concluding "Research Note" in *Woodrow Wilson and Colonel House* by citing Edmund Wilson's description of the career of Wilson:

> As President of the United States, he repeated after the War his whole tragedy as president of Princeton—with Lodge in the role of West, the League of Nations in the place of the quad system, and the Senate in the place of the Princeton trustees. It is possible to observe in certain lives, where conspicuously superior abilities are united with serious deficiencies, not the progress in career or vocation that carries the talented man to a solid position or a definite goal, but a curve plotted over and over again and always dropping from some flight of achievement into a steep descent into failure.[20]

Alexander George calls this the "self-defeating pattern" and "self-defeating dynamism" in Wilson's career.[21] One of the authors' chief concerns in their study of Wilson is to explain this pattern.

Their way of doing so involves a certain shift of explanatory perspective. Lasswell's compensatory hypothesis has been invoked to explain Wilson's quest for power, his need to dominate people in order to assuage inadequacy feelings. The self-defeating pattern manifested itself, however, *after* Wilson had attained various leader-roles and was exercising the authority that they conferred upon him. Specifically, when as leader he was confronted with determined opposition to a project which he had proposed and was trying to put through—the Graduate College location issue at Princeton and the League issue are the two principal instances—he would grow rigid and uncompromisingly insistent upon having

his way *in toto* and upon utterly defeating and humbling those who led the opposition against him—even though this meant the loss of the project itself in a
form that intrinsically ought to have been acceptable to him.

The Georges recognize that Wilson's conduct in these recurring situations of
challenge to his authority as leader calls for a more concrete, a more *ad hoc*
explanation than the generalized urge for power and achievement which they
see as stemming from low estimates of self. In constructing this explanation, they
shift their emphasis from a need for domination to a need for "freedom *from*
domination" or a "fear *of* being dominated."[22] This in turn is speculatively derived
from the vicissitudes of Wilson's childhood relationship to his father. The argument runs as follows: children generally experience a certain amount of resentment of their parents, and this tendency would have been intensified in
Wilson's case by his father's harsh ridicule of him. But the anxiety aroused by
these hostile feelings caused Wilson to repress them from consciousness and
assume an attitude of "surpassing devotion" to his father, so that "there is not
a shred of evidence that he ever once openly rebelled against his father's authority. Instead, he submitted and became an extravagently devoted son," so much
so that "even in successful maturity, he retained a feeling of incompetence in
his father's presence."[23]

The final step in the argument is that the Dean Wests of Wilson's career as a
leader—those who opposed and threatened to defeat his cherished projects—
were father-figures against whom he was determined to express the rebellious
and hostile feelings that he had suppressed in relation to his real father, on the
implicit motto of "never again." The authors' statement of the argument runs as
follows:

> He bristled at the slightest challenge to his authority. Such a characteristic might well
> have represented a rebellion against the domination of his father, whose authority he
> had never dared openly to challenge. Throughout his life his relationships with others
> seemed shaped by an inner command never again to bend his will to another man's.
> He seems to have experienced men who were determined to make their viewpoints
> prevail against his own—men like Dean West at Princeton or, later, Senator Lodge—
> as an unbearable threat. They seem to have stirred in him ancient memories of his
> capitulation to his father and he resisted with ferocity. *He* must dominate, out of fear
> of being dominated.[24]

The fact that the authors have introduced a new line of reasoning (outside of
or going beyond the Lasswellian compensatory formula) to explain Wilson's self-
defeating pattern is not objectionable, although it would seem desirable, if possible, to account for the latter in terms of the same *system of explanation* that
applies to Wilson's other characteristic patterns of behavior. The new line of reasoning does, however, present some problems. As acknowledged in the first of
the statements cited above, it is speculative. There is no direct evidence for "the
violence he had once felt but never ventured to express in response to his father's
overwhelming domination," and the only indirect evidence—his notable slowness

to learn the alphabet and to read—is presumably interpretable in more than one way. As the Georges emphasize, Wilson's lifelong demeanor toward his father was admiring and deferential; in short, anything but hostile, violent, rebellious. They interpret this as signifying repressed violent feelings against the elder Wilson.[25] This is no more subject to disproof than it is to proof. Certain questions might, however, be raised. If Wilson so successfully (through reaction-formation) managed to suppress his underlying rebelliousness against his dominating father, might he not have shown a like tendency in relations with father-like dominating figures encountered later in life, the very Wests and Lodges against whom he fought so uncompromisingly? Or, if we allow that he was driven to act out against other would-be dominators the rebellious violence that he had repressed in himself with reference to his own father, why do we not see a pattern of rebellious violence against numerous potential father-figures encountered earlier in life, e.g., school teachers, or superiors in academic life with whom he had dealings prior to his presidency at Princeton? Why did the suppressed aggressive violence come out in him only in these few instances in middle and later life?

None of what has been said here invalidates the Georges' interpretive approach to Wilson. At most it suggests that the problem of working out a fully satisfactory psychological interpretation of him remains unsolved, and that an alternative to the Georges' approach may be worth trying out. It seems to me that the most promising basis for such an alternative is the conception of the neurotic personality presented by Karen Horney in her final and most important work of synthesis, *Neurosis and Human Growth*. That Woodrow Wilson was a neurotic personality and that much of his behavior which is of special interest to students of politics invites interpretation on this hypothesis will be the burden of the argument in what follows, and the evidence will be drawn from the Georges' study itself.

AN ALTERNATIVE INTERPRETATION

In his review of the Georges' book cited above, Bernard Brodie writes: "Wilson was intensely neurotic—though the authors refrain from using this or like terms throughout the book—and to get into the dynamics of his actions inevitably requires recourse to concepts and insights that have developed out of the discoveries of Sigmund Freud."[26] Brodie was correct, I believe, in saying that Wilson was "intensely neurotic," although the Georges avoidance of the term apparently reflects doubt about this on their part. The Horneyan conception of the neurotic personality, at any rate, was not, in their view, fully applicable to Wilson. As Alexander George says elsewhere,

> If Wilson is not the simple clinical stereotype of a compulsive, neither can he be regarded as a full-blown neurotic. True, one cannot read, for example, Karen Horney's insightful and penetrating descriptions of neurotic drives and of the neurotic character structure without being struck by the applicability of much of what she says to Wilson. But these

descriptions are applicable only to a certain point and, upon reflection, one is on balance equally or more impressed with the extent to which Wilson's behavior and career *diverge* from those of her patients. This divergence from the clinical picture concerns precisely the critical question whether the neurotically disposed individual is able to deal adequately with his conflicts and hence retains the ability to function effectively. For Wilson was, after all, a highly successful person. He was able to overcome a severe disturbance in childhood development; thereafter, not only did he keep fairly well in check the compulsive and neurotic components of his personality but he succeeded in large measure in harnessing them constructively to the achievement of socially productive purposes. To the clinical psychologist, therefore, Wilson is interesting as much because he was able to overcome childhood difficulties and to perform as successfully as he did in public life, as he is because of the pathological pattern of self-defeating behavior he tended to repeat on several occasions during his public career.[27]

I have quoted this statement at length not only because it sets forth a distinctly skeptical, not to say negative, view of the applicability of Horneyan theory to Wilson, but also because it raises an important general question.

This is "the critical question whether the neurotically disposed individual is able to deal adequately with his conflicts and hence retains the ability to function effectively." Professor George implies that Horney would answer in the negative— a position that I believe is mistaken. Horney at least allows for the *possibility* of effective functioning on the social plane. In her view, as I read it, neurosis is often a mighty motive force for achievement, including achievement of what for many would be "socially productive purposes" in the political realm. Notwithstanding the egocentricity of the neurotic individual's "search for glory," he may in some instances be spurred on to impressive political success, even triumph, by the driving inner need to prove the idealized self in action and gain public recognition of it.[28] Especially in those societies whose cultural norms or mores place a high value on power, fame, etc., individuals of exceptional ability who are motivated by neurotic ambition may be highly successful in the achievement of their goals and may thereby, through very much of their careers, find in this external success at least the mirage of a solution for their inner conflicts. Of course, the person who is inwardly conflicted ("at war with himself") because of neurosis will pay a high psychological price for this form of solution. Moreover, by virtue of the psychodynamics of neurosis, summarized earlier, the neurotic's inner conflicts will place a heavy strain on his relations with others. They may, in fact, impair his effectiveness in an organizational role. But the neurotically generated social animosities or conflict may at times be, or appear, socially "functional" depending upon the nature and situation of the organization itself, e.g., if in some sense it is a fighting organization with an ideology of militance in terms of which an enmity born of neurosis can credibly be rationalized.

Whatever position we take on this general issue, when we turn to Wilson the case against the thesis that he was a neurotic personality is weak. For here we clearly see both sides of the coin. On the one hand, enormous ambition combined with extraordinary political talents drove him to dizzy heights of success in a career of leadership that ran in a single decade from the presidency of a university to the presidency of the United States. None of this success is incompatible with the possibility that Wilson and his ambition were neurotic in character. On the other hand, his stunningly successful career was bedeviled by repeated searing personal conflicts in which Wilson's response to those who incurred his enmity by opposing his projects comprised a "pattern of self-defeating behavior" which Professor George himself calls "pathological." Such a duality of accomplishment and failure, of greatness come to grief, would suggest the possibility of neurosis even if we knew nothing more about the individual in question. To argue the proposition in positive terms, however, we must turn to the evidence.

Horney discusses the neurotic personality in general terms and at the same time, as indicated earlier, suggests a threefold typology of neurotic personalities. She distinguishes (1) those who seek "expansive" solutions in one or another form of mastery; (2) those who seek "self-effacing" solutions in love; and (3) those whose solution is "resignation" through aloofness from others or freedom. She also suggests that these various "solutions" are at best dominant trends in a neurotic life-course and that many cases (if not all) are mixed ones. Those who seek expansive solutions are, moreover, divided into "narcissistic," "perfectionistic," and "arrogant-vindictive" subtypes characterized respectively by the need for admiration, extreme perfectionism, and the need for a vindictive triumph over those perceived as enemies. A neurotic who makes a career of political leadership will almost self-evidently belong to the expansive category, although it has been hypothesized that the appeal of mastery through political accomplishment could be accompanied in some instances by self-effacing tendencies expressing the appeal of love.[29] That this hypothesis applies to Wilson may be suggested by such a statement as the following in a letter to his first wife: "I have an uncomfortable feeling of carrying a volcano about with me. My salvation is in being loved. . . . There surely never lived a man with whom love was a more critical matter than it is with me!"[30] Yet Wilson's dominant solution was certainly the expansive one, with elements of all three subtypes or subtendencies present. As we shall see, the last of these, i.e., the need for a vindictive triumph over enemies, is especially relevant to the self-defeating pattern.

On the basis of Horney's generalized description of the neurotic process and the detailed biographical material provided by the Georges in their book, Wilson was a classic case of the neurotic personality. It is quite clear from their account of the boy's early life, of "the crushing feelings of inadequacy which had been branded into his spirit as a child,"[31] that he experienced the basic anxiety that in Horney's view fosters neurosis. Second, we see in the young Wilson ample evidence of the self-idealization which Horney explains as the anxiety-ridden youngster's method of finding a sense of personal worth and significance in such circumstances. As a boy at the dinner table, he was heard to say, "papa, when I get to be a man, I'm going to have a lofty position." "He spent his childhood and youth," the Georges write, "industriously preparing to be a great man."[32] Also, he soon began to visualize the political realm as the scene of his destined greatness. At sixteen, while conversing with his cousin Jessie, he referred to a portrait on the wall and said: "That is Gladstone, the greatest statesman that ever lived. I intend to be a statesman, too."[33]

Young Wilson created an image of himself as a future great statesman, and eventually identified himself with it; the idealized image became, in Horney's terms, an "idealized self," which he felt driven to prove in practice. Since the idealized self was a statesman-self, the goal of his compulsive striving to demonstrate it in practice *can* be described as "power," but it would be more accurately designated a quest for great political accomplishment or "search for glory." In the Georges' words, "what attracted him, apparently, was the prospect of exercising leadership *per se*. He was . . . , throughout his career, a leader in search of a cause. One feels, almost, that the various causes for which he fought so passionately in later years were in themselves almost incidental to him. A man cannot exercise power in a vacuum, after all."[34] An indication of the importance of seeing the search for glory as the driving force of Wilson's life is that he especially sought public acknowledgment and applause, which need not have been the case if power *per se* were his object. From boyhood, his ambition was to become a great orator, and as a political man he was, all his life, above all a magnificent *performer*. This was true of him as a teacher as well: "Wilson's performance at Princeton, from the very start, was superlative. His class lectures were celebrated. . . . Sometimes, at the end of a particularly brilliant performance— and they were *performances*—the students would impulsively burst into applause."[35]

What is salient in this personality is a lofty self-estimate, not a low one, although the latter may have lurked below the surface in the form of repressed or semirepressed self-condemnatory tendencies arising from the empirical Wilson's inability always and wholly to *be* the idealized self in actual practice. In short, we have here that very combination of high and low self-estimates which was discussed earlier. Public plaudits, and in particular those of the political communities over which he successively presided as leader, would have represented to Wilson a proof of success in fulfilling his ambition to be a new Gladstone. Political success, as attested by public approval, was confirmation of the idealized self, and all the more necessary because the suppressed self-doubts and self-condemnatory tendencies inevitably made him insecure in his lofty self-estimate and hence in need of constant support in the form of praise and admiration.

Speaking of neurotic pride, Horney writes:

> With all his strenuous efforts toward perfection and with all his belief in perfection attained, the neurotic does not gain what he most desperately needs: self-confidence and self-respect. . . . The great positions to which he may rise, the fame he may acquire, will render him arrogant but will not bring him inner security. He still feels at bottom unwanted, is easily hurt, and needs incessant confirmation of his value.[36]

Wilson emerges in the Georges' account as just such a person. They speak of "that undercurrent of restless dissatisfaction which was the man's fundamental mood."[37] Elsewhere, they write that "Wilson's thirst for accomplishment was unquenchable. A project successfully completed might for a moment still his inner doubts—but only for a moment."[38] Horney's line of reasoning, based on the concept of the idealized image of self and the never-ending and yet never fully successful quest to actualize and gain confirmation of it, explains all this better than the Lasswellian formula does.

The same is true of Wilson's way of responding to approval and admiration from those around him or from strangers, and his way of responding to disapproval or disagreement. Because of the inevitable insecurity of the pride structure, the neurotic personality is, as Horney explains, in constant need of reassurance from others that he *is* the paragon that he believes himself to be; and he is hypersensitive to criticism because it threatens to mobilize and bring him face to face with his suppressed *self*-critical, *self*-condemnatory tendencies. Consequently, he tends to react with vindictive hostility to the source of the criticism or opposition, upon whom his self-condemnation is projected. Wilson's enormous need for reassurance and admiration, and his resulting manner of responding to flattery, of which Colonel House took such active advantage—all this is abundantly documented in the biographical facts cited by the Georges. So is his hostility against his detractors or those who in any way threatened to outdo him in a leader-role, as Dean West did at Princeton. "All of Wilson's close friends—the men, the women, the professors, the politicians, the socialites—shared one characteristic: they were or at least had to seem to him to be *uncritical* admirers of the man and of everything he did."[39] Further, the authors note as "truly remarkable" the "vast number of letters Wilson wrote to friends fervently expressing his gratitude for their faith and affection. So far from reducing his energy for this type of letter-writing, the pressure of public business, particularly when he was under attack, seemed to intensify his need to turn for solace to those who restored him with their uncritical approval."[40] Naturally, he was most in need of this uncritical approval when "under attack," because public attack would intensify the insecurity of his idealized self.

The Georges' way of explaining Wilson's compulsive need for uncritical admiration and agreement with his views differs from the Horneyan explanation suggested in the foregoing paragraph. As they see it:

> Intellectual disagreement or the feeling that a friend disapproved of some project he had in hand aroused intolerable anxieties, the echoes of indelible boyhood impressions. For the boy Wilson had learned that if he did not earn his father's approval by instantly accepting his every opinion and behaving accordingly, he stood in danger of forfeiting his father's love. To the man Wilson, identity of opinion and love were inseparably linked. . . . To him, if a friend disagreed with him about a matter of importance, it signified that the friend no longer cared for him. He reacted in the way he once had feared his father would react in similar circumstances—he broke the relationship.[41]

To me this explanation is not cogent: it simply transposes to the adult Wilson a way of relating to persons that corresponds to his father's way of relating to *him* when he was a child. But it is not self-evident that Wilson would have taken over this trait from his father; he might have rebelled against it. Whereas in terms of Horneyan theory, we do get a dynamic explanation of the behavior in question. Approval of him and his projects, especially by those whose opinions mattered most to him, was a vital need because it ministered to his craving for reassurance that he *was* his "true self," i.e., the idealized one. It was for this reason that he required "the soothing balm of flattery," as the Georges put it in describing Colonel House's way of approaching Wilson.[42] Significantly, the Georges themselves seem at times to see the behavior in these terms:

> He needed his friends to confirm his faith—so easily shaken by outer attack because so savagely preyed upon from within—in *his great destiny,* in *his human worth.* He needed their tributes to his *selfless idealism,* particularly when the detractors rudely stripped away his carefully wrought rationalizations and, with cruelly used insight, broadcast the power-seeking, self-centered, arrogant aspects of his behavior.[43]

THE SELF-DEFEATING PATTERN: TWO VIEWS

We come, finally to Wilson's repeated rigidity and vindictiveness in response to challenges to his authority as expressed in such cherished projects as his Graduate College conception at Princeton and the League of Nations Covenant. I have summarized the Georges' interpretation of this behavior as Wilson's effort to gain "freedom from domination" by figures whom he may have experienced as reincarnations of his domineering father, and I have questioned that view, believing that an alternative interpretation in Horneyan terms is more persuasive.

The Georges draw a useful distinction between "Wilson the power-seeker" and "Wilson the power-holder." As power-seeker, he was "free to devote every ounce of his intelligence and energy to waging a realistic campaign to attain his goal." Indeed, "he proved himself a practical politician without peer, a prodigy in the art of elevating himself to power."[44] Certainly, Wilson demonstrated notable flexibility in the process of power seeking, and a capacity to adapt his policy positions to the requirements for success. This was shown, for example, in his shift from a conservative political stance before winning the governorship to the reformism which powerfully assisted him along the path to the presidency. His flexibility was repeated in his quick shift to an antibossism posture in state politics after encouraging the Democratic party bosses of New Jersey who groomed him for the governorship to believe that he would remain loyal to them. His troubles always emerged *after* he had won a position of power. Of Wilson the power-holder the Georges write that "having attained an opportunity for exercise of power, first as President of Princeton and finally as President of the United States, he was no longer able to suppress his inner impulses toward aggressive leadership."[45] Further: "Having legitimized his drive to exercise power by laborious self-preparation and by adopting worthy goals, Wilson felt free to indulge his wish to force others into immediate and complete compliance with his demands."[46]

But Wilson the power-holder did not become immediately and indiscriminately aggressive in his leadership tactics. As the Georges take care to point out:

> In each of the major executive posts he occupied during his life there was an initial period during which the type of leadership he exercised in response to his inner needs coincided with the type of leadership the external situation required for impressive accomplishment. He drove the faculty and trustees at Princeton to accomplish an unprecedented series of reforms. The New Jersey legislature of 1911 was a triumph of productivity in his hands. Later, he was to exact a brilliant performance from the Sixty-Third Congress of the United States.

They go on:

> Wilson's difficulties arose when he encountered opposition, often evoked partly in reaction to his own driving demands, and when the chance for further success hinged upon his ability to alter his tactics.... Indeed, he was usually least capable of flexible responses in the situations which most required them. For angry opposition only intensified his anxieties and the more surely dictated a stubborn determination to subjugate his foes.[47]

This passage suggests that the opposition to which Wilson responded in this manner was wittingly or unwittingly provoked ("often evoked partly in response to his own driving demands") by the man himself. The Georges reinforce this inference when they say a little further on: "His *provocative behavior* attracted the personal hostilities of his opponents. They, then, attacked him and his programs in a vindictive spirit."[48]

Now if, in the initial periods, Wilson as leader was capable of prodigious accomplishment (and the flexibility it requires), the distinction between Wilson the power-seeker and Wilson the power-holder, for all its usefulness as a starting point, does not take us to the core of the problem. What has to be explained is not a generalized aggressiveness in Wilson's enactment of his leader-roles, but specifically his opposition-provoking behavior *in office* and the vindictiveness which this opposition typically aroused in him—with politically self-defeating consequences. Approaching this problem in terms of the hypothesis that Wilson was a neurotic personality in Horney's terms, a solution suggests itself along the following lines. His motivation, as has been argued, was never a desire for power *per se;* it was the search for glory, and more concretely the drive to prove the idealized Wilson in action through leadership success. The prime test of such success was winning a leadership role that would bring him fame, honor, acclaim and acknowledgment of his talents, along with the opportunity to reap more such rewards by demonstrating in the office won his greatness as a leader.

Accordingly, no sooner had he obtained a particular leadership role than he would take advantage of it to espouse and strive to put through new ideas, new departures in policy, new programs which, if successful, would bring greater glory and possibly, also, open the way to a still higher leadership role with its still greater opportunities for further leadership success. Since in his initial periods in office he found not only real needs for change but also real opportunities to persuade the given establishment and community of the desirability of the proposed reforms, the initial scale of Wilson's accomplishment was impressive. But he would be driven by his compulsive need for glory, reinforced now by the initial leadership success, to press for further dramatic and acclaim-producing leadership projects despite the inevitable growth of resistance to further change; or else, as in the governorship, he would lose interest after exploiting the potentialities of the post for his purposes and thus allow the success in the legislative session of 1911 to give way to the failure of that in 1912.

To cite an especially important instance of Wilson's motivation as leader, we may refer to his espousal of the League of Nations. Colonel House appealed to Wilson's desire for glory in this connection: "All through the war, in seeking to stimulate Wilson's interest in international affairs, House shrewdly assured him that he could achieve immortality by pioneering a world organization which would insure peace."[49] And further: "He had always wanted—*needed*—to do immortal work. Devising a peace settlement which would prevent future wars was a task which appealed to everything within him which strove for self-vindication through accomplishment. For what greater good could a man do than engineer the end to human strife?"[50] But the moral motivation was inextricably intertwined with the egocentricity of Wilson's search for glory. Once he had taken up the project, Wilson was highly possessive about it. As House confided to his diary:

> I wish again to call attention to the selfishness which seems to lurk in the minds of those in authority. The President is anxious to state his peace terms before Lloyd George and Clemenceau have an opportunity to forestall him. It is not team work.... It is the thing I have complained of so often in this diary, that is, that it is not so much general accomplishment that those in authority seem to desire as accomplishment which may redound to their personal advantage.[51]

Whoever rose to challenge Wilson in such a situation, by opposing the plan or Wilson's particular version of the plan, aroused him to a vindictive fury as compulsive as the need for glory which underlay his espousal of the plan. For such a challenge was implicitly a challenge to the validity of Wilson's exalted self-appraisal, his idealized statesman-self and its attributes of wisdom, nobility, farsightedness. Having difficulty in imagining that the plan (and hence he, himself, as its sponsor) was deficient in any way, Wilson could only interpret the opposition as motivated by the ugly ulterior designs of an evil opponent. Such a rationalization was his only means of defending the idealized self in that situation.

Consequently, Wilson became not only utterly intransigent toward the challenge, he also became enraged against the challenger. Very likely this rage was compounded by the projection upon the opponent of Wilson's own repressed self-hate. His only recourse now was to do everything possible to expose the opponent as malign and to defeat him humiliatingly. Gaining such a pride-restoring vindictive triumph eventually became more important to Wilson than putting through the project itself, no matter how much effort he had invested in it. As Horney notes in discussing such motivation in the neurotic personality, "compulsively he has to drag his rival down or defeat him."[52] I submit that the psychodynamics of Wilson's self-defeating pattern find explanation in these terms.

To conclude with a speculative postscript to this argument, let us recall the Georges' distinction between Wilson the power-seeker and Wilson the power-holder and their reference to his "provocative behavior" while in power. We might hypothesize that underlying the provocative behavior was not only the search for glory through great leadership that led him to drive too hard, but also *an unconscious need to provoke opposition in order that, by overcoming it, he could experience the winning of the leader-role again,* for example by appealing to his mass constituency over the heads of his establishmentarian opposition. As the Georges say in their final paragraph, "Wilson sought vindication."[53] This meant, we might add, not alone the sought-for vindictive triumph over the evil challenger, but the rewinning of legitimate power in the very process of gaining that political victory.

This reasoning would suggest that Wilson had an unconscious fantasy of being challenged and of overcoming the challenge gloriously, thereby gaining vindication both of himself and some immediate threatened project expressive of his greatness as a leader. His provocative behavior may be seen from this viewpoint as a way of creating, while in the leader-role, situations that made it necessary for him, as it were, to win it all over again. His tendency, then, was *not* to defeat himself, but to produce challenges to himself that would enable him to win the leadership, and the plaudits, again in the face of the very resistance that he himself had provoked. So, *after* winning a leader-role, Wilson was driven, while enacting that role, to go on reenacting the experience of winning it, to go on being a "power-seeker."[54]

This re-examination of the Georges' psychological interpretation of Woodrow Wilson has been accompanied by the outlining of an alternative approach based on the hypothesis that Wilson was a neurotic personality. Earlier, some criteria were suggested for measuring the relative explanatory values of differing psychological approaches in psychobiography. Perhaps the most fitting words with which to bring the essay to a close would be those of the Georges: "Let the reader consider whether these patterns of behavior become more consistently comprehensible in terms of the explanations herein offered than in terms of other explanations. That will be the best test of their usefulness."[55]

NOTES

1 Harold D. Lasswell, *Psychopathology and Politics,* new ed. (New York: Viking Press, 1960), p. 9. Here and throughout italics are in the original unless otherwise indicated in footnotes.

2 Paul Murray Kendall, *The Art of Biography* (New York: Norton, 1965), p. 15.
3 A. O. J. Cockshut, *Truth to Life: The Art of Biography in the Nineteenth Century* (New York: Harcourt, Brace Jovanovich, 1974), p. 16.
4 Alexander L. George, "Some Uses of Dynamic Psychology in Political Biography: Case Materials on Woodrow Wilson," in *A Source Book for the Study of Personality and Politics,* ed. Fred I. Greenstein and Michael Lerner (Chicago: Markham, 1971), p. 80.
5 In his "Afterthoughts—Thirty Years Later," appended to the 1960 new edition of *Psychopathology and Politics,* he himself noted that ". . . the study of politicians (and of politics in general) by methods largely inspired by psychoanalysis has made but modest progress to date" (p. 290). Since 1960, however, the psychobiographical study of political leaders has shown notable signs of progress, in Erik H. Erikson, *Gandhi's Truth: On the Origins of Militant Non-Violence* (New York: Norton, 1969), and a number of other studies.
6 For example, according to Betty Glad, "Contributions of Psychobiography," *Handbook of Political Psychology,* ed. Jeanne N. Knutson (San Francisco: Jossey-Bass, 1973), p. 298, "the systematic use of psychobiography for the exploration of the interface between personality, attitudes, and political behavior did not really begin until 1956, with the publication of the Georges' book—*Woodrow Wilson and Colonel House*—and Smith, Bruner, and White's *Opinions and Personality.*" Fred Greenstein devotes most of a chapter of his *Personality and Politics.* 2nd ed. (New York: Norton, 1975) to an analysis of the Georges' study as a model of procedure in psychobiography.
7 Bernard Brodie, "A Psychoanalytic Interpretation of Woodrow Wilson," in *Psychoanalysis and History,* ed. Bruce Mazlish (Englewood Cliffs: Prentice-Hall, 1963), p. 123. This review appeared originally in *World Politics,* 9 (1957), 413–22.
8 Lasswell, *Psychopathology and Politics,* pp. 74–75.
9 Harold D. Lasswell, *Power and Personality* (New York: Norton, 1948), p. 39.
10 *Woodrow Wilson and Colonel House,* p. 320.
11 Alexander L. George, "Power as a Compensatory Value for Political Leaders," *The Journal of Social Issues,* Vol. XXIV, no 3 (July, 1968), p. 35.
12 Greenstein has reasoned along similar lines in *Personality and Politics,* pp. 68–69, 92–93.
13 Lasswell, *Power and Personality,* p. 53. Italics added.
14 Karen Horney, *Neurosis and Human Growth: The Struggle Toward Self-Realization* (New York: Norton, 1950), pp. 18, 22. The following exposition of the concept of the neurotic personality is a summary of Horney's analysis in this book.
15 *Woodrow Wilson and Colonel House,* p. 6.
16 Ibid., p. 8.
17 *Woodrow Wilson and Colonel House,* p. 114.
18 Ibid., p. 151.
19 Arthur S. Link, *Woodrow Wilson: The Road to the White House* (Princeton: University Press, 1947), pp. 206–07.
20 *Woodrow Wilson and Colonel House,* p. 317.
21 George, "Some Uses of Dynamic Psychology," p. 92.
22 *Woodrow Wilson and Colonel House,* pp. 43, 12. Italics added.
23 *Woodrow Wilson and Colonel House,* p. 9.
24 Ibid., pp. 11–12.
25 Noting the importance placed by the Georges on the pattern of reading retardation in boyhood, Greenstein finds that the Georges' interpretation of Wilson's idealization of his father involved "reaction-formation" (*Personality and Politics,* p. 84). This is fully plausible although the Georges do not use the term itself. In Freudian theory, reaction-formation represents an individual's attempt to defend against a certain repudiated tendency in himself by going to the opposite extreme.
26 Brodie, "A Psychoanalytic Interpretation of Woodrow Wilson," p. 115.
27 George, "Some Uses of Dynamic Psychology," p. 83. From one of the references to this article (p. 97) it appears that the quoted comment on Horney was based on a reading of

two of her earlier works: *The Neurotic Personality of Our Time* (New York: Norton, 1937) and *Our Inner Conflicts* (New York: Norton, 1945). The latter work presaged in many ways the fuller and more systematic account of the dynamics of the neurotic personality presented in *Neurosis and Human Growth*.

28 A notable historical example which I have attempted to document in detail, in terms basically of Horneyan theory, is Stalin. See Robert C. Tucker, *Stalin As Revolutionary 1879–1929: A Study in History and Personality* (New York: Norton, 1973), chaps. 3–4 and 12–14.

29 This hypothesis has been suggested by Mr. Harry Hirsch of the Princeton Politics Depaitment in a seminar discussion. For Horney's classification of neurotic personality types and analysis of the main types and subtypes, see *Neurosis and Human Growth*, chaps. 8, 10 and 11.

30 *Woodrow Wilson and Colonel House,* p. 21. One's interpretation of this statement would turn on what one took to be the precise meaning that Wilson placed on "love." It could have carried, for example, the connotation of admiration or adulation, which in turn would be consonant with the "expansive" solution.

31 Ibid., p. 114.

32 Ibid., pp. 8, 9.

33 Ibid., p. 3.

34 Ibid., p. 29.

35 *Woodrow Wilson and Colonel House,* p. 28. During his Princeton period Wilson made this statement, which I believe was unwittingly self-revelatory: ". . . I am covetous for Princeton of all the glory that there is, and the chief glory of a university is always intellectual glory. The chief glory of a university is the leadership of the nation in the things that attach to the highest ambitions that nations can set themselves, those ideals which lift nations into the atmosphere of things that are permanent and do not fade from generation to generation" (Link, *Wilson: The Road to the White House,* p. 44).

36 Horney, *Neurosis and Human Growth,* p. 86.

37 *Woodrow Wilson and Colonel House,* p. 24.

38 Ibid., p. 119.

39 Ibid., p. 31.

40 Ibid., p. 122.

41 *Woodrow Wilson and Colonel House,* pp. 31–32.

42 Ibid., p. 126.

43 Ibid., p. 122. Italics added.

44 Ibid., pp. 58, 116.

45 Ibid., p. 116.

46 Ibid., pp. 117–118.

47 *Woodrow Wilson and Colonel House,* pp. 118–19. On these points the Georges are in full agreement with Link. See Link, *Woodrow Wilson: The Road to the White House,* p. 45.

48 *Woodrow Wilson and Colonel House,* p. 121. Italics added. See also the authors' statement in the Introduction (p. xx) that: "As President of the United States, his provocative behavior all but invited the catastrophic defeat he suffered when the Senate refused to ratify the Versailles Peace Treaty with the League of Nations in it."

49 *Woodrow Wilson and Colonel House,* p. 189.

50 Ibid., p. 197.

51 Quoted in *Woodrow Wilson and Colonel House,* p. 189. By "those in authority" House, of course, meant the president.

52 Horney, *Neurosis and Human Growth,* p. 198.

53 *Woodrow Wilson and Colonel House,* p. 315.

54 I am indebted to Dr. Joseph Slap for elucidating in a personal communication the way in which unconscious fantasies can underlie certain repetitive forms of conduct or lead an individual to recreate situations which activate such forms of conduct.

55 *Woodrow Wilson and Colonel House,* p. 12.

12

Woodrow Wilson's Political Personality: A Reappraisal

Edwin A. Weinstein
James William Anderson
Arthur S. Link

Historians, biographers, and political scientists, as well as psychiatrists and psychologists, have long been intrigued by Woodrow Wilson's personality and its relationship to the events of his academic, political, and diplomatic careers. Although interpretations have varied, there is universal agreement that Wilson's personality was of major importance in both his successes and failures.

Along with the conventional descriptions of Woodrow Wilson's character by his major biographers, Ray Stannard Baker and Arthur S. Link, there have been two book-length psychoanalytic studies. The first, *Thomas Woodrow Wilson,* by Sigmund Freud and William C. Bullitt, was written during the 1930s but not published until 1967.[1] This study, a biased application of a simplistic and distorted version of psychoanalytic theory, is not regarded either by historians or psychoanalysts as a scholarly contribution. In one review,[2] Link demonstrated that the evidence on which the psychological interpretations are based is wildly inaccurate and at times even fabricated. In another review,[3] the psychoanalyst, Erik H. Erikson, pointed out that the crude psychological propositions used in the book were certainly not the handiwork of Freud; he added, however, that Freud's involvement with the book, no matter how minimal,[4] remains an embarrassment to psychoanalysts.

The second study, *Woodrow Wilson and Colonel House: A Personality Study,* by Alexander L. and Juliette L. George, was published in 1956 and reprinted with a new preface in 1964.[5] In contrast to the Freud-Bullitt book, the Georges' study has received wide acclaim, and political scientists interested in psychology have

Reprinted with permission from *Political Science Quarterly,* 93(Winter 1978–79):585–98.

held it up as a model of a psychodynamically oriented political biography. For example, Bernard Brodie calls the book "the first interpretation of the character of [Wilson] which impressed one as having depth, coherence, and consistency."[6] Fred I. Greenstein and Michael Lerner write that it is "one of the most rigorous and convincing of the psychobiographies of political figures."[7] Elmer E. Cornwell, Jr., in a recent review of books on the presidency, characterized *Woodrow Wilson and Colonel House* as "perhaps the best portrait ... drawn." "Their analysis of the impact on the future President of a strict Calvinistic creed and demanding Presbyterian-minister father," Cornwell adds, "remains the most successful 'psychohistorical' treatment of any President."[8]

It is our view, however, that the Georges' book (along with an explanatory article that Alexander George published in 1960), although not deserving of immediate dismissal, as is the Freud-Bullitt work, presents an essentially incorrect interpretation of the personality of Woodrow Wilson and its effect on his career.

The style of the book is graceful and concise, and the Georges have an unusual ability to translate psychological concepts into readily grasped, non-technical language. They are basically sympathetic to Wilson and have great admiration for his achievements. In addition, as Robert C. Tucker has noted in a recent essay on the book,[9] the Georges deserve credit for advancing, through their case study of Wilson, the understanding that a political leader's personality may play a large or even decisive role in determining his conduct in public affairs. The Georges also made a contribution to the development of the methodology of psychobiography. The two authors, in their Research Note and in the 1964 Preface, and Alexander George in the essay of 1960, described the methods they had used while writing the book and their reasons for adopting these methods; they were the first psychobiographers to attempt to conceptualize the process of applying psychology to biography. Finally, some of the book's shortcomings reflect the time in which it was written. Psychological theory has advanced since the mid-1950s, and a great deal of new evidence about Wilson's life has been discovered since the book's original publication in 1956. The Georges, of course, had to work with the psychological theories and the historical sources which were available at the time.[10]

Nonetheless, the Georges' book, in our opinion, suffers from three major deficiencies, which, taken together, result in an inaccurate portrayal of Wilson's personality. The principal failing of the book is that the research on which it rests is inadequate. Second, the Georges fail to recognize the limitations of their psychological model and misrepresent evidence to fit their theory. Third, they ignore Wilson's neurological disorders as conditions affecting his behavior.

The remainder of this essay will examine in detail two of the topics most crucial to the Georges' interpretation of Wilson's personality—Wilson's childhood and the Princeton graduate college controversy; present data, which though available to them, was not investigated; and comment on their use of psychological theory.

I

The Georges claim that Wilson suffered from a troubled relationship with his father, the Rev. Dr. Joseph Ruggles Wilson, a distinguished southern Presbyterian minister. Although Woodrow Wilson overcame his childhood difficulties to some extent, they state, pathological patterns continued to plague him periodically throughout his political career. The main evidence offered for this view is Wilson's early learning experience. The facts are well-known: Wilson did not learn the alphabet until he was nine and did not read with even minimal facility until he was eleven. He entered school at the age of ten and performed poorly. The explanation offered by the Georges reads:

> Perhaps the Doctor's scorn of fumbling first errors was so painful (or perhaps the mere expectation of such a reaction was so distressing) that the boy renounced the effort altogether. Perhaps, too, failing—refusing—to learn was one way in which the boy dared to express his [unconscious] resentment against his father.[11]

It is improbable that Wilson's slowness in learning to read was due to emotional factors and highly likely that it was a manifestation of developmental dyslexia. Undiagnosed in Wilson's childhood, the condition was well-known to neurologists at the time that the Georges wrote their book. However, a number of psychiatrists and psychologists still believed that the condition was an emotional rather than a neurological problem, and the Georges simply chose an explanation that was currently popular. The condition is a frequent one, occurring in about 10 percent of the school population, significantly more frequently in boys. Research over the past seventy years indicates that developmental dyslexia is caused by a delay in the establishment of the dominance of one cerebral hemisphere—usually the left—for language. One theory is that, with the maturational lag, there is representation of language in both hemispheres and performance suffers in the competition for control of the same function.

The specific evidence that Wilson had developmental dyslexia can be summed up in three groups. First, by his own admission he was a slow reader into adult life. At the Johns Hopkins, the amount of assigned reading was his bane. "Steady reading," he wrote his fiancée, "always demands of me more expenditure of resolution and dogged energy than any other sort of work."[12] Second, difficulties in calculation are commonly associated with developmental dyslexia, and Wilson was extremely poor in arithmetic. Third, when, as a result of a stroke in 1896, he could not write with his right hand, he was able, within a few days and without practice, to write with his left hand in perfectly formed script. This ability strongly suggests that he had mixed cerebral dominance for language.

The reading disability affected Wilson's development and his relationship with his parents, but hardly in the way that the Georges state. It probably made him more dependent on his family. Also, he may have feared that his reading problems indicated that he was stupid or lazy. The condition probably made Dr. Wilson more pedagogic and insistent on drilling his "lazy" son. To judge from Wilson's pleasant memories of having his family read to him, they seem to have been tolerant of his problem. During the Civil War, Dr. Wilson was away from home some of the time serving as a chaplain in the Confederate Army. Much of the reading was done by other family members and, if the Georges' hypothesis were true, Wilson must have been expressing his "unconscious hostility" toward his mother, sisters, and other relatives. We do not have a good record of Wilson's childhood such as might be gained from contemporary letters, diaries, or autobiographies; like any other child, he may have felt insecurities. However, it is certain that they did not come about in the manner postulated by the Georges.

According to the Georges, Wilson's relationship with his father was nothing less than devastating. They say that Wilson's father "ridiculed his intellectual capacities and made him feel mediocre." They add that Wilson had to endure "barbed criticism," "sarcastically made demands" and "aspersions on his moral and intellectual worth," and that Wilson interpreted these criticisms "as humiliating evidence, that, try as he might, he was inadequate." As a result of this treatment, they conclude, Wilson feared that he was "stupid, ugly, worthless and unlovable."[13] The Georges' entire interpretation of Wilson's personality revolves around their portrayal of his relationship with his father. They argue that, because of this relationship, Wilson forever harbored a deep sense of worthlessness and also carried a burden of rage which he later turned against adversaries, such as Dean Andrew F. West and Senator Henry Cabot Lodge of Massachusetts.

The sole evidence for this view of Wilson's relationship with his father, aside from the Georges' interpretation of Wilson's reading disability, consists of comments made to Baker in the mid-1920s. Wilson's daughter, Margaret, talking of Dr. Wilson said: "His idea was that if a lad was of fine tempered steel, the more he was beaten, the better he was."[14] The metaphor, a favorite of both Wilson and his father, may be interpreted in various ways and at several levels of concreteness. Probably Dr. Wilson was boasting about Woodrow. But any interpretation should take into account Margaret Wilson's feelings about her grandfather. Margaret did not know Dr. Wilson well until she was fourteen years old, when, because of his deteriorating health, he came to live with his son in Princeton. Affected by severe cerebral arteriosclerosis, Dr. Wilson had become testy and puerile, and his grandchildren were afraid of him.[15] Margaret Wilson's statement can hardly be regarded as indicative of Wilson's relationship with his father while the boy was growing up.

The other recollection is a more substantial one. Wilson's cousin, Helen Woodrow Bones, told Baker:

> Uncle Joseph was a cruel tease, with a caustic wit and a sharp tongue, and I remember hearing my own family tell indignantly of how Cousin Woodrow suffered under his teasing. He was proud of WW, especially after his son began to show how unusual he was, but only a man as sweet as Cousin Woodrow could have forgotten the severity of the criticism to the value of which he so often paid tribute, in after life.[16]

This recollection, more than fifty years after the alleged events, may or may not have been accurate. However, Helen Bones (who was the first Mrs. Wilson's private secretary from March 1913 until Mrs. Wilson's death in August 1914, served as mistress of the White House until Wilson married again in December 1915, and continued to live off and on with the president and his second wife) was fiercely and passionately devoted to Wilson. She deeply resented any criticism of the man she idolized.[17] She would probably have exaggerated and magnified the importance of such stories about Dr. Wilson's treatment of his son. She most likely heard the stories from her parents, and there is evidence of bad blood between them and Dr. and Mrs. Wilson.

The Georges cite an additional recollection to give an idea of the nature of this teasing. One morning, according to another cousin, Jessie Bones Brower (Helen Bones's sister), Wilson's father apologized when his son arrived late for breakfast and explained that he had been so greatly excited at the discovery of another hair in his mustache that it had taken him longer to wash and dress. "I remember very distinctly the painful flush that came over the boy's face," the cousin recalled.[18] If this is typical of Dr. Wilson's teasing, it does not sound harsh or excessive and certainly does not suggest the type of father-son relationship that would handicap Wilson for the rest of his life. Wilson's father was a great wit and punster and used his family as an audience, but there is no indication that he was malicious.

Let us grant that these recollections offer some support for the Georges' interpretation. However, they must be weighed against contrary evidence, which is much more substantial. There are many reports from people who knew Wilson and his father well—sources available to the Georges—about the extraordinarily warm relationship that existed between Wilson and his father during Wilson's childhood.[19] They spent a great deal of time together, and Dr. Wilson read to him and talked to him at length. Early in the week, Wilson's father would visit parishioners while they were at work, and he would take his son along to share the experiences. As evidence of Wilson's submissive attitude toward his father, the Georges cite his helping his father, as a young man, with the dull task of writing the minutes of the General Assembly of the southern Presbyterian Church. If one is to judge by the bitter controversy that led to Dr. Wilson's resignation from the Columbia Theological Seminary,[20] the minutes were anything but dull. In pursuit of their theme of Wilson's "unconscious hostility" toward and fear of his father, the Georges go so far as to interpret Wilson's tender care of his father, over the last years of his life, and his singing of the old man's favorite hymns to him, as evidence of Wilson's guilt and submission!

The Georges emphasize that Wilson was extremely dependent on his father until the latter's death. In support of their view, they cite the observation of a Princeton colleague, Winthrop More Daniels, that Wilson was always the pupil of his father. They fail to cite evidence to the contrary, such as that of Bliss Perry, who commented on the comradely relationship between the two men.[21] It is true that Wilson was financially dependent on his father into his late twenties. However, after the death of Wilson's mother in 1888, he, Woodrow Wilson, became the effective head of the family and the one to whom his brother, sisters, and *father* came for advice and support. Yet the Georges maintain that Wilson's early dependence never changed. As further evidence, they cite the famous "my incomparable father" letter written when Wilson was thirty-two and in the first year of his professorship at Wesleyan. The letter reads:

My precious father,
My thoughts are full of you and dear "Dode" [Wilson's younger brother, Joseph] all the time. Tennessee seems *so* far away for a chap as hungry as I am for a sight of the two men whom I love. As the Christmas recess approaches I realize, as I have so often before, the *pain* there is in a season of holiday and rejoicing away from you. As you know, one of the chief things about which I feel most warranted in rejoicing is that I am your son. I realize the benefit of being your son more and more as my talents and experience grow: I recognize the strength growing in me as of the nature of your strength: I become more and more conscious of the hereditary wealth I possess, the capital of principle, of literary force and skill, of capacity for first-hand thought; and I feel daily more and more bent toward creating in my own children that combined respect and tender devotion for their father that you gave your children for you. Oh, how happy I should be, if I could make them think of me as I think of you! You have given me a love that grows, that is stronger in me now that I am a man than it was when I was a boy, and which will be stronger in me when I am an old man than it is now—a love, in brief, that is rooted and grounded in *reason,* and not in filial instinct merely—a love resting upon abiding foundations of *service,* recognizing you as in a certain very real sense the author of all I have to be grateful for! I bless God for my noble, strong, and saintly mother and for my incomparable father. Ask "Dode" if he does not subscribe? and tell him that I love my brother passionately.
. . .Ellie joins me in unbounded love to you both.

Your devoted son,
Woodrow[22]

Although still an important figure in the southern Presbyterian Church, Dr. Wilson had encountered disappointments in his work and was frequently discouraged and depressed. His career had not advanced, while Woodrow's had, and he had become increasingly identified with and somewhat envious of his son. Wilson, busy in his new position at Wesleyan and involved with writing *The State* (1889), had not written to his father for some time. Could not Wilson, feeling his neglect of his father, now a lonely widower, have written the letter to raise the old man's spirits and self-esteem? And could he not in fact have been expressing his feelings toward his father?

The Georges claim that Dr. Wilson became proud of his son only after the latter began to show how unusual he was. There could be some argument about when Woodrow Wilson began to display extraordinary talent. Probably it was during his senior year at Princeton, when he was managing editor of *The Princetonian* and had an article accepted by a national review. Yet the many letters that Joseph R. Wilson wrote to his son before 1878–79 reveal affection, admiration, pride in his son, and helpful criticism, but never denigration.[23] Wilson dedicated *Congressional Government* to his father. He wrote:

> To his father, the patient guide of his youth, the gracious companion of his manhood, his best instructor and most lenient critic, this book is affectionately dedicated by the author.

Dr. Wilson had a tremendous influence on his son, and probably no boy grows up without some resentment toward his father. However, on the basis of the evidence there is no reason to believe that the dedication of *Congressional Government* [24] was not a valid representation of Wilson's feelings toward his father.

It is almost incredible that a psychobiography tracing the development of Wilson's personality should make so little mention of his mother, Janet, or Jessie, Woodrow Wilson, about whom a great deal was known when the Georges wrote their book. They spend less than half a page on the subject, quoting from the memories of her that Wilson expressed at the time of her death: "As the first shock and the acute pain of the great, the irreparable blow passes off, my heart is filling up with tenderest memories of my sweet mother, memories that seem to hallow my whole life—which seem to explain to me how it came about that I was given the sweetest, most satisfying of wives for my daily companion. My mother, with her sweet womanliness, her purity, her intelligence, prepared me for my wife. I remember how I clung to her (a laughed-at 'mamma's boy') till I was a great big fellow: but love of the best womanhood came to me and entered my heart through her apron-strings."[25]

A discerning reading of all the evidence about Jessie available to the Georges and of the Wilson family correspondence, which was not available to them, would have shown that this description of Wilson's relationship with his mother was far from complete. Jessie Wilson was indeed a saintly, intelligent woman, devoted to her family, and Wilson was a very loving son. But she was extremely overprotective, and the mutual dependence that she fostered was responsible for the relatively late age at which Wilson achieved emotional and heterosexual maturity. Shy, reserved, and deferential to the outgoing Dr. Wilson, she was intensely ambitious for her husband and son. She was also extraordinarily sensitive to what she felt were slights of others; and, when Wilson or his father encountered setbacks, she invariably attributed them to the spite and malice of their opponents. While Wilson's father pointed out his son's faults and tried to temper his impatience and aggressiveness, she was completely uncritical. Much more than Dr. Wilson, she gave Woodrow the feeling that he was not only intellectually, but morally, superior to his colleagues—a trait that contributed to one of Wilson's greatest failings, his overconfidence. Her influence had a great deal to do with Wilson's shyness and uneasiness with people who were not close to him, and his particular dependence on women. Mrs. Wilson was often ill—probably on a psychosomatic basis—and extremely anxious and worrisome about Woodrow's health. Wilson's attitudes toward illness, derived from both parents, had most important consequences for his career. There is also good evidence that Mrs. Wilson suffered from chronic depression; her son later said many times that he had inherited his tendency toward melancholy from his mother's side.

II

No study of Wilson's behavior during the great crises of his career can be complete without taking into account the effects of the cerebral vascular disease from which he suffered, intermittently, from the age of thirty-nine until his death in 1924. In 1896, Wilson had a stroke which caused a marked weakness of his right hand, and he had recurrences in 1900, 1904, 1906, and 1907. The stroke of 1906 caused not only weakness of his right arm but almost complete blindness of his left eye, a syndrome indicative of an embolus from the left internal carotid artery. Wilson's attempts to adapt to the consequences of the stroke caused changes in his behavior and helped set into motion events relevant to his defeats in the quadrangle plan and graduate college controversies at Princeton. The course of carotid artery disease is very variable, with frequent remissions, and, in the light of today's knowledge, it is not surprising that Wilson was in good health while governor of New Jersey and when he became president of the United States. The disease, however, is ultimately a progressive one and, by the end of World War I, Wilson was showing signs of generalized cerebral involvement. In Paris, he had an attack of influenza, probably a virus encephalopathy, which, superimposed on pre-existing brain damage, produced changes in behavior which may have influenced the outcome of the peace negotiations. In October 1919 he had a massive stroke that completely paralyzed the left side of his body and produced mental attitudes and personality changes which were important factors in his failure to obtain ratification of the Treaty of Versailles.[26]

The Georges are not neurologists or psychiatrists, and some of the information on which the above reconstruction is based was not available to them. Yet even lay observers, such as Herbert Hoover, had commented on the changes of Wilson's mental functioning after the Paris illness. Any behavioral scientist should have wondered about the effects of the massive stroke of 1919. Similarly, the Georges ignored Wilson's stroke of 1906 as a factor in his behavior and explained his problems during the quadrangle (or "quad") plan and graduate college controversies as stemming from an emotionally disturbed childhood.

The controversy over the location and character of the graduate college was the most dramatic event of Woodrow Wilson's term as president of Princeton University. A wealthy alumnus, William C. Procter, in 1909 offered to donate $500,000 to help build a graduate college to house graduate students, but he included an important stipulation—that the building be located on the golf course, nearly a mile from the center of the campus. It was the site which the dean of the small existing graduate school, Andrew Fleming West, a close friend of Procter, had selected. West favored an off-campus site so that graduate students might study undisturbed by undergraduates. Wilson consistently argued that they should live close together, in order, as he put it, that the graduate students might energize the intellectual life of the undergraduates.[27] It was the same idea that had led Wilson to institute the preceptorial system and to propose his quadrangle plan. Originally, both West and Wilson had advocated a central location, but West had changed his view. West believed that Wilson had delayed action on the graduate college in favor of his preceptorial and quad plans—which indeed he had—and charged that Wilson had gone back on his promise of support, given in 1906, at the time when West turned down an offer of the presidency of the Massachusetts Institute of Technology. Wilson believed, with ample reason, that West was an intellectual dilettante, who wished to maintain dominion over an elitist world of his own. Some months before the Procter offer, Wilson had reorganized the faculty committee on the graduate school and broken West's absolute control of the policies of the graduate school.

The Georges see the conflict as based on Wilson's perception of West as a father figure. In their view, the situation caused Wilson to give vent to the unconscious hostility which he had felt, but had never been able to release, toward his own father. They regard the issue of the location of the college as merely an excuse for Wilson to release this unconscious hostility by doing battle with West. At some level, they say, West evoked in Wilson the image of his father. Therefore Wilson resisted West "with all the violence he had once felt, but never ventured to express, in response to his father's overwhelming domination." But, they add, Wilson could not confess, even to himself, that he experienced West as "an unbearable threat," and, consequently, he "disguised all his volcanic feelings against West in terms of a great moral crusade in which he championed the 'right.' "[28]

We have already examined the Georges' previous evidence for Wilson's "unconscious hostility" toward his father. Before considering further their interpretation of the graduate college controversy, additional background is necessary. The situation was already a tense one because of the bitter struggle that had occurred over the quadrangle plan. This was a proposal by Wilson to abolish the exclusive undergraduate eating clubs and construct quadrangles, or residential colleges, assignment to which would be made by lot. Opposition, often violent, soon developed and was led by the eastern alumni. The trustees, who had approved the plan "in principle," when Wilson presented it in June 1907, withdrew their support in October. Wilson continued to press for it, and the battle became so acrimonious that a wealthy trustee and generous contributor to the university, M. Taylor Pyne, threatened to withdraw his support if Wilson ever mentioned the quad plan again.[29] Dean West led the minority faction of the faculty who were in opposition, which, to Wilson's great sorrow, included his best friend, John Grier Hibben.

Wilson's illness was an important factor in the defeat of his quad plan and also laid the groundwork for his defeat in the graduate college controversy. In 1906 he was at the height of his popularity and power at Princeton: the curriculum had been reformed, the faculty upgraded, and the preceptorial system successfully launched. Except for an episode of weakness in his right arm lasting several months in 1904, he had been in excellent health during his presidency. The stroke of 1906 was the first one to be recognized as such, and Wilson received a gloomy prognosis. He and his wife were aware that the condition was similar to that which had robbed his father of his mental faculties. Characteristically, Wilson's reaction was to immerse himself in his work. Originally, he had thought that the quad plan would take twenty years; now he thought it immediately attainable. In the interests of his health, he cut down on his social life. He took regular naps, reduced his personal contacts, and, in contrast to his previous habits, now decided to meet members of the Princeton community only on official business. Prior to the formal announcement to the trustees of the plan in June 1907, he had mentioned the idea to only three intimate friends on the faculty and not at all to the alumni. This lack of preparation contrasted markedly with the way he had organized support for the preceptorial system and must be judged an important cause of his failure. Wilson's increased overconfidence was one of a number of behavioral changes that occurred after the stroke in 1906; he became less empathic, more stubborn, and more prone to overgeneralize and personalize his problems.

The question of the site of the graduate college was far more than a pretext for Wilson to destroy West. At stake were Wilson's control of the university and the character of its educational program. It is debatable whether close association between graduates and undergraduates would have yielded the advantage that Wilson envisaged. However, his emphasis on such an association in the preceptorial and quadrangle plans indicates that the issue was important in itself. The Georges' treatment of the graduate college controversy makes it seem that Wilson stood practically alone in pressing his arguments. Actually, many others shared his point of view. Approximately half of the trustees supported Wilson, and the various votes related to the controversy were all close. Although the evidence is not conclusive, it appears that a large majority of the faculty, particularly the professors who were doing most of the graduate instruction, preferred that the college be built in the midst of the campus. In fact, members of the faculty (and of the board of trustees) were constantly pressing Wilson to stand firm and even to remove West or reduce his influence over the graduate program and college.[30]

Wilson's personality and his pattern of behavior under stress had a great deal to do with the events of the controversies over the quad plan and graduate college. But Wilson's aversion to Dean West did not come about because of unconscious feelings toward his father. Wilson detested West because West was the condensed symbol of so many of the social, educational, economic, and political problems that Wilson faced at Princeton. Moreover, Wilson did not "disguise" his feelings toward West. He expressed them quite openly.[31]

It is impossible in a single article to provide detailed analysis of and commentary on an entire book. It must suffice to say that we believe that the Georges' view of the relationship between Wilson and Edward M. House was highly distorted by overreliance on the House diary, which often presents a one-sided and unreliable account of events; that we find their explanation for Wilson's attempts to remain out of World War I almost arcane; and that recent research has considerably revised their explanation for the so-called break between Wilson and House at the Paris Peace Conference.[32]

III

By today's standard, the Georges' use of psychological theory is inadequate. Their formulations have been largely superseded by the views of ego psychology and by considerations of the development of the self and of social roles and interactions. While the Georges cannot be criticized for not anticipating these approaches, it should be pointed out that the works of Harry Stack Sullivan, Karen Horney, and Erich Fromm were available to them. Also, the common-sense view that most children identify with their parents and grow to resemble them does not seem to have played a part in their thinking. By the 1950s, the idea of fixed childhood hostilities, locked deep in the unconscious, impervious to change, and ready to burst forth in pristine fury, was being challenged. For the Georges to suggest that Wilson simply and directly transferred his hatred of his father to West and Senator Lodge during the fight over the Versailles Treaty is highly mechanistic, reductionistic, and deterministic. The formulation leaves no room for consideration of character development or identity formation.

The authors could have given a more realistic view of Wilson's relationship with his parents had they taken up family values and cultural norms. For example, Wilson's reluctance to express any negative feelings toward members of his family was shared by them and was a facet of their subculture. It is difficult to accept any theory of personality that does not take into consideration a subject's relationship with his mother, particularly Wilson's mother, who instilled so much anxiety in him. Then, the Georges give the impression that all that one has to know about Wilson is that his self-esteem was disastrously low. Yet self-esteem is rarely unitary. One may feel confident in some areas, insecure in others. Wilson was bothered by feelings that he was ugly; he seems to have identified himself in this respect with his rather physically unattractive mother. Yet he rarely had doubts about his intellectual and leadership qualities after reaching maturity.

Even without detailed knowledge of Wilson's childhood, one would assume, from his compulsive personality traits and his need to control his environment, that he had anxieties and insecurities. Yet to translate such insecurities into an insatiable drive for political power is to provide far too simple an explanation for a complex, multidetermined process. Further, the Georges state:

His [Wilson's] stern Calvinistic conscience forbade an unabashed pursuit of power for personal gratification. He could express his desire for power only insofar as he convincingly rationalized it in terms of altruistic service and fused it with laudable social objectives.[33]

It is true that Wilson often validated pragmatically arrived at decisions in moral terms, but when in the world of human affairs is concern for the public good divorced from personal gratification?

Woodrow Wilson and Colonel House has important implications for writers of psychobiography. They should be aware that personality theories derive, not only from scientific investigations, but also from ideology, the social milieu, and the personal problems of their authors. Theories are dated, as the Georges themselves point out; theories not only change with the years, but proponents of the same theory differ in their interpretations of it. In an interdisciplinary endeavor, more than superficial knowledge of areas outside of one's primary field is necessary. The historian or political scientist should be familiar, not only with psychoanalytic theory, but also with the many aspects of behavioral science, which, in recent years, have so profoundly influenced psychoanalysis. Above all, the psychobiographer should immerse himself in the primary biographical sources, not least of all for the reason that the criteria for clinical evidence may be quite different from those for historical work.[34] The great acclaim accorded the Georges' book may have helped give the impression that psychobiography can be written by furnishing "deep" interpretations of the work of others. No psychobiography is better than the research on which it rests.

NOTES

1 Sigmund Freud and William C. Bullitt, *Thomas Woodrow Wilson* (Boston: Houghton Mifflin, 1967).

2 Arthur S. Link, "The Case for Woodrow Wilson," *Harper's*, April 1967. pp. 85–93.

3 Erik H. Erikson, in *The New York Review of Books*, February 9, 1967, pp. 3–6; reprinted in *The International Journal of Psychoanalysis* 48(1967):462–68.

4 The degree of Freud's involvement will not be known until the Bullitt Papers at Yale are opened and we can see what Freud actually wrote. It is well known that Freud disliked Americans in general and Wilson in particular, who he thought was the embodiment of the Puritan moralist and was responsible for the breakup of the Austro-Hungarian Empire.

5 Alexander L. George and Juliette L. George, *Woodrow Wilson and Colonel House: A Personality Study* (New York: Dover Publications, Inc., 1964). Although the book includes an analysis of Wilson's relationship with Colonel House, the central concern is to provide a portrait of Wilson's personality and political behavior (see p. xxi), and it is this portrait, not the analysis of the relationship between Wilson and House, that is the focus of the present essay.

6 Bernard Brodie, "A Psychoanalytic Interpretation of Woodrow Wilson," in Bruce Mazlish, ed., *Psychoanalysis and History* (New York: Grossett & Dunlap, 1971), pp. 115–23.

7 Fred I. Greenstein and Michael Lerner, eds. *A Source Book for the Study of Personality and Politics* (Chicago: Markham, 1971), p. 77.

8 *The Wilson Quarterly* 1 (Winter 1977):68.

9 Robert C. Tucker, "The Georges' Wilson Reexamined: An Essay on Psychobiography," *American Political Science Review* 71(June 1977):606–18.

10 However, Alexander George, in an article published ten years ago ("Power as a Compensatory Value for Political Leaders," *Journal of Social Issues* (July 1968):29–49), still confidently advanced the theory that Wilson's damaged self-esteem, caused by his tyrannical and demanding father, was an important factor in propelling him into politics. The first, second, and perhaps the third, volumes of *The Papers of Woodrow Wilson,* which shed much new light on the relationship between Wilson and his father, were available when George's article was written. He presumably did not read these volumes; in any event, he did not cite them.

11 George and George, *Woodrow Wilson and Colonel House,* p. 7.

12 Wilson to Ellen Louise Axson, March 29, 1884, Arthur S. Link et al., *The Papers of Woodrow Wilson,* 28 vols. to date (Princeton, N.J.: Princeton University Press, 1966–) 3: 496; hereinafter cited as *PWW.*

13 George and George, *Woodrow Wilson and Colonel House,* pp. 114, 272, 6, 8.

14 Ibid., p. 8.

15 Margaret Axson Elliot, *My Aunt Louisa and Woodrow Wilson* (Chapel Hill, N.C.: University of North Carolina Press, 1944), p. 122.

16 George and George, *Woodrow Wilson and Colonel House,* p. 8.

17 Expressions of her feelings occur again and again in Helen W. Bones to Jessie Bones Brower, February 12 and 23, April 1 and 12, May 3, and June 1, 7, and 18, 1913. Woodrow Wilson Collection, Princeton University Library.

18 George and George, *Woodrow Wilson and Colonel House,* p. 8.

19 See for example, Ray Stannard Baker, *Woodrow Wilson, Life and Letters: Youth, 1856–1890* (Garden City, N.Y.: Doubleday, Page and Co., 1927); Josephus Daniels, *The Life of Woodrow Wilson* (Philadelphia: The John C. Winston Co., 1924); William Bayard Hale, *Woodrow Wilson; The Story of His Life* (Garden City, N.Y.: Doubleday, Page and Co., 1912); William Allen White, *Woodrow Wilson* (Boston and New York: Houghton Mifflin, 1924).

20 About this episode, see John M. Mulder, *Woodrow Wilson: The Years of Preparation* (Princeton, N.J.: Princeton University Press, 1978), pp. 15–17.

21 Bliss Perry, *And Gladly Teach* (Boston: Houghton Mifflin, 1935), p. 153.

22 Wilson to Joseph Ruggles Wilson, December 16, 1888, *PWW,* 6:30–31.

23 None of these letters was written during Wilson's early childhood; they date from the year 1875, when Wilson was eighteen years old, and they include seventy-six letters written before September 1885, when Wilson began his first teaching job at Bryn Mawr College. They are printed in *PWW,* vols. 1–5.

24 *Congressional Government: A Study in American Politics* (Boston: Houghton Mifflin, 1885), p. iii.

Thirty years later, long after his father's death, we hear Wilson saying about his father: "I remember my father as essentially humble and devout before God, spirited and confident before men. A natural leader, with a singular gift of clear, eloquent, convincing speech. Generous, playful, full of high spirits, and yet given to most laborious industry, alike in the use of books and in the administration of church affairs. A man who believed much more in the efficacy of Christian simple and pure living than in dogmatic advice or spiritual conversation—a robust Christian.

"The description I naturally associate with his name would be something like this: "Generous, high-spirited, thoughtful, studious, a master of men and of thought, who sought the life of dogma in conduct and preferred a pure life to a pious profession" (c. May 25, 1914).

And again: "As I look back on my boyhood, it seems to me that all the sense I got, I got by association with my father. He was good fun: he was a good comrade; and the experience he had had put a lot of sense in him that I had not been endowed with by birth, at any rate; and by constant association with him, I saw the world and the tasks of the world through his eyes, and because I believed in him I aspired to do and be the thing that he believed in" (May 29, 1914).

25 WW to Ellen A. Wilson, April 18, 1888, *PWW,* 5:719.

26 See Edwin A. Weinstein, "Woodrow Wilson's Neurological Illness," *Journal of American History* 57(September 1970):324–51. On a basis of new evidence, it is not likely, as was stated in this article, that Wilson had a stroke in Paris.

27 As Wilson put it in an address before the Princeton Club of New York on April 7, 1910: "As I look back upon my own studies as a graduate student, I realize that ... the intellectual limitations of the men with whom I was associated in the great graduate school I attended, was that their thought was so centered upon special lines of study that they had become impatient of everything that drew them away from them. I have heard these men again and again deplore the necessity they would some day be under of going through the drudgery of teaching stupid undergraduates,—a state of mind and a point of view which utterly unfitted them for the very profession they were approaching. That was due, in my mind, to the dissociation of graduate study in the life of the university from the undergraduate body.

"Not only that, but I believe that our universities lack the impulse of advanced study, so far as their undergraduates are concerned, largely because their undergraduates are not sufficiently brought into contact with the graduates. You know, gentlemen, that the process of education is a process of contagion. If you want to educate a man, put him in close association with the kind of intellectual fire you wish him to be touched by" (*PWW*, 20–345).

28 George and George, *Woodrow Wilson and Colonel House*, pp. 40, 43.

29 Melancthon W. Jacobus to Wilson, November 5, 1907, *PWW*, 17:468–69.

30 Arthur S. Link wishes to state that much new evidence discovered since the publication of his *Wilson: The Road to the White House* in 1947 has convinced him that his treatment of Wilson and West and the graduate college controversy is inadequate and unbalanced.

31 The entire graduate college controversy is amply documented in *PWW*, vols. 18–20.

32 The most authoritative study of House at the Paris Peace Conference, Inga Floro, *Colonel House in Paris: A Study of American Policy at the Paris Peace Conference 1919* (Aarhus, Denmark: Universitetsforlaget, 1973), proves conclusively that the cause of the so called break between the two men was House's failure to follow Wilson's explicit instructions while the latter was in the United States.

33 George and George, *Woodrow Wilson and Colonel House*, p. 117.

34 The best example in the past few years of a psychiatrist's use of primary historical sources is John E. Mack, *A Prince of Our Disorder: The Life of T. E. Lawrence* (Boston: Little, Brown, 1976).

13

Woodrow Wilson and Colonel House: A Reply to Weinstein, Anderson, and Link

Juliette L. George
Alexander L. George

Arthur S. Link of Princeton University has been studying and writing about Woodrow Wilson for some forty years, and he is the editor of *The Papers of Woodrow Wilson*. The thirty-six volumes thus far published in this series are a tribute to his prodigious scholarship. By common consent, Professor Link is the preeminent Wilson scholar of our time. If Link finds serious fault with an interpretation of Wilson, it behooves those who advanced it to reexamine their work in the light of his criticisms. As authors of *Woodrow Wilson and Colonel House: A Personality Study*, we felt placed under such an obligation upon the publication in *Political Science Quarterly* three years ago of an article by Link in collaboration with Edwin A. Weinstein (a psychiatrist and neurologist who has been studying and writing about Wilson for almost fifteen years), and James William Anderson (a clinical psychologist). In their article, Weinstein, Anderson, and Link characterized *Woodrow Wilson and Colonel House* as "an essentially incorrect interpretation of the personality of Woodrow Wilson and its effect on his career."[1]

Over the past few years, therefore, we have reviewed our work and have incorporated into our research a great deal of manuscript material that has become available since the publication of *Woodrow Wilson and Colonel House* in 1956. This review in the light of all the evidence, old and new, has served to confirm our belief in the validity of the interpretation of Wilson we offered in *Woodrow Wilson and Colonel House*. Indeed, the data now available permit a much fuller delineation of the relationship between Wilson and his father—of the extraordinary bond that existed between them, the very intensity of which, in our view, is related to the intensity of Wilson's early self-doubt, his suffering and need for approval (all of which now also may be more fully documented). We continue

Reprinted with permission from *Political Science Quarterly*, 96(Winter 1981–82):641–65.

191

to view Wilson as a great tragic figure whose "tragic flaw"—a ruinously self-defeating refusal to compromise with his opponents on certain issues that had become emotionally charged for him—evolved out of low self-estimates that we believe he developed as a child in response to his father's demands.

We consider it unfortunate, moreover, that Weinstein, Anderson, and Link present as though it were an indisputable fact Dr. Weinstein's *hypothesis* that beginning in 1896, Woodrow Wilson suffered a series of brain-damaging strokes that significantly and adversely affected his political functioning even so early as during his Princeton presidency. That Weinstein's retrospective interpretation of Wilson's medical problems is open to question among qualified medical specialists is obvious from the statement by Michael F. Marmor, M.D., of the Stanford University School of Medicine (see appendix). Of even greater concern, however, is the fact that Professor Link has permitted himself to state unequivocally in *The Papers of Woodrow Wilson* that Wilson suffered such strokes. In numerous notes and other editorial apparatus to several volumes of *The Papers,* Link asserts that Wilson had small strokes in 1896 and 1907 and "a major stroke" in 1906.[2] We believe he has thereby compromised the objectivity of that otherwise superb series and therefore compromised its value to historians, both present and future.

Weinstein, Anderson, and Link state in their critique that *Woodrow Wilson and Colonel House*

> suffers from three major deficiencies, which, taken together, result in an inaccurate portrayal of Wilson's personality. The principal failing of the book is that the research on which it rests is inadequate. Second, the Georges fail to recognize the limitations of their psychological model and misrepresent evidence to fit their theory. Third, they ignore Wilson's neurological disorders as conditions affecting his behavior.[3]

We shall address these criticisms in turn.

SOURCE MATERIALS FOR *WOODROW WILSON AND COLONEL HOUSE*

Weinstein, Anderson, and Link disparage our research—*Woodrow Wilson and Colonel House* furnishes " 'deep' interpretations of the work of others."[4] In our book, we characterized our work as "largely a synthesis and reinterpretation of well-known facts of Wilson's career."[5] We did not claim to be historians, nor was it our aim to uncover new data: rather, we hoped to cast a fresh eye on that which was already known. Indeed, we extracted a great deal of useful information from the published literature. To the extent that we could gain access to them at the time we were doing our research, however, we also studied the major primary sources.

The three principal relevant manuscript collections were: the Wilson papers at the Library of Congress, the papers of Ray Stannard Baker at the Library of Congress, and the papers of Colonel House at the Sterling Memorial Library at Yale University. Mrs. Wilson, who was notoriously chary of granting scholars access to the Wilson papers, rejected our periodically renewed requests until our study was almost complete. Then we were allowed to read a series of documents which, Katharine E. Brand (Mrs. Wilson's representative in the Manuscript Division of the Library of Congress) assured us, was all the collection contained for the years of Wilson's childhood and youth. We found little of significance in what we were allowed to see that Baker had not already published.

Miss Brand herself had charge of Baker's papers and she granted us access to them. We studied the Baker papers, over a period of years, to the great enrichment of our comprehension of Woodrow Wilson. For Baker, with Mrs. Wilson's help, had collected the reminiscences of scores of Wilson's family, friends, and associates. His papers remain an indispensable source for Wilson researchers.

Access to Colonel House's papers was controlled by Charles Seymour, president-emeritus of Yale University. Shortly after Seymour announced that Colonel House's diary would be open to scholars, we applied for, and were granted, permission to read it. It is a source of abiding satisfaction to us that, although we do not consider ourselves historians, we found and published for the first time numerous passages in House's diary (which Seymour had omitted from *The Intimate Papers of Colonel House*) revealing of certain significant aspects of the Colonel's attitude toward Wilson.

Inga Floto, whose book *Colonel House in Paris: A Study of American Policy at the Paris Peace Conference 1919* Weinstein, Anderson, and Link refer to as "the most authoritative study of House at the Paris Peace Conference," characterizes *Woodrow Wilson and Colonel House* as "epoch making," a " 'coup' from an historian's point of view."[6] We find it awkward to cite her generous praise but consider the disparagement of our research by Weinstein, Anderson, and Link justification for doing so. *Woodrow Wilson and Colonel House*, Floto writes, is "the first attempt at a consistent utilization of House's voluminous diary in its full, chronological scope," and she credits us with having made available material of "decisive importance."[7]

Weinstein, Anderson, and Link make no reference whatever to our use of primary source materials, let alone to the fact that we unearthed new data. We consider this an unfair omission and their criticism of our research unjustified.

WOODROW WILSON'S PERSONALITY

We turn now to the second of our "principal failings": "...the Georges fail to recognize the limitations of their psychological model and misrepresent evidence to fit their theory."[8] It seems to us that we were not only aware but scrupulous to convey to readers an awareness that what we were presenting for their consideration is an interpretation of Wilson based on certain hypotheses, which we articulated and invited them to examine on the basis of data, which we also presented. We explicitly stated in our book that the validity of our interpretations is necessarily a matter of opinion: `

No incontrovertible proof can be offered. Nor can any one incident be relied upon to sustain this or any other theory of Wilson's motivation. It is only when the man's career is viewed as a whole that a repetition of certain basically similar behavior is discernible. Let the reader consider whether these patterns of behavior become more consistently comprehensible in terms of the explanations herein offered than in terms of other explanations. That will be the best test of their usefulness.[9]

Weinstein, Anderson, and Link evince no such restraint in the presentation of their hypotheses. Consider, for example, the way they conclude their statement concerning Wilson's inability to read until he was eleven, which they attribute to developmental dyslexia, physiologically determined, and which we, on the other hand, suggest in *Woodrow Wilson and Colonel House* may have derived from feelings of inadequacy and been an unconscious expression of resentment of his father's perfectionist demands.[10] Say Weinstein, Anderson, and Link: "We do not have a good record of Wilson's childhood such as might be gained from contemporary letters, diaries, or autobiographies; like any other child, he may have felt insecurities. However, it is certain that they did not come about in the manner postulated by the Georges."[11] Whence, in the absence of adequate data, these authors' certainty? Is peremptory assertion a substitute for reasoned argument? So apparently Weinstein, Anderson, and Link think; for so many of their interpretations and medical diagnoses are couched in categorical language— language that we consider inappropriate to the speculative nature of their enterprise.

The Dyslexia Hypothesis

Let us get down to specific cases: we do not think our hypothesis about Wilson's delayed acquisition of reading skills can be thus handily dispatched. Nor do we consider it irrelevant that Link's present certainty about the cause of Wilson's reading problem follows decades of his failing to recognize that a problem requiring explanation even existed. In *Wilson: The Road to the White House,* published in 1947, he did not even refer to Wilson's early learning difficulties and wrote that "Wilson's boyhood was notable, if for nothing else, because of his normal development."[12] (This notwithstanding that years before, Baker, whose work Link cites, had specifically drawn attention to Wilson's early slow development.)[13]

Twenty years later, in 1967—long after we, in *Woodrow Wilson and Colonel House,* had again drawn attention to the data of Wilson's early learning problems and he himself had mentioned in passing that Wilson "was a late starter"—Link was still arguing that "all evidence indicates that Wilson had a normal boyhood, at least as normal as was possible for boys growing up in the South during the Civil War and Reconstruction."[14]

By 1968, Link was at least referring, however doubtfully, to the "family tradition" which "may or may not be correct" according to which Wilson "did not learn to read until he was nine." (Actually the data indicate he had learned only his letters when he was nine. He could not read until he was eleven.) To be sure, Link was now willing to acknowledge that the boy "seems to have suffered from insecurity on account of his inability to achieve as rapidly as he thought he should," but he was quick to pronounce it "normal insecurity." "His personal advantages and precocity aside," Link wrote, "Wilson seems to have been a remarkably normal person during the first forty years of his life. His childhood was serene. . . ."[15]

The article in *Political Science Quarterly* by Weinstein, Anderson, and Link provides gratifying indication that Link has at last taken notice of what he joins his colleagues in correctly describing as the "well-known" facts of Wilson's boyhood learning difficulties. However, the diagnosis he joins them in offering—developmental dyslexia—seems to us to collapse under scrutiny.

Weinstein, Anderson, and Link speak of developmental dyslexia as if it were a now thoroughly understood disability of established etiology.

> Undiagnosed in Wilson's childhood, the condition was well-known to neurologists at the time that the Georges wrote their book. However, a number of psychiatrists and psychologists still believed that the condition was an emotional rather than a neurological problem, and the Georges simply chose an explanation that was currently popular. The condition is a frequent one, occurring in about 10 percent of the school population, significantly more frequently in boys. Research over the past seventy years indicates that developmental dyslexia is caused by a delay in the establishment of the dominance of one cerebral hemisphere—usually the left—for language.[16]

A far less confident tone about the nature of reading disabilities and various types of dyslexia is taken by several of the experts who participated in the conference on dyslexia conducted in 1977 by the National Institute of Mental Health. For example, Michael Rutter, a British psychiatrist, contends that the term "dyslexia" has not yet been even satisfactorily defined and that "the presumption of a neurological basis is just that—namely a presumption." He considers it "meaningless" at this time to attempt any estimate of the prevalence of dyslexia.[17] While there is great interest in the hypothesis that a delay in the acquisition of left-hemisphere dominance may be associated with some cases of reading difficulty, Rutter believes that "the evidence on this point remains inconclusive." John Hughes of the Department of Neurology, University of Illinois School of Medicine, writes: "Satz (1976) has summarized the data relating cerebral dominance and dyslexia and has claimed that information is still lacking on this crucial issue." As for the etiology of reading disorders, a number of eminent psychiatrists *continue* to believe that emotional factors are the basis for some of them.[18]

Our purpose in citing the continuing perplexities of specialists in dyslexia research is to counter the impression that readers might well gain from Weinstein, Anderson, and Link that medical research has solved the mystery of reading disabilities and that psychological explanations have been eliminated for all varieties. According to Rutter the very concept of developmental dyslexia "constitutes a hypothesis—the hypothesis that within the large overall group of disabled readers there is a subgroup with a distinct constitutionally determined condition."[19] Very well. Weinstein, Anderson, and Link claim that "Tommy" Wilson was such an intrinsically impaired child. What is their evidence?

"Specific evidence" of developmental dyslexia, Weinstein, Anderson, and Link claim, is that Wilson "was a slow reader into adult life. At the Johns Hopkins, the amount of assigned reading was his bane. 'Steady reading,' he wrote his fiancée, 'always demands of me more expenditure of resolution and dogged energy than any other sort of work.' "[20]

The sentence from Wilson's letter to his fiancée, Ellen Axson, that Weinstein, Anderson, and Link quote in support of their thesis is incorrectly cited as having been written on 29 March 1884. This is an error of some consequence, since its correct date, 29 *November* 1884, places it within the period that Wilson was making a heroic effort to toil through the reading required for obtaining a Ph.D. It was an effort he detested, which only weeks before he had decided to abandon on the grounds, he had written Ellen Axson, that "a forced march through fourteen thousand pages of dry reading" would jeopardize his health. "I am quite sure that I shall profit much more substantially from a line of reading of my own choosing, in the lines of my own original work. . . ."[21]

Nonetheless, in those days, as in these, a degree made a man more marketable. Wilson, avid to equip himself for a job that would give him the wherewithal to marry, reluctantly embarked on the hateful "forced march" shortly after he had renounced it. The drudgery was all but unbearable. His letters to Ellen Axson during these weeks and until mid-February, 1885, chronicle his growing distress. He is tempted "to throw down these heavy volumes and run out into the glories of the open air." He berates himself for not accepting the necessity of complying with the requirements. Try as he will to submit, "I often grow savagely out of humour with my present state of pupilage. . . ."[22]

Reading for the Ph.D. was not the full measure of his problem. "I am handicapped for my degree," he wrote to a friend, "because of the extra work with which I was indiscreet enough to saddle myself." He had committed himself to collaborate on a history of political economy with one of his professors. "I am to wade—am wading, indeed—through innumerable American text writers," he continued, "for the purpose of writing . . . about one-third of the projected treatise." As for the degree, "it's this year or never."[23] The burden proved too great and, finally, on 19 February 1885, he wrote to his fiancée: "I have given up—this time conclusively—the struggle for the degree. . . . Cramming kills me; reading in development of a subject improves and invigorates me."[24]

Is the sentence that Weinstein, Anderson, and Link pluck from one of the letters Wilson wrote in the midst of the struggle described above credible evidence of developmental dyslexia? That construction of it strikes us as tortured. It seems to us much more likely that Wilson's statement indicates his distress at the *kind* of reading that was being demanded of him and the crushing amount of it.

If the record suggested that Wilson was generally a reluctant reader, slow because the very act of reading was difficult for him, the case for Weinstein, Anderson, and Link's hypothesis of developmental dyslexia would gain some ground. The record fails them, however. One has but to look through the diary he kept during the summer after his freshman year at Princeton to see that he was in fact an omnivorous reader, provided only that he had a taste for the matter at hand: Macaulay, Shakespeare, Gibbon, Plutarch, Pepys, Dickens, novels, magazines, encyclopedia articles—all passed under his frequently enthusiastic but, by preference, unhurried scrutiny.[25] The argument may be summed up in a simple statistic: it takes no less than thirty pages of quite fine print in the index to the first twelve volumes of *The Papers of Woodrow Wilson* to cover the subject category, "Woodrow Wilson—Reading."[26]

Weinstein, Anderson, and Link claim two other "groups" of "specific evidence that Wilson had developmental dyslexia": he was "extremely poor in arithmetic," an ineptitude commonly associated with developmental dyslexia; and he quickly "and without practice" mastered writing with his left hand when in 1896 (as the result of a stroke, they say, an assertion about which more later) he was unable to write with his right hand. This ability "strongly suggests that he had mixed cerebral dominance for language."[27]

We question that the dyslexia hypothesis finds support from these "groups" of evidence. Being "extremely poor in arithmetic" can have a score of explanations other than developmental dyslexia; moreover, whatever his difficulties with arithmetic, Wilson's capabilities ranged from keeping meticulous personal financial records to overseeing the formulation of national economic policy and the negotiation of intricate international economic questions. As for his left-handed writing, given Wilson's considerable artistic talents and his intense perseverence, it is not surprising that he succeeded in acquiring that skill. It was not the easy accomplishment that Weinstein, Anderson, and Link suggest, however. We know from Stockton Axson's account that Wilson set about the task with "customary determination."[28] We know from Wilson himself that he practiced "laboriously," notwithstanding which writing with his left hand remained "clumsy and uncertain," "awkward," "tedious," "a painfully slow process"—"it takes me half an hour to [write] one of these pages."[29] In short, Wilson does not seem to have been naturally ambidextrous. Even with practice, writing with his left hand seems to have remained an uncomfortable occasional necessity rather than an easy alternative to the use of his clearly preferred right hand.

The dyslexia hypothesis suffers further when one considers two aspects of dyslexia about which the experts generally agree: that it is strongly associated with disordered handwriting and with persistently atrocious spelling.[30] Wilson's handwriting—as surely Weinstein, Anderson, and Link would agree—is a very model of beautiful penmanship. Even his check registers look like copperplate. And he was an excellent speller. His errors were few and far between.

For the purpose of pursuing our critics' train of thought, however, let us grant for a moment that "Tommy" Wilson suffered from some inborn defect, that it was indeed developmental dyslexia that impeded his learning to read. What would the psychological consequences of such a disability have been, both upon the boy and his parents? The literature on dyslexia is clear that every poor reader, no matter what the cause of his problem, is predisposed to feeling inadequate, "bad," or "stupid."[31]

Weinstein, Anderson, and Link give passing recognition to the fact that "the reading disability affected Wilson's development and his relationship with his parents," but they immediately add "but hardly in the way that the Georges state." How, then, *was* the boy affected? "It probably made him more dependent on his family," they say. They acknowledge that "he may have feared that his reading problems indicated that he was stupid or lazy" and that "the condition probably made Dr. Wilson more pedagogic and insistent on drilling his 'lazy' son." Having edged up to the dread explanation, Weinstein, Anderson, and Link hurry away and remove Dr. Wilson with them: during the Civil War he was sometimes away from home; other family members read to Wilson and he enjoyed that; and the data are lacking, but whatever insecurities Wilson might have felt "it is certain that they did not come about in the manner postulated by the Georges."[32]

This account by Weinstein, Anderson, and Link leaves some nagging loose ends that not only deserve but demand consideration. What would the effect be on a boy to fear that he was stupid or lazy—and, by the way, there is no "may have" about it: years later when he was president, Wilson often reminisced about his boyhood with his physician and friend, Cary Grayson, and Grayson recalls that "he often spoke of himself as being a lazy boy."[33] What attitudes toward himself would his father's "insistent drilling" have engendered—his father, a master of the English language, a brilliant expositor of Calvinist doctrine, which says nothing about developmental dyslexia but a great deal about wickedness and sin and dereliction of duty? Would this devoted father, a man of his times, not have had an especially poignant stake in the intellectual progress of this, his third child but first son, and been frustrated and disappointed at the boy's poor performance? And would "Tommy's" self-concept not almost inevitably have suffered? Would he not have felt humiliated, unworthy, inadequate? In short, would this family situation not have fostered the ripening in a boy's heart of those low estimates of himself that these authors deny existed? It seems to us they overlook the ample evidence that this was the case and refuse to draw the conclusion obvious even from their prettified account of the family interaction.

Woodrow Wilson and His Father

For the sake of evaluating Weinstein, Anderson, and Link's thesis on its own ground, we have thus far omitted the ingredient of Dr. Wilson's propensity for sarcasm and severe criticism and how these are likely to have impinged upon his son's development. "The Georges claim that Wilson suffered from a troubled relationship with his father," write Weinstein, Anderson, and Link, and they reject the idea.[34] Having attempted to subtract Wilson's reading problem as indication of father-son stress, they try to belittle the significance of the testimony of young family members that Joseph R. Wilson, a man of many virtues to be sure, was also a sarcastic tease.

The evidence cannot be so handily dispatched, however. And now there is a good deal more of it than was available at the time we were writing *Woodrow*

Wilson and Colonel House. There is, for example, an unpublished manuscript by Dr. Stockton Axson, the much younger brother of the first Mrs. Wilson, who lived with the Woodrow Wilsons for a number of years. Axson was not only Woodrow Wilson's devoted friend for over forty years; he was also a great favorite of Wilson's father. The two were fast friends to the day Joseph Ruggles Wilson died, and Stockton Axson thought the old minister a great man. Yet he wrote at length of the forbidding side of Dr. Joseph Wilson and of how, when displeased, his humor "bubbled *hot*" in "scalding sarcasms" which could be "really withering." He had in him, Axson tells us, "a certain savage humor which caused him to say sometimes cruel things even to those who loved him and whom he loved." Notwithstanding his qualities of greatness, he was a "ruthless sort of a man," Axson wrote, "a man with a distinct streak of perversity in him." In his sarcasm, he reminded Axson of Jonathan Swift.[35]

The sarcasm, the mordant wit, the cruel teasing, the relentless drilling to which he subjected his son obviously constituted only one facet of Dr. Joseph Wilson's personality. We do not for a moment deny—nor did we in *Woodrow Wilson and Colonel House*—that there is rich and persuasive evidence of the comradeship between Wilson and his father, of abiding love, and of the transmission from father to son of moral values and of a range of skills and perceptions that fostered the greatness of Woodrow Wilson.[36] Recognizing and giving full weight to this evidence, however, does not necessitate refusing to recognize, as we think our critics refuse to do, that *all* facets of Joseph Wilson entered into his interaction with his son and that the syndrome we tried to trace in *Woodrow Wilson and Colonel House* also had important consequences. Weinstein, Anderson, and Link write as though they consider it beyond the realm of possibility that the demanding father may have generated in his sensitive son feelings of inadequacy and also of unconscious resentment. Is it likely that the boy never inwardly rebelled at the stern religious teachings graven into his soul? Did Woodrow Wilson enjoy some divine dispensation from experiencing conflicting emotions about a beloved parent? Is it really unthinkable to Weinstein, Anderson, and Link that Wilson may have had to deal with ambivalence?

There is the briefest intimation—half a sentence—that such questions crossed our critics' minds. "Dr. Wilson had a tremendous influence on his son," they write, "and probably no boy grows up without *some* resentment toward his father."[37] Weinstein, Anderson, and Link write as though any unconscious resentment Wilson felt toward his father was of minor dimensions and without significant repercussions for the understanding of his political behavior. They write as though his early learning difficulties neither resulted from nor led to psychological problems that importantly affected his development. They leave unmentioned and show no sign of having considered the implications of many self-revealing statements Wilson made in private conversations or of dozens of self-characterizations to be found in his letters, in his diaries, and sometimes even in his public utterances which bespeak great inner turmoil.

Wilson's Enduring Anxieties

We shall cite just one such statement to convey the flavor of the evidence. In 1884, at age twenty-eight—long before any of the "strokes" that Weinstein, Anderson, and Link claim altered his personality—Wilson wrote to his fiancée:

> It isn't pleasant or convenient to have strong passions: and it is particularly hard in my case to have to deal with unamiable feelings; because the only whip with which I can subdue them is the whip of hard study and that lacerates *me* as often as it conquers my crooked dispositions. I hope that none of my friends—and much more none of my enemies!—will ever find out *how much it costs me to give up my own way.* I have the uncomfortable feeling that I am carrying a volcano about with me.[38]

In other letters to Ellen Axson Wilson he refers to himself as "a man of a sensitive, restless, overwrought disposition." He speaks of his "sombre, morbid nature," his "fears," "anxieties," "morose moods," of "my poor, mixed, inexplicable nature." "Deep perturbations are natural to me, deep disturbances of spirit." He writes of "my natural self-distrust," of having "never been sanguine," of often falling when irritated into "the stern, indignant, defiant humour, the scarcely suppressed belligerent temper for which there are abundant materials in my disposition." "I have to guard my emotions from painful overflow," he confides.[39]

Such feelings, so persistently and intensely expressed, require explanation. Weinstein, Anderson, and Link offer none. We believe that these emotions were related to his ceaseless effort to maintain his self-esteem; that for Wilson carving out a sphere of competence in public life and striving for high achievement were a means of overcoming feelings of unimportance, of moral inferiority, of weakness, of mediocrity, of intellectual inadequacy; that in certain crucial situations in his public career, Wilson's self-defeating stubbornness and unwillingness to defer (or at least make expedient gestures of deference) to men whose cooperation was essential to the accomplishment of his goals were irrational manifestations of underlying low self-estimates against which he had constantly to struggle. It remains our conviction that the hypotheses advanced in *Woodrow Wilson and Colonel House,* applied to the vast body of data concerning Woodrow Wilson, have consistent explanatory power.[40]

WOODROW WILSON'S MEDICAL PROBLEMS

The third "principal failing" of *Woodrow Wilson and Colonel House,* according to Weinstein, Anderson, and Link, is that we "ignore Wilson's neurological disorders as conditions affecting his behavior." Undaunted by the virtual absence of medical records for this period of Wilson's life, they assert unequivocally that he suffered strokes in 1896, 1900, 1904, 1906, and 1907. They say that "by the end of World War I, Wilson was showing signs of generalized cerebral involvement." They state further that an episode of illness (which Weinstein had earlier diagnosed as a stroke) in April 1919 while he was negotiating the Versailles Peace

Treaty in Paris was not only influenza but "probably a virus encephalopathy, which, superimposed on pre-existing brain damage, produced changes in behavior which may have influenced the outcome of the peace negotiations." The massive stroke of October 1919 which, as is well known, paralyzed Wilson's left side also, according to Weinstein, Anderson, and Link, resulted in personality changes "which were important factors in his failure to obtain ratification of the Treaty of Versailles."[41]

It is certainly the case that we did not think that brain damage became a factor to consider in Wilson's political behavior until the autumn of 1919. While doing our research for *Woodrow Wilson and Colonel House*, we were alert to the possibility that personality changes affecting his handling of the League controversy in the Senate may have followed the catastrophic stroke of October 2. There was indeed evidence that he was given to outbursts of tears and of temper. His pathetic hope that the Democratic convention might renominate him and that he could win a third term in 1920 suggested impairment of his judgment of the political realities. A moving memorandum by Katharine E. Brand detailing Woodrow Wilson's last years made it clear that in many ways he was but a shadow of his former self. Nonetheless it was our conclusion then and it is our conclusion now that his behavior on the League issue remained intact. Whatever the nature of the brain damage he sustained in the fall of 1919, it altered neither his grasp of his problem with the Senate nor his strategy to deal with it. He had struck his unyielding position long before October 1919—a position that anguished practically everyone who cared personally about him or supported U.S. entry into the League of Nations. Wilson's conduct in this respect after the stroke was entirely consistent with his behavior before it. Both before and after, ample warnings were conveyed to him of the all but inevitable consequences of his refusal at every turn to compromise. Both before and after the stroke, he rejected these warnings, using the same arguments against compromise and cogently communicating them from his sickbed. The stroke seemed not to modify his behavior one whit in this respect.

Of course, it is possible to argue that he *would* have changed his position had he not been stricken. One can only speculate. Our own guess, given his history, is that he would not have yielded, that his stubbornness was in the deepest sense an expression of the integrity of his functioning on the public issue of supreme value to him. To the day he died, he expressed the conviction that history would vindicate him. To those who knew and loved him best, his refusal to compromise was a source of sorrow rather than of surprise. A sense of some terrible inner logic to his self-defeating behavior in terms of stable, persistent characteristics that they had long since recognized pervades their narratives.

His implacable enemy, Senator Henry Cabot Lodge, too, sensed that Wilson was held to his course by some invincible inner compulsion. The leading opponent of Senate ratification of the Treaty as submitted by Wilson, Lodge based his strategy upon a shrewd assessment of Wilson's personality. He calculated that Wilson would never agree to accept even minor reservations, that rather than compromise with the Senate and particularly with him (Lodge), Wilson would allow the treaty—League of Nations and all—to be defeated.[42]

The drama unfolded quite as Lodge had foreseen. His tactical finesse in maneuvering Wilson from one excruciating refusal to compromise to another testifies to his deadly insight into the tragic flaw in Wilson's character. He was not confounded by any perplexing "changes" in Wilson. His success at predicting Wilson's reactions suggests their constancy through all the vicissitudes of Wilson's health.

There was a time when Link recognized the relationship between Wilson's character and the recurrent defeats he suffered. In his book, *Wilson: The Road to the White House,* Link wrote:

> The Princeton period was the microcosm of a later macrocosm, and a political observer, had he studied carefully Wilson's career as president of Princeton University, might have forecast accurately the shape of things to come during the period when Wilson was president of the United States. What striking similarities there are between the Princeton and the national periods![43]

Link's comment pertained to the quad and graduate school controversies that fractured the Princeton community in 1907 and continued to reverberate bitterly for years after Wilson's resignation from the Princeton presidency in 1910. The quad controversy revolved about Wilson's plan to build quadrangles in which upper and lower classmen, some graduate students, and unmarried preceptors would live and eat together thereby, Wilson argued, stimulating intellectual exchange outside of the classroom. Opponents, among whom were wealthy alumni on whose contributions any construction would depend, viewed the plan as a threat to the eating clubs to which many were sentimentally attached and as having high-handedly been presented to the Board of Trustees before discussion with faculty and alumni. Moreover, they regarded Wilson's quad plan as a brazen attempt to divert attention and resources from the long-planned development of the graduate college under the leadership of its dean, Andrew Fleming West. In 1906, at Wilson's own behest, West had declined an invitation to become president of the Massachusetts Institute of Technology in favor of remaining at Princeton in order to put the graduate college into operation. A bitter dispute erupted between Wilson and his supporters and West and his supporters which crystallized around the ostensible issue of where the proposed graduate college should be located. Various concessions to Wilson's views were offered including substantial reform of the eating clubs, stripping Dean West of much of his authority, and compromising on the site issue. Wilson refused them all.

Writing in *Wilson: The Road to the White House* about what he then considered Wilson's unreasonable behavior, Link said: "The vagaries of his mind during this period are unfathomable." At that time he found the most striking fact about the whole Princeton controversy "the absence of any clear-cut issue" and that Wilson had shifted from one issue to another so that "it was almost impossible to tell where he really stood."[44] He attributed Wilson's difficulties at Princeton and later in his career explicitly to his *character* rather than to the logic of the situations he confronted:

> Wilson was a headstrong and determined man who was usually able to rationalize his actions in terms of the moral law and to identify his position with the divine will. . . . The time came at Princeton, Trenton, and Washington when Wilson did not command the support of the groups to whom he was responsible. Naturally, he was not able to change his character even had he wanted to change it, with the result that controversy and disastrous defeat occurred in varying degrees in all three cases.[45]

Link now holds a different view of the Princeton imbroglio, as he indicates in a footnote to the article by Weinstein, Anderson, and Link: "Arthur S. Link wishes to state that much new evidence discovered since the publication of his *Wilson: The Road to the White House* in 1947 has convinced him that his treatment of Wilson and West and the graduate college controversy is inadequate and un-balanced."[46]

The account of the Princeton controversy given by Weinstein, Anderson, and Link suggests that Wilson's actions in fact derived from a reasonable assessment of the situation rather than from characterological idiosyncrasies. If this is indeed Link's current interpretation, it collides with the simultaneous claim that "changes" in Wilson's behavior due to brain damage from the alleged strokes of 1896, 1900, 1904, 1906, and 1907 impaired his performance and played a critical role in his defeat. To us it seems that to the extent that they consider Wilson's refusal to compromise in the quad and graduate college battles a reasonable defense of his principles, they reduce the grounds for arguing the significance of the alleged personality and behavioral changes in consequence of the alleged strokes.

Wilson's Behavior in Paris

If in their article Professor Link repudiates the interpretive structure of *Wilson: The Road to the White House,* Dr. Weinstein also discloses a significant change of view involving one of his key diagnoses: that of Wilson's brief illness in Paris in April 1919. In his widely read and widely quoted article, "Woodrow Wilson's Neurological Illness," published in 1970, Weinstein stated that the most likely cause of Wilson's illness during the Peace Conference was a "cerebral vascular occlusion (blood clot in the brain)"—in short, a stroke. He construed certain aspects of Wilson's behavior during and after his illness as evidence of the kind of behavioral change that would confirm brain damage caused by a stroke. Weinstein described the "cerebral vascular occlusion" as "a lesion in the right cerebral hemisphere extending to include deeper structures in the limbic-retic-ular system. With the history of lesions of the left side of the brain, indicated by the attacks of right-sided paresthesia and left monocular blindness from 1896 to 1908, he now had evidence of bilateral damage, a condition affecting emotional and social behavior more severely than a unilateral lesion."[47]

This medical description was so precise and authoritative in tone that few laymen would dare to take issue with it. The problem is that the major evidence on which it relied—the allegedly strange changes in Wilson's behavior—is tittle-tattle which has gained momentum and grown in absurdity in its passage from one source to another. The historical record, as we shall shortly attempt to show, provides a background against which Wilson's "strange behavior," viewed in context, seems reasonable and rational.

The speculative nature of Weinstein's diagnoses is revealed by the fact that in the article by Weinstein, Anderson, and Link the minutely described stroke of his earlier article is withdrawn. A footnote states that new evidence indicates that it is not likely to have occurred after all.[48] Now readers are informed that Wilson had an attack of influenza in Paris in April 1919 (as most historians have thought all along). A crucial aspect of the brain-damage thesis is salvaged, however, for Weinstein, Anderson, and Link also say that it was not merely influenza but "probably a virus encephalopathy." In short, as a result of one disease or another, according to Weinstein, Woodrow Wilson sustained brain damage in April 1919 that significantly affected his judgment in the conduct of the negotiations. In both articles "strange" changes of behavior are cited as evidence of altered brain function.[49]

Let us examine some of this allegedly irrational behavior: one manifestation cited by Weinstein in his earlier article (which presumably constitutes part of the documentation of the "changes in behavior" alleged by Weinstein, Anderson, and Link) was Wilson's instruction to his personal staff in Paris that they use official limousines only for official business. Irwin "Ike" Hoover, White House head usher who served as chief of Wilson's household staff in Paris, is the source of this tale, which he recorded in his book, *42 Years in the White House.* This gentlemen, as his letters to his wife indicate, had grown accustomed to taking joyrides practically every day—sometimes two and three times a day. ("It is fine to order up a big limousine, say 'to the hotel' and off it goes," he wrote to his wife. "Come out, say 'home' and you are on the way back." Of the scores of letters he wrote home, there is scarcely a handful—except when he was at sea en route to or from the conference—in which he did not articulate his use or non-use of the limousines for the particular day covered. "Ike" missed his family—and also his Dodge automobile to which he referred affectionately in several letters.)[50] Other staff members fell into the same habit of rushing for the cars the moment the president and Mrs. Wilson went out.

One day during his illness in April 1919 the president sent for one member of his staff after the other and found that they were all out in the cars. This angered him and he ordered the staff to curtail use of the cars for personal pleasure.[51] We see nothing "strange" or "irrational" in Wilson's crackdown—unless it be that he did not sooner lose his temper at Hoover's profligate abuse of privilege.

On the basis of "Ike" Hoover's account, Weinstein also accepted as "markedly irrational behavior" after his April 1919 illness that Wilson was concerned that the French servants in the house the French government had placed at his disposal were spies. The fact is that many Americans at the conference were worried about spies. Joseph Grew, secretary of the American commission, issued directives warning of the need for the secure handling of confidential papers, for burning trash, for being alert to the possibility that telephones were being tapped, and that French employees might be spying for their government. During the very week of Wilson's illness, Dr. Grayson wrote in his diary that one of the servants who claimed not to speak English had been found to know English fluently and that the French government was engaged in spying on the president. Mrs. Wilson's secretary, Edith Benham, noted in her diary on 29 March 1919 that conversations at meals had to be restrained because "Colonel House says there are spies here in the house who report everything to the Foreign Office." Colonel House noted in his diary at the beginning of the conference that the private wire between his study and Wilson's "is constantly 'covered' to see that it is not tapped."[52]

It seems to us grotesque that Wilson's concern for security at the conference should be interpreted by Weinstein and others as evidence of brain damage. Was Joseph Grew also brain damaged? And Dr. Grayson, Colonel House, and Miss Benham too?

The Question of Strokes

And what about the earlier episodes of illness in 1896, 1900, 1904, 1906, and 1907 which Weinstein, Anderson, and Link state were strokes, the one in 1906 being "the first one to be recognized as such"?[53] By all accounts, Wilson's illness in 1906 was the most serious of his prepresidential years. One spring morning in that year, he awakened unable to see out of his left eye. He immediately consulted two eminent Philadelphia specialists (an ophthalmologist and an internist). The medical records, unfortunately, are missing. Surviving letters and later reminiscences, however, indicate that Wilson was told that a burst blood vessel had caused a hemorrhage in the eye, that he had arteriosclerosis and high blood pressure, and that he needed prolonged rest. Wilson obediently delegated his duties to Princeton colleagues, spent a quiet summer in England and, with medical approval, resumed his work in the fall.

Nowhere could we find evidence that this illness had been diagnosed as a stroke or "recognized as such." We wrote to Weinstein and asked when Wilson's illness in 1906 was recognized as a stroke and by whom. In his reply, Weinstein cited sources that simply contain no mention of a stroke.[54] He further wrote in this letter that Wilson's ophthalmologist and internist knew that he had arteriosclerosis and high blood pressure and that strokes are very common in these conditions; and that they may not have told Wilson in so many words that he had had a stroke but used a euphemism instead. Such speculation on Weinstein's part consisting of what he thinks must have been in other people's minds strikes us as utterly inadequate justification for the unqualified claim by Weinstein, Anderson, and Link that the 1906 illness was a stroke "recognized as such," much less for Link's assertion in *The Papers of Woodrow Wilson* that it was "a major stroke."

Of course the question to which all the foregoing discussion leads is: how would competent, independent medical authority evaluate Woodrow Wilson's illnesses throughout his career and Weinstein's diagnoses of them? For a response to this question, we turned to Michael F. Marmor, M.D., associate professor of Ophthalmology at the Stanford University School of Medicine. We placed at Marmor's disposal all the data in our possession relating to Wilson's health[55] and made available to him the relevant volumes of *The Papers of Woodrow Wilson* as well as the source materials cited by Weinstein in his various articles.

Marmor embodied the results of his review in a letter to us dated 18 May 1981 (see appendix for the text). The letter speaks for itself and we need only note here Marmor's main conclusions: that in the absence of documented findings or medical records, Weinstein's analysis is necessarily speculative; that his own reading of the evidence leads him to question both the medical interpretations of Weinstein and the propriety of presenting such views as historical fact.

As a matter of fact, questions about the validity of Weinstein's diagnoses have been raised previously and were brought to the attention of both Link and Weinstein a decade ago. In 1971, Robert T. Monroe, M.D., an internist long associated with the Harvard University School of Medicine, wrote four pages of comments on Weinstein's article, "Woodrow Wilson's Neurological Illness," which had been published the preceding year. He detailed the medical grounds for doubting Weinstein's interpretations and expressed his overall evaluation as follows: "Professor Weinstein seeks to prove that Wilson 'had a long history of cerebral vascular disease,' and that it 'was associated with alterations in behavior and personality.' In my view he has failed on both counts." Weinstein dismissed Monroe's comments as uninformed, and the following year, volume sixteen of *The Papers of Woodrow Wilson* appeared with the statement in the preface that Wilson's illness in 1906 was "a major stroke."[56]

IMPLICATIONS FOR *THE PAPERS OF WOODROW WILSON*

In conclusion, we should like to say a few words about *The Papers of Woodrow Wilson,* of which Professor Link is editor. The publication of Wilson's papers is one of the major projects in historiography in our time. These volumes are meant to preserve for posterity a true and unbiased record concerning Woodrow Wilson. Scholars today consult *The Papers of Woodrow Wilson* on the assumption—an assumption upon which they ought to be able to rely—that the facts stated in the informational notes to various documents are true and accurate. Scholars will continue to consult *The Papers of Woodrow Wilson* on this assumption for many generations to come. As we noted at the beginning of this article, the editorial matter of several volumes of *The Papers* contains (in prefaces and in numerous notes as well as in listings in various indices) unqualified allusions to Wilson's so-called strokes between the years 1896 and 1907. (The volumes covering the period of the Paris Peace Conference into which Wilson's illness of April 1919 falls have not yet been published.) We believe that these allusions have prejudiced the objectivity of *The Papers of Woodrow Wilson* and have already misled a number of writers.[57] We also believe that those in charge of the project have a reverence for the truth and a fidelity to their scholarly duties. We suggest that a reconsideration and emendation of the editorial matter that elevates Dr. Weinstein's controversial medical hypotheses to the status of historical fact is in order.*

POSTSCRIPT

A book by Edwin A. Weinstein, *Woodrow Wilson: A Medical and Psychological Biography,* has appeared since this article was completed. We can only note here that Weinstein persists in presenting, as if it were indisputable fact, his theory that Wilson suffered a series of disabling strokes dating back to 1896. The book contains numerous statements implying the existence of medical data and opinion which, so far as we know, simply are not available in the historical record.[58] An even more serious concern is that Weinstein has omitted data of critical diagnostic significance, thus precluding an objective evaluation of his hypotheses by his medical peers. His account of Wilson's episode of visual loss in 1906 is an important case in point.

In describing the 1906 episode, Weinstein writes that Mrs. Wilson "searched for evidence that would bear out the Doctor's opinion that her husband's stroke had been brought on by strain and overwork." He also writes that the Princeton trustees "agreed that the stroke had been caused by overwork." However, we know of no evidence (and Weinstein offers none) that Wilson's doctors, Mrs. Wilson, or the Princeton trustees stated, implied, or even believed that Wilson had suffered a stroke.

Weinstein titles his chapter about the 1906 episode, "A Major Stroke and Its Consequences," and he begins with a general description of carotid occlusive disease. In this disorder, blood clots or arteriosclerotic plaques in the neck may

*We wish to express our cordial thanks to the staff of the Manuscript Division, Library of Congress, for facilitating our research there and especially to Dr. David Wigdor, specialist, twentieth-century political history. At the Yale University Library, Arthur Walworth took precious time from his own work on Woodrow Wilson and the Paris Peace Conference to direct our attention to documents of particular interest from his own files and in the papers of Colonel House. Professor Link and Dr. David W. Hirst accorded us many courtesies, for which we thank them, at the Firestone Library, Princeton University. At all stages of our work on this project we have benefited from the expert knowledge and wisdom of Margaret M. Stuart, M.D. We are indebted to Joseph M. Goldsen, A.E. Hanson, Elise F. Kendrick, and Lee R. Lombard for helpful comments on the first version of this article, which was presented at the annual meeting of the International Society of Political Psychology in Mannheim, Germany, in June 1981.

fragment and form emboli that lodge in smaller arteries such as those within the eye. He then writes that Wilson's ophthalmologist (Dr. George E. de Schweinitz) "told him that he had sustained a blood clot in the eye," the obvious implication being that "clot" refers to an embolus from the carotid. We believe this is a misleading description because important evidence has been omitted. What de Schweinitz actually told Wilson is not known. It can only be inferred from letters written by Wilson and Mrs. Wilson at the time, and from the later recollections of such knowledgeable people as John Grier Hibben (who had accompanied Wilson to Dr. de Schweinitz's office), Stockton Axson, Drs. Cary Grayson and E.P. Davis, and Eleanor Wilson McAdoo. *All* of these sources say that Wilson's loss of vision was caused by a hemorrhage or burst blood vessel within his eye. Yet Weinstein omits any mention of hemorrhage in his book, even though the distinction between hemorrhage and embolic clot is critical, because bleeding within the eye is *not* characteristic of carotid occlusive disease and indeed militates against that diagnosis. Weinstein's only cited source for the word "clot" is a letter from Ellen Axson Wilson to a cousin in which she says: "Two weeks ago yesterday Woodrow waked up perfectly blind in one eye!—it turned out from the bursting of a blood vessel in it. . . . The clot in the eye is being absorbed with extraordinary rapidity." The word "clot" in the context of Mrs. Wilson's letter seems clearly to refer to a coagulum from the burst blood vessel rather than to an embolus.

We (Michael F. Marmor, Juliette L. George, and Alexander L. George) hope to comment more fully on Weinstein's book elsewhere.

APPENDIX

May 18, 1981

Dr. and Mrs. Alexander George
Department of Political Science
Stanford University
Stanford, California 94305

Dear Dr. and Mrs. George:

I have reviewed at length the medical and historical source material which bears upon the possibility that Woodrow Wilson had neurologic disease. I am preparing a comprehensive analysis of this material for publication and this letter represents a summary of my impressions and conclusions.* You have my permission to quote from this letter, with the proviso that statements should not be taken out of context or used without sufficient material to provide a balanced picture of my views.

*See Michael F. Marmor, "Wilson, Strokes, and Zebras," *New England Journal of Medicine,* 307 (August 26, 1982) 528–35. See also Marmor, "The Eyes of Woodrow Wilson," *Ophthalmology,* 92 (March 1985) 454–65—eds.

Let me say at the outset that the medical analysis of historical figures is by nature a speculative process. In the absence of documented findings or medical records, one must rely upon guesswork and judgment to analyze lay descriptions of disease. Physicians are trained to consider all of the rare and unlikely disease which might afflict their patients, lest one be missed. However, in looking back over history, the approach should probably be the opposite: given the symptoms, search for the most common and likely causes. Under these constraints, historical diagnoses will rarely have the certainty of scientific fact, and should in general be considered hypothesis.

In a series of articles, psychiatrist Edwin Weinstein has argued that Wilson suffered from serious cerebrovascular disease over a period of nearly thirty years, and that discrete strokes accounted for behavioral changes at several critical junctures in Wilson's professional life. This view has been accepted by the eminent historian Arthur Link, who has referred to these "strokes" without qualification in the current edition of *The Papers of Woodrow Wilson*. My own reading of the evidence leads me to question both the medical interpretations of Dr. Weinstein, and the propriety of presenting such views as historical fact.

Weinstein's thesis is that Wilson suffered for many years from cerebrovascular disease, primarily carotid artery insufficiency, and had discrete strokes which influenced his professional behavior. Weinstein contends cerebrovascular disease first became manifest as disability of the right arm, resulting from one or more small strokes in 1896. The strongest and most direct evidence for stroke is considered to be Wilson's episode of left visual loss in 1906, which Weinstein describes as diagnostic of left carotid occlusive disease. Finally the illness which Wilson suffered during the 1919 Peace Conference is viewed as viral encephalopathy superimposed on preexisting brain damage. Each of these points merits careful analysis.

Wilson had difficulty with his right hand and arm for more than twenty years, and referred on numerous occasions to "writer's cramp" which was apparently diagnosed as a "neuritis." The precise symptoms are not spelled out, but the hand and arm were often painful, especially while writing. These symptoms began long before the alleged stroke of 1896, and references to this complaint can be found in the Wilson papers as far back as 1884. There are no references to suggest a sudden onset of symptoms (as from a stroke) in either 1884 or 1896, and the symptoms are too chronic to call them a result of transient ischemic attacks. Furthermore, Wilson also had occasional discomfort and pain in his *left* arm.

"Writer's cramp" is poorly understood as a clinical entity. Some cases may have an organic basis from pathology such as arthritic joint damage or inflammation of the nerves, but many are thought to represent an occupational neurosis. Characteristically, the patient has difficulty writing more than a few words, but lacks any major disability for other activities. This fits the descriptions of Wilson's disorder, and there is evidence that even during his severe periods of disability he was able to write brief ledger entries with his right hand which rules out any serious paralysis or limitation of movement. To accept this condition as writer's cramp (even without a precise definition of that term) seems perfectly reasonable in view of the nature and duration of the symptoms, whereas to fit these symptoms into a stroke syndrome places them in the category of unusual manifestations.

The 1906 episode is interpreted by Weinstein as direct evidence for cerebrovascular disease, since right-sided weakness and left-sided blindness are often associated with insufficiency or occlusion of the left carotid artery. However, the ocular findings in Wilson's case argue *against* a diagnosis of carotid occlusion. Wilson awoke one morning aware of poor vision in his left eye, which numerous sources indicate was found to result from bursting of a blood vessel and hemorrhage inside the eye. The fact of the matter is that retinal hemorrhage is *not* a sign of carotid occlusive disease. Carotid disease most characteristically leads to occlusion of the retinal arteries which causes a loss of vision but produces a very different picture (without hemorrhage) inside the eye. Arterial occlusion would not have been described in the language used by Wilson and his family members.

Wilson's doctors noted signs of arteriosclerosis and mild hypertension, and there seems little doubt that he had systemic vascular disease. The most likely cause for Wilson's eye disease would be a retinal vein occlusion, which is often associated with hypertensive vascular disease, and which produces diffuse hemorrhages in the retina. Other possibilities include hemorrhagic macular degeneration. The point to emphasize is that these ocular hemorrhages occur frequently as isolated events; they give evidence of generalized vascular pathology but they do not constitute strokes or carry any direct implication of cerebral ischemia or symptomatology.

There are other reasons to doubt a stroke in 1906. The stroke would have affected the left cerebral hemisphere which has major control over language and speech, yet Wilson clearly suffered no impairment in these areas. Weinstein implies that a stroke caused personality changes that affected Wilson's subsequent activities, but the literature on strokes is quite clear in emphasizing that personality changes are not a characteristic of the stroke syndrome in the absence of cognitive changes or dementia. Weinstein carefully qualifies his argument to state that Wilson's behavioral changes in 1906 were an adaptation to his illness and could result from stress as well as brain damage. Considering that Wilson had indeed suffered an ocular hemorrhage, and that he was working with intensity as president of Princeton University, why should it be necessary to invoke strokes or cerebral pathology to account for his actions?

Similar problems arise in analyzing the illness that began on April 3, 1919, during the Peace Conference. Weinstein initially concluded that Wilson had suffered a stroke to explain his behavior during the conference, but the tenuousness of the stroke hypothesis is shown by Weinstein's shift to a diagnosis of viral encephalopathy when new evidence made it clear that Wilson had had respiratory disease. I fail to see the need for postulating any diagnoses beyond severe influenza to account for Wilson's behavior. Wilson was ill with respiratory symptoms and high fever, and there are surely few of us who cannot attest to the debilitating effect of severe flu. Wilson was confined to bed for five days but was incapacitated only on the first day, after which he resumed conferring and decision making from his bedroom. The term "viral encephalopathy" may apply to a broad range of symptoms, from minimal headache and irritability, to severe somnolence, convulsions, and death. Wilson clearly did not have the latter, and some would argue that the former are in fact a routine component of the flu syndrome. Wilson's activities for the remainder of April 1919 seem quite consistent with a history of severe but uncomplicated influenza, and I should think the burden of proof would be to show otherwise.

Wilson probably had systemic vascular disease for a good part of his life, and there is no question that he ultimately suffered a severe stroke in the fall of 1919. Neither of these observations, however, can be construed as evidence for multiple strokes or for significant neurologic dysfunction during the earlier years of his career. Chronic vascular disease may cause subtle changes in mentation, ultimately resulting in dementia. Could Wilson have had very mild degrees of change accumulating over the years? Certainly this is possible, but how does one distinguish this type of subtle degeneration from other aspects of maturation and aging which are evident in everyone? This man actively ran one of the major universities in the United States, campaigned articulately for the presidency, and was clearly a lucid and powerful thinker in political affairs up to the moment of his serious stroke in 1919.

The interpretations which I have chosen to emphasize focus upon common and ordinary conditions, rather than the unusual or the extreme. I think the odds favor such an interpretation, but these views are admittedly hypothetical and open to review or criticism by others. I hope that my arguments will, at the least, raise reasonable doubts about the stroke theory and return it to a position of hypothesis rather than fact in historical source material.

With warm regards,

(Signed) Michael F. Marmor, M.D.*
Associate Professor
Division of Ophthalmology
Chief, Ophthalmology Section
Veterans Administration Medical Center
Palo Alto, California

*Doctor Marmor is currently Head, Division of Ophthalmology, Stanford University School of Medicine—eds.

NOTES

1 See Edwin A. Weinstein, James William Anderson, and Arthur S. Link, "Woodrow Wilson's Political Personality: A Reappraisal," *Political Science Quarterly* 93(Winter 1978–79):586; and Alexander L. George and Juliette L. George, *Woodrow Wilson and Colonel House: A Personality Study* (New York: John Day Company, 1956: Dover Publications, 1964). We are exiled in good company. Some years ago Arthur Link wrote of Ray Stannard Baker that his eight-volume *Woodrow Wilson: Life and Letters* (Garden City, New York: Doubleday, Page and Co., 1927–1939) suffered from Baker's having "to a large degree imposed his own personality profile upon Wilson." Moreover, claims Link (without justification, in our opinion), Baker portrayed Wilson "as being mainly feminine in personality, if not virtually a sexual neuter." This of the man in whose early volumes Woodrow Wilson fairly springs to life. Baker's prodigious research resulted in the collection of that rich raw data upon which Link's own work—and that of every other Wilson scholar—heavily rests. See Arthur S. Link, ed., *Woodrow Wilson: A Profile* (New York: Hill and Wang, 1968), pp. vii–viii.

2 We shall here cite two of the two dozen instances we have thus far found in Arthur S. Link et al., ed. *The Papers of Woodrow Wilson*, 36 vols. to date (Princeton, N.J.: Princeton University Press, 1966–). Of Wilson's illness in May 1906, it is stated in the introduction to vol. 16: "Years of excessive work take their toll in late May 1906, when Wilson suffers a major stroke that seems for a moment to threaten his life. . . ." (p. vii). In December 1907, Moses Taylor Pyne, a Princeton trustee, wrote to Wilson saying he was sorry to learn "that you were suffering from an attack of Neuritis" (ibid., vol. 17, p. 549). Link's editorial footnote to the word "Neuritis" reads: "In fact, Wilson had unquestionably suffered a slight stroke" (ibid., p. 550).

3 Weinstein, Anderson, and Link, "A Reappraisal," p. 587.

4 Ibid., p. 598.

5 George and George, *Woodrow Wilson and Colonel House*, p. 323.

6 Inga Floto, *Colonel House in Paris: A Study of American Policy at the Paris Peace Conference 1919* (Aarhus, Denmark: Universitetsforlaget, 1973; Princeton, N.J.: Princeton University Press, 1980); Weinstein, Anderson, and Link, "A Reappraisal," p. 597.

7 Floto, *Colonel House in Paris*, pp. 13, 20, 21. We cite Floto solely on the question of our research and do not mean to suggest that she endorses our interpretation of the House-Wilson relationship. To be sure, she credits us with "elucidating the 'mechanism' " of the friendship in an "unassailable" fashion, but she is critical of our analysis of the "break." Her book is an important contribution to a continuing discussion among historians. We think, however, that the assertion by Weinstein, Anderson, and Link that Floto "proves conclusively that the cause of the so-called break between the two men was House's failure to follow Wilson's explicit instructions while the latter was in the United States" ("A Reappraisal," p. 597) is an oversimplification.

8 Weinstein, Anderson, and Link, "A Reappraisal," p. 587.

9 George and George, *Woodrow Wilson and Colonel House*, p. 12. See also ibid., p. 114.

10 See ibid., p. 7.

11 Weinstein, Anderson, and Link, "A Reappraisal," pp. 588–89.

12 Arthur S. Link, *Wilson: The Road to the White House* (Princeton, N.J.: Princeton University Press, 1947), p. 2.

13 Baker, *Life and Letters*, vol. 1, pp. 36–37.

14 George and George, *Woodrow Wilson and Colonel House*, p. 7; and Arthur S. Link, "The Case for Woodrow Wilson," *Harper's Magazine* 234(April 1967):91. In anticipation of the argument that Wilson did poorly because his schooling was disrupted in consequence of the disrupted times, let us point out that "Tommy" was a conspicuously poor student compared to his peers. According to Baker, " Tommy' Wilson's school work was decidedly below average" and his teacher compained to Dr. Joseph Wilson that "Tommy" was at the foot of his class not for want of ability but because he would not study (Baker, *Life and Letters*,

vol. 1, p. 42; also the Papers of Ray Stannard Baker, Series 1B, Box 3, "Memo for the Augusta Period," Library of Congress, Washington, D.C., p. 10). Link had referred to Wilson as a "late starter" in *Woodrow Wilson: A Brief Biography,* Cleveland, Ohio: World Publishing Co., 1963), p. 18.

15 Link, *A Profile,* pp. xiv–xv.

16 Weinstein, Anderson, and Link, "A Reappraisal," p. 588.

17 Michael Rutter, "Prevalence and Types of Dyslexia," in *Dyslexia: An Appraisal of Current Knowledge,* eds. A. L. Benton and D. Pearl (New York: Oxford University Press, 1978), pp. 5, 24. The chapters in this book were written for the National Institute of Mental Health conference.

18 Ibid., p. 9; John R. Hughes, "Electroencephalographic and Neurophysiological Studies in Dyslexia," p. 234 and O. Spreen, "The Dyslexias: A Discussion of Neurobehavioral Research," pp. 178–79, both in *Dyslexia,* Benton and Pearl; also see Leon Eisenberg, "Psychiatric Aspects of Language Disability," in *Reading, Perception and Language: Papers from the World Congress on Dyslexia,* ed., D. D. Duane and M. B. Rawson (Baltimore, Md.: York Press, 1975), p. 225.

19 Rutter, "Prevalence and Types of Dyslexia," p. 24.

20 Weinstein, Anderson, and Link, "A Reappraisal," p. 588.

21 Wilson to Ellen Axson, 8 November 1884, *Papers of Woodrow Wilson,* vol. 3, p. 415.

22 Wilson to Ellen Axson, 20 January 1885, ibid., p. 623; 13 February 1885, ibid. vol. 4, pp. 244–45.

23 Wilson to Heath Dabney, 14 February 1885, ibid., vol. 4, pp. 248–49.

24 Wilson to Ellen Axson, 19 February 1885, ibid., p. 269.

25 See ibid., vol. 1, pp. 83–128, and 132ff. for a still earlier diary and "Commonplace Book" in which Wilson recorded his enjoyment of reading. See also Wilson to his sister, Annie Howe, on 19 April 1876 in which he reports "employing most of the last week in reading" and finding "a great deal of enjoyment" in it (ibid., p. 128).

26 See ibid., vol. 13, pp. 267–97.

27 Weinstein, Anderson, and Link, "A Reappraisal," p. 588.

28 "Material on Woodrow Wilson Prepared by Dr. Stockton Axson with Occasional Assistance of Admiral Cary T. Grayson," a memoir owned personally by Professor Link. See chapter entitled "Health and Recreations," p. 15. We wish to thank Professor Link for granting us access to this manuscript.

29 Wilson to Dr. Azel W. Hazen, 29 March 1897, *Papers of Woodrow Wilson,* vol. 10, p. 201. Wilson to Ellen Axson Wilson, 17, 21, and 23 June 1896, and 3 July, 18 August 1896, ibid., vol. 9, pp. 519, 523, 527, 532, 573. Also see Wilson to Ellen Axson Wilson, 29 June 1908, ibid., vol. 18, p. 345.

30 Macdonald Critchley, *The Dyslexic Child* (Springfield, Ill.: Charles C. Thomas, Publisher, 1970), pp. 36–40. See also Rutter "Prevalence and Types of Dyslexia," p. 18.

31 Eisenberg, "Psychiatric Aspects of Language Disability," p. 220. See also D. Duane, "Summary of the World Congress on Dyslexia," in *Reading, Perception and Language,* Duane and Rawson, p. 5; and Critchley, *The Dyslexic Child,* p. 97.

32 Weinstein, Anderson, and Link, "A Reappraisal," pp. 588–89.

33 "Memorandum of Interviews with Dr. Cary T. Grayson on February 18, 19, 1926 at Washington," Papers of Ray Stannard Baker, Box 109.

34 Weinstein, Anderson, and Link, "A Reappraisal," p. 587. Space limitations preclude further discussion of Wilson's childhood and relationship with his father. For relevant data, see George and George, *Woodrow Wilson and Colonel House,* pp. 6–13, 31–32, 271–72; see also George and George, *"Woodrow Wilson and Colonel House:* A Reply to Weinstein, Anderson and Link" (Paper delivered at the 1981 meeting of the International Society of Political Psychology, Mannheim, Germany, June 1981), pp. 10–78. We hope to publish elsewhere a fuller account, made possible by the data now available, about Wilson's father as his re-

lentlessly driving (as well as wonderfully incisive) critic; and of Wilson's longing to do—as he put it—"immortal work," work of such noble service to humanity that to further it he felt morally justified to indulge his aggressions against those who stood in his way in that sphere of authority in which he sought compensatory gratifications.

One interesting vein of data—a good deal of which Professor Link, unfortunately, has omitted from *The Papers of Woodrow Wilson*—is contained in letters to Wilson from his parents about their difficulties in raising Wilson's much younger brother Joseph R. Wilson, Jr. ("Josie"), ten years Wilson's junior. Dr. and Mrs. Wilson complain to the now studious and increasingly successful "Woodrow" that "Josie" is "lazy"—even as Wilson himself, as a boy, had been made to feel. They disparage "Josie's" nascent competences, express concern about his lack of will to study, seek Wilson's advice about what to "do" about the hapless boy (as, when Wilson was a lad, his father had conferred with the family's distinguished elders about what to "do" about his poor performance in school). They poke fun at "Josie," squelch his wish to play, disparage his popularity with his fellows, express surprise and amusement at his accomplishments. In short, years after publication of our book, further documentation has emerged of a parental style that includes the seriously ego-damaging characteristics which we—on the basis of practically no evidence, according to Weinstein, Anderson, and Link— were able to describe in *Woodrow Wilson and Colonel House.*

35 "Material on Woodrow Wilson Prepared by Dr. Stockton Axson," chapter entitled "Woodrow Wilson and His Father," pp. 5, 8, 15–16; chapter entitled "Dr. Joseph R. Wilson," pp. 1, 2, 9, 12–13; chapter entitled "The Personality of Woodrow Wilson," Part II, p. 24; and untitled chapter, pp. 4–5.

36 George and George, *Woodrow Wilson and Colonel House,* pp. 3, 12–13.

37 Weinstein, Anderson, and Link, "A Reappraisal," p. 592 (emphasis added).

38 Wilson to Ellen Axson, 7 December 1884, *Papers of Woodrow Wilson,* vol. 3, p. 522 (emphasis added).

39 See in ibid. Wilson to Ellen Axson (Wilson), 17 February 1885 (vol. 4, p. 263), 13 March 1892 (vol. 7, p. 483), 20 July 1908 (vol. 18, p. 372), 9 August 1902 (vol. 14, p. 68), 23 February 1900 (vol. 11, p. 436), 28 January 1895 (vol. 9, p. 137), 20 March 1885 (vol. 4, p. 389), and 29 August 1902 (vol. 14, p. 118).

40 See also Alexander L. George, "Power as a Compensatory Value for Political Leaders," *Journal of Social Issues* 24(July 1968):29–49.

41 Weinstein, Anderson, and Link, "A Reappraisal," pp. 587, 594. It is useful throughout this discussion to bear in mind Dr. Weinstein's criteria for accepting impaired brain function as an etiological or causal agent in political behavior. He stated them in his article, "Woodrow Wilson's Neurological Illness," *Journal of American History* 57(1970), as follows: "First, the appearance of clinical evidence of brain damage should coincide with behavioral change. Second, the behavioral change should involve some impairment in performance. Third, it should be possible to classify actions in the political field into behavioral syndromes known to be associated with certain types of brain damage" (p. 325).

42 See Henry Cabot Lodge, *The Senate and the League of Nations* (New York: Charles Scribner's Sons, 1925). Wilson, Lodge wrote, "was simply an element to be calmly and coolly considered in a great problem of international politics" (p. 226). It was "of vital moment to me" to make "a correct analysis of Mr. Wilson's probable attitude" (p. 219; see also pp. 212–13). Lodge's insight was based upon years of hostile but astute observations stretching back to the beginning of Wilson's administration—a period during which, if we understand Weinstein, Anderson, and Link correctly, they believe Wilson to have been relatively free of manifestations of the brain damage from which they say he suffered.

43 Link, *The Road to the White House,* p. 90.

44 Ibid., pp. 76, 78.

45 Ibid., pp. viii–ix.

46 Weinstein, Anderson, and Link, "A Reappraisal," p. 596, n. 30.
47 Weinstein, "Woodrow Wilson's Neurological Illness," pp. 341–42.
48 Weinstein, Anderson, and Link, "A Reappraisal," p. 594, n. 26. We wished to include as part of the data we were assembling for independent medical review the "new evidence" that led Dr. Weinstein to abandon his "stroke" diagnosis. For over a year and a half, however, we were unable to gain access to it. Both Professor Link and Dr. Weinstein stated in reply to our several requests that they were bound by a promise of confidentiality not to reveal it. We were especially interested to know how the new evidence related to Dr. Weinstein's current diagnosis of "virus encephalopathy," upon which the hypothesis that Wilson sustained brain damage in Paris must now rest. We therefore wrote Dr. Weinstein and asked whether the new evidence proved or suggested the diagnosis of virus encephalopathy. In a letter dated 12 September 1979, he replied that the confidential data did not go beyond confirming the diagnosis of influenza.

On 22 October 1980, Professor Link wrote to us that he had been released from the pledge of confidentiality and he granted us access to the diary of Dr. Cary T. Grayson, Wilson's physician throughout his presidency. We thank him for this courtesy.
49 Weinstein, Anderson, and Link make repeated references to physiologically induced behavior and personality changes in Wilson without delineating the characteristic behavior patterns, the underlying personality, upon which the alleged changes impinged. Changes, after all, are comprehensible only in terms of that which preexists. Did the postulated brain damage accentuate certain aspects of a well-established behavior system or did it, in these authors' view, cause quite alien behavior to become manifest?
50 Papers of Irwin Hoover, Box 2, Library of Congress.
51 Diary of Cary T. Grayson, 5 April 1919; Gilbert Close to Arthur Walworth, 7 May 1951. Papers of Arthur Walworth, Yale University Library, New Haven, Conn.
52 Memoranda nos. 29, 32, 47 from Secretary of the American Commission to Negotiage Peace to members of the commission and their staffs, Papers of Tasker H. Bliss, Container 286, Library of Congress; Diary of Cary T. Grayson, 8 April 1919; Diary of Edith Benham Helm, 29 March 1919, Library of Congress; Diary of Edward M. House, 7 January 1919, Yale University Library.
53 Weinstein, Anderson, and Link, "A Reappraisal," p. 596.
54 Alexander L. George and Juliette L. George to Edwin A. Weinstein, M.D., 19 July 1979 and his reply 12 September 1979. Dr. Weinstein cited Baker, Mrs. Wilson, Stockton Axson, and Moses Taylor Pyne. In a subsequent letter (3 October 1979), Dr. Weinstein said he had no other sources.
55 This included the diary of Dr. Cary T. Grayson as well as our correspondence with both Professor Link and Dr. Weinstein concerning the data upon which they relied for the preparation of their article and, most particularly, for Dr. Weinstein's diagnoses of Wilson's illnesses in 1906 and in Paris in April 1919. Professor Link informed us (letter dated 1 March 1979) that he had no medical records concerning Wilson that have not already been published in the *Papers of Woodrow Wilson* or are not available in the Wilson papers at the Library of Congress.
56 See the Papers of Arthur Walworth, Yale University Library, for Dr. Monroe's comments and Dr. Weinstein's reaction to them.
57 See, for example, John Mulder, *Woodrow Wilson: The Years of Preparation* (Princeton, N.J.: Princeton University Press, 1978), pp. 143, 145, and 147 for unequivocal references to Wilson's "stroke" of 1896 and its supposed effect on his thinking; see also his account of Wilson's illness in 1906 in which the stroke hypothesis also appears (pp. 185–86). There are numerous other references to the effects of Wilson's alleged strokes on his thinking and behavior. For a further discussion of this issue, see Juliette L. George, Michael F. Marmor, and Alexander L. George, "Issues in Wilson Scholarship: References to Early 'Strokes' in the *Papers of*

Woodrow Wilson," Journal of American History 70(March 1984):845–53; Arthur S. Link et al., "Communication," ibid., 945–55; George, Marmor, George rejoinder, ibid. 955–56. See also George, Marmor, George, "Communication," ibid., 71(June 1984):198–212—eds.

58 Edwin A. Weinstein, *Woodrow Wilson: A Medical and Psychological Biography* (Princeton, N.J.: Princeton University Press, 1981), pp. 165–67. See also Ellen Axson Wilson to Mary Hoyt, 12 June [1906], *Papers of Woodrow Wilson,* vol. 16, p. 423; Wilson to Nicholas Murray Butler, I June 1906, ibid., p. 413; "Memorandum of Interviews with Grayson," Papers of Ray Stannard Baker, Box 109, p. 3; ibid., Box 5, Notebook XXII, pp. 56–57; Cary T. Grayson, *Woodrow Wilson: An Intimate Memoir* (New York: Holt, Rinehart and Winston, 1960 and 1977), p. 81; Stockton Axson, "Material on Woodrow Wilson," chapter entitled "Health and Recreations," p. 23, and chapter entitled "The Physical Man," p. 10. In the Papers of Ray Stannard Baker, see conversation with John Grier Hibben, 18 June 1925, Box 111; conversation with E. P. Davis, M.D., 12 November 1925, Box 106; E. P. Davis, "Memoranda Concerning Woodrow Wilson"; and Gilbert Close to Ray Stannard Baker, 26 September 1925, Box 103. See also Eleanor Wilson McAdoo, *The Priceless Gift* (New York: McGraw-Hill Book Company, 1962), p. 241. It is interesting to note that Weinstein himself, in his article "Woodrow Wilson's Neurological Illness," stated: "De Schweinitz found that the blindness had been caused by the bursting of a blood vessel in the eye" (p. 334). De Schweinitz's finding of a burst blood vessel is also reported in a footnote in *The Papers of Woodrow Wilson,* vol. 16, p. 412, n.1.

Part II
Bibliography

Suggestions for additional readings in psychobiography are grouped below under two headings. The first contains general works on the relationship between psychoanalysis and biography. These readings amplify some of the arguments put forth by Mack, Coles, and Runyan in the selections reprinted above. The second heading consists of comparative readings and contrasting interpretations of notable historical figures; they are arranged roughly chronologically.

Psychohistorians rarely discuss in theoretical terms the relationship between psychology and biography. Erik Erikson is perhaps the most notable exception. As a clinician, he is not surprisingly strongly influenced in his view of the past by the scientific and clinical ideas attributed to psychoanalysis. In *Childhood and Society* (New York, 2d ed., 1963), he wrote: "psychologies and psychologists are subject to historical laws and ... historians and historical records are subject to those of psychology" (p. 403). For a succinct statement, see Erikson's *Insight and Responsibility* (New York, 1964), pp. 201–08. A growing connection between clinical work and psychobiography was reported by John Gedo in "The Methodology of Psychoanalytic Biography," *Journal of the American Psychoanalytic Association,* vol. 20 (1972), pp. 638–49. However, the literary biographer Leon Edel maintains that biographers should not be influenced by the therapeutic intent: see his "The Biographer and Psycho-Analysis," *International Journal of Psychoanalysis,* vol. 42 (1961), pp. 458–66. Similarly, W. F. Mandle warns the biographer against the therapeutic overtones of psychoanalytic theory. A biographer is not in any way a therapist, he wrote; his task rather is "to understand and explain the past" ("Psychology and History," *The New Zealand Journal of History,* vol. 2, no. 1 [April, 1968], pp. 1–17). The most thorough recent discussion of theory and method in psychobiography is William McKinley Runyan's *Life Histories and Psychobiography* (New York, 1982), from which chapter three, "Why Did Van Gogh Cut Off His Ear?" has been reprinted above. Two other important works which review psychobiographies and their methods should be mentioned here. They are: John Mack, "Psychoanalysis and Historical Biography," *Journal of the American Psychoanalytic Association*, vol. 19 (1971), pp. 143–79; and Miles Shore, "Biography in the 1980's: A Psychoanalytic Perspective," *Journal of Interdisciplinary History*, vol. 12, no. 1 (Summer 1981), pp. 89–113.

II

Psychobiographers have ranged widely over the past and with varying degrees of success in attempting to explain past lives. Their difficulties have been exacerbated by a scarcity of historical evidence. Only a few psychohistorians have been bold enough to tackle ancient history, where more than the usual evidentiary problems exist. The case for a psychohistorical interpretation of this early period has been made by Thomas W. Africa, "Psychohistory, Ancient History, and Freud," *Arethusa*, vol. 12, no. 1 (Spring 1979), pp. 5–33. Africa's attempt at a psychobiography of the Roman era may be found in "The Mask of an Assassin: A Psychohistorical Study of M. Junius Brutus," *Journal of Interdisciplinary History*, vol. 8, no. 4 (Spring 1978), pp. 599–626.

Erik Erikson's *Young Man Luther* (New York, 1958)—generally considered to be the model for contemporary psychobiography—is not without its deficiencies in historical evidence. For critical reviews of this important work see, for example, the *Journal for the Scientific Study of Religion*, vol. 2, no. 2 (April 1963), pp. 238–52. Other comments may be found in Roland H. Bainton, "Luther: A Psychiatric Portrait," *The Yale Review*, vol. 48 (1959), pp. 405–10; Lewis W. Spitz, "Psychohistory and History: The Case of Young Man Luther," *Soundings*, vol. 56 (1974), pp. 182–209; and a special issue of *The Psychohistory Review* on Erikson, vol. 5, no. 3 (December 1976). Especially useful is R. A. Johnson (ed.), *Psychohistory and Religion: The Case of Young Man Luther* (Philadelphia, 1977). For a general critical treatment of Erikson, see Joel Kovel, "Erik Erikson's Psychohistory," *Social Policy*, vol. 5 (1974), pp. 60–64.

The tendency of some psychobiographers to emphasize theory over fact is best exemplified by J. C. Flugel's early study (first published in 1920) of a contemporary of Luther's, King Henry VIII of England. Flugel makes much of Henry's unconscious "desires," "feelings," "complexes," "mind," and "tendencies"—as they are variously described in his "On the Character and Married Life of Henry VIII," in Bruce Mazlish (ed.), *Psychoanalysis and History* (Englewood Cliffs, 1963). A more recent psychological portrait of Henry is less reductive. Miles Shore combines Eriksonian stage-modeling with Heniz Kohut's psychology of narcissism in "Henry VIII and the Crisis of Generativity," *Journal of Interdisciplinary History*, vol. 2 (1972), pp. 359–90.

To overcome the scarcity of relevant personal detail so important to psychobiography, Elizabeth Marvick utilizes an early medical record kept during the childhood of her subject Louis XIII, king of France from 1610 to 1642. See her two articles "The Character of Louis XIII: The Role of his Physician," *Journal of Interdisciplinary History*, vol. 4, no. 3 (Winter 1974), pp. 347–74; and "Childhood History and Decisions of State: The Case of Louis XIII," in L. de Mause (ed.), *The New Psychohistory* (New York, 1975). Another seventeenth-century figure has captured the attention of Roger Howell, who cautiously reviews the evidence for a psychobiographical study of that elusive Puritan, Oliver Cromwell, in "Cromwell's Personality: The Problems and Promises of a Psychohistorical Approach," *Biography*, vol. 1, no. 1 (Winter 1978), pp. 41–60.

Ernst Lewy uses evidence—which he considers "as reliable as material supplied by patients"—in combination with Freudian Oedipal theory to discuss an eighteenth-century Prussian monarch: see "The Transformation of Frederick the Great: A Psychoanalytic Study," in *The Psychoanalytic Study of Society*, vol. 4 (1967), pp. 252–311. Less explicit about his theoretical structure, Harold T. Parker explains Napoleon Bonaparte's ambition and rise to power as a need for approval from his mother and later (by extension) approval from France. Parker's argument is in "The Formation of Napoleon's Personality: An Exploratory Essay," *French Historical Studies*, vol. 7 (1971), pp. 6–26.

A particularly useful article because it is unusually self-conscious about its methodology is the collaborative work by Frederick Wyatt and William B. Willcox, "Sir Henry Clinton: A Psychological Exploration in History," *William and Mary Quarterly*, vol. 16 (1959), pp. 3–26. Wyatt (a clinical psychologist) and Willcox (a historian) observe that Clinton, who was a commander of the British forces during the American Revolution, had a career marked by curious episodes of maladaptive behavior. They argue that it can be explained by "an unconscious conflict over authority." Clinton's colonial opponent, Benjamin Franklin, was well known for an opposite trait: Franklin was a diplomat and negotiator of great skill. In a satisfyingly modest approach, Richard L. Bushman avoids speculation about Franklin's infancy and childhood and explains the life from firmly established adult behavior patterns: see "On the Uses of Psychology: Conflict and Conciliation in Benjamin Franklin," *History and Theory*, vol. 5 (1966), pp. 225–40.

Another military figure in American history who, like Clinton, was not known for his conciliatory nature was General George Custer. Custer's last stand has gone down in history as a courageous battle against insurmountable odds, but to Charles K. Hofling, it was another "rash and self-destructive" act characteristic of Custer's life. Hofling, following the theories of self psychology advocated by Heinz Kohut, believes that Custer had a narcissistic personality disorder: see Hofling's *Custer and the Little Big Horn* (Detroit, 1981).

Kohutian interpretations seem to have made significant headway in recent psychobiographical studies. Charles Strozier's *Lincoln's Quest for Union* (New York, 1982) places Lincoln's leadership within a broad framework of a Kohutian "cohesive group self" (the United States in the 1850s). Lincoln's rage and fears of a dominant Southern slave power was emblematic of the North as a whole, and contributed to a war spirit. Other aspects of Lincoln's personality—such as his self-deprecating humor—Strozier sees as part of a Kohutian self-therapy to ward off depression. See also Strozier's article, "Heinz Kohut and the Historical Imagination," *Psychohistory Review*, vol. 7, no. 2 (Fall 1978), pp. 36–39. A more contemporary subject explained in Kohutian terms is the former Australian prime minister, Gough Whitlam. James Walter's *The Leader: A Political Biography of Gough Whitlam* (University of Queensland, 1980) portrays Whitlam as a "narcissistic personality type": see especially chapter six.

One of the few psychohistorical studies with a woman as its subject is Donald R. Allen's analysis of Florence Nightingale. Relying on Helene Deutsch's notion of feminine masochism, Allen believes that a strong masochistic strain in Nightingale "helped her to choose and pursue a career in nursing" at a time when this was not a respectable occupation for upper-class women. The discussion may be found in detail in Allen's article, "Florence Nightingale: Toward a Psychohistorical Interpretation," *Journal of Interdisciplinary History*, vol. 4, no. 1 (Summer 1975), pp. 23–45. Other recent psychobiographies have diverged from Deutsch's orthodox Freudian view of women: see John Cody, *After Great Pain: The Inner Life of Emily Dickinson* (Cambridge, Mass., 1971); Jean Strouse, *Alice James: A Biography* (Boston, 1980); and Alice Wexler, *Emma Goldman: An Intimate Life* (New York, 1984).

As one might expect, historical subjects living closer to our own time promise a greater harvest of useful evidence. But this has led neither to a consensus of methodological approach nor to an agreement in interpretation. Even within the psychodynamic tradition, there is great variation. Good examples are three differing treatments of Otto von Bismarck, the nineteenth-century German statesman. Otto Pflanze gives a rather eclectic psychodynamic portrayal, Reichian in parts, in his "Toward a Psychoanalytic Interpretation of Bismarck," *American Historical Review*, vol. 77 (1974), pp. 419–44. Charlotte Sempel's "Bismarck's Childhood: A Psychohistorical Study," *History of Childhood Quarterly*, vol. 2 (1974), pp. 107–24 draws upon Anna Freud, Erikson, and selected articles in the *Psychoanalytic Study of the Child* for its theoretical framework. (See also Sempel's "1866: Bismarck's Gamble," *Psychohistory Review*, vol. 7, no. 2 [Fall, 1978], pp. 25–29.) Judith M. Hughes, "Toward the Psychological Drama of High Politics: The Case of Bismarck," *Central European History*, vol. 10 (1978), pp. 271–85, relies on object relations theory. Hughes has expanded her article into a longer study, *Emotion and High Politics* (Berkeley, 1983)—a somewhat insoluble mixture of diplomatic policy and personality in late-nineteenth-century Germany and Britain.

It is upon another German, Adolf Hitler, that the most extensive psychohistorical scrutiny of all has fallen. While Hitler was still in power psychological studies were begun, notably Walter Langer's classified wartime study for the OSS, *The Mind of Adolf Hitler* (New York, 1972); and Erik Erikson's "Hitler's Imagery and German Youth," *Psychiatry*, vol. 5 (1942), pp. 475–93. Langer's book applies an orthodox Freudian scheme to public and intelligence material available during the war. Correctly noting the importance of Hitler's fantasies, Langer's analysis nevertheless suffers from theoretical rigidity. Erikson's essay, later published in revised form in his *Childhood and Society* (New York, 1950), portrays the mixture of unconscious urges and shrewd propaganda that filled Hitler's *Mein Kampf* and suggests the historically determined unconscious reasons for the Germans' response to their Führer's dreams and appeals.

More recent psychohistorical studies of Hitler include Robert Waite, *The Psychopathic God* (New York, 1977) and Rudolph Binion, *Hitler and the Germans* (New York, 1976). Waite's book relies heavily upon Langer's study, which was declassified and published in 1972. Waite sees Hitler as a "borderline personality," suffering from a sadomasochistic guilt complex, a severe Oedipus complex, castration anxiety, and an undescended testicle. Waite provides a great deal of clinical material to support his interpretation of the evidence and there is much that rings true in his depiction of the private Hitler. Some of his conclusions, however, are based more upon theoretical assumptions than upon direct evidence from Hitler's childhood and adolescent years. Binion's work is a unique attempt to isolate the determinative causes for Hitler's rise and fall. By immersing himself in the relevant documents, Binion claims to detect empathically a link between Hitler's trauma over his mother's death at the hands of a Jewish doctor and the trauma suffered by the German people in 1918, twin traumas that led, respectively, to Auschwitz and Stalingrad. Binion's method is probably too intensely subjective for most historians: see, for example, Fred Weinstein's critique in *Psychohistory Review*, vol. 6, no. 1 (Summer 1977), pp. 50–61.

Works on Hitler constitute only the most prominent outcropping of the mountain of psychohistorical work on Nazi Germany. Psychohistorians have also undertaken the study of other subjects connected with Nazism. Historian and psychoanalyst Peter Loewenberg has produced representative studies such as "The Unsuccessful Adolescence of Heinrich Himmler," *American Historical Review*, vol. 76 (1971), pp. 612–41; "The Psychohistorical

Origins of the Nazi Youth Cohort," *American Historical Review,* vol. 76 (1971), pp. 1457–1502; and a comprehensive review essay, "Psychohistorical Perspectives on Modern German History," *Journal of Modern History,* vol. 47 (1975), pp. 229–79.

Political and social disorders of the twentieth century, represented by Hitler's rise to power, have given psychohistorians much to think about. Revolutionary studies especially would seem to be a promising field. The relationship between personal psychological traits and revolution is treated by George D. Jackson's "Lenin and the Problems of Psychohistory," *Canadian Slavonic Papers,* vol. 19, no. 2 (June 1977), pp. 207–22. Jackson puts aside the simplistic Freudian theories of E. Victor Wolfenstein's *The Revolutionary Personality* (Princeton, 1971) and suggests instead a more clinical approach based on the work of Carl Rogers and Abraham Maslow. This, Jackson claims, would avoid the misleading monolithic intepretations of personality based on childhood traumas and substitute a study of personalities at a given point of time in a life. A different psychobiographical approach to revolutions is suggested by Bruce Mazlish's *The Revolutionary Ascetic* (New York, 1976). Mazlish believes that the "Robespierres win out over Dantons" in revolutions because the puritanical revolutionary with a "displaced libido" who denies bonds of friendship and feeling can devote everything to the revolution. Among Mazlish's examples are Oliver Cromwell, Robespierre, Lenin, and Mao Tse-tung. Mazlish's thesis has been questioned. Peter Loewenberg suggests in the *American Historical Review,* vol. 82, no. 2 (April 1977), pp. 336–37 that Mazlish relied too heavily on the Oedipal dynamics of Freudian libido theory: Loewenberg recommends object relations theory. Chalmers Johnson is more critical, and wonders how Mao can be considered an ascetic with "his pot belly, his chain smoking, and his three wives." See "Pregnant with 'Meaning!' Mao and the Revolutionary Ascetic," *Journal of Interdisciplinary History,* vol. 7, no. 3 (Winter 1977), pp. 499–508.

An ascetic mode of leadership would also seem to characterize Woodrow Wilson's presidency. Wilson is second only to Hitler as a psychobiographical subject. In addition to the three articles reprinted above, readers may want to peruse the biography that initiated the present debate on the psychological travails of Wilson, Alexander and Juliette George's *Woodrow Wilson and Colonel House: A Personality Study* (New York, 1956). We recommend the Dover edition (1964): here the Georges add a helpful preface and a concluding research note. Alexander George elaborates on his theoretical model in "Power As a Compensatory Value for Political Leaders," *Journal of Social Issues,* vol. 24, no. 3 (1968), pp. 29–49. A recent issue of *Political Psychology,* vol. 4, no. 2 (June 1983), pp. 289–331, debates the various interpretations of Wilson. Dorothy Ross provides a timely survey of the issues in her "Review Essay/Woodrow Wilson and the Case for Psychohistory," *Journal of American History,* vol. 69, no. 3 (December 1982), pp. 659–68. Much of the controversy swirls around Edwin Weinstein's evaluation of Wilson's health during critical moments of his presidency. Weinstein's views are given in the article reprinted above, but readers desiring additional information should read Weinstein's recent book, *Woodrow Wilson: A Medical and Psychological Biography* (Princeton, 1981), cited in note 13 of our introduction.

The life of T. E. Lawrence, scholar, author, and as "Lawrence of Arabia," a guerrilla leader against the Turks in World War I, has become an intriguing psychobiographical subject. Digging deeply into Lawrence's background and utilizing a sophisticated eclectic—though essentially psychodynamic—model, John Mack places a debased self-esteem at the center of Lawrence's curious fall from fame into obscurity after the war. Mack's first advanced his thesis in "T. E. Lawrence: A Study of Heroism and Conflict," *American Journal of Psy-*

chiatry, vol. 125 (1969), pp. 1083–92: Mack later expanded his ideas into a full-scale biography of Lawrence, *A Prince of Our Disorder* (Boston, 1976).

The perils of writing a psychobiography of a contemporary figure are well illustrated in the case of Richard Nixon. Many attempts have been methodologically unsophisticated and politically biased. A representative work is David Abrahamsen's *Nixon vs Nixon: An Emotional Tragedy* (New York, 1976). An analyst, Abrahamsen claims to be basing his study upon "years of training and experience" and to rest his conclusions upon "a vast body of scientific knowledge," yet he seems unable to distinguish between historical fact and bald speculation. Bruce Mazlish obtains somewhat better results in his "Toward a Psychohistorical Inquiry: The 'Real' Richard Nixon," *Journal of Interdisciplinary History*, vol. 1 (1970), pp. 49–105. In Mazlish's longer psychobiography, *In Search of Nixon* (New York, 1972), especially worth noting is chapter six, "The Psychohistorical Approach." Stanley Allen Renshon's review article, "Psychological Analysis and Presidential Personality: The Case of Richard Nixon," *History of Childhood Quarterly*, vol. 2 (1975), pp. 415–50 provides a thoughtful comparison of four psychological approaches to Nixon.

PART III

THE PSYCHOLOGY OF
THE GROUP IN HISTORY

14

Group Psychology and Problems of Contemporary History

Bruce Mazlish

Events of recent history have begged for explanation in terms of group psychology and group behaviour. The omnipresent reality of totalitarianism, especially, calls for its interpretation in the very terms—growing "irrationality," and hence psychology—that shape the phenomenon itself. Somehow, we must make what seems almost totally irrational submit to rational explanation. The term "cult of personality" itself emphasizes the psychological dimension. So, too, our increased interest in, and awareness of, racial situations provokes an inquiry into the inter-personal relations that underlie an otherwise irrational, and often uneconomical, system. Colonial relations, messianic cults, all ask similar questions.

Yet, since the publication of William McDougall's *Introduction to Social Psychology* in 1908, perhaps the earliest text in the field, little seems to have been done here that satisfies the historian's quest for greater understanding. As for psychoanalytically-oriented work, the theories of Freudian individual psychology, even for those convinced of their validity, seem not to have been satisfactorily connected to the problems of group psychology. Thus the stern and demanding challenge of group psychology and its relation to history still confronts us, unsmilingly. The cheerful note in this situation is that a fresh look at the problem, however unsuccessful, can hardly be compared too unfavourably to its predecessors.

I propose, therefore, to note some of the new theories of group psychology and group behaviour as applied to contemporary history; then to glance at their possible application to national character; at their application in work on group psychoses and neuroses, as well as inter-group rivalry and persecutions (all closely related phenomena); and, lastly, to discuss briefly a case study in inter-

This article first appeared in the *Journal of Contemporary History*, 3,2 (April 1968), pp. 163–77.

group relations, O. Mannoni's study of the colonial relationship in Madagascar. The new theories of group psychology, or at least the non-Freudian ones, appear to me to have little applicability to history. What is known as the theory of cognitive dissonance does not help to explain historical phenomena.[1] Similarly, the work done at the Massachusetts Institute of Technology by Richard Held and his colleagues on the connection between motor activity and the perception of reality, on the distortion of even the simplest perceptions when action is inhibited, is fascinating, but it is difficult to see how it can be usefully applied by the historian. The same applies to the recent work by other psychologists, showing that one's judgment is affected by what others around one think: if six "primed" subjects claim a black object is white, the innocent seventh subject will in all probability also pronounce it white. Suggestions about the lack of motor activities in totalitarian countries leading to distortion, or about the influence of propagandized peers on a person, while undoubtedly true, simply do not advance us far in history.

It may be that the failure is mine. However, in what follows I shall only be able to remark on a few instances of what is, generally speaking, non-Freudian group psychology as applied to historical material.

David McClelland's *The Achieving Society* (1961) is by now a well-known book. Its thesis is simple: the ethos of "achieving" is crucial to a flourishing society, and its presence in personality can be measured empirically, even for past societies. The method of application is elaborate: scales and tables, based on present-day questionnaires and polling techniques, are used to investigate Greek pottery as well as the German school system, and to see how high on the "achieving scale" they measure. Obviously, the book attracts as an effort to shed light on the psychological factor in developing underdeveloped countries today, and as an empirical corrective and extension to Max Weber's theory of the Protestant ethos. Alas, most critics have not been persuaded by either the tables (which too often seem to have shaky conclusions drawn from them) or the sweeping nature of the theory.

McClelland's book does point to the increasing interest in the factor of group psychology as part of the economic development process. It has gradually become clear even to the econometricians that human beings are what make economies tick, and that economic development does not take place on paper, in terms of nicely manipulated figures. Thus, in addition to generalized theories of growth in which the psychological factor is merely presumed, such as Rostow's theories of economic stages, there are important efforts, such as Everett Hagen's *Theory of Social Change* (1962), in which the psychological is explicitly made central to the theory. As Hagen, a professional economist, says elsewhere, "The theory of the economics of economic development will mainly elaborate details, rather than making major advances, until advances in sociology and personality theory give it new insights."[2]

Along with economic development, political development has become a subject of current interest. Here, too, the psychological has received much emphasis, centring to a large extent on the idea of identity. Perhaps it is only natural that the 'search for identity' by new nations attracts more attention than the analysis of the identity of established nations. Thus, Lucian Pye deals with the "identity crisis," both on the individual and the public level, in Burma, in his book *Politics, Personality, and Nation Building;* and Harold Isaacs has done a whole series of studies based on this concept, covering the untouchables, Americans in Israel, the Filipinos, American Negroes, and so forth. Isaacs' other overriding interest in these studies is to observe how individuals and groups perceive others, and how they are, in turn, perceived (see, for example, *Scratches on our Minds: American Images of China and India*); and he relates this aspect of the psychology of perception (used at a low level of theory) to his examination of the search for identity; part of a group's self-identity, for example, is based on how it is perceived by other groups.

Leaving development aside for the moment, psychological and semi-psychological studies have been made also on how existing political systems function in terms of their leadership element (and, of course, such studies can quickly be extended to the developing nations).[3] An instance is Lewis J. Edinger's *Kurt Schumacher: A Study in Personality and Political Behavior* (1965). The basic theory behind this book is clearly Harold Lasswell's classic notion (e.g., in *Psychopathology and Politics,* 1930) that the political actor, to use Edinger's phrases, "strives to satisfy personal needs through the assumption and performance of certain roles"(p. 5). One then asks what expectations the "actor" brings to his roles, and what are the expectations of the "counter-players." Alas, the "satisfaction of conscious or unconscious personal goals may not correspond to rationally posited or group-oriented goals and norms" (p. 4). Worse, the "actor" in the leading role may even reject new information when it clashes with cherished beliefs, needs, etc. (our old friend perception again). Other conclusions are that what works in one situation may not work in another: what was manifestly functional for Schumacher in securing leadership of the SPD was dysfunctional in the larger context of post-war German politics (p. 306); and a concluding hypothesis: "that behaviour which may have been self-defeating in terms of Schumacher's manifest aspirations may have served latent personality needs" (p. 282).

Obviously, work such as Edinger's is not very Freudian. It is more concerned with actors, roles, communication networks, and group-oriented goals. It will be interesting to see, therefore, what comes out of the conference on "Leadership," planned by Dankwart Rustow, Columbia University. (The papers are to appear as an issue of *Daedalus.*) Its stated purpose is to "look at rulers, at founders of states, or at founders of social or intellectual movements from a variety of perspectives, including the interplay between private personality and public role, the relationship between leaders, followers, rivals, and antagonists, the tactics of leadership, and a leader's successes, failures, and place in history." A central problem is conceived to be that of "the social and psychological congruence between leaders and followers," and in pursuing the psychological theme, we are informed, correctly of course, that "David Truman, summing up the trend of studies in social psychology, has stressed that 'the conception of leadership as a functional relationship rules out the possibility that all leaders have in common certain "traits" that set them off from followers.' " Robert C. Tucker will deliver a paper on The Theory of Charismatic Leadership; Stanley Hoffman on General de Gaulle; Dankwart Rustow on Ataturk as State Founder, and so forth, all emphasizing social, or group, psychology, Freudian or otherwise.

What of the more Freudian, or Neo-Freudian, efforts? We can take the work of Erik Erikson as the most outstanding contribution. His *Young Man Luther* (1959) was a brilliant, pioneering example of the new work in the emerging field of psycho-historical process. Now Erikson has turned to contemporary history, in the figure of Mahatma Gandhi. As yet only bits and pieces of this study have emerged, but the full-scale work is promised soon. It will provide an examination of the methodological problems involved in such work, much deeper even than that of the Luther volume, and will analyse Gandhi explicitly in the political and religious group settings in which he functioned. For those interested in contemporary history, the book may well have an even wider interest, for Erikson uses Gandhi, and his theory of non-violence, as a way of analysing the phenomena of war and violence in our time. Erikson is taking his theories of basic trust and of mutuality in the individual and seeking to extend them to the public arena. Deeply affected, I believe, by Konrad Lorenz's *On Aggression* (1966), he is trying to provide a "ritualization" for aggressive impulses, a training in "mutuality" that will keep man from going for the jugular, so to speak, and thus to supply the deficiency created by our lack of instinctive restraints. Gandhi shows the way.

Further discussion will have to await the appearance of Erikson's book. If, as I suspect, it takes up where Freud left off (one thinks, for example, of his "Thoughts for the Times on War and Death," 1915), we may well have an important theoretical contribution, not only to the study of Gandhi's leadership and to the problem of Indian identity, which it is sure to be, but to what is perhaps the most important phenomenon of contemporary history: war. If so, one hopes that it will stimulate further empirical studies.[4]

National character has always been an intriguing subject simply because everyone can play. The dour Scotsman, the energetic American, the volatile Italian, each can be nicely ticketed. Serious scholars, such as David Potter *(People of Plenty)*, Margaret Mead *(And Keep Your Powder Dry)*, Geoffrey Gorer and John Rickman *(The People of Great Russia)*, and even Erik Erikson (see his essays on American, German, and Russian character in *Childhood and Society*), have also tried their hand at the subject.

In my judgment it is an impossible subject. The only thing to do with so-called national character is to dissolve it into its parts. Certainly, in trying to understand contemporary domestic or international history, the concept of a unitary national character is a poor—indeed, non-existent—analytic tool.[5] To begin with, the subject of nationalism itself is still one of the least well-defined and manageable topics. The very definition of a "nation" and the basis on which it rests is up in the air. (At one extremity, we have African "nations" only a few years old, trying to compress into one generation changes that took centuries in Europe; and at the other extremity we have centuries-old European nations trying to transcend their present existence and achieve a supranational "European" identity.) Why not first study "tribal" character? Or regional character? And then examine how these are synthesized into something larger, called "national character" (e.g., what "characteristics" are held in common, in America, by a New Englander; a Mississippian—white or Negro; a Texan; and a Minnesotan?).

"National character," in other words, may mask the hard questions of dynamic process and functional relationship. For example, take character: on the individual level, a classic psychoanalytic definition is Fenichel's "The habitual mode of bringing into harmony the tasks presented by internal demands and by the external world" (*The Psychoanalytic Theory of Neurosis,* 1945, p. 467). The first part of this definition refers to defences, and is a useful notion in so far as most individuals develop characteristic patterns of defence (denial, projection, repression, etc.). Internal demands might seem constant but, as Erikson has insisted, they at least manifest themselves differently at different stages of the individual's life cycle. And the external world—that is in fact the realm of history (in this case, personal history). The point of all this is that, today, the emphasis in psychoanalysis is on "character" as a dynamic process, where even the defences shift during different periods of life and in relation to changing external demands.

How can these notions be extended to group psychology? The Eriksonian position, for example, and it is conceptually admirable, is that the individual's character is developed mainly in terms of the group character, that is, of the values and patterns of behaviour of the group as these are manifested in bringing up children: hence *Childhood and Society* (1951). Thus, by studying a "great man," a Luther or Gandhi, we may come to understand as well the society within which he is nurtured and to which he in turn contributes his creativity. There is much to be said for this approach; but it is no longer effectively in terms of "national character."

What about functional relationship? Let us assume an American "national character." If, for example, we are trying to understand American military policy today, can we use the generalized national character as a base from which to begin analysis? Or must we ask whether a distinct sub-group—say, a Southern "character"—plays a disproportionate role in formulating and carrying out military policy? Moreover, must we ask more narrowly how the Southern sub-group character and the Eastern sub-group character interact with one another, so that an outcome unintended by either emerges from the confrontation of character?

And, given the structure of American executive power, ought we to ask about the "character" of the President, and how it interrelates to something called the national character? In short, national character is an overgeneralized notion, when what counts most is the character of the men who actually wield power. (How representative of Japanese national character were the militarists who wielded power in the second world war? Were the surprise attacks preceding almost all Japanese military involvements in modern times a characteristic Japanese "defence," or a particular policy and offensive tactic of the generals?)

What national character points at is important. We do want to inquire about characteristic defences of a people, but we need to see these as dynamic, changing according to who the leaders are, to the demands of external reality, and to the period of history and the particular generation concerned. In short, concepts such as "national character," "spirit of the age," and so forth, start at the wrong end. They are stereotyped and posit as explanatory concepts what may only emerge, momentarily, as a result of particular empirical relations in a functioning system, subject to rapid change again. Consequently, we need to inquire into what is behind "national character," not into "national character" itself.

Under the heading, "Group Psychoses and Neuroses, and Intergroup Rivalry and Persecution," we find such unalluring topics as anti-Semitism and the authoritarian personality. As parts of the totalitarian phenomena of our time, these topics press for explanation in the same "irrational" terms as appear to produce them. "Sane," "rational" interest politics of the nineteenth century have given way to "cultural" or "status" politics, and the latter tend to rest on unconscious, rather than conscious, foundations: hence the appeal to social psychology, especially psychoanalysis.[6]

Anti-Semitism, of course, existed long before totalitarianism, but it is only with the advent of modern psychology that we have tried to probe its nature deeply. Such works as Ernst Simmel's "Anti-Semitism and Mass Psychopathology," along with essays by various scholars in the book he edited, *Anti-Semitism, a Social Disease* (1946); Ackerman and Jahoda, *Anti-Semitism and Emotional Disorder: A Psychoanalytic Interpretation* (1950); and numerous other studies have done much to illuminate the subject. Such studies form part of a general inquiry into racial or religious prejudice (anti-Negroism, anti-Catholicism, and so forth), and we can regard them as prototypic.

The first thing to note is that anti-Semitism is not to be classified as an individual mental disease. In fact it is a character defence, used to prevent mental illness. Unfortunate as this may be, it is true. Emotional conflicts typically displayed by anti-Semites—unsatisfactory relations with the opposite sex, unsatisfactory resolution of feelings towards the father and mother, strong tendency to regress to primitive and childlike destructive impulses, general immaturity, and general confusion as to development of self (lack of "identity")—all these are dealt with by various defence mechanisms (especially projection and introjection) in an effort to substitute prejudice for more threatening neurotic, or psychotic, symptoms. The same conflicts, however, may lead to other "ideological" solutions. In any case, it is the social setting that turns, or does not turn, a personal solution into, say, the "final solution" of history. Norman Cohn sees this very well, in his *Warrant for Genocide* (1967): "Though the individuals who make up a group of Jew-killers are well within the bounds of reality, and most of them are not even fanatics, and even the fanatics are far from mad—yet it is perfectly true that the group as a whole behaves like a paranoiac in the grip of his delusion." Such a group "psychosis" arises, however, only where there is a hard core of fanatics, supported by public indifference, and allowed to run amuck, or even encouraged, by the government. In this sense, then, Simmel is absolutely right in calling anti-Semitism a "social disease."

Let us now turn to *The Authoritarian Personality* (1950), as typical of a certain range of studies. While it, too, deals with anti-Semitism, it seeks to describe a larger entity: the authoritarian, or fascist, personality. Like McClelland's *Achieving Society*, it tries to set up an objective scale, derived from questionnaires, by which to measure the presence of the phenomenon. To this, however, it adds the "confirming evidence" of depth interviews. Methodologically, it has raised many important questions, and these have been gone into exhaustively by other scholars. So, too, has the point that should concern us most here, both about this particular study and the anti-Semitic studies touched on above: admit, for argument's sake, that some people have a "tendency" to an "authoritarian" or "anti-Semitic" personality, how do we go from this to political or social action, which is what we are interested in? What is the actual link between such personality factors and the public arena (note that this is the same question asked about Lasswell's formulation thirty years earlier of the relation between private motivations and public acts, where the individual "displaced" the former onto the latter)?[7] The answers to these questions have not been forthcoming and this points to the real difficulties. Psychological explanation is not the same as historical explanation.

While the studies on anti-Semitism and authoritarian personalities are most interesting and valuable, they do not shed much light on the phenomena of contemporary history. To begin with, such personality traits have existed for a long time: it is like trying to explain culture by climate, when the climate has stayed the same for centuries. If we add to this the sort of criticisms implicit in the brief discussion above, we find ourselves not far advanced. In short, the problem of group psychology and contemporary history cannot be resolved until we look more closely at this particular problem in the light of the general problem of historical explanation.

One of the crucial points in the specifically psychoanalytic approach in relation to history concerns causation and determinism; and it is a point that disturbs unsympathetic critics of psychoanalysis. Freud insisted that strict determination prevailed in respect of psychic acts; there are no "accidents." For example, "free association," the basis of dream analysis and of therapy, is "free" only in the sense that it is not hampered by the censorship of "logical," "rational" thought and mores. It is not, however, undetermined. In fact, free association, as almost all the other processes in psychoanalysis, is *over-determined*. Indeed, it is the latter phenomenon—the fact that the same word or symbol refers to many elements in the unconscious thought process, on the one hand, and that the single unconscious drive or pattern of behaviour will manifest itself in innumerable different conscious manifestations, on the other hand—that warrants the historian in his use of the evidence. Because the psychological phenomena are over-determined, the evidence can be abundant and self-confirming.

Nevertheless, determined and over-determined as it is, psychoanalytic evidence is not generally *causal* in nature; and this is the first fallacy. Psycho-historical inquiry does not offer us causal explanations, but only explanations in terms of correspondence and co-existing processes. This fact is clearer, for example, in Erikson than in Freud. In discussing the case of a little boy, Erikson declares:

> We cannot escape the conviction that the meaning of an item which may be "located" in one of the three processes [the somatic, the ego, and the societal] is co-determined by its meaning in the other two. An item in one process gains relevance by giving significance to and receiving significance from items in the others. Gradually, I hope, we may find better words for such relativity in human existence. Of the catastrophe described in our first specimen, then, we know no "cause." Instead we find a convergence in all three processes of specific intolerances which made the catastrophe retrospectively intelligible, retrospectively probable. The plausibility thus gained does not permit us to go back and undo causes. It only permits us to understand a continuum, on which the catastrophe marked a decisive event, which now throws its shadow back over the very items which seem to have caused it (*Childhood and Society*, 1963, pp. 37–8).

Put another way, "Being unable to arrive at any simple sequence and causal chain with a clear location and a circumscribed beginning, only triple bookkeeping (or, if you wish, a systematic going around in circles) can gradually clarify the relevances and the relativities of all the known data" (p. 46). In sum, psycho-historical inquiry helps us to understand the "meaning" of an event, but does not—in fact, cannot—offer us a simple causal explanation of it.

It follows directly that history cannot be *reduced* to psychoanalytic explanation. This reductionism is the second great fallacy in the field. As we have seen in discussing *The Authoritarian Personality*, psychoanalysis adds to other explanations in history; it is no substitute for them.

The third fallacy is the pathological one. Analysis of a "leader" (or, indeed, of a whole people, "national character"), may simply reduce the subject to its neurotic or psychotic elements, and it becomes a matter of wonder how he functions at all; the sources of his creativity, of his positive appeal to his followers, seem never to be exposed. Without labouring this point, it must be said that mere description, for example of an Oedipal complex, while valuable, is not enough;

we need to see it in its adaptive aspect, and to study it as part of what Erikson called his "triple bookkeeping," where our prime concern is with "relativity" and "meaning."

One of the most interesting efforts in analysing a group situation, especially because it does not approach the subject via a great man and his relations to his followers, is to be found in O. Mannoni's fascinating work, *The Psychology of Colonization* (1950), a pioneering, imaginative, and marvellously intuitive book. Put simply, Mannoni's analysis of the relationship in Madagascar, around 1948 (and the uprising that then occurred), between the natives and the colonial rulers is that the former have a need for dependency relations, starting from their cult of the dead, but inculcated in them by all their family arrangements, while the latter act in terms of a "superiority complex" (in reality, a fear of inferiority). To the colonialist, the native's dependency looks like inferiority, and, in certain cases, lack of gratitude (the natives, for example, take support for granted). To the native, the colonialist's effort to shake himself free of the dependency relationship (by giving him "freedom") is perceived as betrayal. And so on, in a complex series of misunderstandings (and "understandings"?).

Without exploring the book's thesis any further, it will be useful to look briefly at the methodology, for it points to some of the problems in relating group psychology to contemporary history. The first thing to notice is Mannoni's admitted personal involvement in the situation. As he tells us, he was himself being analysed, and the events of 1948 were a sort of "conversion crisis" for him; his experience raises the question of what, for shorthand purposes, we can call the "counter-transference" problem. To what extent does the historian distort his materials because of his own psychological reactions? Obviously, the problem of distortion exists in all historical work, but when it draws on the deepest elements of unconscious processes, it is more difficult to deal with. New techniques, new training, and new methodology will have to be evolved to deal with this situation.

Next, Mannoni's analysis of the natives is based on his own ethnological observation. He brought to this book various theories from Alfred Adler and Melanie Klein, but, as he admits, the natives would never tell him their dreams nor submit to psychoanalysis. How trustworthy, then, is such an analysis? How adequate the Adlerian theories used? Mannoni does offer some explanations of otherwise inexplicable native behaviour that seem suggestive; but we have no way of checking on them. What does become obvious is that he talks of the natives as if they were a homogeneous group, when in fact they are composed of more than a score of separate tribes, each, apparently, with somewhat different customs and motivations. Certainly the Hova are different: they came to Madagascar as conquerors and rulers, just as did the Europeans, and think of themselves as rather superior to the "natives." Yet today they are in the culturally marginal situation of being between the colonial rulers (French) and the "natives." In short, we are up against some of the social-context problems raised earlier in relation to national character.

As for the colonialists, what materials does Mannoni use in analysing them? His appeal is to European literature, and he offers us, for example, fascinating analyses of Defoe's *Robinson Crusoe* and Shakespeare's *The Tempest*, as well as of Descartes's character.[8] Mannoni's intention is to demonstrate the European fear of dependency and abandonment, successfully kept at bay, however, by a deliberate confrontation of isolation and by a resolution of Oedipal feelings into characteristics of independence and superiority. Once again, persuasive as this work is, we must ask how suitable it is as explanation? Were the twentieth-century Europeans who became colonialists "typical" sixteenth or eighteenth-century characters? Or with rather special drives and needs? Why not analyse *them*, directly? In short, again we need particular empirical work in terms of a significant sociological context: the correct identification and then analysis of the actual colonial elite.

Whatever the weaknesses in Mannoni's book (and I have touched on them merely to illustrate some general problems), it has one overpowering virtue: he places his colonialists and natives in a direct psychological confrontation. This is perhaps the crux of his special addition to psycho-historical inquiry. Character is not something isolated and static, but is something developed and expressed in relation to other persons and groups.

To take as illustration the case of Hitler, the nazis, and the German people: it is not enough to analyse them in terms of the role of guilt in their personal and collective behaviour (incidentally, a fascinating topic). One must also analyse the role of guilt in those with whom they are interacted, say, the English and French at Munich. The "guilt" of Versailles, after all, was experienced, though differently, by both sides, and both sides were trying to "do" and "undo," as they "acted out" their deepest psychological impulses.[9] It is this confrontation aspect of psycho-historical inquiry that Mannoni's work brings so strongly to the fore, and which is methodologically its most important contribution.

Out of such a confrontation and interaction comes, as it does for individuals, a sense of identity (or else a failure of such a sense), and this brings us back full circle to the problems of national character and the economic and political development of underdeveloped countries. Perhaps now we can see that it is identity—a sense of inner sameness and continuity, perceived as such by oneself and confirmed by the perception of others—that we must study, rather than national character. Such sameness as found in identity is, of course, paradoxically, a dynamic characteristic (requiring moreover constant reaffirmation), of a person or group.[10]

We would no doubt all agree that many of the major problems of contemporary history can be summarized under such headings as totalitarianism, war, modernization, development, and revolution.[11] Existing studies using the theories and techniques of some form of group psychology oblige the historian to deal with such an approach as he seeks to understand the historical phenomena surrounding him. It is to be hoped, however, that the historian will seek comprehension in contemporary history not only by the utilization of existing studies (which, admittedly, are lamentably few in number and deficient in methodology and data), but by entering the field himself. Once it is seen that group psychology (especially of the psychoanalytic kind) is neither a substitute for history, nor a cosmetic to be applied externally to Clio, but an intrinsic and meaningful part of historical explanation, it will be difficult for any really honest historian to evade a confrontation on this level with himself and, consequently, with his fellow men and their destinies.

NOTES

1 See Leon Festinger, *A Theory of Cognitive Dissonance* (1957). Professor F. C. Iklé offers a summary: "Studies show that in certain circumstances people tend to reduce discrepancies between their behavior and what they know by distorting what they know. A person who has chosen among alternatives that seemed equally attractive to him tends to suppress or modify information that suggests his choice was wrong. He will inflate the data that makes the chosen alternative look preferable and belittle the advantages of the rejected alternative that he belatedly discovers," F. C. Iklé, "Can Social Predictions Be Evaluated," *Daedalus,* Summer 1967, p. 734.

2 Professor Hagen made this statement when delivering a yet unpublished paper to the Group for Applied Psychoanalysis in Boston, 1967.

3 Perhaps the best known of such studies is Nathan Leites's *A Study of Bolshevism* (1953). Here, a "code" of Bolshevik behavior, a way of psychological response, was worked out. But the book is much more an example of content analysis than of psychoanalysis. The dynamic element is simply missing. If, however, one does take the book seriously in its own terms—content analysis—then one is forced to ask why no comparable work on the "code" of American behavior has been forthcoming? And this immediately leads to the point that the "code" of Bolshevik and the "code" of American behavior would have to be studied as a highly dynamic psychological interplay in international affairs rather than as a rigid, self-contained set of rules for one party only.

4 Brief mention should be made of two of Erikson's disciples. The first is Robert Lifton, best known for his study, *Thought Reform and the Psychology of Totalism* (1961), which seeks to examine, by means of modified Freudian theory, the general subject of totalitarian thought control (incidentally, from a non-Freudian, Pavlovian point of view, there is the interesting, and even earlier, work, *Battle for the Mind,* by William Sargent, which seems to reach similar conclusions). Lifton is now engaged on a study of Hiroshima and the impact of the atom bomb, which joins in a significant way with Erikson's interest in war and its psychology. In his "Death and Death Symbolism," already published, Lifton seeks to use new data—immediate historical materials—to inspire new concepts of psychology and historical behavior, concepts which relate to twentieth-century themes of violence, inhumanity, guilt, and anxiety, and which contrast with the sexual vocabulary of Freud originating in the Victorian era of the late nineteenth century. In short, new times and experiences are seen as calling forth new psychological concepts by which to explain them.
The second disciple is Susanne Rudolph, who has produced two articles on Gandhi. The first one, in *World Politics* (October 1963), on "The New Courage: An Essay on Gandhi's Psychology," implicitly raises the problem of using western theories and perceptions in relation to non-western groups and cultures; it also explores from a psychological viewpoint

the topic of "marginality." The other paper, "Self-Control and Political Potency" (*The American Scholar*, Winter 1965–6), is on the general phenomenon of asceticism, with particular reference to Gandhi, as a means of political power; here, too, the problem of differing cultural values enters meaningfully. In this last paper we also have an effort to extend Freud's notion of the leader as free of libidinal ties.

5 Of course, this is not to say that intuitions about national character, such as are found in most of the studies I have named, are not both interesting and valuable. The admirable article on the subject by Alex Inkeles and Daniel J. Levison, "National Character: The Study of Modal Personality and Sociocultural Systems" (*Handbook of Social Psychology*, ed. G. Lindsey, vol. 2, 1954), is more sanguine about the possibilities of the subject, though the authors admit that even a successful *a priori* definition of "national character" does not mean that the entity necessarily exists empirically.

6 On the shift away from "interest" politics, see, for example, Hannah Arendt, *The Origins of Totalitarianism* (1961), or *The New American Right*, ed. Daniel Bell (1955).

7 One of the best criticisms along these lines is Edward Shill's article in the collection on the *Authoritarian Personality*, ed. by Christie and Jahoda. See also Lucian Pye, "Personal Identity and Political Ideology" (1962), reprinted in *Psychoanalysis and History*, ed. B. Mazlish (1963).

8 For further analysis of Shakespeare's *The Tempest* and the psychology of race relations, see Philip Mason, *Prospero's Magic* (1962).

9 Obviously, such an analysis must take into account not only the "confrontation" aspect of the situation—what the behavior of one party triggers off psychologically in the behaviour of the other—but the reality aspect, the political, military, economic, and social circumstances surrounding the two parties.

10 The difficulties of achieving such an identity for underdeveloped countries are also well expressed by Lucian Pye: "Erikson's concept of identity thus suggests that the problem of consensus in transitional societies runs deeper than mere agreement over political forms and over the appropriate ends and means of political action; it involves the creation of an inner coherence of values, theories and actions for the entire polity. The implication is that in underdeveloped countries there is a vicious circle at the subjective level, which is more crucial to the problem of national development than the more manifest vicious circle of poverty, ill-health and illiteracy. Those who hope that national identity can come from modernization cannot escape the pressing psychological fact that modernity, in the mind of these people, has always been the monopoly of those who were their former masters. If they hated their colonial rulers, then they cannot expect to find their identities by following the same path. If they did not hate their former rulers, there might still be the problem of preferring dependency to autonomy, which would confuse the quest for identity. National identity cannot be built upon doing less well what one's former master excelled at" ("Personal Identity and Political Ideology," in *Psychoanalysis and History*, p. 172).

11 Chalmers Johnson, however, cautions us about the use of psychology in relation to revolutions: "The aspect of psychological studies of revolution that we do not find useful is the misinformed generalization of micro-data without reference to a macro-model—namely, the derivation of revolution from psychological studies of individual revolutionaries and the resultant value judgment that because some revolutionaries are lunatics, revolution is a form of social lunacy." Johnson then concludes: "Psychological data on revolutionaries must be related to the social system; otherwise they are only of propaganda value, useful in denigrating movements of which we may disapprove" (*Revolution and the Social System*, 1964, pp. 25–6). It should be clear from what I said earlier that I agree with Johnson about the need for relating psychological data to the social system. I am distressed, however, at his implied notion that all psychological studies of revolutionaries are "denigrating"; this is to embrace the pathological fallacy.

15

The Sociological Endeavor
and Psychoanalytic Thought

Gerald M. Platt

Attempts at integrating psychoanalytic and sociological thought have focused upon aggregate behavior, that is, on "national character" studies, on studies of collective action in political and religious movements, or on revolutionary activity, and so on. However, analyses of such group action employing psychosocial frameworks have not fared well in sociology: either they did not meet the scientific standards of the sociological discipline or they did not seem to lead anywhere. Today there is mostly apathy, ambivalence, or outright hostility toward psychoanalytically oriented frameworks in sociology.

However, not all the forms of integration between the two disciplines are held in equal disesteem, and even within the several forms there are more and less well-regarded works. This essay will suggest four forms of integration between psychoanalysis and sociology and will use these as categories in terms of which we may amplify the discussion. A word of caution is in order: psychosocial thought is not neatly organized around a topic such as American Studies. Sociologists want to develop universals applicable to the here and now and to distant times and places. Thus, it will be difficult to confine this discourse to American society, although special attention will be given to this substantive focus.

PSYCHOBIOGRAPHY OF ELITES: THE ONTOGENETIC MODEL

Suggesting that sociologists have not pursued ontogenetic studies of prominent figures should not imply that they are uninterested in this approach or that they eschew it simply on sectarian grounds. There are certainly sufficient numbers of psychobiographical "leadership" studies so that a sociologist could construct

First published in the *American Quarterly*, 28 (1976), pp. 343–59. Copyright © 1976, American Studies Association.

a course entitled, "The Sociology of American Elites." American presidents, for example, have especially attracted psychobiographers and it would be possible in a sociology course of this nature to review the lives, personalities, and political styles of Jefferson, Lincoln, Theodore Roosevelt, Wilson, Kennedy, and Nixon.[1] Why then do not sociologists more thoroughly delve into this intellectual endeavor?

The answer to this question resides in a number of issues all connected with the theoretical framework employed by psychobiographers. For example, no matter how often psychobiographers write that the objective of "psychobiographical investigation is to try to relate the particular identity need of a given leader to the 'typical identity needs' of his historical times,"[2] sociologists will not accept such an assertion. Robert Bellah points out that it is problematic to infer the personality of the mass from the analysis of an elite figure, no matter how sensitive and detailed the analysis.[3] Thus, sociologists recoil from generalizations like "these qualities and experiences [regarding Theodore Roosevelt] were shared by many of his contemporaries."[4]

At one level this is no more than a criticism based upon statistical representativeness; sociologists would never infer from a single case to a total population. But this criticism has a deeper and more important meaning. Sociologists know that such generalizations violate the very ontogenetic theory the psychobiographer employs. In the ontogenetic model the adult personality is a result of the organization of drives and defenses as these became fixed through infant handling by caretaker persons during the early phases of child rearing. But that theory stresses the idiosyncratic development of personality and sociologists have suggested two systematic features of the caretaking process which contribute to personal idiosyncrasy: variation in meaning and thus in the effect of the same caretaking event; and variation in caretaking events as a result of spatial and temporal differences, such as those produced by birth order and familial differentiation within a society.

These two sources of variation in concerted effect upon personality can be illustrated by referring again to the Theodore Roosevelt biography; in this instance we are reviewing the different meaning of caretaking events in relation to birth order in personality formation. It has been argued that Theodore Roosevelt's aggressive political style was a result of anger engendered in him through maternal oral deprivation in combination with emulation of paternal phallic character (i.e., "hardness"). Interestingly, however, the passive retreatism, personal and occupational failure, and alcoholism of Teddy's younger brother Elliott are explained in terms of the same constellation of parental caretaking events. Thus, if two children raised in a single family and assumedly experiencing similar caretaking events can develop such divergent personalities, the theory cannot claim for a population congruent personalities even if they are touched by similar child rearing experiences, unless the theory can specify the conditions under which similar treatment or environmental impingements will produce personality convergence and/or divergence. But psychoanalytic literature admits to the lack of understanding of why one psychic economy rather than another emerges out of similar circumstances.[5]

In sum, psychobiographers have not convinced sociologists that it is possible to assert psychological congruence between a leader and mass simply by studying the leader, no matter how effectively the leader is related to the mass. The willingness of a population to be moved and the capacity to move a population can be explained entirely in sociological terms.

Tenuous inferences regarding the relation of the leader's personality to that of the mass is not the only issue which has turned sociologists away from psychoanalytically oriented work. Additionally, sociologists wish to understand how contemporary and historical actors realistically deal with the circumstances they face. But the ontogenetic model employed in describing such uniquely capable adult personalities must resort to anomalous child rearing practices and consequences to explain such development. The result of this is that such persons described in these terms, no matter how cogent their actions and how exceptional their accomplishments, end up being "neurotics."[6]

This creates a dilemma for psychobiographers which they have never resolved. How are such regressed persons so acutely perceptive, so able to evaluate the problems they face, so capable of acting upon realistic grounds, so cognitively controlled when their egos are hemmed in by drives and defenses? The capacity to perceive and to deal with the world objectively at any time, but especially when the ego is confronted with realistic difficulties and perplexities, as so many of the central figures in psychobiographies are, necessitates some concept of ego processes independent of sexual energies, that is, an ego relatively autonomous from drives and from excessive moralizing.[7]

But the typical psychobiography describes its protagonist in exactly the opposite manner, that is, as an individual relating to contemporary problems and persons in terms of fixed energies and displaced symbols of a personal past. The dilemma is exacerbated by the incaution psychobiographers manifest in locating the point of fixation in the ontogenetic process. Characters described in oral and anal terms would be hard pressed to operate in everyday life, let alone solve significant social and intellectual problems. The oedipally fixed individual would be obsessive and rigid, lacking the fluidity for creative solutions associated with psychobiographical heroes. By contrast, it is to Erikson's credit that he fixed his identity crisis in terms of social features for performance; at a minimum this associates personal conflict with a social reality.[8]

Thus, the ontogenetic model itself is at the root of many of the difficulties that sociologists associate with psychobiographical endeavors. But the model in fact has been used in two ways. The first and most prevalent way is the literal clinical view, i.e., in which child rearing determines adult personality. The second way has been to treat the parent-child relationship as a metaphoric prism through which to view other human relationships in society. Thus, a psychobiographer may seek in adult relationships features which resemble the parent-child relationship—identifying oedipal struggles over authority, dependence, autonomy, intellectual and cultural commitments, etc., as Mazlish has done in his excellent study of James and John Mill.[9]

The literal use of psychoanalytic theory has been rightfully labeled "reductionist" because every present situation is treated as a return of a repressed personal past.[10] However, the second, metaphoric, form of the theory's use has led to important theoretical and empirical accomplishments in overcoming the criticisms of spurious inference, or of deriving creativity from mental illness. The metaphoric use of the ontogenetic model should dominate psychohistory in the coming decade.

SHARED SOCIALIZATION, SHARED PERSONALITY

Sociology conceives of society as differentiated into segments associated by distinguishable bases of solidarity, attitudes, and behaviors. The bases of solidarity are variables—like age, sex, class, ethnicity—and institutions—like family, education, religion, the political and economic orders. Socialization is a term employed in connection with child rearing but more generally refers to any social context in which individuals experience cognitive, emotive, and moral learning and undergo personal transformation. Social differentiation and socialization are independent conceptions and thus it has been possible to examine their coincident effects, such as age-socialization, sex-socialization, class-socialization and so on.

Sociological works explicitly addressed to age-socialization have only recently begun to appear.[11] Sex-socialization has had a long history in psychoanalytic work, now negatively evaluated by contemporary scholars. A reinvigorated interest in sex-socialization has been stimulated by the women's movement.[12] Socialization studies in institutions, especially occupational socialization, have received a great deal of attention in sociology since the 1950s.[13] However, class and ethnic childhood socialization has been a sociological preoccupation for almost half a century.[14]

Freud's analysis of the relationship between adult character and the treatment of infantile sexuality and aggression began to pervade class and ethnic socialization studies in the 1940s. One group of sociologists investigated breast feeding, weaning, toilet training, sexual play, and so on among families distinguished by class and ethnic background. The "mediating variables" for such activities were parental permissiveness, control, punishment, expressivity, and authority. The investigators were also interested in the effects of child rearing practices on adult personality formation.

Another group of sociologists, anthropologists, and psychoanalysts with neo-Freudian orientations studied similar relationships among preliterate peoples and in foreign nations. These two groups of social scientists shared an important dimension in their approach to the topic. Both wanted to find consistent treatment of infantile impulses in relation to consistent adult behavioral expressions. Psychoanalytic theory would thus be integrated with sociology by demonstrating that social patterns of behavior were derivative of fixed personality dispositions developed from child rearing practices.

While the two groups shared a single objective, they were distinguishable by their methodologies. The former group was composed of research sociologists and social psychologists investigating statistically sampled populations, usually within our society, and employing the techniques of personal interviews, personality inventories, and projective tests. The latter group was composed of sociologists, anthropologists and psychoanalysts doing ethnographic field observation, collecting dreams, myths, and folklore, though also using projective instruments.

The distinction between the two groups is not clear cut, but it is worth making because it permits us to discuss the findings of each group separately. The generalizations reported by the experimental group in 1946 indicated that the American lower classes were more permissive in socialization practices than the middle classes, and that, holding class constant, black Americans tended to be more permissive than whites. Further, middle class parents produced more psychologically troubled children and adults.[15]

Almost immediately following the publication of these findings a series of contradictory child rearing studies appeared. These publications suggested that the earlier psychoanalytically informed socialization studies were incorrect and that there was no difference in infant treatment by class. Later studies reported that the middle classes were more permissive and tolerant of their children than were the lower classes.[16] Finally, Urie Bronfenbrenner compiled all of these studies, restructured the data so that they were comparable, and reanalyzed the findings. Bronfenbrenner hypothesized that the middle classes were more susceptible to influences from popular culture and thus changed their child rearing patterns more quickly than the lower classes. Martha Wolfenstein had already demonstrated that popular advice to parents since 1914 had been in the direction of greater permissiveness in child rearing.[17]

In light of the durability of class and ethnic culture, and the instability of child rearing practices, the assumed causative association between the two was rendered problematic. And William Sewell, an experimental sociologist, was particularly incensed by the indictment of the middle classes as productive of "neurotic" individuals. Sewell and his students set out, in a series of carefully designed studies, to test whether any association between infant caretaking and adult personality existed. His work was devastating for psychoanalytic theory. In a summary article published in 1961 he reported that childhood treatment and adult personality characteristics were statistically unrelated. More specifically, Sewell was saying that most relationships such as longer and shorter breastfeeding periods, or harsh or permissive toilet training, led to no measurable differences in adult 'personality. A very small number of associations were statistically significant but the majority of these relationships contradicted expectational associations that derived from psychoanalytic theory. Sewell and his students pursued this research well over ten years and calculated hundreds of associations between specific child handling practices and adult personality characteristics. Every experiment, whether directed at the study of orality, anality, or whatever, led to the same conclusion: there was no evidence for the assumed psychoanalytic relationship between child rearing and adult personality.[18]

Finally, in a summary article on class and ethnic influences on socialization published in 1970, Robert Hess reported, "No recent studies of any scope deal with the questions of social class differences in patterns of child rearing. The familiar variables—toilet training, feeding, concern about sex play, and the like— no longer dominate the research stage."[19] In part the decline of these studies can be explained in terms of their scientific, i.e., statistical failure. But as noted in the discussion of psychobiography the underlying problem is in psychoanalytic theory itself.

Concepts of breast feeding, toilet training, sex play, permissiveness, authority, family, social class, ethnicity are all important to study in themselves, but they are too global to serve as bases for understanding adult actions in particular situations. Too much intervenes between childhood and adult years. In sum, then, the research sociologists attempted to relate social differentiation, socialization, and psychoanalytic theory while still employing the ontogenetic family model, hoping to find congruent personality dispositions and thus consistent social action on this basis. But even if class and ethnic caretaking events had held constant over time (and they did not), this framework would still be confronted with other sources of variation in personality formation, as explained above.[20]

PSYCHOANALYTIC THEORY IN CULTURE AND PERSONALITY STUDIES

The logic governing the integration of psychoanalytic theory with anthropological studies has been noted, i.e., infantile discipline shapes adult dispositions to action and thus determines consistent group patterns of behavior. This field tends to be characterized by an intelligent caution regarding the limitations of psychoanalytic integration with anthropology.[21] There is, however, considerable variation in the quality of the work and the degree and kind of psychoanalytic conceptualizations employed.

The integration of psychoanalysis and anthropology started early in this century and the production has been intimidating.[22] For example, in 1959, John Honigmann, in a summary paper entitled "Psychocultural Studies," recorded 407 publications in the years 1955 to 1958; the vast bulk of these integrated psychoanalytic theory with cultural anthropology. In 1961 and 1963 considerable production was again reported in this area, and summary articles entitled "Culture and Personality" showed that the field was still dominated by psychoanalytic psychology. However, by 1965, the biennial summary entitled "Psychology and Anthropology" indicated that anthropologists were drawing from a much broader spectrum of psychological orientations. By 1971, only a small proportion of the items cited in the relevant article of the *Biennial Review of Anthropology* employed psychoanalytic theory.[23]

This change in the field of culture and personality raises two questions; first, the more theoretical: why the decline of interest in psychoanalytic theory in culture and personality studies? second, the more practical: how is it possible to review this enormous production? We will address the latter question first; the focus of this article permits circumscription of the culture and personality works to those which analyze American society. The more difficult theoretical question will be addressed later.

Culture and personality studies of America can be divided into three broad substantive categories: psychocultural studies of, respectively, American WASP society, of American blacks, and of American Indian societies.[24] One of the best known psychocultural American national character studies is Geoffrey Gorer's *The American People: A Study of National Character.*[25] Gorer begins his analysis with America's relationship to Britain and to Europe, characterized as a form of father rejection (read "destruction"). And once America accomplished this break with its paternal past, the rest of the Oedipal drama ensued: American men became dominated by their own morality, castrates in their homes, slaves to their ambitious strivings, and alienated adjuncts of their machines and offices. Americans seek after individualism but fear isolation. Their heterosexual relationships are dependent and filled with ambivalence. American character, in the presence of material abundance, is held together by a thin psychological thread. All of this followed because America became a child-centered, mother-dominated society; indeed, American superego was "maternalized."

Gorer disclaimed any moralizing intention on several occasions,[26] but after a quarter-century it is not difficult to see his bias. Gorer at one point unfolds the American wife-husband relationship by analogy with the "Blondie" cartoon, and this says more about the usefulness of the analysis than do all the scholarly pages in the volume together. In brief, Gorer's work is a thinly disguised British intellectual's characterization of white middle class Protestant American society as neurotically and crudely materialist.

Only a few years after Gorer's portrayal of American character, Erik Erikson's chapter on "American Identity" appeared in *Childhood and Society.* Erikson's characterization was similar to Gorer's, especially in its emphasis on "mom" in the development of American personality. But unlike Gorer's depiction of a "smotherer," Erikson's mother is in the business of producing compulsive male adults capable of working in an industrial society. For Erikson, mother represents society's morality; one envisions a 1950s suburban matron as drill sergeant, preparing her children for the rigors of competitive social warfare.[27] Although these works by Gorer and Erikson were not of primary interest to Sewell, he did note in passing the slipshod quality of their analyses and inferences.[28]

References to Gorer's and Erikson's depictions of American national character are now largely absent from the sociological literature.[29] However, the framework on which they were based did survive to some degree, especially in the study of American student life. In 1960 Kenneth Keniston explained alienated youth in terms of dominating mothers and passive fathers. In the years 1968–1973, though, Keniston reversed himself, characterizing student activists as heightened in their consciousness, that is, as being concerned for others and as being desirous of creating an open, flexible community—because they had been socialized, after all, in democratic families.[30] While Lewis Feuer could still see student activism in very traditional ontogenetic terms (i.e., angry sons symbolically killing symbolic fathers),[31] Stanley Rothman and his colleagues described Jewish student radicals as attacking a hated WASP establishment which had undermined their fathers and had wished to emasculate them.[32] Needless to say, it would be difficult to reconcile Keniston's image of mobilized, determined, and independent youth with Gorer's and Erikson's notion of their socialization.

With regard to the earlier period in American national life, John Demos has suggested that Puritans socialized their children by stressing "law and order" in the anal phase of development (Demos, following Erikson, actually refers to this stage in terms of "autonomy"). However, Demos is quick to note that Puritan parental efforts which structure this stage of life are continuous throughout the socialization process, so that the emphasis on obedience to a rigid moral code is "maintained with little significant change for quite a number of years."[33]

An excellent companion work to Demos is Kai T. Erikson's *Wayward Puritans: A Study in the Sociology of Deviance.*[34] Though Kai Erikson's work is only minimally psychoanalytic, he demonstrates that deviance is a form of behavior which helped define the boundaries of Puritan morality and thus helped keep the community intact. The narrowness of appropriate forms of Puritan behavior underscores the salience of Demos' analysis.

Sociologists do not typically employ psychoanalytic concepts in their own historical studies.[35] Psychosocial studies of slavery, however, being consistent with a concern for present-day black identity, have particularly interested sociologists. Stanley Elkins' *Slavery* is most notable in this regard.[36] Elkins' Sullivanian analysis, grounded in the thought of George Herbert Mead, the eminent American sociological theorist, helped his work achieve its impact. It should be noted, for example, that Erving Goffman's conception of "total institution," an important corrective to the concentration camp analogy employed by Elkins (it suggests less stress on internationalization and more stress on variant forms of slave role-playing) nevertheless seems to be based on the fundamental logic laid out by Elkins.[37]

The study of the development of oppressive social conditions analogous to slavery in the post-Civil War period has yielded a number of psychosocial works regarding the consequences for black identity. Works by John Dollard, Abram Kardiner and Lionel Ovesey, Robert Coles, Kenneth B. Clark, Joel Kovel and

Thomas J. Cottle are able to integrate psychological with sociological levels of analysis without reducing one to the other.[38] Because these analyses give credence to social variables, they are popular among sociologists.[39]

Black identity studies, of course, have a built-in corrective against reductionism; the pervasive racial discrimination which must affect black identity can hardly be denied. However, the workers who studied American Indian societies, which are relatively segregated from white culture, were less constrained by these social realities. The result is that psychosocial studies of American Indians exhibit a great deal of variation in the degree to which they exclusively employ the child rearing model to explain social organization. The massive amount of ethnographic works precludes an exhaustive review; we can at best illustrate only some of the extremes in approach.

Geza Roheim, one of the most orthodox psychoanalytically oriented workers in this group, wrote of preliterate societies in general that: "Culture or sublimation in a group are evolved through the same processes as in the individual"; "Cultural areas are conditioned by typical infantile situations in each area"; "Human culture as a whole is the consequence of our prolonged infancy"; "Typically human forms of adjustment are derived from the infantile situation."[40] Compare these comments to Cora DuBois' remarks regarding orality among the Alor:

> To avoid the possibility of simplistic interpretations, it must be stressed again that no single tension like hunger and the habits associated with its gratification will explain either the totality of the culture or the dominant and stressed personality traits of its bearers. It will be only by examining the whole variety of such individual life experiences and searching for the formalized and unformalized cultural correlates that any progress will be made, not only in defining more sharply the interaction of personality and culture, but also in elucidating the stability of attitudes and value systems.[41]

There are, then, some common themes among the works of the culture and personality group, but obviously there are also important differences. The work of this group is not unidimensional in orientation nor in quality. The general principle for judging quality, besides that of professional standards of scholarly excellence, is the degree to which culture and personality studies avoid a reductionist psychoanalytic explanation of societal or group patterns of behavior.

This standard is shared by many critics of the culture and personality school. The most extensive criticism of the approach was offered by Harold Orlansky in 1949. Following an exceedingly detailed review of the literature in the field, Orlansky suggested that

> we are led to reject the thesis that specific ... disciplines have specific, invariant psychological impact upon the child. Instead, it appears that the effect of a particular discipline can be determined only from knowledge of the parental attitude associated with it, the value which the culture places upon discipline, the organic constitution of the infant, and the entire socio-cultural situation in which the individual is located. In short, it is contended that personality is not the resultant of instinctual infantile libidinal drives

mechanically channelled by parental disciplines, but rather that it is a dynamic product of the interaction of a unique organism undergoing maturation and a unique physical and social environment.[42]

Orlansky's stance was not new to the field, but it was an unpopular position at the time of its publication. Still his argument for the autonomy of the effects of cultural and social variables sufficed to promote a negative attitude toward psychoanalytic theory in ethnographic work. But there was an additional pressure on anthropological and sociological ethnographers to break the psychoanalytic alliance. This was, and is, the pressure on these social scientists to offer descriptions of societies which are both richly empirical and readily recognizable as "correct" from the perspective of societal members, i.e., the subjects of their investigations. A less elaborate image of a society, subjectively inconsistent with the knowledge and experience of its members, is referred to in sociology as a "gloss." Ethnographic descriptions which articulate only with professional categories of description are referred to as a "professional gloss." Regrettably, much of what passed for "scientific" psychoanalytically oriented national character and culture and personality studies came to be viewed in terms of "professional gloss." These studies could be considered valid descriptions only by psychoanalytic "true believers."

A NEW SYNTHESIS

At the same time, however, a few sociologists began to reexamine the theoretical bases for the integration of psychoanalysis and sociology. Talcott Parsons contributed significantly to the revisions which followed. In a series of papers on the topic, most of which are reprinted in his *Social Structure and Personality*, Parsons asserted that causal relationships had to proceed from society to personality.[43] Parsons went much further in other important ways, suggesting, for example, that there was no level of the personality unaffected by society and culture, including the instinctual. Parsons, however, did not break with the familial ontogenetic model.

It was, rather, the implicit suggestion of a group of psychoanalytically oriented social psychologists, who were performing laboratory studies on interactive patterns in small groups, that caused a break with the ontogenetic familial model. Their writings indicated that symbolic enactments of Freudian sociological descriptions could be generated in group therapy sessions. The analysis suggested, however, that symbol systems could be independent of instinctual sublimation and it thus rendered problematic the need for a family socialization model to explain shared morality in a group.[44]

Influenced by these sources, I began with Fred Weinstein to rethink psychosocial approaches to social organization, to collective action, and to historical studies. The culmination of this was our publication of *The Wish to Be Free* and *Psychoanalytic Sociology*.[45] There are important theoretical discontinuities between our two works, but their general points of agreement include: establishing the primacy of cultural and social factors in collective action; a stress upon reality orientations in mass movements; the explanation of psychic forces in collective action in terms of responses to particular conditions of strain and as binding and unifying mechanisms; the capacity to explain class, age, family background, etc.,—that is, to explain heterogeneity of membership in collective movements— as a situationally produced and hence contingent feature, bypassing any need for an ontogenetic socialization model; a theoretical framework that allows for the organization of empirical work in a manner consistent with sociological and historical demands for validity and in conformity with members' descriptions of their own experience. We have our doubts that a closed theoretical system is possible in social science; at this point, however, we have not come to any firm conclusions on the matter.[46]

The field of psychohistory and psychosocial studies is evolving. The production is now almost too massive to catalogue. I have approached the topic of the relationship of psychoanalysis to sociology from the perspective of modes or styles of integration, as a technique for categorizing different efforts. Some modes of integration properly have disappeared from the literature, while others have changed and improved.

NOTES

1 Carl Binger, "Conflicts in the Life of Thomas Jefferson," *American Journal of Psychiatry*, 125 (1969), 1,098–1,107; Fawn Brodie, "Jefferson Biographers and the Psychology of Canonization," *Journal of Interdisciplinary History*, 2 (1971), 155–72; and *Thomas Jefferson: An Intimate History* (New York: Norton, 1973); Ramon I. Harris, "Thomas Jefferson: Female Identification," *American Imago*, 25 (1968), 371–88; Pierce L. Clark, *Lincoln: A Psycho-Biography* (New York: Scribner, 1933), and "Unconscious Motives Underlying the Personalities of Great Statesmen and Their Relation to Epoch-Making Events: A Psychoanalytic Study of Abraham Lincoln," *Psychoanalytic Review*, 8 (1921), 1–21; Bronson A. Feldman, "Lincoln: The Psychology of a Cult," *Journal of the National Psychological Association for Psychoanalysis*, I (1952), 7–24; Edward J. Kempf, *Abraham Lincoln's Philosophy of Common Sense: An Analytical Biography of a Great Mind* (New York: Academy of Sciences, 1965); George W. Wilson, "A Prophetic Dream Reported by Abraham Lincoln," *American Imago*, 1 (1940), 92–98; Glenn Davis, "The Early Years of Theodore Roosevelt: A Study of Character Formation," *History of Childhood Quarterly*, 2 (1975), 461–92; Glenn Davis, "The Maturation of Theodore Roosevelt: The Rise of an Affective Leader," *History of Childhood Quarterly*, 3 (1975), 43–74; Morton Prince, "A Scientific Vivisection of Mr. (T.) Roosevelt," *Current Literature*, 52 (1912), 518–22; Bernard Brodie, "A Psychoanalytic Interpretation of Woodrow Wilson," in *Psychoanalysis and History*, Bruce Mazlish, ed., rev. ed., (New York: Grosset and Dunlap, 1971), 115–23; Sigmund Freud and William G. Bullitt, *Thomas Woodrow Wilson: A Psychological Study* (Boston: Houghton Mifflin, 1967); Alexander L. and Juliette L. George, *Woodrow Wilson and Colonel House: A Personality Study* (New York: Day, 1956); William Bayard Hale, *The Story of Style: A Psychoanalytic Study of Woodrow Wilson* (New York: Viking, 1920); Philip Rieff, "Fourteen Points on Wilson," *Encounter*, (1967), 85; David Shannon, "Woodrow Wilson's Youth and Personality: An Essay Review," *Pacific Northwest Quarterly*, 58 (1967), 205–07; Nancy G. Clinch, *The Kennedy Neurosis* (New York: Grosset and Dunlap, 1973);

Joseph Katz, "President Kennedy's Assassination," *Psychoanalytic Review*, 51 (1964–65, #4), 121–24; James Barber, "President Nixon and Richard Nixon: Character Traps," *Psychology Today*, 8 (Oct. 1974), 112–21; Eli Chesen, *President Nixon's Psychiatric Profile* (New York: Wyden, 1973); Bruce Mazlish, *In Search of Nixon: A Psychohistorical Inquiry* (New York: Basic Books, 1972); Stanley Allen Renshon, "Psychological Analysis and Presidential Personality: The Case of Richard Nixon," *History of Childhood Quarterly*, 2 (1975), 115–50. Also see Erwin Hargrove, *Presidential Leadership: Personality and Political Leadership* (New York: Macmillan, 1966); James Barber, *The Presidential Character: Predicting Performance in the White House* (Englewood Cliffs, N.J.: Prentice-Hall, Inc.. 1972).

2 Richard Evans, *Dialogue with Erik Erikson* (New York: Norton, 1967), 66.

3 Robert Bellah, *Beyond Belief: Essays on Religion in a Post-Traditional World* (New York: Harper, 1970), 13.

4 Glenn Davis, "The Early Years of Theodore Roosevelt."

5 George R. Krupp, "The Bereavement Reaction," in Warner Muensterberger and Sidney Axelrad, eds., *The Psychoanalytic Study of Society* (1962), Vol. 2, 42–74; the relevant passages are on pp. 43–44. David Shapiro, *Neurotic Styles* (New York: Basic Books, 1965), 5. Robert Wallerstein, "Psychoanalytic Reflections on the Problem of Reality," *Journal of American Psychoanalytic Association*, 21 (1973), 5–33. Also see F. Weinstein and G. M. Platt, *Psychoanalytic Sociology: An Essay on the Interpretation of Historical Data and the Phenomena of Collective Behavior* (Baltimore: Johns Hopkins University Press, 1973), 45.

6 On the problem of reality and realistic action in psychoanalytic discourse, see Weinstein and Platt, op. cit. On the need for reality orientation in historical studies, see Gerald Izenberg, "Psychohistory and Intellectual History," *History and Theory*, (1975), 139–55. See also Fred Weinstein's review of Arthur Mitzman's *Iron Cage*, *American Historical Review*, (June 1971), 1,399–1,401. Weinstein suggests that Weber, as portrayed by Mitzman, would have been hard pressed to make his intellectual contributions given this psychological characterization.

7 General statement on the place of ego in psychoanalytic theory can be found in Robert White, "Ego and Reality in Psychoanalytic Theory," *Psychological Issues* (monograph 11, 1963); also see George S. Klein, "The Ego in Psychoanalysis: A Concept in Search of an Identity," *Psychoanalytic Review*, 56 (1969–70), 511–25. The concept "ego"—indeed, the entire "ego psychology" is theoretically problematic. That is, concepts—introduced by Freud and elaborated by Heinz Hartmann, Ernst Kris, Rudolph Lowenstein, and Anna Freud—pertaining to the "structural theory" and psychoanalytic metapsychology lend themselves too easily to reification and distortion. The leading critics of "ego psychology" and the structural theory are George Klein, Roy Schafer, and Robert R. Holt. For a summary view, see Robert R. Holt, "The Past and Future of Ego Psychology," *Psychoanalytic Quarterly*, 44 (1975), 550–76, and the companion article by Emanuel Peterfreund, "The Need for a New General Theoretical Frame of Reference for Psychoanalysis," ibid., 534–49. While I approve of the criticism, I will continue to use the customary language, pending some agreement on replacements for the structural terms. Changing the language here would only lead to confusion. Any reader interested in the way terms might change is referred to, e.g. Roy Schafer, "Action: Its Place in Psychoanalytic Interpretation and Theory," *Annual of Psychoanalysis*, 1 (1973), 159–96. More traditional psychoanalysts have always eschewed the main implications of the ego psychology. Thus, Edward Glover referred to Heinz Hartmann—generally considered to be the leading ego psychoanalytic theoretician in the post-Freudian era—as a neo-Freudian and said that Hartmann's concept of "secondary autonomy" is "a comforting narcissistic myth." See Glover, "Metapsychology or Metaphysics?" *Psychoanalytic Quarterly*, 35 (1966), 173–90. Beyond these criticisms it is still necessary to address ourselves to the main problem, the ability of people to define and cope with their problems in everyday life.

8 For a sociological exploration of this problem, see G. Platt and F. Weinstein, "Alienation and the Problem of Social Action," in Edward A. Tiryakian, ed., *The Phenomenon of Sociology*

(New York: Appleton-Century-Crofts, 1971), 284–310. For Erik H. Erikson's most detailed statement on identity, see his "Identity and the Life Cycle: Selected Papers" (with a Historical Introduction by David Rapaport), in *Psychological Issues* (New York: International Universities Press, 1959), 1–171. Also see in this connection Kathleen Dalton, "Theodore Roosevelt, 1858–1901; A Social Psychological Interpretation," (Diss. Johns Hopkins University).

9 Bruce Mazlish, *James and John Stuart Mill: Father and Son in the Nineteenth Century* (New York: Basic Books, 1975).

10 William Gilmore, "The Problem and Danger of 'Originitis' in Psycho-History: The Early Years of Orestes Brownson," paper presented at the annual convention of the Organization of American Historians, April 13, 1973, Chicago, Ill. See also Peter Blos, "The Epigenesis of Adult Neurosis," *Psychoanalytic Studies of the Child*, 27 (1972), 105–35; and Erik Erikson, *Young Man Luther* (New York: Norton, 1958), 18.

11 See Matilda White Riley, Marilyn Johnson, and Anne Foner, *Aging and Society: A Sociology of Age Stratification* (New York: Russell Sage Foundation, 1972), Vol. III. Also see Anne Foner, "Age in Society," *American Behavioral Scientist*, 19 (1975), 144–65; and see "Lifelong Education and Age Stratification," ibid., 206–23; Joan M. Waring, "Social Replenishment and Social Change," ibid., 237–56; Bernice L. Neugarten, Joan W. Moore, and John C. Lowe, "Age Norms, Age Constraints, and Adult Socialization," *American Journal of Sociology*, 70 (1965), 710–17. In the field of psychology see Kenneth Keniston, "Youth: A 'New' Stage of Life," *American Scholar* (Autumn 1970), 631–54; this same topic is discussed from a sociological perspective by T. Parsons and G. M. Platt, "General Education and Studentry Socialization: The Undergraduate College," Ch. 4, *The American University* (Cambridge: Harvard University Press, 1973).

12 Eleanor E. Maccoby, ed., *The Development of Sex Differences* (Stanford: Stanford University Press, 1966); Paul H. Mussen, "Early Sex-Role Development," in David A. Goslin, ed., *Handbook of Socialization Theory and Research* (Chicago: Rand McNally, 1969), 707–29; Walter Mischel, "Sex-Typing and Socialization," in Paul H. Mussen, ed., *Carmichael's Manual of Child Psychology*, 3rd. ed. (New York: Wiley, 1970), vol. 2, Ch. 20, 3–72; Alice Rossi, "Feminist History in Perspective: Sociological Contributions to Biographic Analysis," in Dorothy Gies McMuigan, ed., *A Sampler of Women's Studies* (Ann Arbor: University of Michigan, Center for Continuing Education of Women, 1973), 85–108; Nancy Chodorow, "Family Structure and Feminine Personality," in Michael Zimbalist Rosaldo and Louise Lamphere, eds., *Women, Culture and Society* (Stanford: Stanford University Press, 1974), 43–66; Carroll Smith-Rosenberg, "Puberty to Menopause: The Cycle of Femininity in Nineteenth-Century America," in Mary Hartman and Lois W. Banner, ed., *Clio's Consciousness Raised: New Perspectives on the History of Women* (New York: Harper Torchbooks, 1974), 23–37. A recent review essay on psychology offers several sources related to sex-socialization: Mary Brown Parlee, "Psychology," *Signs: A Journal of Women in Culture and Society*, 1 (1975), No. 1, 119–38.

13 For general and recent statements on "adult socialization," see Orville Brim and Stanton Wheeler, *Socialization After Childhood: Two Essays* (New York: Wiley, 1966); John A. Clausen, ed., *Socialization and Society* (Boston: Little, Brown, 1968); Howard S. Becker, "The Self and Adult Socialization," in *Sociological Work: Method and Substance* (Chicago: Aldine, 1970), 289–303; Howard S. Becker and Anselm L. Strauss, "Careers, Personality and Adult Socialization," *American Journal of Sociology*, 57 (1952), 470–77; Robert R. Faulkner, "Coming of Age in Organizations: A Comparative Study of Career Contingencies and Adult Socialization," *Sociology of Work and Occupations*, 1, No. 2 (May 1974), 131–73.

14 Bronfenbrenner reports class-socialization studies performed in 1928 and 1932, the former out of Berkeley, the latter a national study. See Urie Bronfenbrenner, "Socialization and Social Class Through Time and Space," in Eleanor E. Maccoby, Theodore M. Newcomb, and Eugene L. Hartley, ed., *Readings in Social Psychology*, 3d ed. (New York: Henry Holt, 1958), 400–25.

15 Arnold W. Green, "The Middle Class Male Child and Neurosis," *American Sociological Review,* 11 (1946), 31–41; Allison Davis and Robert J. Havighurst, "Social Class and Color Differences in Child-Rearing," ibid., 698–710; Martha C. Ericson, "Child-rearing and Social Status," *American Journal of Sociology,* 52 (1946), 190–92.

16 Eleanor E. Maccoby and Patricia K. Gibbs, "Methods of Child Rearing in Two Social Classes," in W. E. Martin and C. B. Stendler, eds., *Readings in Child Development* (New York: Harcourt, Brace, 1954); Robert R. Sears, Eleanor E. Maccoby, and Harry Levin, *Patterns of Child Rearing* (Evanston, Ill.: Pow, Patterson and Co., 1957); Daniel R. Miller and Guy E. Swanson, *The Changing American Parent: A Study on the Detroit Area* (New York: Wiley, 1958), and *Inner Conflict and Defense* (New York: Schocken, 1966). See also in this connection, Robert J. Havighurst and Allison Davis, "A Comparison of the Chicago and Harvard Studies of Social Class Differences in Child Rearing," *American Sociological Review,* 20 (1955), 438–42.

17 Urie Bronfenbrenner, "Socialization and Social Class Through Time and Space"; Martha Wolfenstein, "Trends in Infant Care," *American Journal of Orthopsychiatry,* 23 (1953), 120–30.

18 William H. Sewell, "Social Class and Childhood Personality," *Sociometry,* 24 (1961), 340–56; most of the relevant bibliography of Sewell and his co-workers is cited in this article.

19 "Social Class and Ethnic Influences upon Socialization," in Carmichael's *Manual of Child Psychology,* 457–557.

20 This methodological difficulty plagues even impressive psychohistorical works such as Peter Lowenberg's study of "The Psychohistorical Origins of the Nazi Youth Cohort," *American Historical Review,* 76 (1971), 1,457–1,502. In light of these considerations a position such as de M·use's—that all social meaning derives from child care—flies in the face of established social scientific knowledge. Indeed, it would be impossible to explain social order if we took such a statement as deMause's seriously. See Lloyd deMause, *The History of Childhood* (New York: Psychohistory Press, 1974).

21 Kluckhohn points to a summary of the criticism raised regarding the integration of psychoanalysis into anthropology in his "The Influence of Psychiatry on Anthropology in America During the Past One Hundred Years," in J. K. Hall, G. Zilboorg, and H. A. Bunker, eds., *One Hundred Years of American Psychiatry* (New York: American Psychiatric Association. Columbia University Press, 1944), 580–617, esp. 614–15. The best of these efforts avoided analytic reductionism and integrated social, economic, and political institutions and cultural patterning with the psychodynamic variables. In this connection, see from the anthropological side, Cora DuBois, *The People of Alor* (Minneapolis: University of Minnesota Press, 1941), and from the psychoanalytic side, Abram Kardiner, *The Psychological Frontiers of Society* (New York: Columbia University Press, 1945).

22 Edward Sapir was initiator of the culture and personality field; he published a series of papers starting in 1929. See Edward Sapir, *The Unconscious: A Symposium* (New York: Knopf, 1929), 114–42; "Cultural Anthropology and Psychiatry," *Journal of Abnormal and Social Psychology,* 27 (1932), 234–35; "The Emergence of the Concept of Personality in the Study of Cultures," *Journal of Social Psychology,* 5 (1934), 408–15; "The Constribtion of Psychiatry to Understanding Behavior in Society," *American Journal of Sociology,* 29 (1937), 862–71; "Anthropology and the Psychiatrist," *Psychiatry,* 1 (1938), 7–13.

23 John J. Honigmann, "Psychocultural Studies," *Biennial Review of Anthropology,* 1 (1959), 67–106; Anthony F. C. Wallace and Raymond D. Fogelson, "Culture and Personality," *Biennial Review of Anthropology,* 2 (1961), 42–78; Robert A. LeVine, "Culture and Personality," *Biennial Review of Anthropology,* 3 (1963) 107–45. J. L. Fischer, "Psychology and Anthropology," *Biennial Review of Anthropology,* 4 (1965), 211–61, Harry C. Triandis, Roy S. Malpass, and Andrew R. Davidson, "Cross-Cultural Psychology," *Biennial Review of Anthropology,* 7 (1971), 1–84.

24 The outstanding anthologies of the culture-personality orientation were Clyde Kluckhohn,

Henry A. Murray, and David M. Schneidner, eds., *Personality in Nature, Society and Culture* (New York: Knopf, 1956: first published in 1948), and Douglas G. Haring, ed., *Personal Character and Cultural Milieu* (Syracuse: Syracuse University Press, 1956). Additional materials can be found in the *Biennial Reviews of Anthropology* (formerly the *Annual Review of Anthropology*). See also, A. Irving Hallowell, "Culture, Personality, and Society," in *Anthropology Today*, 597–620; Margaret Mead, "National Character," and Alex Inkeles, "National Character and Modern Political Systems," in F. Hsu, ed., *Psychoanalytic Anthropology* (Homewood: Dorsey, 1961), 172–208. And there have been some recent anthologies on psychoanalysis and society and culture; see Hendrik M. Ruitenbeek, ed., *Psychoanalysis and Social Science* (New York: Dutton, 1962), and *Varieties of Modern Social Theory* (New York: Dutton, 1963); Warner Muensterberger, ed., *Man and His Culture: Psychoanalytic Anthropology after "Totem and Taboo"* (London: Rapp and Whiting, 1969).

25 (New York: Norton, 1948).

26 Gorer, *The American People*, 144.

27 (New York: Norton, 1950).

28 William H. Sewell, "Infant Training and the Personality of the Child," *American Journal of Sociology*, 58 (1952), 150–59.

29 Margaret Mead, *And Keep Your Powder Dry: An Anthropologist Looks at Amerca* (New York: Morrow, 1942) is an earlier and much less psychoanalytically influenced American national character study which has worn better than these two. Other sociologically influential national character studies employ psychoanalytic concepts, but they are not so literal in terms of the clinical ontogenetic socialization model. See, for example, David Riesman, *The Lonely Crowd* (New Haven: Yale University Press. 1950); Winston White, *Beyond Conformity* (New York: Free Press, 1961); Snell and Gail Putney, *Normal Neurosis: The Adjusted American* (New York: Harper and Row, 1964); Alexander Mitscherlich, *Society Without Father: A Contribution to Social Psychology*, trans. Eric Moxbacker (New York: Harcourt, 1963); Hendrick M. Ruitenbeek, *The Individual and the Crowd: A Study of Identity in America* (New York: Nelson, 1964). Summaries of relevant bibliography can be found in Michael McGiffert, *American Quarterly*, 15 (1963), summer supplement #2, part 2), 330–49; Thomas L. Hartshorne, "Recent Interpretations of the American Character," *American Studies International* (supplement to the December 1975 *AQ*), 10–17.

30 Kenneth Keniston, *The Uncommitted* (New York: Harcourt, 1960), *Young Radicals* (New York: Harcourt, 1968), *Youth and Dissent* (New York: Harcourt, 1971), and *Radicals and Militants* (Lexington, Mass.: Heath, 1973).

31 Lewis Feuer, *The Conflict of Generations* (New York: Basic Books, 1969).

32 Stanley Rothman, Anne H. Bedlington, Phillip Isenberg, and Robert Schnitzer, "Ethnic Variations in Student Radicalism: Some New Perspectives," unpublished paper, 1976. For a thesis similar to Rothman, et al., see John Murray Cuddihy, *Ordeal of Civility: Freud, Marx and Levi-Strauss, and the Jewish Struggle with Modernity* (New York: Basic Books, 1974).

33 John Demos, *A Little Community: Family Life in Plymouth Colony* (New York: Oxford University Press, 1970), 139.

34 (New York: Wiley, 1966).

35 See in this connection, Werner J. Cahnman and Alvin Boskoff, eds., *Sociology and History: Theory and Research* (New York: Free Press, 1964). Philip Rieff constitutes an exception to this rule. See his "History, Psychoanalysis, and the Social Sciences," *Ethics*, 63 (1953), 107–20, reprinted in Edward N. Saveth, ed., *American History and the Social Sciences* (New York: Free Press, 1964), 110–26.

36 Stanley M. Elkins, *Slavery: A Problem in American Institutional and Intellectual Life* (Chicago: University of Chicago Press, 1959). For example, David Brion Davis, *The Slave Power Conspiracy and the Paranoid Style* (Baton Route: Louisiana State University Press, 1969), and Earl E. Thorpe, *Eros and Freedom in Southern Life and Thought* (Durham, N.C.: Seeman

Printery, 1967), are hardly known among sociologists. However, other historical and social scientific works on the South and slavery are used by sociologists, especially the writings of Tannenbaum, Stampp, and Genovese. Recently Robert W. Fogel and Stanley L. Engerman made a flap in sociology, but this was primarily because of their complex statistical analysis: see their *Time on the Cross: The Economics of American Negro Slavery* (Boston: Little, Brown, 1974). For a concise historical overview of the debate regarding the origins of slavery, see Joseph Boskin, *Into Slavery: Racial Decisions in the Virginia Colony* (Philadelphia: Lippincott, 1976)

37 Ann J. Lane, *The Debate Over Slavery: Stanley Elkins and His Critics* (Urbana: University of Illinois Press, 1971).

38 John Dollard, *Caste and Class in a Southern Town* (New York: Doubleday, 1937); Abram Kardiner and Lionel Ovesey, *The Mark of Oppression: Explorations in the Personality of the American Negro* (New York: World Publishing, 1951); Robert Coles, *Children of Crisis: A Study of Courage and Fear* (Boston: Little, Brown, 1964) Vol. 1; Kenneth B. Clark, *Dark Ghetto: Dilemmas of Social Power* (New York: Harper Torchbooks, 1965); Joel Kovel, *White Racism: A Psychohistory* (New York, Pantheon, 1970); Thomas J. Cottle, *Black Children, White Dreams* (Boston: Houghton Mifflin, 1974). We should also mention in this connection Allison Davis and John Dollard, *Children of Bondage: The Personality Development of Negro Children in the Urban South* (Washington, D.C.: American Council on Education, 1940); William H. Grier and Price M. Cobbs, *Black Rage* (New York: Basic Books, 1968); Frantz Fanon, *The Wretched of the Earth* (New York: Grove Press, 1968), and *Black Skin, White Masks* (New York: Grove Press, 1967).

39 Although not directly concerned with black identity but rather with ethnic prejudice, the classic *Authoritarian Personality* needs to be noted for its ground-breaking work in the integration of personality and culture and society. See T. W. Adorno, Else Frenkel-Brunswik, Daniel J. Levinson, and R. Nevitt Sanford, *The Authoritarian Personality* (New York: Harper, 1950). Also see in this connection, Richard Christie and Marie Jahoda, *Studies in the Scope and Method of "The Authoritarian Personality": Continuities in Social Research* (Glencoe, Ill.: Free Press, 1954), and Milton Rokeach, *The Open and Closed Mind* (New York: Basic Books, 1960).

40 Geza Roheim, "The Psychoanalytic Interpretation of Culture," originally published *International Journal of Psychoanalysis,* 22 (1941) and reprinted in Warner Muensterberger, ed., *Man and his Culture,* 31–51; quotes from p. 50.

41 Cora DuBois, "Attitudes Toward Food and Hunger in Alor," originally published in Leslie Spier, A. Irving Hallowell, and Stanley S. Newman, eds., *Language, Culture and Personality: Essays in Memory of Edward Sapir* (1941), 272–81, and reprinted in Douglas G. Haring, ed., *Personal Character and Cultural Milieu* (Syracuse, N.Y.: Syracuse University Press, 1948), 240–53, quote from p. 253. See also Esther Goldfrank, "Socialization, Personality, and the Structure of Pueblo Society (with particular reference to Hopi and Zuni)," originally published in *American Anthropologist,* 47 (1945), 516–39, and reprinted in Douglas G. Haring, ed., *Personal Character and Cultural Milieu,* 303–27, quote from p. 322.

42 "Infant Care and Personality," *Psychological Bulletin,* 46 (1949), 1–48; A. R. Lindesmith and A. L. Strauss, "A Critique of Culture-Personality Writings," *American Sociological Review,* 15 (1950), 587–600. For a pointed refutation of Orlansky's work from a traditional psychoanalytic point of view, see Sidney Axelrad, "Infant Care and Personality Reconsidered: A Rejoinder to Orlansky," *The Psychoanalytic Study of Society,* Vol. II (New York: International Universities Press, 1962), 75–132.

43 (New York: Free Press, 1964). Some exceedingly interesting papers on the relation of personality to culture and society are included in Anne Parsons, ed., *Belief, Magic and Anomie: Essays in Psychosocial Anthropology* (New York: Free Press, 1969).

44 Philip E. Slater, *Microcosm: Structural, Psychological and Religious Evolution in Groups*

(New York: Wiley, 1966); Theodore Mills, "Authority and Group Emotion," in W. Bennis and E. Schein, ed., *Interpersonal Dynamics* (Homewood, Ill.: Dorsey, 1964), 94–108; Theodore Mills, *Transformation: An Analysis of a Learning Group* (Englewood Cliffs, N.J.: Prentice-Hall, 1964); W. G. Bennis, "Defenses Against "Depressive Anxiety' in Groups: The Case of the Absent Leader," *Merrill-Palmer Quarterly* 7 (1961), 3–30; W. G. Bennis and H. A. Shepart, "A Theory of Group Development," *Human Relations,* 9 (1957), 415–37.

45 *The Wish to Be Free: Society, Psyche and Value Change* (Berkeley: University of California Press, 1969); *Psychoanalytic Society* (1960); see also, "The Coming Crisis in Psychohistory," *Journal of Modern History,* 47 (June 1975).

46 For related psychosocial investigations, see Edwin G. Burrows and Michael Wallace, "The American Revolution: The Ideology and Psychology of National Liberation," *Perspectives in American History,* 6 (1972); Jack P. Greene, "Autonomy and Stability: New England and the British Colonial Experience in Early Modern America," *Journal of Social History,* 7 (1974), 171–94; Edward Shorter, "Illegitimacy, Sexual Revolution, and Social Change in Modern Europe," *Journal of Interdisciplinary History,* 2 (1971), 237–72; Bruce Mazlish, *James and John Stuart Mill;* E. A. Wrigley, "The Process of Modernization and the Industrial Revolution in England," *Journal of Interdisciplinary History,* 3 (1972), 225–59; Peter Shaw, *The Character of John Adams* (Chapel Hill: University of North Carolina Press, 1976).

16

Accusers, Victims, Bystanders: The Innerlife Dimension

John Demos

The organizing structures of inner life have little to do with logic, proportion, balance, and the like; seemingly disparate elements are frequently joined on the basis of symbolic or experiential association. And there is one thematic cluster in the witchcraft materials that vividly exemplifies this point. The main ingredients, described at length in the preceding pages, can be summarized as follows. (1) Infants seemed to make an especially likely, and vulnerable, target for witchcraft; among all the fatalities explained in this way there was clearly disproportionate representation for the very young. (2) Many witches were believed to have an inordinate, and envious, interest in infants and small children. (Some were, in fact, childless.) (3) A number of witches were accused of interfering in the process of infant "nursing." (They would cause soreness or ulcers in the breast; they would make the milk dry up.) (4) Another notorious target of witchcraft was livestock, including (and especially?) milk cows. (5) Witches themselves were thought to "give suck" to their imps and familiars. (6) Courts, local officials, and private citizens would search the bodies of suspected witches for the preternatural "teats" that marked them as the Devil's own.

There is a central preoccupation here with maternal function, especially in regard to infants and small children, which invites further study. Of course, infants of this time and place were very much at risk, relative to other age-groups in the population.[1] Moreover, the forms of their morbidity and mortality may have seemed especially perplexing. (Infant illness was often sudden and dramatic; and communication—in particular, verbal communication—between patient and caretaker was limited or nil.) In short, there was good reason to be anxious about the care of the very young, and it hardly seems surprising that witchcraft belief should have picked up this anxiety. But something else was involved as well. The figure of the witch suckling her imps conveyed a scornful reflection on maternity itself: what has been termed above the witch-as-nurse displayed, in the unconscious, a reverse face—the nurse-as-witch. Here one senses the viewpoint of an aggrieved and angry child, caught up in an archaic form of "sibling rivalry": "I hate my mother who has so unfairly shifted her love from (all-deserving) me to her other (wicked and undeserving) children." Hence the aforementioned cluster of witch-related beliefs seems to have expressed, more or less simultaneously, a parent's fear that infant children may sicken and die, and a child's wish that infant siblings would suffer precisely that fate.

Here once again is the issue of attack-aggression-rage, which looms so large throughout the witchcraft material. Its importance in the psychology of victims; accusers, bystanders (and even the accused themselves) can scarcely be overemphasized: this was what witchcraft most chiefly concerned. Yet infantile sibling rivalry will not alone suffice as explanation; it needs some larger framework of understanding. The succeeding paragraphs propose such a framework—and, by a very roundabout route, return eventually to the subject of aggression.

Recall, for a start, the figure of the witch-as-intruder: this, too, embraced a very large theme. It was as if the witch and her victim were battling back and forth across a vital territory where *boundaries* had assumed the greatest possible significance. On the manifest level the victim and his supporters would labor strenuously to keep the witch at a distance, while she, for her part, was forever "thrusting in." Countermagical strategies were designed to establish clear and impermeable boundaries (for example, the placement of bay leaves or horseshoes, usually near the threshold of the victim's house). At the level of fantasy, as well, the same theme was powerfully evident. Time and again a spectral witch attacked her victim at home and in bed (coming "through the window" or "in at the keyhole"); there was no way to prevent a "shape" from gaining whatever access she desired. Her favorite targets included the victim's children, his livestock, his personal effects; in short, no part of his household was beyond reach. His private conversation, indeed his very thoughts, might be known to her—also embarrassing events in his past, and important prospects in his future. Of course, the most dramatic of all forms of victimization was outright "possession" by the Devil, a process in which the center of personality was invaded from outside. Here was a total failure of boundary-maintenance.

But concern for boundaries was inseparable from the matter of *control.* The intrusions of the witch were meant to demonstrate, and to enlarge, her power over important aspects of the victim's experience. This issue was articulated with special clarity in the course of fits and the various "spectral" encounters. Could the witch force others to do her bidding (that is, to sign the Devil's book)? Could she manipulate their feelings? (Said one shape, "I will make you afraid before I have done with you.")[2] Could she dictate the details of their behavior? (Said one victim, *"They* say I must not speak it [God's name].... They say I must not go in.... They say I shall not eat it ..." etc. And an afflicted girl, under the watchful care of Cotton Mather, asked her tormentors simply, "Is my life in your hands?")[3] Affliction itself was a direct manifestation of the power of the witch. She attacked in places, and by methods, of her own choosing—and the results corresponded in detail to her plan. Her touch, her look, her words could be instantly efficacious. Occasionally she reduced her victims to small images—to "puppets," in both the literal and the figurative meanings of that term. On the other hand, the witch herself could sometimes be manipulated; a careful application of countermagic might simply reverse the roles of puppet and puppeteer.

Considered from an explicitly psychological standpoint, these elements denote a distinctive mode of "object relations." Subject and object, self and non-self, are poorly distinguished—or, at best, are separated only by brittle, easily movable borders. Connections across (or through) such borders are fluid, dense, more or less continuous. Control is indeed a lively issue here—along with its obverse, autonomy. Important sectors of experience are compressed into the two categories of pleasure and pain; and motives are reduced to love and hate (expressed as succor and attack). To all this is added a heavy reliance on the "defense mechanism" of projection.

But to put matters thus is to raise further questions of cause, of source, of origins. Where, in short, did such patterns come from? The prominence throughout the witchcraft material of projective process offers an important clue. Projection (along with introjection) belongs with the most "archaic" of the defenses; its roots lie buried in the earliest phase of life. Freud himself identified the key link: "The original pleasure ego wants to introject into itself everything that is good and to eject from itself everything that is bad.... Expressed in the language of the oldest—the oral—instinctual impulses, the judgement is: 'I should like to eat this,' or 'I should like to spit this out.' "[4] Amidst the turmoil of infant sensation, projection and introjection provide a modicum of order. At best they serve the long-term goal of "structure building" (sorting and connecting constituent parts within the early self); at the least, they help to sharpen the boundaries between self and non-self (since their operation depends on boundaries of some sort).[5]

They remain, forever afterwards, associated with a cluster of "unconscious ego activities."[6] And they carry an implicit reference to the most primitive perceptual experiences of the very young child, who regards his "primary object" (caretaker) as a virtual appendage bound to perform his entire bidding. When this expectation runs afoul of reality, rage is the certain result. Expressed subjectively, the initial impression "She will not do as I want" quickly becomes "She does not love me," which is further elaborated into "She hates me and seeks to hurt me." In later life sudden reversals—such as illness or other misfortune—may recall the feelings of helplessness and frustration of infancy. And these, in turn, may reactivate the characteristically infantile modes of perception. Then—and again later—the sense of being well seems to depend on the care, the loving compliance, of others. Conversely, being unwell has the subjective meaning of being unloved and unprotected, or even of being hated.

These processes can be directly related to the development of the "self-system." They belong to that very early and formative period which Freud designated by the term "primary narcissism" but left for later psychoanalytic theorists—most especially Heinz Kohut—to explore in detail.[7] The building of the "nuclear self" is indeed a central theme here. From the diffuse and disorganized experiences of the newborn infant a core of personality gradually evolves. This core has increasing qualities of cohesiveness (in its internal composition), of boundedness (vis-à-vis the external world), and of continuity (over time). Objects (internal representations of other people) are distinguished with growing clarity, but from an inherently "narcissistic" viewpoint. The budding self conceives a "grandiose fantasy," encompassing power, knowledge, beauty, perfection—and looks for confirmation in all this from the available objects. At the same time the self invests the objects with a perfection of their own—in which it may then share by way of an enduring attachment. (This is, in brief, a matter of "idealization," of primitive hero-worship.) Encounters with reality, and a growing appreciation of intrinsic limitations, bring about the gradual modification of these early narcissistic structures. Infantile grandiosity is rescaled and reworked into "healthy ambition," and infantile idealization yields a stable system of (internalized) values. Meanwhile the nuclear self becomes an effective center for the myriad experiences of later life and the locus of a continuing "esteem" (especially *self*-esteem).[8]

This is but a schematic outline based on *optimal* development, and of course the particulars of individual experience are never so tidy or so happily successful. Indeed, the chief concern here is the negative side—the failures, the deficits, the distortions in the self-system. For witchcraft expressed such things, was rooted in them, to a quite unmistakable degree. The implicit concern with boundary-maintenance was itself a diagnostic sign. Victims were thought to be attached to witches, invaded by witches, overcome by witches—notions that suggest a certain fragility in the nuclear self. The presence of so much angry affect points in a similar direction. However, anger is an insufficiently strong description of the attitudes expressed toward—or, more frequently, projected into—the figure of the witch. There was something raw, uncompromising, altogether "primitive" about these attitudes—a quality readily associated with the clinical category "narcissistic rage."[9] Behind narcissistic rage there usually lies an experience of "narcissistic injury" or insult. And this, in turn, calls attention to the numerous situations of conflict with which accusations of witchcraft were typically bound up. Slighting remarks, threats, petty aspersions on character or behavior often evoked a strong response. There was a prickly side to the early New Englanders which shows through in many sectors of their experience, not least in their concern with witches.[10] Consider, too, the matter of display, the claims of "special-ness" implicit in attack by witchcraft. Such claims were most vividly dramatized in full-blown "fits," but, in a lesser measure, they may be imputed to all self-described victims: "The forces of evil have chosen *me* as their target. And you—the standers-by—must attend to me in my hour of affliction."

This discussion has alluded more than once to infantile "ties" with a "primary object." But such terminology may seem excessively abstract, even obfuscating. *Who ordinarily was—and is—the actual, flesh-and-blood "primary object"?* And what is the lasting significance of the "ties" involved here? To raise these questions is to return to a most important problem. Recall the conclusion of Chapter 3 that accused witches were predominantly adult women; recall, too, the difficulty of understanding *why*. Social conditions—the (partially) inferior status of New England women vis-à-vis men—seemed to "fit" with the witch/woman equation, but hardly to explain it.[11] The transcultural aspect of this phenomenon—the common tendency in otherwise disparate societies to define witches as *female*—suggested that interpretive effort might need to reach beyond the particular circumstances of a single time and place. The involvement of both sexes—women no less than men—in prosecuting witches implied another set of parameters. But sociological inquiry yielded no clear line of interpretation, no answers, satisfying these general specifications.

Now, as the problem of gender appears once again, there is a more promising outlook. For the theory of early object relations does furnish some answers (which is to say that the problem itself belongs more to the psychology than to the sociology of witchcraft). The key point is what Dorothy Dinnerstein has called the "female monopoly of early child care," the fact that "for virtually every human the central infant-parent relationship, in which we form our earliest, intense and wordless, feelings toward existence, is a relationship with a woman."[12] Beneath the manifold forms of this relationship (across different cultures, and for different individuals within the same culture), there are certain fundamental regularities.

Infants are, in the first place, entirely dependent on their mothers: for food, for warmth, for nurturance, for entertainment, for virtually all the "good" they know. A mother's power to supply these needs, or not to supply them (depending on her own wishes and resources), lies at the center of infantile experience. She seems, from the infant's own standpoint, "omnipotent and responsible for every blessing and curse of existence."[13] For the blessings she is gratefully loved—but for the curses she is angrily blamed. And every child, no matter how well cared for, knows some discomfort, some disappointment, some moments of loss and separation. These are, moreover, experienced with an immediacy and intensity unmatched in any subsequent phase of life.

But there is more to the infant-mother relationship than helplessness and dependence on the one side and (seemingly) limitless powers on the other. For the mother is critically implicated in the infant's evolving experience of its own center, its own will, its own subjectivity. She is the "non-self" from which self is progressively distinguished; she plays "it" to the infantile "I." She is "the over-whelming, external will"—again the words are Dinnerstein's—"in the face of which the child first learns the necessity for submission." She disposes a vital power "to foster or forbid, to humble or respect, our first steps toward auton-omous activity."[14]

As an overall result, "female sentience . . . carries permanently for most of us the atmosphere of that unbounded, shadowy presence toward which all our needs were originally directed." And, also as a result, we attribute to "female intentionality" a menacing aspect of

> the rampant and limitless, the alien and unknowable. It is an intentionality that needs to be . . . corralled and subjugated if we . . . are to feel at all safe in its presence. It needs to be corralled . . . not only because its boundaries are unclear, but also because its wrath is all-potent and the riches it can offer or refuse us [are] bottomless.[15]

These images—to repeat—arise and flourish in all "mother-raised children," that is, in women as well as men. Their lasting power derives from their very early provenance. Their association with "pre-verbal" development is, in fact, of the greatest importance; for since they are "formed entirely without words," they continue thereafter to have a "subterranean life of their own, unmodified by that limited part of human sensibility which we call intelligence."[16] Their force and their distinctiveness are highlighted when they are set alongside the comparable imagery of men. "Male sentience" and "male intentionality" have—within the same context of innerlife experience—a much clearer shape, a far more even coloration. Men appear to stand for reason, for logic, for balance, for whatever is most "cleanly human." This, in turn, reflects developmental circumstance. Men (fathers) are not ordinarily much of a factor in infantile experience. And when (later on) men do begin significantly to impinge on the child's life, they enter an "object world" which is in all ways more developed. The child has some ca-pacity to appreciate their separate "subjectivity"—they are more "you" than "it"— and to take their measure as creatures of human, although still quite outsized, dimensions. Fathers, in short, seem far less "magically formidable" than mothers, from the standpoint of the child.[17]

The "magically formidable" qualities of mothers—enlarged to embrace women in general—are, of course, of the greatest importance here. Indeed, the term would serve nicely to describe witches, as perceived by their victims and accusers. Other elements in the figure of the witch have an equally clear reference to infantile experience: the (seeming) malevolence, the intrusiveness, the capacity to inflict all-consuming hurt and harm. To be sure, impressions received *after* infancy must also be credited: most especially, castration anxiety (in its two dif-ferent, gender-related forms), and the (awesome, mysterious) role of women as bearers of new life.* But these serve, by and large, to elaborate on themes rooted in the earliest object-world.

There is little doubt, finally, that New England was populated by "mother-raised children."** Childbirth itself was entirely in the hands of women (midwives, and female kin and friends of the mother); it seems, indeed, that men and all younger children were effectively excluded from such occasions.[19] Breast-feeding—which continued, in the average case, for about one year—would establish a special bond between the mother and her newborn.[20] And this bond seems to have been maintained also in other areas of infant care (judging from scattered notations in personal and local records).[21] By contrast, fathers do not appear in any significant relationship to children until the latter are at least two or three years old. Of course, this division of responsibility for infant nurture is characteristic of virtually every known culture, past and present. It fosters, in turn, a virtually universal "antagonism to women," a misogynous substrate of transcultural dimensions. Its visible outgrowths were—and are—extremely varied, even within a single social setting. But among all such outgrowths none has been more compelling than the figure of the witch. Here was something that the New Englanders shared with countless other specimens of humankind.

There is one additional way to consider this material, involving a shift of reference from the self system and early object relations to what Erik Erikson has called "psychosocial adaptation."[22] Erikson's well-known schedule of developmental stages posits an unfolding of specific "ego qualities" (each encompassing positive and negative "potentialities"). And among such qualities the one associated with the second stage invites particular attention. The issue in this period (roughly the second and third years of life) is defined as "autonomy vs. shame

---

*The link between castration anxiety and more generalized fears of women has been sum-, marized as follows by Karen Horney: "It [castration anxiety] is an anxiety of psychogenic origin that goes back to feelings of guilt and old childhood fears. Its anatomical-psychological nucleus lies in the fact that during intercourse the male has to entrust his genitals to the female body, that he presents her with his semen and interprets this as a surrender of vital strength to the woman, similar to his experiencing the subsiding of erection after intercourse as evidence of having been weakened by the woman." Woman's biological role in bearing children elicits both fear and jealousy. On the one hand, there is the [preconscious] idea that a person who gives life is also capable of taking it away. (Thus, as Simone de Beauvoir has written, "From the day of his birth man begins to die: this is the truth incarnated in the Mother.") On the other hand, childbearing seems awesome, wonderful, enviable. There is a considerable scientific literature on these issues, and on their relation to misogynous feeling at large.[18] Their presence among the psychological forces that generated witchcraft belief can scarcely be doubted. However, they reflect a specifically *male* viewpoint, and could apply, at most, to the men within the victim-group. And since the *animus* toward witches so clearly embraced persons of both sexes, other factors (e.g. the residues of "early object relations") have greater explanatory power in the present context.

**The implicit reference of the term "raised" continues, for these purposes, to be very *early* childhood.

and doubt." If all goes well, boundaries are defined, and "limits" are set, around a "vital perimeter of personal space." Within this space the child seeks "a gradual and well-guided experience of the autonomy of free choice." And the legacy to later life—again, given a favorable result—is "a sense of self-control without loss of self-esteem," accompanied by "a lasting sense of good will and pride." But often, of course, the result is not so favorable, and the "negative potentialities" come into play. Thus an inordinate propensity to shame is usually grounded in the experience of this developmental stage. But it is "doubt" which seems especially pertinent here. Erikson writes,

> Doubt is the brother of shame. Where shame is dependent on the consciousness of being upright and exposed, doubt . . . has much to do with a consciousness of having a front and a back . . . and especially a "behind." For the reverse area of the body . . . cannot be seen by the child, and yet it can be dominated by the will of others. The "behind" is the small being's dark continent, an area of the body which can be magically dominated and effectively invaded by those who would attack one's power of autonomy. . . . This basic sense of doubt . . . finds its adult expression in paranoiac fears concerning hidden persecutors and secret persecutions threatening from behind.*[23]

This *potpourri* of interpretive deduction yields some common implications about development—about source-points of the stresses and conflicts that found outward expression in witchcraft belief. To recapitulate: (1) "Projection" was everywhere central to witchcraft accusations. And projection, with its "oral" foundation, rates as one of the earliest of all the psychological "defenses." (2) Witchcraft belief displayed important elements of "magical thinking," especially with respect to implicit stereotypes of women. And these have their roots in the "preverbal" substrate of infantile experience. (3) The symptoms and fantasies associated with witchcraft suggest a certain vulnerability in the "self system." Here, too, the genetic line leads far back toward infancy. (4) The same evidence, considered from the standpoint of "ego qualities," underscores the issue of "autonomy" (and its negative correlate "doubt"). And this issue is said to belong especially to the "second stage" of psychosocial adaptation, encompassing roughly the second and third years of life. (5) The extreme symptoms of one particular victim-group, the "af-

---

*The passage, as quoted, implies a biological reference for the psychosocial "potentialities" of the second stage. In short, Erikson links specifically "anal" concerns to the child's struggle for autonomy and his corresponding vulnerability to shame and doubt. However, the strength of this link presumably varies, depending on the personal (and cultural) reinforcement in any given case. In settings where much is made of "toilet training," the anal reference is likely to be central and obvious. But in a different context—i.e., where such matters are downplayed—it may have only minimal importance. For an anthropological example of a culture in which the developmental attainment of autonomy is not much joined to anal preoccupation, see Jean L. Briggs, "The Issues of Autonomy and Aggression in the Three-year-old: The Utku Eskimo Case," in *Seminars in Psychiatry,* IV (1972), 317–29. In this respect, Puritan child-rearing was more like the "Eskimo case" than, e.g., the usual pattern of our own time.

flicted girls," denote unresolved conflicts in relation to "maternal objects." And the cast of those conflicts seems largely "pre-oedipal."

Of course, no such interpretations can be made to yield a precise set of chronological markings, for individual development necessarily sets something of its own pace. Yet the convergent emphasis on *very early* experience seems impressive. Terms like "preverbal" and "pre-oedipal" imply an upper bound of about age three. On the other hand, these tasks and concerns do not belong to the condition of neonates. They require some glimmerings of psychic structure, or at least some movement in that direction; hence age one seems plausible as an approximate lower bound.

Do these numbers find explicit confirmation in the witchcraft materials themselves? There is one documentary fragment which deserves at least a mention: an allegation, from the Salem trials, that one of the accused witches "appeared [i.e. in her spectral shape] as little as a child of two years old."[24] In general, however, the records are devoid of developmental reference—hence the need to revert once again to procedures of inference. What is known generally about the experience of early childhood in seventeenth-century New England? And can this experience be plausibly connected with the themes explored above in relation to witchcraft?

There are, in fact, grounds for thinking that age two was an especially important—and difficult—time in the life of a Puritan child. It was about then that he was most likely to face the arrival of a younger sibling, since in most New England families pregnancies were spaced at intervals of twenty to thirty months.[25] This would mean, in turn, the loss of his mother's special attention: no longer was he the littlest, and most vulnerable, member of the family. But beyond such intimations from demography lie important and explicit prescriptions of Puritan child-rearing. The central task for parents, as defined by the leading exemplars of New England culture, was "training the will" of their young. Indeed, their phrase "training the will" was regularly equated with "breaking the will." Every child was thought to come into the world with inherent tendencies to "stubbornness and stoutness of mind": these must be "beaten down" at all costs.[26] One aspect of such tendencies was the wilful expression of *anger*—and anger was, by Puritan reckoning, the most dangerous and damnable of human affects.[27] Children must therefore be trained to compliance, to submission, to "peace." To effect such training, drastic means were sometimes needed. Puritan parents were not inclined to spare the rod; but more important than physical coercion was the regular resort to shaming.[28] (Here lies another line of connection to the vital "second stage" in Erikson's formulation, defined as it is around the polarity of "autonomy vs. shame and doubt.")

Published statements about child-rearing from the period emphasize that this regime must start early, in order to be fully effective. And while they are not additionally specific, they do direct attention to the second and third years of life. For these are the years when much of development seems to center on the expression of personal "will." The child stands, and walks, and moves more or less freely about; he achieves great progress in the coordination of hand and eye; he begins consciously to control important bodily processes (e.g. the eliminative ones). Much of cognition remains preverbal; yet he gains at least the rudiments of speech (e.g. those which permit him to give or withhold his assent— "yes" and, above all, "no"). Most two-year-old children are eager to test their new-found capacities in relation to other people. And such testing inevitably yields a quotient of frustration and anger, even where it contributes most directly to the growth of "autonomy."

Now imagine how all this might seem against a backdrop of Puritan values. Wilfulness, self-assertion, competitive struggle, surges of infantile grandiosity, sudden outbursts of anger: thus the markings of "original sin," displayed in unvarnished form. To allow such traits room for growth was to open a way for the Devil, whose own character was defined in virtually the same terms. There could be little doubt where parental and social obligation lay. . . .

Developmental theory and clinical data from our own time; seventeenth-century notions of child-rearing; Puritan values in a larger sense; and the particulars of witchcraft proceedings: such are the ingredients of our interpretive model. The model does not constitute "proof" in the traditional manner of historical research, for the connections between one element and the next lie, in part, beyond a scholar's sight-range. Yet there is a sense of fit about the whole, which carries its own persuasiveness.

Some cautions and disclaimers are needed, by way of conclusion. It would be unwise to assign an exclusive "causal" significance to specifically traumatic events forced on New England children in the first few years of life. Any such "reductionist" argument misleads—on at least two counts. For one, it underestimates the importance of manifest cultural tradition. Witchcraft, in all its rich detail, was a subject of *explicit communication,* between persons, communities, and whole generations. Expressed differently: witchcraft was a matter of conscious belief no less than inward (and unconscious) propensity. In addition, the earliest developmental impressions must not be overemphasized at the expense of all succeeding ones. The present investigation has been pressed to the level of roots and sources, but there is no doubting the importance of subsequent reinforcement. Indeed, such reinforcement can be virtually assumed: if New England children encountered in earliest life a strenuous resistance to their deepest autonomous strivings, they must surely have had similar experiences in later childhood. The value-system which supported all this made no intrinsic distinctions as to age. Older children and "youths" would hear from all sides the Puritan message of "peace," of "harmony," of submission—with its corollary warnings against anger and the open assertion of self. Presumably the same message was received, without words, in countless personal transactions.

These psychological inferences must not, finally, be construed as a diagnosis of outright pathology. The great majority of the New Englanders who believed in witchcraft were in no meaningful sense "sick" or otherwise "disturbed." Most of them, like most of us, fell within some normal range of mental and emotional adaptation. On the other hand, most of them—again, like most of us—knew certain areas of inner conflict and vulnerability. And—perhaps to a greater degree for them than is true for us—such areas obtained similar shape and substance among otherwise different individuals; for theirs was a more unified, less heterogeneous culture.

To be sure, some few among them showed in their attitudes toward witchcraft a vulnerability that ran very deep and proved ultimately disabling. For these few—and the "afflicted girls" come first to mind—the language of sickness does indeed apply. Their troubles bear direct comparison to clinical experience today; their fits and related behavior were the outward signs of a disturbance at the center of personality. Though little is known of their individual histories prior to their involvement in witchcraft proceedings, one many reasonably infer psychic "lesions" of a large, and long-standing, kind.

And yet pathology is always a matter of *relative,* not absolute, distinctions. Hence even the most extreme instances of affliction would remain in some sense comprehensible to the whole community of New Englanders. A girl "in her fits," an older person attributing specific misfortune to the malefic power of his neighbor, the legion of ordinary folk who maintained a general belief in the reality and power of witchcraft: all were joined by strong bonds of inner preoccupation. The difference and distance between them embraced quantity, not quality; as individuals they represented a variety of points along a single psychological spectrum. Every attack by witchcraft summoned deeply responsive echoes in a host of "bystanders," for the victim was acting out—although (sometimes) to an "extremity"—pressure-points and vulnerabilities that were widely shared.

Two points deserve a final restatement. Strong, purposeful, effective as they undeniably were, many of the New Englanders seem to have felt persistently vulnerable in their core sense of self. Tremors of uncertainty plagued their struggle to grow and endure as free-standing individuals; they could not feel confident of maintaining the existential boundaries of their lives. And, in ways examined above at great length, such feelings were evoked with particular intensity by the figure of the witch.

By a separate but parallel route she evoked other feelings as well. The intrusive, demanding traits so widely attributed to her are best viewed as projections. Her victims were presumably uncomfortable about similar tendencies in themselves, about their own wishes to intrude, to encroach, to dominate, to attack—their whole assertive side. As frequently happens in such situations, they dealt with their conflict by externalizing it. Not they, but rather their neighbor—the "witch"—possessed the traits they so deeply despised.

NOTES

1 Maris A. Vinovskis, "Mortality Rates and Trends in Massachusetts before 1830," *Journal of Economic History*, XXXII (1972), 195–201; David E. Stannard, *The Puritan Way of Death*, 54–55; Demos, *A Little Commonwealth*, 131–32; Kenneth A. Lockridge, "The Population of Dedham, Massachusetts, 1636–1736," in *Economic History Review*, 2nd ser., XIX (1966), 329; James K. Somerville, "A Demographic Profile of the Salem Family, 1660–1700," unpublished paper presented at the conference on social history, Stony Brook, New York. (1969).

2 Deposition by Mary Hale, in the trial of Katherine Harrison; Willys Papers, W017, Brown University Library.

3 Cotton Mather, "Memorable Providences, Relating to Witchcrafts and Possessions," in Charles Lincoln Burr, ed., *Narratives of the Witchcraft Cases* (repr. New York, 1968), 112, 116, III; Cotton Mather, "A Brand Plucked Out of the Burning," in ibid., 269.

4 Sigmund Freud, "Negation," in Strachey, ed., *The Standard Edition of the Complete Psychological Works of Sigmund Freud*, XIX, 237.

5 Anna Freud, *The Ego and the Mechanisms of Defense*, 51–52.

6 The term—and the main elements of the argument presented in this paragraph—are taken from the work of Abraham Kardiner. See his *The Individual and His Society* (New York, 1939), 305–10.

7 Sigmund Freud, "On Narcissism," in Strachey, ed., *The Standard Edition of the Complete Psychological Works of Sigmund Freud*, XIV, 69–102, and "An Outline of Psychoanalysis," in ibid., XXIII, 150ff. Kohut's work is most fully presented in his two books, *The Analysis of the Self* (New York, 1971) and *The Restoration of the Self* (New York, 1977). See also Otto Kernberg, *Borderline Conditions and Pathological Narcissism* (New York, 1975).

8 For an excellent summary of recent work by Kohut and his colleagues, see Ernest S. Wolf, "Recent Advances in the Psychology of the Self: An Outline of Basic Concepts," in *Comprehensive Psychiatry*, XVII (1976), 37–46.

9 Heinz Kohut, "Thoughts on Narcissism and Narcissistic Rage," in *The Psychoanalytic Study of the Child*, XXVII (1972), 360–400; see also Kohut, *The Restoration of the Self*, 116ff.

10 Demos, *A Little Commonwealth*, 49–51; Richard L. Bushman, *From Puritan to Yankee: Character and the Social Order in Connecticut, 1690–1765* (Cambridge, 1967), ch. 1.

11 See pp. 63–64.

12 Dorothy Dinnerstein, *The Mermaid and the Minotaur: Sexual Arrangements and Human Malaise* (New York, 1976), 33. Dinnerstein's extraordinary book—easily the best of all studies on the psychological underpinnings of misogyny—provides the basis for this discussion of the woman/witch equation.

13 Ibid., 108.

14 Ibid., 28–29, 165.

15 Ibid., 164.

16 Ibid., 84.

17 Ibid., 175–76.

18 Karen Horney, *Feminine Psychology*, Harold Kelman, ed. (New York, 1967); see especially "The Distrust Between the Sexes," 107–18. Wolfgang Lederer, *The Fear of Women* (New York, 1968). H. R. Hays, *The Dangerous Sex* (New York, 1964). Joseph Rheingold, *The Fear of Being a Woman* (New York, 1964). Bruno Bettelheim, *Symbolic Wounds* (New York, 1954). Marjorie C. Barnett, " 'I Can't' versus 'He Won't,' " in *Journal of the American Psychoanalytic Association*, XVI (1968), 588–600. Edith Jacobson, "Development of the Wish for a Child in Boys," in *The Psychoanalytic Study of the Child*, V (1950), 139–52. Daniel S. Jaffe, "The Masculine Envy of Woman's Procreative Function," in *Journal of the American Psychoanalytic Association*, XVI (1968), 121–48. Kato van Leeuwen, "Pregnancy Envy in the Male," in *International Journal of Psychoanalysis*, XLVII (1966), 319–24. Robert C. Bak, "The Phallic Woman," in *The Psychoanalytic Study of the Child*, XXIII (1968), 15–36.

19 This, at any rate, is the strong impression gained from personal and legal records dealing with episodes of childbirth, and from manuals of midwifery. See the brief account of colonial practice in Richard W. Wertz and Dorothy C. Wertz, *Lying In: A History of Childbirth in America* (New York, 1977).
20 Demos, *A Little Commonwealth*, 133.
21 Whenever infants are mentioned in records from the period, their mothers are invariably found with them.
22 See Erik H. Erikson, *Childhood and Society*, 2nd ed. (New York, 1963), ch. 7, "Eight Ages of Man."
23 Ibid., 253–54.
24 Testimony by Hannah Post, printed in Massachusetts Historical Society, *Collections*, III, 224.
25 Demos, *A Little Commonwealth*, 68.
26 Robert Ashton, ed., *The Works of John Robinson*, 2 vols. (Boston, 1851), I, 245–47.
27 Ibid., I, 226.
28 See, for example, the opinions of Cotton Mather on discipline of the young in his little treatise "Some Special Points Relating to the Education of My Children," reprinted in Perry Miller and Thomas A. Johnson, ed., *The Puritans*, 2 vols. (New York, 1963), II, 724–27. See also the words which Mather attributed (elsewhere) to his clerical colleague, Nathaniel Ward: "Of young persons he would himself give this advice: 'Whatever you do, be sure to maintain shame in them,' for if that once be gone, there is no hope that they'll ever come to good"; *Magnalia Christi Americana* (Hartford, 1853), I, 522.

17

Non-Psychoanalytic Approaches to National Socialism

Harvey Asher

This paper attempts to answer the questions of why and how the Germans were led so far by Hitler and the Nazis, without recourse to psychological theories that focus primarily on abnormal behavior. Instead, attention will be directed to those findings of social psychologists that support the notion that many Germans followed a regime whose ideas they did not necessarily share and whose actions they may have abhorred.

It can of course be argued that the policies Hitler pursued exposed the wishes (sometimes unconsciously held) of the populace, and that the link between leaders and led was the German historical tradition, a shared set of beliefs, attitudes, and values created by exposure to common experiences, institutions, crises, and behaviors. With varying degrees of sophistication, historians subscribing to revelationist positions try to isolate those thinkers in the German past whose ideas they believe resemble or seem potentially compatible with Hitler's *Weltanschauung*.[1] Or they may point to idiosyncratic German ways of apprehending reality that were sufficiently congruent with the Nazi outlook so as to be politically exploitable.[2] Specific historical events responsible for the distorted mind set of the Germans may be cited, such as the bitter reaction to the wars of the French Revolution, which led to an exaggerated rejection of rationalism and cosmopolitanism.

The notion that the German past prepared the way for Hitler is not restricted to a discussion of intellectual precursors. It also takes the form of trying to establish continuity between the political heritage of an earlier era, e.g., Bismarckian authoritarianism, and a modern version of the same paradigm, e.g., Nazi authoritarianism. At its extreme, the revelationist school asserts that the German past irrevocably prepared the way for Hitler, that the Germans got what they

Reprinted from *Psychohistory Review,* 7:3 (Winter, 1978), pp. 13–21.

deserved.[3] More sensibly, it is noted that an anachronistic authoritarian state—by preventing the mature development of liberalism, democratic socialism, left-wing Catholicism, and responsible conservatism—provided the prototype for Nazism or made it impossible to offer effective resistance to a Fascist onslaught.[4]

The importance of historical continuity is also stressed in efforts directed toward establishing a German national character, as displayed in an authoritarian personality, family, or similar characterological syndrome.[5] Such studies are of three basic types: (1) in-depth personality assessments seeking to explore the latent or underlying character structure of individual Germans; (2) analyses of German collective, institutional, and political phenomena; and (3) social anthropological accounts of childrearing patterns among Germans, and their manifestation in the adult personality.[6] Authoritarian personality traits on the individual level are supposedly created and reinforced by familial patterns of paternal dominance and maternal submission, producing a national character high in submission and obedience to authority which Hitler manipulated for his own "warped" ends. The psychological consequences of these authoritarian developments on German history include repressed hostility (individual and collective), and the inhibition of soft, so-called feminine feelings such as tenderness and love.

In turn, the Germans' repressed hostility was projected onto others and "acted out" under the Nazis. The implication is that Germans supported the Third Reich because the Nazis embodied their collective frustration and more importantly, because they offered the psychiatric casualties of unhealthy childrearing patterns the opportunity to release those pent-up frustrations. More astute writers of the character distortion school specify particular historical conditions which activated resentments that had hitherto remained latent. Particular groups in German society are singled out as being especially susceptible to infection.[7] In any case, the Nazis and their supporters remain linked by mutual pathology. Tragically for mankind and the Germans "a successful leader (Hitler) gives expression to the subliminal needs of the culture and is able to project an image that fuses with and meets these cultural attitudes (abnormalities)."[8]

And yet, even if we could establish the existence of pathology on the individual or small-group level,[9] some serious difficulties remain. One is that most Germans failed to join the Party.[10] Of equal concern, the Germans never gave Hitler an electoral majority.[11] Nor can it be demonstrated conclusively that most Nazis came from authoritarian homes;[12] or, since so many who did come from authoritarian homes did not become Nazis, it is not possible to single out this factor as the main etiological agent.[13]

While it is virtually impossible to prove that most Germans were Nazi supporters by virtue of shared psychological pathology and common authoritarian upbringing, might it not be that in Hitler's Germany a large number of deviants (ten to fifteen percent of the population) gained control over a majority of "normal" people? Selzer makes just such an argument, but his explanation of the

Nazi success is both weak and confusing. Having rejected authoritarian cultural and social characteristics in the German population as the primary link between the Nazis and the masses, Selzer then suggests that "the Nazi ethos appealed to certain aspects of their personality, even though they did not conform to the Nazi type."[14] Elsewhere he remarks on how "the chance emergence of a highly effective leadership resulted in the politicization to a most unusual degree of the psychologically aberrant population of Germany."[15] *Chance* turns out to be the connection between Hitler and the German masses, who, it turns out, do share at least some of the personality traits of their pathological leaders after all.

The use of national character to account for German submission to Hitler and the Nazis is fraught with problems: (1) authoritarianism is not peculiar to Germans; (2) it is not clear if all Germans succumbed to it; and (3) it is not possible to specify how much of the authoritarian trait the individual must possess to become a Nazi supporter or sympathizer. National character arguments essentially account for Hitler's hold over the Germans by postulating reciprocal pathologies, overt for the former, covert for the latter; the Nazis represent a distorted and disguised mirror-image of their authoritarian German brethren. The Freudian perspective is evident here—all men are basically evil, though some are more so than others. They possess uncontrollable impulses and death instincts which constantly threaten to crash through the shaky barriers that uphold civilization.[16] The Nazis are the example *par excellence* of this universal tendency; the authoritarian structure of the Reich produced circumstances under which if one scratched a German, one found a potential Nazi.

Freudian notions also appear in those theories which focus on mass movements and the politics of mass mobilization to explain German acceptance of Hitler. These writers argue that the breakdown of class structure and the disappearance of autonomous groups with limited goals produced anomie and rootlessness, reactions to the massive dislocations spawned by industrialization. The victims of uncontrolled technology respond by becoming irrational and malleable; they are then seduced by manipulative leaders who capture the dispossessed and alienated with histrionic strategies.[17] Predictably, the virulence of the German reaction to these disruptive forces is attributed to national history. In truth then, we wind up with a subtler version of the national character thesis, with somewhat greater emphasis on a charismatic leadership harnessing the energies of *mindless* and hate-ridden masses—a twentieth century Teutonic version of collective insanity.

Theories centering on irrational mass-man in many ways represent a throwback to Gustav Le Bon's earlier work on crowd behavior.[18] The Frenchman described the impulsivity of crowds which he ascribed to a weakening in intellectual aptitude and the suspension of critical judgment. The individual in the crowd becomes an automaton, displaying extreme credulity, fleeting sentiments, irritability, intolerance, and absence of reason; in short, behaviors "which are almost always observed in beings belonging to inferior forms of evolution—in women, savages, and children." (p. 16) Le Bon endorses the primacy of the unconscious personality in guiding crowd behavior: "The heterogeneous is swamped by the homogenous and the unconscious qualities obtain the upper hand." (p. 8) The loosening of rational bonds make the group particularly susceptible to suggestion and contagion, mindless automatons dominated by strong-willed leaders who exercise "a veritible magnetic fascination on those around them" (p. 120) by "calling up in the souls' of their fellows that formidable force known as faith, which renders a man the absolute slave of his dream." (p. 114)

Of special interest here is Le Bon's belief that "an entire nation may become a crowd under the action of certain influences," (p. 3) a view which sounds rather similar to the national character position described earlier. That crowds display different forms of irrational behavior is, in Le Bon's opinion, due to racial differences. (p. 159) The similarity of this line of thought to modern versions highlighting the German national character and its collective "madness" is transparent.

Although his terminology is different, Freud expressed many of the same views on crowd behavior as Le Bon.[19] "In a group the individual is brought under conditions which allow him to throw off the repressions of his unconscious instinctual impulses." (p. 74) Freud explains how inhibitions and individual instincts are removed in the group. He contends that the suggestibility of group members results from their having "put one and the same object (the Leader) in place of their ego ideal (personal aspirations) and have consequently identified themselves with one another in their ego (leading to espirit de corps, group identity)." (p. 116) Group actions recapitulate the dynamics of the ancient primal horde, that archaic heritage which in times immemorial made the individual compliant toward his parents. (p. 123) "The leader of the group is still the dreaded primal father" (p. 123) to whom the individual surrenders his ego ideal. (p. 129)

Several difficulties prevent Le Bon and Freud's versions of contagion theory from being employed as a sufficient explanation of the relationship between Hitler, the Nazis, and the Germans. For one thing they assert that in a crowd, all individuals experience the same emotions and engage in the same kind of response to a single, compelling source of suggestion.[20] Always seeing the group as a total unit blinds these authors "to any diversity or differing degree of individual conviction backing up the apparent behavior of the group."[21] It is assumed that all individuals in the group share common motives and attitudes, all possess the same unconscious impulses, and all display regressive behavior. More colloquially, the picture drawn is of people going crazy together, no longer able to function with the least bit of rationality.

While this theory is somewhat efficacious for explaining short-term mob actions such as Kristallnacht, in the case of Nazi Germany we are concerned with explaining a long-term relationship between leaders and led which showed few signs of severance even after it became clear that the leader was pursuing a disastrous course. While it may be shown that Hitler exhibited self-destructive tendencies,[22] it would be virtually impossible to demonstrate that the Germans continued to support him because he was leading them in pursuit of Thanatos, a conclusion strongly suggested by the Freudian model.

Some modern day psychohistorical studies of Hitler also aim at increasing our understanding of the relationship between the Nazis and the German masses, although such is not always their primary intent. Those that do have such intent share a common interest in demonstrating the close affinity between Hitler's personal pathology (variously diagnosed), his political decisions, his Weltanschauung, and style of leadership. Most germane to our purpose is the contention, shared by several psychohistorians, that what likely saved Hitler from psychotic disintegration was his ability to get the German people to buy into his projections, albeit for reasons transcending his own pathology.[23] In other words Hitler avoided going crazy by getting the Germans to equate his bizarre perceptions with reality, which they did because of some unresolved, unconscious conflicts in their own past that in some mysterious way overlapped with Hitler's personal hangups.[24] Rudolph Binion attempts to demystify the situation by specifying the content of the traumas experienced by Hitler and the Germans and by showing how they intertwined. He cites three traumas: (1) Klara Hitler's over the death of her children; (2) Adolf Hitler's over the death of his mother; and (3) the German people's over their unwillingness to accept defeat in World War I. While a complete discussion of the Binion theses is beyond the scope of this article,[25] we can at least question his assertion that *all* Germans were traumatized and that following Hitler was the *only* way the trauma could be resolved.

This brief survey of several traditional and psychoanalytic studies of Hitler's hold over the Germans revealed a number of methodological difficulties and questionable assumptions. I now want to look at the contributions of social learning theory to the subject. Social learning theorists are highly critical of fundamental Freudian constructs, e.g., the unconscious. They are concerned with overt behavior—how responses are learned, maintained, increased or extinguished. They advocate a strong empirical grounding to confirm their hypotheses. Very broadly speaking, this orientation can be labeled behavioristic;[26] the individual is seen as responding to factors in the external world rather than projecting his own internal states (drives) onto the environment.

One dimension of learning theory relevant to our discussion is the concept of modeling. According to Bandura and Walters, there are at least three possible effects of exposure to a model: (1) to imitate precisely responses *not previously* in the observer's repertoire (new behaviors); (2) to inhibit or increase the frequency and/or intensity of a *previously* acquired response more or less similar to those exhibited by the model; and (3) to serve as a cue, whereby the model's responses elicit *similar* observer responses that are neither entirely novel nor inhibited as a result of prior learning.[27] Cumbersome language aside, what this social learning model suggests is that the behavior of some Germans toward Hitler's regime was acquired not as the result of character deficiency or historical conditioning to authority, but through imitating the behavior of the new Nazi authority figures, behavior which was encouraged and rewarded by the Führer and his entourage. New behaviors were learned, for example, to act out aggression or to disavow reason. Previously learned behaviors increased in frequency or intensity—prejudice against Jews justified beating them up and eventually exterminating them. Much of Hitler and his cohorts' hold over the masses flowed from the dynamics of the interaction itself—that is, Nazis served as new models for citizens to emulate. How the Nazis acquired power is largely an historical question. That *the achievement of power* gave them greater potency as model is beyond question. Quite possibly the tradition of obedience among Germans augmented the process of imitating strong political authority figures. It is a truism that winners are more imitated than are losers: an important aspect of Hitler's control was that behaviors he endorsed were rewarded by the regime, for example by increased status, or a better job. It is likely that specific individuals and constituencies who did not necessarily approve of Nazi attitudes or behaviors adopted them not out of fervent conviction or mindless conformity, but by the process of imitation. The standards of acceptable behavior were redefined by a new group of models who gained maximum exposure through their monopolistic control of the mass media. Skillful use of propaganda and the provision of opportune setting, e.g., Nuremburg rallies, in which to act out the new rituals and responses increased the likelihood of imitation.

The concept of imitation helps to remind us that loss of critical faculties need not be the only or primary reason a person surrenders his individuality; he can do so while remaining critically aware and knowledgeable. While a Heydrich, Himmler, or Goebbels may have jumped on the Nazi band-wagon because it provided a vehicle for coping with his own particular pathology,[28] it does not follow that all or most Germans were similarly motivated unless one assumes, as do many Freudians, that one can generalize from the abnormal to the so-called normal. Imitation of potent models rather than psychopathy or a flawed personality thesis helps augment our understanding of the average German's response to the Nazis.

Individuals may imitate a group for several reasons. Their emulation may result from:

a. Reward power, based on a member's perception that others have the ability to mediate rewards for him.
b. Coercive power, based on the member's perception that others have the ability to mediate punishment for him.
c. Legitimate power, based on the perception by members that others have a legitimate right to prescribe behavior for them.
d. Referent power, based on the member's identification with others.
e. Expert power, based on the perception that the other has some special knowledge or expertise.[29]

Most of the theories discussed in the early part of this article focus exclusively on legitimate and referent power. Earlier totalitarian theories exphasized coercive power.[30] Traditional biographers have referred to expert power, e.g., Hitler's ability to dazzle army leaders by rattling off military statistics.[31] The importance of reward powers for understanding part of the relationship between Hitler and the Germans has been noted. We will also be looking at categories of legitimate and referent powers, but in a somewhat different manner than traditional or psychoanalytic historians.

Cognitive dissonance is another social psychological tool useful for explaining why some Germans followed the Nazis. The supposition here is that cognitive systems tend toward a state of harmony, balance, consistency, or consonance. Cognitive dissonance arises when people at any one time *know* things that have opposing behavioral implications. If one stimulus implies "do this" and another indicates "do the opposite" then the individual is in a state of cognitive dissonance.[32] To cope with discrepancies between opposing cognitions, or cognitions and behaviors held simultaneously, the dissonant person has recourse to several strategies. He can exaggerate the value of what was chosen. In the Germans' case, the citizen could glorify the value of submitting to the Führer over the value of independent action, or he could devalue the rejected alternative, for example by assessing the Weimar Republic as completely bankrupt.

Still another way of reducing dissonance is to find others who agree with us or who are in the same situation as we are. This technique, called bolstering, enables the person to say: "There is nothing wrong with me; see how many are just like me."[33] In contradistinction to the Freudian defense mechanism of projection, the individual who "bolsters" need not *unconsciously* cast out the unwanted "evil" by attributing it to others. Rather he consciously accommodates others to his position: "Yes, I may be treating Jews terribly, but so is everyone else, which makes me no worse than them."

Obviously the three responses can be used in various combinations.[34] The point is that when a person is induced to do or say something which is contrary to his private opinion, there will be a tendency for him to change his opinion so as to align it with what he has done or said. It seems plausible to suggest that the Nazi experiment increased the proclivity to cognitive dissonance among Germans because Hitler and the Nazi value system *were not compatible* with their personal beliefs. While certainly not a complete explanation of the willingness of many to perform actions they *consciously* loathed, the theory of cognitive dissonance offers a helpful qualification to those theories which assume the primacy of unconscious processes or postulate national character deficiencies. It highlights the willingness of human beings to pursue consistency in thought, though sometimes at the expense of a realistic world view.

In line with cognitive dissonance theory, there is some evidence that "individuals who go through a severe initiation to gain admission to a club or organization . . . tend to think more highly of that organization than those who do not go through severe initiation to gain admittance."[35] If motivation is held constant, severity of initiation may be the decisive factor in determining one's assessment of the group experience, not what the group actually *does*. While most relevant for explaining the loyalty of the Nazi elite, this tendency suggests that some who joined the Party retained their membership and positive appraisal not because of what the party did for them, nor out of ideological conviction, but because of what they gave up to join.

Here a word is also in order about how inaccurate views may be sustained in light of contrary evidence. The problem is how to prevent new knowledge from effecting a change of opinion or action.[36] One way is by contextual twisting. This involves the reinterpretation of contradictory information in the context of what is already known. Undoubtedly, some Germans knew Jews whose characteristics did not fit Hitler's stereotype. A maneuver to justify ignoring this piece of information would have been to proclaim that Jew an exception to the rule, thereby allowing the stereotype to be maintained. Or the disturbing fact may be placed in the context of data compatible with the prevalent attitude. Instead of acknowledging that some Jews possessed "intelligence" and "business acumen" these key characteristics were perceived and classified as "shrewdness" and "exploitativeness"—enabling the stereotype to remain unassailed. New information as such is not even processed, let alone evaluated. One might also reject an unpleasant fact on the grounds that it conflicts with other, presumably more complete data. Although the Jews in a given German community might not have exhibited a particularly invidious trait, their brethren elsewhere were assumed to display the hated characteristic conspicuously.[37]

Another tactic for retaining a static world view is to discredit those sources which would challenge it. In the German context, this involved denying that extermination was being implemented, because the source of information, whether the foreign press or an acquaintance, was unreliable.

A last resort is simply to discard the relevance of new information. People may have "learned" that the Jewish stereotype was false or that a "final solution" was being enacted. Given the fact that the new information did not interfere with their daily activities, their comments may have been, "So what?" Such conduct is a way of leaving a field of potential conflict by withdrawing from it both physically and psychologically.

The procedures just described are far from passive; it requires effort to desensitize oneself to facts, to avoid perceiving them or to keep them out of focus.

> To protect himself from coming in conflict with the social order, the individual adopts measures the consequences of which are *not* to observe, *not* to understand, *not* to feel.[38]

It is not the purpose of this article to discuss the psychic costs levied by these distortive processes. What I have attempted is to counter the facile notion of passive, uniform German masses unconsciously seduced by fiendish deviants who found responsive chords in a defective population infected by "historical pathology."[39] Rather, I have made an effort to illustrate some of the conscious ways in which many Germans avoided unpleasant situations.

I remain all too aware that in the German case we are at times dealing with the behavior of evil people. I am also cognizant that Nazi goals and conduct were elsewhere emulated, that there were other fascist experiments, and that virulent anti-Semitism was not confined to Germany—some Poles, Ukrainians, and Frenchmen enthusiastically joined the SS.[40] It is also likely that people partly meet those who manipulate them, and that propaganda and coercion enhance the process. Yet it remains equally true that much of German collective behavior toward National Socialism operated on a conscious level, is rationally analyzable, and that psychosocial approaches are efficacious in dealing with these behaviors. While the historian employing psychosocial theory must be chary of making the facts fit the generalization, knowledge of group behavior augments his ability to grapple with the dynamics of the historical process. Psychosocial concepts offer a corrective to contagion theories—the argument that collective behavior follows from the more or less automatic transmission and unconscious, uncritical reception of moods and emotions from person to person. Likewise, it eliminates nebulous concepts such as multiple trauma and collective neurosis, while avoiding the overuse of paradox which frequently permeates psychoanalytic explanations of connections between leaders and led.

The effects of group pressure must be assigned weight in accounting for the willingness of some Germans to submit to Hitler and the Nazis. The experiments of Solomon Asch are suggestive here.[41] A group of individuals were asked to judge the size of various lines. Outside of the experimental setting subjects made mistakes one percent of the time. Then the situation was changed so that all but one member of the group were told to make wrong judgments. In thirty-three percent of the cases, the duped subject yielded to the majority. One fifth of the subjects were entirely independent; forty-two percent of the group were not appreciably affected by the experimental conditions. (p. 458) The reasons the deceived victims gave for yielding ranged from not wanting to offend, to fear of interfering with the experiment, to an imperative need not to be different, to actually coming to see reality the way the majority reported it. (pp. 468–73)

Asch did not believe that the contradiction between sense perception and group pressure was due to the past experience of the subject. Even those who remained independent throughout, exuding confidence, were still disturbed and assailed by doubts and the temptation to join with the others. (p. 466) In a later experiment, Asch increased the magnitude of line discrepancy to see if it would help the critical subjects to assert their independence and to repudiate the majority more decisively. The results were that "increasing the objective discrepancies did not abolish the majority effect or appreciably decrease it." (p. 475) However, when conditions were altered by reducing the opposition to one person, the change was sufficient almost to abolish the experimental effect. Asch concludes that the results described earlier were a function of the presence of a majority. (p. 476)

One further modification of the initial experiment bears mentioning. When Asch introduced a partner in the group who was supportive of the critical subject two changes occurred: (1) the majority effect was markedly weakened; and (2) the degree to which any single subject yielded diminished strikingly.

The Asch experiments underscore the importance of receiving confirmation from others for attitudes we hold, decisions we make, or actions we perform. Without such support it is very difficult for the individual to retain his independence against the group even if his values are different. Asch's work offers another corrective to undue focus on Hitler's charisma or the "religious" nature of the Nazi movement. Germans often followed the Nazis not out of any great sense of idealism or spiritual fervor, but because they did not want to offend a larger or more powerful group, especially when they perceived themselves as standing alone. While the Nuremberg rallies attracted men who obeyed because they were true believers,[42] the compliance of others was governed by the more mundane considerations of the Asch experiments.

To deny the prevailing view in society, however that view comes to predominate, requires of the individual a serious severance of social bonds, that familiar milieu which he knows and moves in and through which he acquires a sense of worth. An individual's decision to buck the system cannot always be made in reference to a specific issue of disagreement, such as the Nuremberg Laws. The price for assertion of self is costly. And as was the case with many Germans, although they *knew* better, they *chose* not to protest.

The work of Solomon Asch also suggests that much of the behavior (symptomology) exhibited by individuals and groups is a function of factors in the situation itself. If one manipulates external variables in a group interaction (such as proximity, location, and social support), it is possible to elicit behavior that individuals would not ordinarily exhibit. Unlike the psychoanalytic historian who moves from the world of the individual to the external environment and consequently must deduce states of internal mentation,[43] the social psychologist manipulates the external environment and observes behavioral change. Traditional descriptive history which analyzes specific external variables and assesses their impact, such as Hindenburg's decision to appoint Hitler Chancellor, would seem to be the natural ally of the social psychological approaches described in this article. Historians provide the raw data (events, decisions, statistics); the social psychologist can show how major historical episodes became operational at the group level. That is how one moves from the event to changes in human behavior.

In 1935, Muzafer Sherif began a number of experiments to study social factors in perception as a means of getting at the problem of norm formation.[44] In a completely darkened room, a single point of light appears to move when in fact it does not. This phenomenon is called the autokinetic effect. Judgment of the distance of apparent light movement differs markedly from individual to individual and in different spatial arrangements of the room. This unstructured situation arouses considerable anxiety in the individual. (pp. 202–03)

One group of subjects was first asked to estimate the light movement individually and then brought into a group setting to make "new" estimates. A second batch began its estimates within a group setting and proceeded to render individual judgment. Sherif found that in the absence of an objective range or scale of stimuli and an externally given reference, both groups (individual and collective) built up their own ranges on an internal reference point, that is they established a range within which all subsequent judgments were rendered. Although in both cases the ranges and norms of individuals tended to converge, convergence was greater when subjects first worked in a group setting. (p. 206) Moreover, when a group member was subsequently experimented on alone, "he perceived the situation in terms of the range and norm that he brought with him from the group." (p. 206)

In the Asch experiments (a more structured situation), the conditions produced error in the majority direction in only one third of the cases despite the obvious discrepencies. In the more ambiguous design of Sherif, *every* subject converged toward an introduced standard unless it was extraordinarily discrepant, e.g., twelve times the person's largest previous judgment. (p. 121)

While caution is indicated in extrapolating the results of these experiments to historical phenomena, they remain suggestive for our subject. They indicate that norms form when individuals interact in problem situations that involve uncertainties and choice among alternative modes of action. Norm formation develops in out-of-the-ordinary situations, where the usual rules and routine of daily living are not applicable. This would seem to be a fit description of the situation in Germany after World War I, suggesting that the *key* variable for understanding the Nazi phenomenon is not to be found in a long established national tradition but in those external events which made previous ways of responding to the environment difficult, inappropriate, or useless. It was the perceived ambiguity of the post World War I situation induced by concrete historical events, that led to a breakdown in the traditional authoritarian structure. Rather than augmenting receptivity to Nazism, the so-called authoritarian tradition may have acted to prevent submission to the Nazi model.

It is important to remember that the Freudian construct of bipolar traits allows that the defenses employed by the authoritarian character give rise to results that may be socially constructive as well as destructive. It is true, as many psychohistorians contend, that the defense mechanisms of the authoritarian personality can lead to submission, repressed aggression and sadism—qualities compatible with a "Nazi personality type." It is also true, but less emphasized, that "the culturally productive variations of the same defenses (can) result in control and discipline, precision and accuracy, dedicated performance and order,"[45] traits which under the appropriate circumstances may be antithetical to Nazism.

The question which psychoanalytic accounts of Nazism fail to answer, in my judgment, is why and how the "pathological" pole of a given trait came to predominate. Even if the dynamics of the process can be traced for a given individual or small group, is it not asking too much to assume that all Germans infected by authoritarianism came down with the same disease? Sherif's experiments suggest that any general conclusion about an alleged German collective pathology will have to be of a most general sort; at best we can say that the perceptions of the populace and of Hitler and the Nazis were not completely discrepant. This does not mean they were similar or that Hitler articulated what most Germans felt, if only unconsciously. Rather we must concentrate first and foremost on the specifics of the external environment which contributed to the Nazi success, such as the deficiencies of Weimar and the bitterness over Versailles. Then attention should move to those observable policies of the Nazis which increased their sources of support, e.g., reduction of class antagonism, foreign policy successes, reduction of unemployment, and terror. The final step is to turn to social psychological theories for an understanding of the different ways and motivations that led most Germans to enthusiastically support or reluctantly go along with the regime.

It also needs to be noted that the dynamics involved in the Nazis' *coming* to power and their *staying* in power are not synonymous. Common sense would indicate that many who are not enthusiastic about a cause will jump on the wagon if it seems to be moving forward, or if there is only one wagon available. The various psychosocial concepts discussed in this article have dealt with both sets of contingencies: how some Germans came to support the Nazis in their bid for power and why they didn't jump off the wagon when it began to go out of control.

On the latter contingency, the willingness of most Germans to stay with Hitler to the bitter end, the brilliant experiments of Stanley Milgram are instructive.[46] His studies were conducted on American subjects, and dealt with obedience that was willingly assumed in the absence of any sort of threat, "obedience that is maintained through the simple assertion by authority that it has the right to exercise control over the person." (p. xii)

The paradigmatic experiment, from which Milgram ran numerous variants, involved soliciting subjects to test the effects of punishment on learning. The "learner" was an accomplice of the experimenter. The "teacher" was a naive subject who was instructed to teach the learner word pairings, e.g., "green"/"ball." The learner-accomplice was seated in a chair, his arms strapped to prevent excessive movement, and an electrode attached to his wrist.

In the experiment, the "teacher" sat behind a generator with thirty switches, ranging from fifteen volts to four hundred fifty volts. There were also verbal designations which ranged from Slight Shock to Danger—Severe Shock. The "teacher" was told to increase the level of shock each time the learner responded incorrectly. At seventy-five volts the learner grunted; at one hundred twenty volts he complained verbally; at one hundred fifty he demanded to be released; at two hundred eighty-five volts "his response can only be described as an agonized scream." (p. 4) The distressing result of the experiment was that "a substantial proportion (of teachers) continued to the last shock on the generator." (p. 5) "It is the extreme willingness of adults to go to almost any lengths on the command of authority that constitutes the chief finding of the study." (loc. cit.)

The primary explanation that Milgram offers for obedience to authority is that a person comes to view himself as the instrument for carrying out another person's wishes and therefore no longer regards himself as responsible for his actions. (p. 8) The individual's moral sense reverts to a consideration of how well he is living up to the expectations authority has of him.

This psychological shift, as Milgram's experiments demonstrate, is not peculiar to Germans. Nor am I contending that it is a complete explanation for German obedience. What I am proposing is that many Germans obeyed Hitler not because they sympathized with his ideas, nor because he performed mass hypnotism, nor because he offered a substitute religion. They were not wicked or evil, or irreversibly conditioned by the German past, or in the thrall of a collective trauma. Rather they obeyed him for the banal reason that for most individuals, as Milgram's findings imply, it is very difficult *not* to obey authority.[47]

In conclusion I would like to state that I do not believe that any single psychological approach to history can by itself definitively answer the questions of why and how the Germans were led so far by the Nazis. I close by offering a three-stage division of labor for historians working on these questions.

a. *Traditional historians.* This group can help to isolate those factors in the German past that made Hitler's accession to power a possibility, e.g., the Bismarckian legacy, the failures of Weimar politicians, historical accidents, Hitler's own skills. They can describe and analyze the import of significant events and personages on the Nazi climb to and retention of power.

b. *Psychoanalytic historians.* These scholars contribute most to increasing our empathic understanding of the private world of Hitler and other Nazi personages. They may discern nonobvious patterns and interconnections between Hitler's childhood, adolescence, and subsequent actions. They enable us to share in the intensity of Hitler's feelings and beliefs and aid us in perceiving how Hitler's internal, subjective world became externalized and politically significant.

c. *Historians using non-Freudian concepts.* These individuals are most effective in showing the dynamics involved in Hitler's and the Nazi's domination over the German masses. They seek to describe the relationship between Hitler and the masses by the same "laws" that govern other known forms of social and group behavior. They are most interested in the rational and conscious aspects of collective behavior and avoid postulating metaphysical collective entities. They provide a most useful way of linking the events of the external world with the behavior of individuals in groups.

Depending on his or her interests and the kind of questions he or she poses about Hitler and National Socialism, the historian may have recourse to some or all of these methodologies.

NOTES

1 Hans Kohn, *The Mind of Modern Germany* (New York, 1960); William Shirer, *The Rise and Fall of the Third Reich* (New York, 1960); Peter Viereck, *Metapolitics: The Roots of National Socialism* (New York, 1965).
2 For example, George G. Iggers, *The German Conception of History: The National Tradition of Historical Thought From Herder to the Present* (Middletown, Conn., 1968), pp. 7–13, notes that German historiography treated the state as an end in itself and rejected thinking in normative terms.
3 A. J. P. Taylor, *The Course of German History* (London, 1945).
4 Klaus Epstein, "A New Study of Fascism [re: Nolte]," in Henry Turner (ed.), *Reappraisals of Fascism* (New York, 1976), p. 16.
5 T. W. Adorno, et. al., *The Authoritarian Personality* (New York, 1950); Erich Fromm, *Escape From Freedom* (Avon edition, New York, 1965) speaks of an "authoritarian character" with sadomasochistic strivings; Bertram Schaffner, M.D., *Fatherland: A Study of Authoritarianism in the German Family* (New York, 1948).
6 Peter Loewenberg, "Psychohistorical Perspectives on Modern German History," *Journal of Modern History*, Vol. 47, No. 2 (June, 1975), p. 247.
7 Peter Loewenberg, "The Psychohistorical Origins of the Nazi Youth Cohort," *American Historical Review*, 76 (1971): pp. 1457–1502. This is a thought-provoking article which contends that the Depression reactivated the earlier trauma experienced by substantial numbers of German children growing up during World War I. As adults this youth cohort became ripe recruits for National Socialism. Loewenberg operates from a psychoanalytic perspective and depicts the actions of the Nazi youth cohort as regressive behavior characterized by external violence, the need for immediate gratification, and longing for a glorified, omnipotent father figure.
8 Loewenberg, "Psychohistorical Perspectives," p. 238.
9 This is a difficult and controversial area. For a judicious summary of efforts to establish the pathology, mainly of the Nazi elite, see George M. Kren, "Psychohistorical Interpretations of National Socialism," *German Studies Review*, Vol. 1, No. 2 (May, 1978), especially pp. 162–66. Among the works discussed by Kren are H. V. Dicks, *Licensed Mass Murder: A Socio-Political Study of Some S.S. Killers* (New York, 1972); G. M. Gilbert, *Nuremberg Diary* (New York, 1947); and F. Miale and M. Selzer, *The Nuremberg Mind: The Psychology of Nazi Leaders* (New York, 1975). My point is that difficulties involved in diagnosing specific individuals multiply enormously when dealing with collective entities.
10 Michael Selzer, "Psychohistorical Approaches to the Study of Nazism," *Journal of Psychohistory*, Vol. 4 No. 2 (Fall 1976), p. 222, notes that two years after acquiring power the party comprised perhaps 3 percent of the population; among German soldiers the proportion of Nazi fanatics appears never to have exceeded 10 percent.
11 Robert Soucy, in his review of Rudolf Binion's *Hitler Among the Germans*, which appeared in the *Journal of Psychohistory*, Vol. 5, No. 3 (Winter 1978), p. 466, points out that in the elections of March 5, 1933, the Nazis polled 43.9 percent of the vote even as institutional Nazification went on unopposed.
12 Peter Merkl, *Political Violence Under the Swastika: 581 Early Nazis*, (Princeton, N.J., 1975).

13 See Else Frenkel-Brunswick, "Environmental Controls and the Impoverishment of Thought," in C. J. Friedrich, (ed.), *Totalitarianism* (New York, 1954), p. 177. Frenkel-Brunswick cautions that "anxiety-inducing social and political situations such as economic depression and war ... [can] create susceptibility to totalitarianism regardless of how democratic the family situation might have been. ... [There is not] a direct or exclusive causal relationship between family structure and the rise of totalitarianism."

14 Selzer, "Psychohistorical Approaches," p. 222.

15 Ibid., p. 221.

16 Sigmund Freud, *Civilization and Its Discontents* (Norton edition, New York, 1961); Fred Weinstein and Gerald M. Platt, "The Coming Crisis in Psychohistory," *Journal of Modern History*, Vol. 47, No 2 (June 1975), p. 210, question the inevitability of conflict between man and society as part of a broader critique of the application of Freudian theory to historical subjects.

17 See James Gregor, *Interpretations of Fascism* (Berkeley, Calif., 1974), especially pp. 78–113. Among the theorists treated are Hannah Arendt, Eric Hoffer, Ortega y Gasset, Emil Lederer, and William Kornhauser.

18 Gustave Le Bon, *The Crowd: A Study of the Popular Mind* (Second edition, Georgia Dunwoody, M.D.). First published in 1895.

19 Sigmund Freud, *Group Psychology and the Analysis of the Ego*, in *The Complete Psychological Works of Sigmund Freud*, trans. by James Strachey (London, 1920–22), Vol. XVIII, pp. 67–143.

20 Ralph H. Turner and Lewis M. Killiam, *Collective Behavior* (Englewood Cliffs, N.J., 1957), p. 5.

21 Ibid., p. 14.

22 J. McRandle, *The Track of the Wolf: Essays on National Socialism and Its Leader Adolf Hitler* (Evanston, Ill., 1965).

23 See for example, Walter Langer, *The Mind of Adolf Hitler: The Secret Wartime Report* (Signet edition, New York, 1973), p. 135; Helm Stierlin, *Adolf Hitler: A Family Perspective* (New York, 1976), pp. 94–96, 109–22.

24 This statement needs qualification; it refers only to those theorists who postulate "unconscious" connections between Hitler's hangups and those of the nation at large. There is no question that Hitler knew how to appeal to the *conscious* desires of the communicant members of the nation. J. P. Stern, *Hitler: The Führer and the People* (Glasgow, 1975) offers a brilliant analysis of Hitler's use of rhetorical language to nourish and sustain his supporters. Ultimately the exchange between the leader and his followers went—*Hitler*: "Deutschland." *Answer*: "Sieg Heil." (p. 36). The audience was not being informed, it was being made to perform. Another talent of Hitler's was to "introduce a conception of personal authenticity into the public sphere and proclaim it as the chief value of politics." (p. 24) Yet can we assume that all Germans were so seduced? Also, what made them so susceptible to Hitler's seduction?

25 See Rudolph Binion, *Hitler Among the Germans* (New York, 1976) and the symposium which appeared in *The Psychohistory Review*, Vol. 6 (Summer 1977), especially the comments of Fred Weinstein and Robert Waite, pp. 44–75. Waite's essay is essentially reproduced in the *Journal of Interdisciplinary History*, Vol. VIII, No. 2 (Autumn 1977), pp. 380–82. Binion's assessment of Waite's book, *The Psychopathic God: Adolf Hitler* (New York, 1977), appears in the *Journal of Psychohistory*, Vol. 5, No. 2 (Fall 1977), pp. 295–301. Waite does not really offer a psychohistorical explanation for the willingness of Germans to follow Hitler and therefore is not discussed. He follows a traditional historical approach of selecting personalities and events in the Germans' past that contributed to the Nazi success. See pp. 244–347 in his book.

26 Salvatore R. Maddi, *Personality Theories: A Comparative Analysis* (Revised edition, Homewood, Ill., 1972). Chapter II contains a fine discussion of different behaviorist theories. Maddi's comments on social learning are particularly germane to this essay. See pp. 537–41.

27 *Social Psychology and Personality Development* (New York, 1963), p. 106. It is important to remember that the observer's perception of the model is instrumental in determining which, if any, of the responses will be elicited. The status of the model, whether the exhibited behavior is rewarded or punished, the model's control over observer rewards, all must be considered. The historian can supply much of the relevant data. And of course, observer characteristics play their part, e.g., the degree to which similar behavior has previously been rewarded or punished.

28 For a series of insightful sketches on the personalities of party stalwarts see Joachim C. Fest, *The Face of the Third Reich: Portraits of the Nazi Leadership*, trans. by Michael Bullock (New York, 1970).

29 J. R. P. French, Jr., and Bertram Raven, "The Bases of Social Power," in D. Cartwright and F. Zander, (eds.), *Group Dynamics: Research and Theory* (Second edition, N.Y., 1960), p. 613.

30 See for example Hannah Arendt, *The Origin of Totalitarianism* (New York 1966); and C. Friedrich and Z. Brzezinski, *Totalitarian Dictatorship and Autocracy,* (New York, 1956).

31 See for example Alan Bullock, *Hitler: A Study in Tyranny* (revised edition, London, 1962).

32 Leon Berkowitz, *A Survey of Social Psychology* (Hinsdale, Ill., 1975), pp. 72–73, 149. Cognitive dissonance is most likely to occur when the conflict involved is between a self-concept and cognitions about a behavior that violates that self-concept. The subject must believe that the behavior was voluntary, so as not to be disturbed by it. Hence many decent Germans acted contrary to their personal inclinations by deceiving themselves rather than by coercion. The theory was developed by Leon Festinger, *A Theory of Cognitive Dissonance* (Stanford, Calif., 1957).

33 Edward E. Sampson, *Social Psychology and Contemporary Society* (New York, 1971), p. 110. It is appropriate here to mention the thoughtful case study by R. C. Raack, "When Plans Fail: Small Group Behavior and Decision-Making in the Conspiracy of 1808 in Germany," *Journal of Conflict Resolution,* Vol. XIV, No. 1 (1970), pp. 3–19. The article offers several insights into how irrational forces are generated by particular small group processes. Most germane for this section is his suggestion that in small groups whose members are extremely disoriented and disadvantaged by societal forces beyond their control, there is a radicalizing tendency which enhances the influence of risk takers and stifles the voices of the more moderate (p. 15). "The very hearing of others' willingness to take risks makes one's like inclinations appear less dangerous." (p. 8). Hence in stressful times it is easier then usual to find fellow passengers willing to take a voyage in a leaky boat.

34 Nor are these the only possibilities for reducing dissonance. For several others, as well as a discussion of the circumstances governing the use of particular forms of dissonance reduction, see Leon Festinger and Elliot Aronson, "The Arousal and Reduction of Dissonance in Social Contexts," in D. Cartwright and A. Zander, (eds.), *Group Dynamics: Research and Theory* (Second edition, N.Y., 1960), pp. 214–31.

35 Elliot Aronson and Judson Mills, "The Effect of Severity of Initiation on Liking for a Group," *Journal of Abnormal and Social Psychology,* Vol. 59 (1959), p. 177.

36 Much of the following discussion is based on William Newman, *American Pluralism: A Study of Minority Groups and Social Theory* (New York, 1973), pp. 240–42.

37 Successful propaganda would be most effective in sustaining this outlook.

38 Solomon E. Asch, *Social Psychology* (Englewood Cliffs, N.Y., 1952), p. 583.

39 It might be noted that Marxist explanations of National Socialism, while not primarily concerned with unconscious motivation, share with psychoanalytic approaches an emphasis on consistency. In the one case it is assumed that class behaviors are uniform, in the other that psychological constructs are universal. For the Marxist view of National Socialism see Renzo De Felice, *Interpretations of Fascism,* trans. by Brenda Huff Everet, (Cambridge Mass., 1977) especially pp. 30–54; Wolfgang Schieder, "Fascism" in C. D. Kernig, (ed.), *Marxism, Com-*

munism and Western Society: A Comparative Encyclopedia, Vol. III (New York, 1972), pp. 291–95.

40 For the varieties of Fascism see the following useful readers: Gilbert Allardyce, (ed.), *The Place of Fascism in European History* (Englewood Cliffs, N.J., 1971); Walter Laqueur, *Fascism: A Reader's Guide* (Berkeley and Los Angeles, 1976); Henry Turner, (ed.), *Reappraisals of Fascism* (New York, 1976); S. J. Wolff, (ed.), *European Fascism* (New York, 1968); and *The Nature of Fascism* (London, 1968).

41 Solomon E. Asch, *Social Psychology,* (Englewood Cliffs, N.J., 1952).

42 See for example Eric Hoffer, *The True Believer* (New York, 1951).

43 That psychoanalytic historians slight the impact of the external environment is a major theme of Fred Weinstein and Gerald Platt, *Psychoanalytic Sociology: An Essay on the Interpretations of Historical Data and the Phenomena of Collective Behavior* (Baltimore, 1973).

44 "A Study of Some Social Factors in Perception," *Archives of Psychology,* Vol. 27, No. 187 (1935). My account draws primarily on Muzafer Sherif and Carolyn W. Sherif, *Social Psychology* (New York, 1969).

45 Loewenberg, "Psychohistorical Perspectives," p. 236.

46 *Obedience to Authority: An Experimental View* (New York, 1974).

47 Milgram notes that obedience was significantly reduced as the victim was rendered more immediate to the subject, e.g., in the same room, or having to force the victim's hand on the shock plate. (pp. 35–36). On the other hand, the only factors compelling the subject to persist were the experimenter's verbal instructions ranging from "please continue" to "you must go on." (p. 21) When Milgram altered the experiment so that the experimenter was strapped into the chair and an accomplice told the "teacher" to continue shocks while the strapped experimenter told the "teacher" to halt, the subject obeyed the experimenter. "The decisive factor is the response to authority, rather than the response to the particular order to administer shocks." (p. 104).

18

Emotionology: Clarifying the History of Emotions and Emotional Standards

Peter N. Stearns with
Carol Z. Stearns

Emotionology: the attitudes or standards that a society, or a definable group within a society, maintains toward basic emotions and their appropriate expression; ways that institutions reflect and encourage these attitudes in human conduct, e.g., courtship practices as expressing the valuation of affect in marriage, or personnel workshops as reflecting the valuation of anger in job relationships.

Emotion: a complex set of interactions among subjective and objective factors, mediated through neural and/or hormonal systems, which gives rise to feelings (affective experiences as of pleasure or displeasure) and also general cognitive processes toward appraising the experience; emotions in this sense lead to physiological adjustments to the conditions that aroused response, and often to expressive and adaptive behavior.[1]

Historians are probably justified in claiming that they are less prone than their colleagues in the social sciences to use jargon and invent new terms that often befuddle the uninitiated. And yet we have long been accustomed to use without second thought terms that were deliberately invented to identify for formal study clusters of related phenomena. "Sociology" itself had such an origin. Furthermore, few historians hesitate any longer to employ some of the terms sociologists have invented, such as "nuclear family," "extended family." What were once neologisms are now standard English and for the very good reason that they convey useful meanings that have heightened the precision with which we can express ourselves. The authors of this essay propose "emotionology" as a useful term with which to distinguish the collective emotional standards of a society from the emotional experiences of individuals and groups. Use of the term as defined

Reprinted from the *American Historical Review,* vol. 90, no. 4 (October 1985) pp. 813–36.

above will focus our attention on the social factors that determine and delimit, either implicitly or explicitly, the manner in which emotions are expressed. Such a study will, we hope, illuminate how and why social agencies and institutions either promote or prohibit some kinds of emotions, while remaining neutral or indifferent to others.

As a subject, emotionology ought to fascinate twentieth-century Americans, who live in a society particularly conscious (or, at least, particularly interested in proclaiming its consciousness) of emotional expressions and restraints. Historical work in this area is partly an effort at self-understanding, possibly because of our increased awareness of emotions as a facet of human experience. But the dependence of historical interest on contemporary issues is familiar, defendable, and not worth belaboring. The point is that all societies have emotional standards, even if they are sometimes largely unspoken or undebated, and societies differ, often significantly, in these standards. Anthropologists have long known and studied this phenomenon.[2] Historians are increasingly aware of it, as we realize that the emotional standards of societies change in time rather than merely differ, constantly, across space. Changes in emotional standards can in turn reveal much about other aspects of social change and may even contribute to such change.

But historians, and some anthropologists, who have properly grasped emotionology as a cultural variable, whose distinctions may affect other features of a society or group, have often confused thinking about emotion with the experience of emotion. For example, in a very interesting study, revealingly entitled *Never in Anger,* anthropologist Jean Briggs described how the Utku Eskimo tribe disapproves of anger and seeks to repress it through socialization. So far so good, for what is involved here is a distinctive value system and the set of informal institutions meant to express that system. But the study does not prove that the Utku are a people without anger. They regularly sulk when challenged (anger turned inward?) and, when even slightly provoked, routinely beat and otherwise abuse dogs and other household animals. These actions are not included in the tribe's proscriptions against anger because of the particular emotionology involved, but an observer may be pardoned for questioning whether the Utku are anger free.[3]

This point could seem fussy, were it not that some historians, in exploring the new field of the history of emotion, have exposed themselves to criticism by ignoring the distinctions between emotion and emotionology. They have written provocative histories about aspects of emotionology but have said far less about emotion than they have claimed. Their vulnerability is needless, or at least avoidable, but the remedy depends on a terminological distinction for which, without the neologism, we lack the vocabulary.

The study of emotion may become one of the hot new topics in social history, a field already known for expanding the range of investigation. The challenge, in sociohistorical terms, is obvious: if not only family structures, protest, and leisure pursuits but also aspects of emotional experience are legitimate subjects for historical inquiry, the social historian can go far toward demonstrating his claim that the study of history is necessary for understanding the context of ordinary human life. One conclusion thus far advanced by historians in this field—that the emotional context of life in Western society has changed significantly in recent centuries—underscores the relevance of historical inquiry. We can use history to help understand our own collective emotional past, a heady prospect in a society encouraged to daily emotional temperature-taking. We may find that, until recent centuries, Western society viewed emotional expectations we take for granted "as a kind of mental illness" (a provocative interpretation that has been applied to the rise of romantic love in the eighteenth century).[4] For if fundamental shifts in emotional standards have occurred, not only in our own recent past but also in different historical cases, we may seek clues in such shifts to other historical changes. To date, understandably enough, historians of emotion (the term emotional historians cannot be fairly suggested) in Western society have concentrated on the link between emotion and other changes in the family. But potentially the linkage can be expanded to include other activities, such as social protest or sports preferences, where emotion may be involved as more than a minor by-product.[5]

Historical study of emotions has the added attraction of linking social history to social and psychological theories that have largely been ignored in favor of more conventional sociological models of stratification and mobility. The history of emotion may help historians overcome, at least in part, a key weakness of psychohistory—the failure to deal persuasively with groups in the past.[6] Further, social historians may be able to do more than simply use familiar psychological theory, which, because of the diversity of theories available and their tendency to be culture-bound, is a debatable practice, though a practice already evident in several relevant studies of emotional change over time.[7] Historians may contribute to theory—that is, to an understanding of the dynamics of emotional behavior—in areas where psychologists have been hampered by their problems in dealing with change. This prospect, recently suggested in a general way by Theodore Zeldin,[8] has been partly confirmed by explorations in American history of changes in the valuation of anger, an emotion not only viewed differently over time but also largely ignored (in favor of concentration on aggressive behavior) by contemporary psychologists, in part because of their own peculiarly modern biases concerning anger.[9] The prospect of new interdisciplinary understanding, possibly one that enhances the historian's contribution, is no small attraction of the extension of social history into emotional as well as rational aspects of past mentalities. Finally, within the discipline of history, attention to emotional standards provides an opportunity for new contacts between social historians and their colleagues in cultural, religious, and intellectual history and may be a bridge between newer sociohistorical findings and more familiar themes, such as the rise of romanticism or the surge of marial piety in late medieval Catholicism. These contacts require caution (social historians must not neglect earlier discoveries about the limits of intellectual history in exploring popular culture and behavior), but, if properly handled, they may enrich the study of past emotional standards. Indeed, one function of the definition of emotionology is to improve the intersection of various historical approaches as they relate to change in, and the impact of change on, emotional values.

Early works in social history, particularly on premodern European mentalities, reflect considerable interest in the emotional component of human experience. Lucien Febvre called for a "historical psychology" that would "give up psychological anachronism" and "establish a detailed inventory of the mental equipment of the time." His call was heard by a number of historians who, while rarely focusing on discrete emotions, tried to explain rituals, beliefs, and institutions in terms of the emotional climate of medieval and early modern Europe. Their interests were not, in the main, adopted by American social historians, who initially preferred to dissect measurable components of emotional outbursts such as witchcraft or avoid emotion-laden periods or incidents altogether. A key distraction was the tendency of American psychohistorians to assume a constant emotional apparatus, usually along Freudian lines, in preference to Febvre's more difficult (but more realistic) concept of a psychology itself subject to change over time.[10]

In fact, modern social history was born in the United States and Britain with a rather rationalist bent, not only in assumptions about scientific methodology but also in a tendency to claim sweet reason in the popular attitudes of the past. One of the first contentions of crowd historians, for example, was that rioters carefully selected their methods and goals—logical choices that can be easily grasped by historians once the rioters' basic assumptions are understood. The historical study of protest, indeed, remains dominated by the claim to rationality, to the extent that some authorities argue that emotion enters their subjects not at all. This is more than a refutation of the conservative, mad mob assumptions of Gustav Le Bon, the rationalists' first target. Charles Tilly has continued to see emotion as an irrelevant by-product of protest, whose contours are firmly determined by organizational potential and rational crowd goals.[11]

Other early sociohistorical works focused on areas where rational motivations could be assumed. Mobility studies, for example, tested responses to an objective social hierarchy; those who did not climb the ladder were presumed blocked by clear impediments, such as discrimination, or, in more subtle renderings, were seen following the rationality of a distinctive value system.

But a number of social historians, pursuing other aspects of the history of the common people, have not eschewed emotion as a component of the past they seek. It is almost impossible to examine the evolution of the family without considering emotional elements, although the effort has been made.[12] Without a parallel examination of emotional ties, structural studies of the links among kin, including extended kin, risk superficiality. The technical nuclearity of many premodern West European households is probably less significant, despite the attention lavished on its discovery, than the emotional ties that existed between elderly parents and adult children, unless, of course, those ties were random. Built around anger-producing child-rearing patterns and later conflicts over property control, the pattern of animosity within the premodern family, which several historians have uncovered, illuminates more of the content of premodern family life than does specification of household composition. And this emotional pattern proved susceptible to change, making it very much the historian's business. Greater affection between adult generations became visible when property relations became less tense, as in seventeenth-century New England, and a further increase in affection toward the elderly in the family has been hypothesized in studies of more recent American history. Structural changes may indeed pass almost unnoticed if they do not seem to disrupt—or if they abet—emotional patterns that researchers find familiar. This may be one explanation for the lack of adverse popular reaction to the growing residential discreteness of the elderly in mid-twentieth-century America, where bonds of affection remained unchanged, given frequent contacts between separate households, and possibly were promoted by the reduction of conflict between in-laws and kin.[13]

Demographic studies have also included analyses of emotional contexts, again almost inevitably. The most sensitive demographic historians have insisted that some change in family motivations must accompany major demographic changes, such as a reduction in birth rates; although certain relevant motivations involve rational economic calculations, others may involve emotions, such as the affection extended toward and expected from children.[14] Regardless of motivation, demographic shifts may themselves cause emotional change. That a reduction in infant death rates accompanies (whether as cause or effect) an increase in the emotional investment in children has become a historical commonplace. Other effects of demographic change on emotion have yet to be fully explored, including changes in the impact of grief as the incidence and manner of death have altered. But demography has already contributed significantly to the consideration of emotional standards within the context of family history.[15]

Most recently a variety of studies, which treat emotion as a legitimate focus of historical investigation, have directly confronted the emotional elements in family history. Historians working on France, Britain, Germany, and colonial America have uncovered a pronounced increase in familial affection in the late seventeenth and eighteenth centuries, which contrasts with the emotional tone seemingly characteristic of families in earlier centuries. John Demos noted an effort in seventeenth-century Plymouth to keep families free from the angry bickering more readily tolerated among neighbors; this effort to control anger was accompanied by the encouragement of conjugal love.[16] Until somewhat later European families tolerated frequent outbursts of anger—or, at least, concentrated their efforts on avoiding behavioral excesses prompted by anger rather than recommending explicit emotional appraisals. Considerable ambiguities about the humanity of young children and concerted efforts at will-breaking fueled familial anger. These child-rearing methods produced behavioral restraints—in that children rarely expressed anger at parents until the latter grew old—but encouraged anger when other outlets were available, including the will-breaking administered to one's own children.[17] Other accounts stress the cold emotional quality of premodern families more than the latent anger within them. The picture of emotional coolness is particularly marked in Edward Shorter's description of family life, for Shorter seems convinced that pronounced contrasts existed between the premodern and modern family, almost to the point that he describes distinct species. The same theme appears in some feminists' efforts to prove that maternal love is an entirely modern emotion and a snare imposed on women by society.[18] But a similar vision emerges in other, less dramatic accounts. Lawrence Stone, for example, compared premodern familial emotion to the level of affect one would expect in a bird's nest.

By the eighteenth century, even in Europe, this emotional pattern began to break up. Historians have disagreed vigorously over which social class pioneered change: the new proletariat, the middle class, and the aristocracy all have advocates.[19] But they have agreed on the basic direction of change. Children began to be treated with greater and more intense affection, particularly, of course, where birth and infant mortality rates dropped.[20] Romantic love began to influence courtship and marital expectations (providing in some cases a novel motivation for the dissolution of marriage).[21] On the eve of its decline as an economic unit, the family took on important new emotional functions, including the strengthening of affectionate relationships among family members. In a parallel development, attitudes toward animals began to shift toward more affection and away from the view that animals were a legitimate target for anger (the common pattern in most agricultural and hunting societies).[22] These emotional shifts have been ascribed to various causes. Most scholars point to the role of religion. Protestantism urged greater attention to love between spouses, and variants of Protestantism, such as moderate evangelicalism in eighteenth-century America, carried the emphasis on familial affection and anger control even further. According to Jean-Louis Flandrin, Jansenism promoted similar religious motivations in France. The Enlightenment, by prompting greater egalitarianism within the family (and more humane attitudes toward animals) and by encouraging an individualism that sought emotional satisfaction, furthered the new emotional trends as well. Less defined but worth attention are economic factors. The rise of market relationships promoted individualism and the need to establish bonds outside the family. At the same time market relationships undermined more traditional emotional ties among male friends, leading men to turn to the family as an emotional haven safe from the competitive jostling that began to characterize male relationships.[23] The need to deal with and depend on strangers in a market economy also encouraged the control of anger, not only within families but also within neighborhoods.

The most intensive work on emotional change has focused on the decades preceding industrialization, which are a watershed in the history of emotion. Historians have been more tentative in analyzing later developments. At the end of his study, Stone sketched the presumable rise of emotional repression in the Victorian era. Flandrin jumped the nineteenth century completely; he found the rise of romantic love in progress but incomplete by the end of the eighteenth century but neatly resumed, indeed completed and fulfilled, in the twentieth. And there is, generally, an assumption that the emotional standards first developed in the seventeenth century do describe a durable emotional framework for modern life, even if Victorianism or the separation of male work from home (leading to new emotional differentiation, in ideal types, between men and women) temporarily complicated realization of this development. Several recent studies of nineteenth-century courtship indeed reveal that ideals of romantic love remained important.[24] Studies of nineteenth-century child rearing, less surprisingly, show that recommendations for parental treatment of children continued to emphasize mutually loving relationships.[25] Other twentieth-century historians, following a new trend of looking nostalgically on the nineteenth-century middle-class family as yet another world we have lost, similarly assume a loving emotional intensity.[26] Questions remain about the impact of Victorianism on emotions, about emotional life among the lower classes, and, now, about the relationship of contemporary familial emotion to eighteenth- and nineteenth-century standards. But the idea of a new period in Western emotional history, corresponding to what we call modern in political or economic history, seems well established.

And this idea is an important contribution to historical study. Historians can now point to major emotional shifts over time, just as anthropologists have pointed to different emotional experiences—and expressions, including even some of the facial expressions used to denote basic emotions—across cultures. Henceforth, emotional changes must be considered, along with other shifts in mentality and behavior, as part of the historian's attempt to convey and explain sociohistorical change. Whether emotional changes *cause* other fundamental changes—as shifts in the emotions involved in child rearing may have done in modern history—or more commonly *reflect* other basic factors, like ideology or economic relationships, must still be discussed. But that emotional change needs to be woven into the historical fabric seems unquestionable. One consequence would be a valuable contribution to psychohistory. The assumption of psychological constants, which allows broad application of presumed contemporary psychological dynamics to past personalities, needs rethinking in light of the discovery of emotional shifts. No longer can we assume without proof, as in a recent study of nineteenth-century grief, that people in the past shared our emotional experience, that we can use contemporary psychology to elucidate past behavior, or that we can use past data, without careful analysis, to bolster contemporary psychological theory.[27] Linkages may be possible, but they require evaluation and evidence. They cannot be taken for granted as premises for research.

Yet, for all the legitimate excitement that the new findings have roused in historians prepared to examine emotional factors in history, the first wave of research has left not only important work to be done but also a nagging sense of dissatisfaction. It is this dissatisfaction that must be addressed, through use of a new terminology, before additional research is undertaken.

Several critics have been troubled by the sharp contrast drawn between a cold premodern and a loving modern society. Have we really shifted from an aversion to infants as greedy, animal-like creatures to child-rearing attitudes based on affection? The idea correctly suggests that some change has occurred and serves as a useful antidote to the time-bound assumption of an eternal kind of maternal affection. But it is probably too stark. Obviously, some allowance must be made for individual variation from the norm. We know that affection for babies is not uniform in our own society. And we might correspondingly assume some deviations from the attitudes of hostility thought to exist in preindustrial times. Beyond the issue of exceptions, however, which some generalizations gloss over, scientific findings need to be integrated, some of which demonstrate that maternalism, though definitely not a historical constant, does have biological components that probably made pre-eighteenth-century practice less distinctive than pre-eighteenth-century rhetoric implies. Thus, glandular changes associated with breast-feeding, which lead to maternal bonding, are not recent developments. To be sure, large numbers of mothers did not breast-feed in the seventeenth century (particularly in parts of Western Europe), and they therefore did not experience this natural bonding. But the majority did, and their experience must be taken into account.[28]

Critics of an early modern "romantic revolution" in courtship and marriage have focused more strictly on individual exceptions to the concept of preromantic coldness, for biological constants are murkier in this area. Cases of dramatic passion for a spouse have been found before the shift to frankly romantic marital criteria, and, although these instances did involve a defiance of accepted norms, their existence must qualify generalizations about emotional style.[29] Even if preromantic emotional standards for courtship are accepted as having been fairly uniform, it is clearly imprudent to assume that romantic love might not have sometimes affected mate choice or developed during marriage, though this kind of affection was not recommended before the seventeenth century. Aside from expectations that some husbands and wives, despite a different emotional context, developed strong affectionate ties after years of cohabitation and shared work, the recent discovery of a high incidence of love-affair complaints in seventeenth-century (that is, preromantic) medical practice in England casts doubt on the uniform coldness of marital and premarital ties.[30]

These qualifications touch the contemporary pole of the comparison as well, where documentation is more readily available. As suggested earlier, several students of the eighteenth-century upsurge in romantic love have written as though the trends then launched revolutionized marital relations; Flandrin, most explicitly, suggested that fruition of the love ideal came about in the twentieth century. But romantic love in twentieth-century marriage is hardly uniform. A poll taken in France in the 1960s revealed that slightly more than half of all boys in secondary school did not expect or desire a romantic marriage (though over 80 percent of the girls did, a disparity that suggested future marital conflict).[31] Studies of working-class marriage, with their emphasis on the mother-daughter bond as the primary affectionate tie even for young married women, raise similar doubts about the triumph of the romantic love ideal.[32] As in the case of child rearing, reality seems to be more complex, change less dramatic, than some of the pioneers in the history of love have indicated.

Other claims made by historians in this field are suspect from another angle. Several have written of a decline in anger concomitant with the eighteenth-century increase in romantic emphasis: "The quality of attachment dramatically improved in the eighteenth century, and, among other things, decreased the level of aggressive violence."[33] At one level—the emotionological—this hypothesis is surely correct: the authors of family and child-rearing manuals urged both emotional goals simultaneously, from the eighteenth to the mid-nineteenth century. But did anger really decline as a result? And has the goal of anger control remained tied in more recent history to recommendations of familial affection? Certainly child-rearing manuals by the late nineteenth century included more positive roles for anger, though not within the family, than their mid-Victorian predecessors had done, yet their emphasis on the need for affection remained unabated. And it is surely possible that growing emotional intensity brought both anger and love in its wake, a notion found in popular culture and in Stone's brief description of the tolerance toward unrestrained displays of emotion— public fighting as much as public displays of affection—in the decades before the Victorian era.[34] Again, the history of emotion seems to be more complex than some of the most striking accounts have yet allowed. Love may not have gained ground so uniformly, because of complications at both ends of the chronological spectrum, and its relationship with other emotions may be more subtle than some observers have believed. We have, in fact, only begun to examine past emotional experience, and the inquiry promises to be arduous. Loving behavior by parents and, still more obviously, by spouses has not increased at the same pace as recommendations of both, and these behavioral patterns did not depart from such a uniformly cold background as has been imagined. Actual patterns of anger cannot be assumed from recommendations of control.

Many historians of emotion have been trapped, ironically, by some of their own cultural assumptions. We live in a society that places an unusually high value on romantic love. It is proper and illuminating to seek the origins of this attitude. But we must also beware of how our own strong assumptions can obscure our view of the past. Surely an idealization of romantic love helped prompt historians of the working class, like E. P. Thompson, to object to Stone's assertion that romantic ideals began nearer the top of society.[35] (Interestingly, no one has objected to recent findings that nineteenth-century workers were less sexually repressed than the bourgeoisie, now that sexual freedom is seen as desirable.) For why argue that workers built romantic love into familial expectations as early as the middle class did, when there is evidence that even now familial affection differs between the two groups, with workers focusing less on husband-wife ties and more on affectionate links in the extended family? Of course, there are major empirical questions involved, concerning present as well as past class differentiations, but it is not inherently demeaning to suggest some differences in emotional style save as historians themselves are wedded to modern middle-class emotionology. As we have suggested, romantic ideals have sometimes prevented observers, historians and others, from recognizing emotional variations, even in studies of the twentieth-century middle class. Certainly the assessment of premodern family styles is complicated by a time-bound reaction to practices that in our culture denote a lack of proper feeling. Affection in premodern society may not have been as different as vocabulary and child-rearing and courtship behaviors suggest to the modern researcher. Expressions of anger may have been more compatible with love for children than our modern values allow.[36] Or affection may have been more dispersed—spread among friends of the same sex, for example—but no less real for being hard to identify by modern observers trained to associate intense affection with marriage or its functional equivalent in extramarital cohabitation (the pattern that once was called concubinage before it was taken up by young middle-class couples). The facts must be faced: the finding most obviously desired from a history of emotion—some plausible chart of the rates of love and anger or the experience of sexuality, joy, and grief—is unlikely to emerge with any precision; it definitely has not emerged to date, despite historians' efforts to postulate trends.

The concept of emotionology is necessary, quite simply, to distinguish between professed values and emotional experience. It also aids researchers seeking to identify contemporary emotional values that could bias any inquiry, historical or otherwise, that attempts to assess the emotional experience of others. As we realize that some of our emotional values—including findings hailed as scientific about the importance of love and of certain kinds of loving expressions in the socialization of children—are influenced, if not created, by the emotionology of our own times, we can more intelligently evaluate past indications of emotional values and assess the origins of our own assumptions.

The emotionology-emotion distinction presumes that in most cases the emotionological range is greater than the variations in emotional experience, from one society or period to the next. Shifts in affection toward infants have probably occurred in Western society over the past three centuries, but they have not been as great as the shifts in emotional standards regarding infants. We can maintain the earlier claim—that psychohistorians must take greater account of changes in emotional behavior over time, given the findings of alterations in behavior even in recent centuries—while admitting that certain psychological findings probably do describe human realities that may be immune to change. After all, we are animals with biological constraints; it is curious that many historians and social scientists have ignored biological factors in their studies of emotion. One of the challenges of research in this field is to sort out the durable (animal) from the transient (culturally caused), while juxtaposing both with prevailing emotional standards.

Most studies of the history of emotion, though not all, have dealt far more with emotionology than with emotional experience. Historians have even neglected one of the central lessons of social history, that formal ideas cannot be automatically equated with wider social values, much less with actual feelings, without a good bit of independent verification. This applies to some of the most facile claims, for example, that maternal love is an eighteenth-century invention or that a major shift in the American valuation of love has occurred in the later twentieth century, an interpretation based on reviewing a handful of highbrow movies.[37] The best work has incorporated aspects of emotionology from research in a variety of sources: formal writings on emotion, like those of Protestant theologians in the seventeenth century; more popularized literature, like the sermons directed at family behavior; and resulting behavioral patterns, such as altered courtship practices or the abandonment of swaddling. But there has nevertheless been too much temptation to assert novel emotional experience, on the basis of admittedly novel emotionology, than the facts warrant. More precise historical aperçus may also have been exaggerated. Were families in Plymouth really exempt from anger, as Demos has asserted (or, to allow for human frailty even among new Americans, largely exempt)? Or should the first distinction be, simply, that the unusual values held up for family behavior—the emotionology—expressed the importance of controlling anger in contrast to prevailing European norms, which would have affected judgments of familial anger without necessarily describing emotional experience within families? Because modern emotionology has influenced the location of emotional expression—what can be shown in public and in private—the task of appraising emotion is particularly complex.[38]

The distinction between emotionology and emotional experience suggests a clearer research strategy than most historians have so far pursued. Inquiry into love, anger, jealousy, and fear[39] should begin with the emotionological context, which is more accessible than emotional experience and important in its own right. Emotionology includes behavior, such as courtship, that reflects and is meant to enforce social norms. In the second stage of inquiry historians should attempt to fathom emotional expressions across time, assuming a correspondence between these trends and those of emotionology but alert to the possibility of variance in direction as well as in degree. In some cases historians may be unable to investigate beyond emotionology; certainly most records of emotional expression, such as diaries, will be filtered by prevailing emotionology. Still, only a distinction between emotion and emotionology will produce the best possible evaluations of past emotional experience.

There is a third task, not an analysis of emotionology proper but related to it, which involves examining peoples' efforts to mediate between emotional standards and emotional experience. This subject may be accessible even when changes in emotions cannot be charted, and it plays a role in family history, where anguish over the presence or absence of certain emotions may change more than the emotions themselves. It is much clearer, for example, that guilt over familial anger has risen since the eighteenth century, as the result of new emotionology, than that the frequency and degree of anger have changed. Yet the presence of guilt is itself important, as part of family life and overall emotional experience. This third stage of inquiry can be readily pursued through diaries and other sources, which are likely to reveal reactions to emotion more than emotion itself. In this process emotionology remains partially discrete from a more general interest in popular mentalities. For emotionology interacts with emotional experience, even when it does not describe this experience exactly, and, therefore, can help reveal the relationship of the experience, appropriately filtered, to other behaviors and perceptions in the past.[40]

In addition to anthropologists who have struggled with the relationship between culture and emotion, a few sociologists have worked on a framework appropriate for the differentiation between emotions and emotionology. William Goode, for example, wrote of an emotionological range between viewing love as a reprehensible aberration, as in the East Asian tradition, and viewing love with considerable approval, such that it is mildly shameful to marry without "being in love." But this range does not prevent deliberately loveless marriage in an age that approves the romantic extreme or vigorous love attachments and literary idealizations of love in an age of emotional repression.[41]

Historians themselves have a clear analogue to the necessary distinction between emotion and emotionology in recent findings on sex. Victorian culture is no longer seen as automatically defining Victorian sexual experience, and not only because of the class divisions that long exempted much of the working class from extensive contact with the culture. Both ideals and experience are significant. Sexual ideals influence practice, attitudes toward practice, and institutional arrangements, such as birth control or the treatment of sexual "deviants," but sexual experience, chartable through illegitimacy rates and to an extent through diaries, autobiographies, and other sources, also causes and reflects important social patterns. A full history of sex—to use the term generically—must include both aspects. Similarly, emotionology is itself important even when it does not define emotional expression. Admittedly, it may prove harder to trace emotion than it is to delineate sexual patterns, only because evidence for the latter may be quantifiable, but the quest is not impossible and can be facilitated by a recognition of the distinction between emotions and the criteria used by society to channel and evaluate them.

For example, during the late eighteenth century, the term "tantrum" first came into the language (its origins are unknown but perhaps derive from the Italian dance tarantella). The word was used disapprovingly in reference to angry behavior by adults. During the nineteenth century the term became widespread—though it entered dictionaries only after 1900—and acquired its current meaning, a rage by children or, in adults, a particularly childish fit. Here, clearly, is a significant shift in emotionology, denoting a new awareness of a particular kind of anger and, through awareness, a new ability to disapprove of it or to try to prevent it through socialization. But surely the behavior described by the word was not new, as the simplest equation between emotionology and emotion might imply. Nor has the invention of the word, or socialization practices designed to modify the behavior, led to a demonstrable diminution of the phenomenon. A few permissive child-rearing experts did indeed claim in the late 1940s that tantrums were on the wane, but they offered no evidence, and their assumption may not be open to serious historical investigation. Clearly, a history of the perception of tantrums, though significant, is not likely to be identical to that of childish behavior.[42]

The emotionology-emotion distinction bears on historical periodization. Emotionology changes, and its changes will normally have some impact on emotional experience or perceptions of it. But emotional experience will not only reflect emotionology juxtaposed to psychological constants but also may reveal the impact of developments such as, in the nineteenth century, the separation of work from home. The relationship between emotionology and emotion thus may not be invariable, which is one reason why so many historians have paused at the end of the eighteenth century without extending their investigations into a subsequent period in which emotionology showed substantial continuity, as in recommendations about love and anger, but without the same rapport with actual emotional life. An effort to define the changing links between emotionology and emotion, as each responds to a somewhat different dynamic, may provide the means to approach appropriate periodization in both areas.

Emotionology is also a vital concept in dealing with the complex impact of class and gender (and possibly age) on emotional experience. The dominant emotionology of a society may set norms for men and women (as in the nineteenth century) or for age groups (as in the preindustrial period, when frequent anger and greed were attributed to the elderly). These norms, though important in their effect on perceptions of proper behavior, do not necessarily describe emotional experience. We know that women have felt anger more frequently than modern emotionology, until recently, countenanced. Their behavior and emotional experience may have been influenced by emotionology, as when anger was concealed within family disputes or revealed in hysteria, but their emotions departed from emotionological standards. A similar distinction between values and reality has been demonstrated in contemporary American society by findings that show a boy's temperament much more predictive of adult personality than a girl's; girls' socialization remains more influenced by emotionological standards, which often yield in adult emotional behavior, as angry women bloom from docile girls.[43] In another important case, old people were not necessarily angrier or greedier in past periods when conventional emotionology pointed specifically to these traits, for the emotionology reflected not just experience but also tensions over property that might change independently of any changes in emotional behavior. That emotional labels applied to the elderly began to change in the nineteenth century is important, but it does not prove corresponding emotional change.

With regard to class, emotionology facilitates understanding of the extent to which emotional criteria are purveyed, explicitly or not, by a dominant class culture. A number of the familiar nineteenth-century middle-class criticisms of working-class culture have an emotionological component; for example, workers were judged insufficiently affectionate to wives, children, and animals. Less familiar, but probably more significant, is a twentieth-century effort to extend new middle-class values concerning the control of anger to the judgment and treatment of the working class.[44] In this case the emotionology of a single class can have general social ramifications, without accurately describing the actual emotional experience, or even the emotionology, of other social groups. Analysis of emotionology can enrich an understanding of class efforts to create a dominant culture and can help sort out disputes over "trickle down" theories of emotional change, like those proposed in studies of eighteenth-century England. That the middle class or the aristocracy pioneered emotionological change on the eve of modern times is hardly surprising, but this does not rob lower classes of an emotional culture of their own (yet to be fully fathomed) and definitely requires an assessment of emotional differences among classes, if any, independent of the professed values of the dominant groups. Emotionology can indeed facilitate study of the emotional experience of lower classes by helping isolate an amazingly persistent middle-class bias, even in twentieth-century efforts to examine working-class emotional standards.[45]

Analysis of emotionology does not, of course, automatically resolve problems of assessing class or gender experience. It does not guarantee the availability of sources needed to study emotion or even emotionological subcultures. It does, however, help guard against generalizations derived from inappropriate sources, while providing the kind of distinction between approved values and actual experience that has informed other studies in social history.

The distinction between emotionology and emotion and the resulting stages of research raise two obvious questions: can the history of emotions be directly tapped? And, if it cannot with any definiteness, is emotionology worth attending to?

It is clear that the effort to deal with changes in emotional experience has barely begun, despite some striking claims by historians. Emotions almost surely retain some important biopsychological continuities. Changes are going to be slower and less concrete than historians, who like dramatic upheavals, would prefer. There may not be change in basic emotions at all. Yet emotion has cognitive components that are open to emotionological influences. It is likely—though not inevitable—that emotionological change will normally have some bearing on emotional experience. When romance is discouraged in courtship, for example, there will probably be less romance (although some) in marriage than when it is encouraged, if only because couples lack appropriate expectations or, in some cases, the vocabulary necessary to express them.[46] Even biological components of emotions may change, for example, when the incidence of breast-feeding shifts or the health (therefore the mood?) of the elderly improves. And if emotions change, even subtly, the possible ramifications on other aspects of behavior, including political, are great enough to command serious attention from historians in several fields.

Because distinctions between standards and emotions have not been sufficiently explicit, we do not yet know how much of the history of emotion we can uncover. After a period in which sharp emotional distinctions were drawn by historians, we seem now to be moving into a revisionist phase in which substantial continuity is stressed. Thus, recent examinations of diaries conclude that reactions to grief have not changed from the nineteenth to the twentieth century and that parental love for children was as lively in the sixteenth century as in the nineteenth.[47] Another interpretation urges that emotional variables play an important role in history, even influencing political behavior, without being subject to change over time. Philip Greven, though once arguing that emotional styles did shift toward a more loving approach to the child,[48] recently pointed to the importance of group variation within a time period, which he treated as more significant than an effort to establish change.[49] Greven saw three fundamental emotional styles present in American families by the late eighteenth century, which have not clearly shifted over time; at most, the balance among them may have altered but in a cyclical fashion more than in long-term changes in direction. This interpretation needs to be tested, of course, in other time periods; as a theoretical construct it has not been fully developed. But its assumptions are conceivable in principle; it correctly calls attention to subgroup variations in emotion that may display greater continuity than do the presumed standards of "society" at large. And Greven's own work demonstrates that the search for key emotional groupings, in a single period, has important implications for a national history.

Efforts to get at emotions, particularly when introducing continuities or complexities not discernible at the strictly emotionological level, have relied heavily on evidence found in diaries. Whether this evidence is representative, and whether it is sufficiently free from emotionological filters, is questionable. Ideally, a history of emotion must use diaries and autobiographies in combination with other sources, including literary portrayals of emotion (though these may primarily reflect the dominant emotionology), other commentaries on emotional expressions in family, work, or leisure life, and, with due caution, behavioral indexes, such as the rates and tenor of protest. A combination of these kinds of sources suggests, for example, real change in the emotional experience of work in the twentieth-century United States, though the suggestion falls short of absolute proof and does not indicate what happens to emotions displaced from the job site.[50] Just as it is interesting that the first studies of emotions posited unduly sharp shifts in experience, based on emotionological change, so it is important to note that recent efforts to demonstrate continuities—maternal love is maternal love all along—hardly commend themselves by the variety of data they have employed. The jury on emotional change, it is fair to say, is still out.

If the task before us in dealing with emotional shifts is difficult, and inevitably somewhat tentative, it is particularly arduous in the study of emotions among the lower classes. Here, commentary by outsiders is almost always biased by emotionological standards. Even the relevant emotional values preached in working-class families—whether followed or not—are not always clear. But the difficulty of examining basic emotions should not, at least as yet, deter the attempt. Careful use of a multiplicity of sources, aided by the distinction between emotional values and emotional experience, may yield clearer signposts than we have to date. It is unwise and unnecessary to use difficulty as an excuse for neglect of a basic ingredient of human history. Nor should problems in studying emotion deter us from continued inquiry into emotionology at various social levels—a subject important in its own right.

In the first place, emotionology is not some simple if specialized artifact of intellectual history. It is clearly influenced by formal ideas, as the work on eighteenth-century love has amply demonstrated. But one challenge in the study of emotionology is to place intellectual aspects in a larger cultural context. Thus, a strictly intellectual history of romantic love logically begins with the tradition of courtly love,[51] but it is most unlikely that a history of emotionology should do so. For the tradition of courtly love, though reechoed in some Renaissance literature, simply did not penetrate far enough into popular culture or into institutional arrangements to count as a genuine emotionology. Similarly, in our own century, an expert, sociological critique of romantic love as the basis for marriage clearly cannot be equated with emotionology, which has largely resisted the hostility of experts.[52] We still manifest a widespread cultural assumption of love before marriage, and for the most part we have institutions to match. A serious shortcoming in Christopher Lasch's challenging comment on recent emotional and familial change is the assumption that a history of ideas about the family, including familial emotion, adds up to a widely shared culture.[53]

In the study of emotionology, in other words, many of the dilemmas involved in bridging the gap between intellectual and social history, which occur and have been studied in other areas, are repeated. Therefore, although emotionology does help relate ideas and popular culture to a powerful theme in human life, it provides no simple equation. The emotionology of a society often responds to economic or demographic change, for example, in efforts to change the valuation of anger to correspond to corporate personnel requirements[54] or in the impact on the emotions of love and grief of changes in child mortality. The best statements of causation in the field thus far have intermingled religious and intellectual change with a sense of shifting organizational context. In this sense emotionology, relating so closely to basic human reactions (though, of course, not necessarily constituting these reactions), pulls together a number of strands of fundamental historical change, at least in certain periods in which key values are in flux.[55]

More important still, emotionology has an impact on other areas of social behavior, apart from any effect it may have on emotions themselves. This is true in the evolution of the modern family, which serves as a center for emotional expression. The rise of divorce (along with other factors) thus mirrors expectations of love in marriage and sometimes low tolerance for the expression of anger in marriage—attitudes, in other words, that follow from a dominant emotionology. Divorce itself, in the twentieth century, is one of the (relatively few?) rituals where the expression of intense anger is readily tolerated. No historian could presume to explain the history of divorce solely by an examination of the impact of emotionology on the family, but none can avoid the topic. Emotionology concerning one set of family relationships may affect others. Thus, romantic love between couples may have followed, emotionologically, from an earlier change in child-rearing standards, as romantic love was essential to permit children to free themselves from what was assumed to be the power of the parental emotional orbit.[56] A more recent suggestion, applied to twentieth-century society, is that romantic love is essential in an individualistic, market-oriented society, because of the irrationality of marriage yet society's need for procreation. This may seem more frivolous.[57] But the force of emotionology in various aspects of family life does remind us of the power of economically irrational behavior in modern history, some of which is spurred and justified by emotionology itself.

Even beyond family dynamics, emotionology has implications that must be explored. The decline in the acceptability of job-based anger for many workers in the twentieth century is no abstract issue, for a host of new techniques in personnel management, such as the retraining of foremen and personality testing, have arisen to express and deal with this change. These trends in themselves alter the work experience. They may relate to a decline in per capita rates of work-based protest.[58] From the viewpoint of employers, when worker discontent becomes emotionologically unacceptable and not just unacceptable in terms of economic implications or attacks on the power structure, mechanisms to deal with unrest, and reactions to unrest once it occurs, may need to be altered. Thus, that white-collar workers are held to different emotional standards than are blue-collar workers plays a role in the management of labor.[59] Certainly there is a fascinating, and linguistically quite precise, correspondence between mid-twentieth-century emotionological trends and Barrington Moore's claim that a decline in "moral indignation" has occurred in contemporary society.[60]

Emotionology surely contributes to definitions of deviance. Expectations of a loving relationship between parents and children affected perceptions of wayward children in the nineteenth century. In our own day, we are urged to tighten our definitions of male sexual aggression in part because of new ideas about anger. The aggressive behaviors had not previously been approved as outlets for anger, but they were not so clearly labeled as unacceptably deviant as they are now.[61]

Emotionology may even relate to trends in the social history of health. Some anthropological evidence exists of a relationship between the most salient targets of disapproval in child rearing and the dominant diseases that arouse concern.[62] If child rearing targets certain emotions for disapproval, might the effect not be explored in a mutual relationship to popular health concerns? Here the rise of new levels of concern about anger in child rearing, particularly in recent decades, parallels the concern for "choleric" diseases of heart and arteries.

Changes in emotionology are related to other important shifts in a society. They describe not only formal intellectual outlook—which can be important in its own right—but also many of the expectations people have about their own emotional behavior, many of the disappointments they perceive at expectations unfulfilled, and many of the reactions they offer to the emotional behavior of others. Changes in the emotionology of anger, for example, easily spill over into reactions to the styles of religious or political leaders, even if actual emotional experience is in the most basic sense unaffected. Thus, in the twentieth-century United States, while anger in politics may not have diminished, its acceptable forms of expression have tightened, which affects the ability of the political process to convey intense feeling. This interaction between values and behavior most clearly distinguishes emotionology from the history of ideas and demonstrates the importance of emotionology to cultural history.

Emotionology also affects the targeting of emotions—the selection of what people or things are appropriate for particular emotional expressions—not only expressions of affection but also anger, fear, even greed. Again this effect can be independent of some actual change in emotional levels. In the eighteenth century, the emotion and expression of love were not necessarily more frequent or more intense than before, but they were concentrated more strictly on family— at least by men. Anger in the twentieth century has not necessarily declined, but, because of emotionological guidance enforced by institutional arrangements particularly in the workplace, men and women have sought new outlets. And shifts in emotional targets are important historical developments in their own right.

In sum, emotionology spurs a variety of personal and institutional arrangements, serving as a factor in definitions of leisure—witness the popularity of boxing at the turn of the century as an approved device for channeling anger[63]— and politics as well as more intimate relationships. By coloring the way one's own emotions and the emotions of others are judged, and by encouraging selection of some emotional targets over others, emotionology can serve as a powerful force in shaping the behavior of individuals and groups. Even changes in the ability to articulate emotional experiences—itself an important development in recent centuries in Western society—alter the way life is perceived and experienced.[64]

Finally, emotionology may well relate to emotion. If historians preserve the initial distinction between the two in their research strategies, they can test for correspondence, even though such correspondence cannot be assumed and may, as suggested above, vary over time.[65] But emotion itself has a cognitive element, combining raw feeling—the "elementary subjective experience"—with judgment and perception, through which an individual evaluates, labels, and controls his feelings.[66] For example, research has shown that biologically similar generalized arousal states are labeled as different emotions depending on the subjects' understanding of the situation that led to the arousal. If emotions were merely glandular or hormonal reactions, they might well not have a history, though even here reactions seem to vary with historically changing factors such as crowding. Despite continued dispute over the appropriate definition of emotions, a substantial consensus exists that emotions are not simply biological reactions but also involve an interplay between body and mind. This is why emotionology legitimately opens the way to a second phase in research, into emotional experience and its possible changes over time.

The study of historical change in emotional values and, to the extent possible and legitimate, in emotional experience itself is ripe for further examination. To be sure, some historians—both traditionalists in political history and practitioners of the new social history—will still prefer their subjects coldly rational, unswayed by considerations of passion.[67] But even the rationalists must be interested in emotionology as a guide to or manipulator of behavior. And, in fact, more is involved. Emotional experience may change over time, and emotional evaluations and targeting certainly change—in changing, they reflect important historical shifts and cause others. Hence, the inquiry, with the definitional distinctions that encourage precision, should proceed.

And this additional inquiry can and should range widely. Recent work has focused on love, understandably enough given our own emotional standards and the desirability of tracing their origins. But there is a need for fuller analysis of other emotions. The possibility of examining anger seems increasingly obvious, for, although the historians of love have tended to assume that anger decreases when recommendations for loving relationships increase, the emotionology of anger has had more interesting deviations than this formula can embrace. Fear, jealousy, joy, and greed merit assessment as well. The rise of an emphasis on love, for example, may have heightened the potential for jealousy, and demographic changes, reducing the number of children per family, may have had the same effect. Yet the desire to see the family as a warm emotional unit may have complicated the expression of jealousy—hence, among other things, the eventual modern fascination with sibling rivalry. Fear may have taken on new meaning, if not in actual experience at least in emotionology, as physical punishment declined and the threat of loss of love loomed larger. The declining use of bogeymen as threats to children and the rise of surrogate sources of fear in twentieth-century children's media and even amusement parks offer considerable scope for historical assessment.[68] We have only begun to fathom the overall emotionological framework, even for modern Western history.

Emotionology also involves standards for emotional behavior outside as well as within the family. To date researchers have needlessly avoided examining emotional standards in work, recreation, and community relations, at least in studies of the eighteenth century onward. Nonfamilial emotions have received only passing comment in assessments of earlier periods—observations of high levels of angry bickering among neighbors or the affectionate attachments encouraged, before Protestantism, among male friends. Without question, the focus on family in more recent emotionology captures an important truth—that many modern people attempted to differentiate between family, which was a haven for emotional intensity, and other relationships, which were to be dominated by sweet reason. Yet at least implicit emotional standards affected nonfamily spheres. The shift in emotionology, toward a more intense focus on the family, almost surely played a role by the later nineteenth century in one key work area— growing confusion over the employment of domestic servants as all parties became less sure of appropriate emotional styles.[69] Some have argued, though mainly on the basis of formal literature, that a shift in the predominant emotional styles of male friendships accompanied the new emotionology of the family, a chord that echoes in some recent critiques of male style.[70] At the same time the relationship between the new family focus and acceptable emotions in women's friendships seems to have been different.[71]

As the larger emotional context is explored, even within the family, by examination of new valuations of emotions like anger and jealousy, the need for extension to extrafamilial settings becomes even more apparent. At what point, if ever, did the standards of anger control newly developed within the family extend to other relationships? When industrial psychologists like Elton Mayo tried to find new devices to limit (and to explain) anger in the workplace, were they not expressing their chagrin at the apparent disjuncture between middle-class emotional values and what they saw in the labor force?[72] A full sense of emotionology and emotion alike dictates examination of changes in emotional standards in a wide variety of areas of social interaction.

By extending the aspects of emotional experience and range of emotions covered and, conjointly, by extending existing findings about emotionological change and its links to emotional experience, historians can, finally, contribute to a richer understanding of the past and a more sophisticated grasp of human psychology. Emotions have been inadequately studied in the behavioral sciences, after a flurry of interest following the work of Darwin and then Freud. Recent work reflects uncertainty about defining emotion itself and about identifying those emotions that are discrete and fundamental—hence, the call for historical inquiry into past psychological theories. But psychological theories do not reflect an adequate sense of the subjection of emotional values to the cultural factors of time and place. Thus, contemporary laboratory research into the experience of feeling anger reports uniform discomfort with the emotion.[73] Is this a constant, as the researchers assume, or the result of a particular culture, in which most anger is disapproved and bodily sensations that might be related to heart or arteries particularly feared? Why, in Homeric culture, could the sensation of anger be termed "sweeter than honey"?[74] Historians can play an active role in grasping a phenomenon demonstrably difficult to grasp and adequately described by no single theory of human behavior.

Much of the historical contribution lies in the future, despite the exciting and provocative start that has been made. Issues of periodization, of the range of emotions beyond love, and of standards for emotion beyond family largely remain to be explored. The concept of emotionology, introducing greater subtlety and greater initial caution into historical inquiry, seems at this point an essential methodological tool. Investigation of emotionological history is itself demanding and has great potential for illuminating aspects of the past and the linkage between past and present. Further probes beyond emotionology, into emotional change, may well be possible if premised on the two-step process of conceptualization and research.

NOTES

1 Paul R. Kleinginna, Jr., and Anne M. Kleinginna, "A Categorized List of Emotion Definitions, with Suggestions for a Consensual Definition," *Motivation and Emotion*, 5(1981):345–79, esp. 354–59.

2 In particular, anthropologists have long grappled with the problem of the influence of culture on emotional experience and expression; we are urging a similar, and more explicit, effort on the part of historians. See, for example, Ruth Benedict, *Patterns of Culture* (New York, 1961); John W. M. Whiting and Irwin L. Child, *Child Training and Personality* (New Haven, 1953); and Joel R. Davitz, *The Language of Emotion* (New York, 1969). Recent sociological inquiry has shown a revival of interest in cultural norms, which one author has termed "feeling rules." See Arlie Russell Hochschild, *The Managed Heart: Commercialization of Human Feeling* (Berkeley and Los Angeles, 1983).

3 Briggs, *Never in Anger: Portrait of an Eskimo Family* (Cambridge, Mass., 1970).

4 Randolph Trumbach, "Europe and Its Families: A Review Essay of Lawrence Stone, *The Family, Sex, and Marriage in England, 1500–1800*," in *Journal of Social History* [hereafter, *JSH*], 13(1979):136.

5 Abram de Swaan, "The Politics of Agoraphobia: On Changes in Emotional and Relational Management," *Theory and Society*, 10(1981):359–85.

6 Richard L. Schoenwald, review of Robert J. Brugger, ed., *Our Selves/Our Past: Psychological Approaches to American History*, in *Social Science History*, 7(1983):345–47.

7 Lawrence Stone, *The Family, Sex, and Marriage in England, 1500–1800* (New York, 1977); and Christopher Lasch, *Haven in a Heartless World: The Family Besieged* (New York, 1977).

8 Zeldin, "Personal History and the History of the Emotions," *JSH*, 15(1982):339–48.
9 Arnold H. Buss and Ann Burkee, "An Inventory for Assessing Different Kinds of Hostility," *Journal of Consulting Psychology*, 21(1957):343–44; and Albert Rothenberg, "On Anger," *American Journal of Psychiatry*, 128(1971):454–60.
10 Febvre, *A New Kind of History*, ed. Peter Burke and trans. F. Folca (New York, 1973), 9. On the implementation of Febvre's idea, principally by French historians, including Febvre himself, Georges Duby, and others, see Stuart Clark, "French Historians and Early Modern Popular Culture," *Past and Present*, 100(1983):62–99; Alphonse Dupront, "Problèms et méthods d'une histoire de la psychologie collective," *Annales-Economies, Sociétés, Civilisations*, 16(1961):3–11; Duby, "Histoire des mentalités," in C. Samaran, ed., *L'histoire et ses méthodes* (Paris, 1961), 937–66; and Jacques Le Goff, "Les mentalités: Une histoire ambiguë," in Jacques Le Goff and P. Nora, eds., *Faire de l'histoire*, 3 (Paris, 1974):76–94.
11 George F. E. Rudé, *The Crowd in History, 1730–1848* (New York, 1964); Tilly et al., *The Rebellious Century, 1830–1930* (Cambridge, Mass., 1975); and Tilly, *From Mobilization to Revolution* (Reading, Mass., 1978).
12 Joan Wallach Scott, "History of the Family as an Affective Unit," *Social History*, 4(1979):509–16.
13 Peter Laslett, *The World We Have Lost* (New York, 1965); Philip J. Greven, Jr., *Four Generations: Population, Land, and Family in Colonial Andover, Massachusetts* (Ithaca, N.Y., 1970); David Hackett Fischer, *Growing Old in America* (New York, 1977); Daniel Scott Smith, "Accounting for Change in other Families of the Elderly in the United States, 1900 to the Present," paper presented at the Conference on the Elderly in a Bureaucratic Society, Case Western Reserve University, Cleveland, Ohio, April 1983; and Suzanne Pacuad and M. D. Lahalle, *Attitudes, comportments, opinions des personnes âgées dans le cadre de la famille moderne* (Paris, 1969).
14 Maria Vinovskis, "From Household Size to the Life Course: Some Observations on Recent Trends in Family History," *American Behavioral Scientist*, 21(1977):263–88.
15 Robert V. Wells, "Family Size and Fertility Control in Eighteenth-Century America," *Population Studies*, 25(1971):73–82.
16 Demos, *A Little Commonwealth: Family Life in Plymouth Colony* (New York, 1970), chap. 9. Also see Lloyd DeMause, ed., *The History of Childhood* (New York, 1974).
17 David Hunt, *Parents and Children in History: The Psychology of Family Life in Early Modern France* (New York, 1970); Jean-Louise Flandrin, *Families in Former Times: Kinship, Household, and Sexuality*, trans. Richard Southern (Cambridge, 1979).
18 Shorter, *The Making of the Modern Family* (New York, 1975); Stone, *Family, Sex, and Marriage*; and Elisabeth Badinter, *L'Amour en plus: Histoire de l'amour maternal (17ᵉ–20ᵉ siècles)* (Paris, 1980).
19 Randolph Trumbach, *The Rise of the Egalitarian Family: Aristocratic Kinship and Domestic Relations in Eighteenth-Century England*, (New York, 1978); J. H. Plumb, "The New World of Children in Eighteenth Century England," *Past and Present*, 67(1975):64–95; Stone, *Family, Sex, and Marriage*; and Shorter, *Making of the Modern Family*. Also see, for the special issue on the history of love, *JSH*, 15, no. 3(1982). Inevitably, the new findings about eighteenth-century emotional change are not, in fact, entirely new. Some time ago Norbett Elias discussed the emotional vagaries of premodern European society, noting the frequency of flashes of temper. His assessment of the rise of more genteel manners, though focused primarily on habits of politeness in dining and so forth, obviously relates to changing emotional expressions in social relationships, including a new effort to discipline temper and adopt a more consistently affectionate tone. See Elias, *The Civilizing Process: The History of Manners*, trans. Edmund Jephcott (New York, 1978), esp. 190–203.
20 Wells, "Family Size and Fertility Control"; Philippe Ariès, *Centuries of Childhood: A Social History of Family Life* (New York, 1962); Plumb, "New World of Children"; and Philip J.

306 Peter N. Stearns with Carol Z. Stearns

Greven, Jr., *The Protestant Temperament: Patterns of Child-Rearing, Religious Experience, and the Self in Early America* (New York, 1977).

21 Trumbach, *Rise of the Egalitarian Family.*

22 Keith Thomas, *Man and the Natural World: A History of the Modern Sensibility* (New York, 1983).

23 Edmund Leites, "The Duty to Desire: Love, Friendship, and Sexuality in Some Puritan Theories of Marriage," *JSH*, 15(1982):383–408; and Flandrin, *Families in Former Times*, 238–39.

24 Ellen K. Rothman, "Sex and Self-Control: Middle-Class Courtship in America, 1770–1870," *JSH*, 15(1982):409–26; and Patricia Branca, *Silent Sisterhood: Middle-Class Women in the Victorian Home* (London, 1975), 122–29. But Zeldin's portrait of the French bourgeois family complicates this pattern by introducing an important national variant; Zeldin, *France, 1848–1945*, volume 1: *Ambition, Love, and Politics* (Oxford, 1973).

25 Bernard Wishy, *The Child and the Republic* (Philadelphia, 1968); and R. Gordon Kelly, *Mother Was a Lady: Self and Society in Selected American Children's Periodicals, 1865–1890* (Westport, Conn., 1974).

26 Lasch, *Haven in a Heartless World.*

27 Paul C. Rosenblatt, *Bitter, Bitter Tears: Nineteenth-Century Diarists and Twentieth-Century Grief Theories* (Minneapolis, 1983).

28 What we suggest here is a balance—its exact dimensions to be determined by careful analysis of data—between the overly categorical claims of the sociobiologists for eternal biological characteristics and the overly sharp claims made recently by some historians that virtual reversals in emotional experience have occurred. Edward O. Wilson, *On Human Nature* (Cambridge, Mass., 1978), and *Sociobiology: The New Synthesis* (Cambridge, Mass., 1975). Our suggestion fits the effort at a humanistic reconciliation of both positions in Kenneth Bock's *Human Nature and History: A Response to Sociobiology* (New York, 1980), 184–85. For a recent historical contribution on emotional constants, see Linda A. Pollock, *Forgotten Children: Parent-Child Relations from 1500 to 1900* (Cambridge, 1984).

29 Barbara J. Harris, "Marriage Sixteenth-Century Style: Elizabeth Stafford and the Third Duke of Norfolk," *JSH*, 15(1892):371–82.

30 Michael MacDonald, *Mystical Bedlam: Madness, Anxiety, and Healing in Seventeenth-Century England* (New York, 1981).

31 Zeldin, *France, 1848–1945*, 1:128; and Evelyne Sullerot, *Women, Society, and Change*, trans. M. Archer (New York, 1971).

32 Mirra Komarovsky, *Blue-Collar Marriage* (New York, 1964); and Peter Willmott and Michael Young, *Family and Kinship in East London* (New York, 1957).

33 Trumbach, "Europe and Its Families," 139.

34 See Stone, *Family, Sex, and Marriage*, 451. Here, and in much of what follows, the discussion of anger is drawn from a forthcoming book on anger in American history, by Carol Z. Stearns and Peter N. Stearns, entitled *Anger: The Struggle for Emotional Control in America's History* (Chicago, 1986).

35 Edward P. Thompson, review of Lawrence Stone's *The Family, Sex, and Marriage in England, 1500–1800*, in *New Society*, 8 (1977):499–501.

36 Herman W. Roodenburg, "The Autobiography of Isabella de Moerloose: Sex, Childrearing, and Popular Belief in Seventeenth-Century Holland," *JSH*, 18(1985):517–40. This study shows the clear presence of maternal love in a premodern family, but it was combined with unembarrassed (if to the child disconcerting) flashes of maternal rage that add up to an emotional package different from what contemporary emotionology would lead us to expect.

37 Ann Swidler, "Love and Adulthood in American Culture," in Neil Smelser and Erik Erikson, eds., *Themes of Work and Love in Adulthood* (Cambridge, Mass., 1980), 120–50; and Badinter, *L'amour en plus.*

38 George R. Bach and Peter Wyden, *The Intimate Enemy: How to Fight Fair in Love and Marriage* (New York, 1968), 17–34. Also see the chapter on family in Stearns and Stearns, *Anger.*

39 Jean Delumeau, *La peur en Occident, XIVe–XVIIIe siècles: Une cité assiégée* (Paris, 1978); Jacques LeBrun, *La peur* (Paris, 1979); and Madeleine Läik, *La peur qu'on a* (Paris, 1979).

40 Emotionology in this sense is more than a word-saving term that eliminates the necessity of repeating phrases like "ideas about fear" or "the popular culture of jealousy." When applied to religious experience, recreation, and popular art, it can be more precisely linked with discrete emotions than can other, more general terms. Excellent studies of premodern mentalities that undeniably describe some emotional content are thus somewhat different, pending a more grandiose synthesis, from studies of emotionology. For example, Johan Huizinga and Max Weber, in their classic works, described popularized intellectual moods, or mentalities, that may feed on emotionology, or derive from it, but they dealt with more purely cognitive or aesthetic reactions—reactions more fully linked to formal culture—than real emotionology entails. See Huizinga, *The Waning of the Middle Ages* (New York, 1955); and Weber, *The Protestant Ethic and the Spirit of Capitalism* (New York, 1977). On other studies that use emotion as part of mentalities, see the reference in note 10 above.

41 Goode, "The Theoretical Importance of Love," *American Sociological Review*, 24(1959):38–47.

42 Leon Kanner, *In Defense of Mothers* (New York, 1944), 37; Dorothy W. Baruch, *New Ways in Discipline: You and Your Child Today* (New York, 1949), 7, 45, 61; Dory Metcalf, *Bringing Up Children* (New York, 1947); and Marion J. Radke, *The Relation of Parental Authority to Children's Behavior and Attitudes* (Minneapolis, 1946), 11–12. Also see the chapters on child rearing in Stearns and Stearns, *Anger*.

43 Jerome Kagan and H. A. Moss, *Birth to Maturity: A Study of Psychological Development* (New York, 1962).

44 Loren Baritz, *The Servants of Power: A History of the Use of Social Science in American Industry* (Middletown, Conn., 1960). Also see the chapter on work in Stearns and Stearns, *Anger*.

45 Daniel R. Miller and Guy Swanson, *The Changing American Parent: A Study in the Detroit Area* (New York, 1964). For some questions about class stereotypes in sociological research on emotional styles, see M. R. Yarrow et al., *Child-Rearing: An Inquiry into Research Methods* (San Francisco, 1968).

46 Recent research on emotions indicates that the cognitive framework within which one classifies an experience affects the emotion, even its autonomic manifestations. For a summary of this phenomenon, see Kleinginna and Kleinginna, "Categorized List of Emotion Definitions," 350. In fact, some of the most promising recent work on the psychotherapy of depression stresses restructuring the patient's cognitive style to teach him to think about his experiences more positively. This, in itself, has helped cure patients overwhelmed by depressive emotions. In view of the Freudian assumptions that underlie most American social sciences, it behooves us to be aware that thought may influence feeling as well as the reverse. See A. John Rush and Donna E. Giles, "Cognitive Therapy: Theory and Research," in A. John Rush, ed., *Short-Term Psychotherapies for Depression* (New York, 1892), 143–81.

47 Pollock, *Forgotten Children;* and Rosenblatt, *Bitter, Bitter Tears*. For more strictly emotionological evidence, see Steven Ozment, *When Fathers Ruled: Family Life in Reformation Europe* (Cambridge, Mass., 1983).

48 Greven, ed., *Childrearing Concepts, 1628–1861* (Itasca, Ill., 1973).

49 Greven, *Protestant Temperament*.

50 Baritz, *The Servants of Power;* and Hochschild, *Managed Heart*.

51 Herman R. Lantz, "Romantic Love in the Pre-Modern Period: A Social Commentary," *JSH*, 15(1982):349–70.

52 William L. Kolb, "Sociologically Established Norms and Democratic Values," *Social Forces*, 26(1948):451–56; and Ronald L. Howard, *A Social History of American Family Sociology, 1865–1940* (Westport, Conn., 1981).

53 Lasch, *The Culture of Narcissism* (New York, 1979), and *Haven in a Heartless World*.

54 Miller and Swanson, *Changing American Parent;* Susan Porter Benson, "The Clerking Sisterhood: Rationalization and the Work Culture of Saleswomen in American Department Stores, 1980–1960," in James Green, ed., *Workers' Struggles, Past and Present: A Radical American Reader* (Philadelphia, 1983), 101–07; and Hochschild, *Managed Heart.* On economic factors in eighteenth-century emotionological change, see Edward Shorter, "Illegitimacy, Sexual Revolution, and Social Change in Modern Europe," *Journal of Interdisciplinary History,* 2(1971–72):237–72; Benjamin Nelson, *The Idea of Usury* (Chicago, 1969); and Leites, "The Duty to Desire," 383–408.

55 Nelson, *Idea of Usury;* and de Swaan, "Politics of Agoraphobia." Walter J. Ong has plausibly argued that rising literacy rates cause new emotional standards, though he offers no direct emotionological evidence. He almost surely erred in implying a uniform emotional style for preliterate peoples. Ong, *Orality and Literacy: The Technology of the Word* (London, 1982).

56 Good, "Importance of Love," 38–41.

57 S. M. Greenfield, "Love and Marriage in Modern America," *Sociological Quarterly,* 6(1965):361–77.

58 De Swaan, "Politics of Agorphobia."

59 C. Wright Mills, *White Collar: The American Middle Classes* (New York, 1953); Mary C. H. Niles, *Middle Management: The Job of the Junior Administrator* (New York, 1941), 72–93; and William H. Whyte, Jr., *The Organization Man* (New York, 1956), 276.

60 Moore, *Injustice: The Social Basis of Obedience and Revolt* (New York, 1978), 500–02. Richard Solomon has described efforts to rouse and manipulate anger, as part of new political protest, in a culture traditionally hostile to angry expression. See Solomon, *Mao's Political Revolution and the Chinese Political Culture* (Berkeley and Los Angeles, 1971), 289–94.

61 Much of the male liberationist literature of the past fifteen years criticizes the presumed sources of unacceptable male anger. For an explicitly feminist discussion, see Jean Baker Miller, *The Construction of Anger in Women and Men* (Wellesley, Mass., 1983), 5–7. The effort to extend the problems attributable to male anger is obvious in the currently fashionable explanation of sexual crimes. See Dolf Zillman and Jennings Bryant, "Pornography, Sexual Callousness, and the Trivialization of Rape," *Journal of Communication,* 14(1982):10–21.

62 Whiting and Child, *Child Training and Personality.*

63 American Institute of Child Life, *The Problem of Temper* (Philadelphia, 1914); and G. Stanley Hall, "A Study of Anger," *American Journal of Psychology,* 10(1899):586.

64 Thus, until the seventeenth century, much emotional distress, when perceived by upper-class patients, was reported as melancholia. In contemporary Western societies, this low-level sadness or anxiety is associated particularly with an uneducated minority. More "sophisticated" people rarely suffer from the rather general symptoms of melancholia, in part because of greater ability to articulate different aspects of emotional experience. This ability is itself an important product of emotionological change over the past several centuries. See Ong, *Orality and Literacy;* and MacDonald, *Mystical Bedlam.*

65 Goode, "Importance of Love."

66 Kleinginna and Kleinginna, "Categorized List of Emotion Definitions," 350; and Joseph R. Royce and Stephen R. Diamond, "A Multifactor-System Dynamics Theory of Emotion," *Motivation and Emotion,* 4(1981):263–98.

67 Gertrude Himmelfarb, "The Rule of Reason," *Harper's,* April 1984, pp. 84–90.

68 Delumeau, *La Peur en Occident;* and Roodneburg, "Autobiography of Isabella de Moerloose."

69 David M. Katzman, *Seven Days a Week: Women and Domestic Servants in Industrializing America* (New York, 1978); Daniel E. Sutherland, *Americans and Their Servants: Domestic Service in the United States from 1800 to 1920* (Baton Rouge, 1981); Catherine E. Beecher, *Treatise on Domestic Economy* (Boston, 1841), 122, 134–40; and Faye E. Dudden, *Serving Women: Household Service in Nineteenth-Century America* (Middletown, Conn., 1983).

70 Nelson, *Idea of Usury*, 139–63; Marc Fasteau, *The Male Machine* (New York, 1974); and Joseph Pleck and Jack Sawyer, ed., *Men and Masculinity* (Englewood Cliffs, N.J., 1974).

71 Carol Smith-Rosenberg, "The Female World of Love and Ritual: Relations between Women in Nineteenth-Century America," *Signs: Journal of Women in Culture and Society*, 1(1975):1–29.

72 Mayo, *The Human Problems of an Industrial Civilization* (New York, 1933), 84. For some similar reactions to workplace anger, see Frederick W. Taylor, *Shop Management* (New York, 1911), and *The Principles of Scientific Management* (New York, 1911).

73 For a summary of commonplaces about the discomfort anger causes, and a brief suggestion of a corrective, see Donald K. Fromme and Clayton S. O'Brien, "A Dimensional Approach to the Circular Ordering of the Emotions," *Motivation and Emotion*, 6(1982):343.

74 "Sweeter wrath is by far than the honeycomb dripping with sweetener, and spreads through the hearts of men"; Homer, *Iliad* 9:109. The abridged quotation is cited by G. Stanley Hall, with qualified approval, in his study of adolescence; Hall, *Adolescence*, 2 (New York, 1904):370.

Part III
Bibliography

Psychohistory is mostly psychobiography: perhaps as little as twenty percent of psychohistory is concerned with social and group movements. The reason is not far to seek. The dominant form of psychohistory is, as we have noted, psychoanalysis—which emphasizes the role of the individual. Yet Freud himself was intrigued with the possibility of extending psychoanalytic principles to society at large, as he demonstrated in both *Group Psychology and the Analysis of the Ego* (New York, 1959) and *Totem and Taboo* (New York, 1960). Freud postulated that groups tend to act through libidinal ties to their leaders because groups undergo collective regressions to an earlier mental stage dominated by a tyrannical father. Through identification, groups thus substitute for the lost father a leader. This attempt to apply a collective psychoanalysis to previous societies has been critically received by Fred Weinstein and Gerald Platt who argue that its theoretical orientation is ahistorical. Freud, they believe, undervalued the realities of the external world. See their argument in detail in *Psychoanalytic Sociology* (Baltimore, 1973) and a shorter restatement in "The Coming Crisis in Psychohistory," *Journal of Modern History,* vol. 47 (June 1975), pp. 202–28.

In spite of obvious difficulties in applying psychodynamic theory to groups, there have been some brave attempts. In most cases, the effort is related to establishing a connection between leaders and groups. The major question, simply put, is: do leaders represent some deep yearning in social groups as Freud believed? And what is the precise link between leader and group? Peter Loewenberg uses the sociological concept of the cohort in combination with psychodynamic theory to suggest an answer for Nazi Germany. German boys, whose fathers were absent as soldiers during World War I, experienced a heightened Oedipal conflict by idealizing the absent father as a heroic warrior. When the fathers returned after the war and displaced the sons, disillusionment set in. Economic dislocation and political insecurity during the interwar period prompted an unconscious longing to recapture the idealized father image of their earlier youth: they found it in Hitler. Loewenberg's argument may be traced in "The Psychohistorical Origins of the Nazi Youth Cohort," *American Historical Review,* vol. 76 (1971), pp. 1457–1502.

The idea of an individual as a psychological symbol for a generation is the theme of a very different time and place in Michael Rogin's *Fathers and Children* (New York, 1976). Rogin depicts Andrew Jackson as a representative for white America's hostile attitude toward its Indian population in the early nineteenth century. Acting out his own rage originating in a paternal deprivation from his childhood, Jackson warred vigorously against the Indians: he won support from Americans who saw Indians as errant children needing the chastening hand of parents. Rogin's method is scrutinized carefully and found wanting by Lewis Parry in his review essay, *History and Theory,* vol. XVI, no. 2 (1977), pp. 174–95. Similar to Rogin's metaphoric notion of a whole society under analysis is George Forgie's *Patricide in the House Divided* (New York, 1979). Here, Abraham Lincoln is seen as the representative type, around whom the psychological needs of an entire generation may coalesce. Mid-nineteenth-century America believed that it lived in a lesser age than the heroic times of the founding fathers. Reverence for the fathers combined, however, with an unconscious realization that freedom from them was necessary to achieve identity and maturity. Only a breaking of the bondage through a bloody civil war could settle psychological accounts. This is clearly an Oedipal analogy. Lincoln, who had put a psychological distance between himself and his own father, likewise symbolically abandoned the founding fathers. In his speeches he gave voice to the conflicted emotions of his generation: thus he helped prepare the nation for war.

Seymour Byman takes a different psychological tack. He is not concerned with the roles of leader and led, but rather with collective behavior. In the actions of Protestant martyrs during Tudor times, he finds consistently compulsive ritual actions as the martyrs faced death at the hands of hostile lay authorities. Relying on the psychoanalytic literature of Freud, Erikson, and Fenichel, Byman believes their rituals, such as kissing the stake and extolling the virtues of God at the hour of death, were a way of allaying anxiety and guilt over their acceptance of martyrdom—an act that came perilously close to suicide, proscribed by the church. In his study, Byman avoids Freud's attribution of primordial urges to group behavior. Byman's argument is in "Ritualistic Acts and Compulsive Behavior: The Pattern of Tudor Martyrdom," *American Historical Review,* vol. 83, no. 2 (June 1978), pp. 625–43).

As Asher suggests in the readings above, non-psychoanalytic methods may prove ultimately more suitable to the study of group behavior in the past. Most appropriate would likely be some form of social psychology, but surprisingly little has been attempted thus far. Historian Richard Raack applies Leon Festinger's theory of cognitive dissonance to explain why German conspirators against Napoleonic domination were unable to recognize the weaknesses of their enterprise. His demonstration that small group dynamics favors the more extreme voices is persuasive. See "When Plans Fail: Small Group Behavior and Decision-Making in the Conspiracy of 1808 in Germany," *Journal of Conflict Resolution,* vol. 14, no. 1 (1970), pp. 3–19. Charles M. Radding suggests a different non-psychoanalytic method in his "Evolution of Medieval Mentalities: A Cognitive-Structural Approach," *American Historical Review,* vol. 83, no. 3 (June 1978), pp. 577–97. He observes the literalmindedness of legal codes in medieval European society. Human thought and intention behind laws were not perceived as important, perhaps because of a universal deference to a higher power. But in the twelfth century, different cognitive structures suddenly emerged, far more concerned with circumstance and intention both in lawmaking and in following the law: rules were no longer absolutely laid down and unquestionably followed. Radding draws on Piaget and Kohlberg's stages of moral development in children to understand this phenomenon. Radding seems to suggest some connection between earlier stages of moral reasoning with less developed societies. Thus, the quickening of economic growth and social change in the eleventh century prepared the way for a more advanced stage of the medieval mentality. But these are, as Radding himself admits, more heuristic than conclusive notions.

Index

About the Contributors

James William Anderson is Assistant Professor, Division of Clinical Psychology, Department of Psychiatry and Behavioral Sciences, Northwestern University Medical School.

Harvey Asher is Professor of History and Political Science, Drury College, Missouri.

Rudolph Binion is Leff Professor of History at Brandeis University.

Robert Coles is Professor of Psychiatry at Harvard University.

Lloyd deMause is Director of the Institute for Psychohistory in New York City.

John Demos is Professor of History at Yale University.

Hans J. Eysenck is Professor Emeritus of Psychology at the University of London.

Alexander L. George is Graham H. Stuart Professor of International Relations and Professor of Political Science at Stanford University.

Juliette L. George is a Senior Scholar, Center for Research in International Studies, Stanford University.

Arthur S. Link is George H. Davis '86 Professor of American History, Princeton University.

Peter Loewenberg is Professor of History at UCLA.

Michael F. Marmor is Head, Division of Ophthamology, Stanford University School of Medicine.

Bruce Mazlish is Professor of History at MIT.

Hans Meyerhoff was Professor of Philosophy, University of California at Los Angeles.

Gerald M. Platt is Professor of Sociology at the University of Massachusetts.

William McKinley Runyan is Associate Professor in the School of Social Welfare and Associate Research Psychologist at the Institute of Personality Assessment and Research, University of California, Berkeley.

Peter Stearns is Heinz Professor of History, Carnegie-Mellon University.

Carol Z. Stearns is a psychiatrist at the Western Psychiatric Institute and Clinic.

Charles B. Strozier is Professor of History at Sangamon State University.

Robert C. Tucker is IBM Professor of International Studies Emeritus and Professor of Politics Emeritus, Princeton University.

Edwin A. Weinstein is Professor Emeritus of Neurology at the Mt. Sinai School of Medicine and Fellow of the William Alanson White Institute of History, Princeton University.

Joseph M. Woods is Associate Professor of History at Atkinson College, York University.